WITHDRAWN

IN SEARCH OF
THE TRUE GYPSY

IN SEARCH OF
THE TRUE GYPSY

From Enlightenment to Final Solution

WIM WILLEMS

Co-ordinator of the Centre for the History of Migrants,
University of Amsterdam

Translated by Don Bloch

FRANK CASS
LONDON · PORTLAND, OR

First Published in 1997 in Great Britain by
FRANK CASS PUBLISHERS
Newbury House, 900 Eastern Avenue
London IG2 7HH

and in the United States of America by
FRANK CASS PUBLISHERS
c/o ISBS, 5804 N.E. Hassalo Street
Portland, Oregon 97213-3644

Website http://www.frankcass.com

British Library Cataloguing in Publication Data

Willems, Wim, 1951–
 In search of the true gypsy : from enlightenment to final
solution
 1. Gypsies
 I. Title
 305.8'91497

ISBN 0-7146-4688-1 (cloth)
ISBN 0-7146-4222-3 (paper)

Library of Congress Cataloging-in-Publication Data

Willems, Wim.
 [Op zoek naar de ware zigeuner. English]
 In search of the true gypsy : from Enlightenment to Final Solution
/ Wim Willems ; translated by Don Bloch.
  p. cm.
 The Dutch original was originally presented as the author's thesis
(doctoral)—Leiden.
 Includes bibliographical references (p.) and index.
 ISBN 0-7146-4688-1 (cloth). — ISBN 0-7146-4222-3 (pbk.)
 1. Gypsies—Europe. 2. Europe—Ethnic relations. I. Title.
DX145.W5513 1997
305.891'49704—dc21   97-22020
                                                          CIP

Typeset by Vitaset, Paddock Wood, Kent
Printed in Great Britain by
Bookcraft (Bath) Ltd, Midsomer Norton, Avon

Contents

Acknowledgements

The reader of European history who goes searching for Gypsies will find them only in footnotes. Even today, we still know little about how Gypsies worked and lived down through the centuries. We are guilty of the same ignorance towards non-sedentary groups in general. That during World War Two hundreds of thousands of itinerants met the same horrendous fate as Jews and other Nazi victims has only been recognized tardily and with reluctance. Gypsies appear to appeal to the imagination simply as social outcasts and scapegoats, or, in a flattering but no more illuminating light, as romantic outsiders. The world is patently intrigued by them, yet at the same time regards them with anxiety as 'undesirable aliens'. People are seldom capable of considering Gypsies as creatures of flesh and blood.

Where does such ambivalence come from? What ideas are involved under the surface of these mixed feelings? Since 1985, together with fellow historians Annemarie Cottaar and Leo Lucassen, I have been trying to come to grips with these questions. Inspired by studies conducted by the University of Leiden on the nature of racism, we resolved to shed light on the neglected history of itinerant groups in the Netherlands, especially Gypsies and caravan dwellers. With the passing of time our studies naturally crossed beyond the Dutch borders. I hope that this volume bears the fruits of our ongoing exchange of ideas.

I would like to advise the reader at the outset that this book is not about Gypsies in the usual sense of the term. Although one will find descriptions of their way of life, culture, norms and values, these are there primarily to indicate how people have thought about Gypsies at different times and in different places. To be sure, the descriptions are invariably accompanied by commentary, although questions concerning who the Gypsies are and how they actually lead their lives are allowed to remain unanswered. Instead I trace contemporary notions about Gypsies back as far as possible to their roots, hoping to lay bare why stigmatization of Gypsies, or rather groups labelled as such, has continued from the distant past even to today.

The original Dutch version of this study appeared early in 1995.

Research for it was financed by the Netherlands Organization for Scientific Research (NWO), the same body that provided the funds to make this gently pruned English translation possible. For thus enabling an international audience to become familiar with the ideas developed cooperatively in our Leiden project, the NWO has earned my special gratitude. I look back with pleasure on the years spent working together with colleagues at the Leiden Institute for Social-Scientific Research (LISWO), part of the University of Leiden. LISWO provided me with an academic home base rich in facilities. I would like to seize the opportunity to express my appreciation to the staff of archives and libraries in many countries who gave me generous assistance in person or replied by return post to my written requests for information. Their memories enabled me to probe further than I had supposed possible.

Indeed more people have been involved in the genesis of this book than I can mention here. A core of four, however, must not go unnamed. First of all my official project supervisors, the cultural anthropologist André Köbben, who emerged as a dedicated guardian of 'the right tone', and the social historian, Jan Lucassen, whose confidence in my ability to deal with historical materials has not, I hope, been damaged irreparably. My thanks, too, to the well-known English gypsiologist Angus Fraser who mustered the patience to provide detailed commentary to the Dutch text, even though I was not shy about admitting I was unable to share his views on Gypsy history. He may be assured of my respect for such magnanimity. And it was, finally, a privilege to work on this English translation with Don Bloch. His feeling for style and expressiveness have, I am convinced, made the book more accessible.

Wim Willems
Centre for the History of Migrants
University of Amsterdam, May 1996

1

Introduction

THE POWER OF LABELLING

In 1991, leafing through a stack of Serbian weeklies, the Dutch cultural anthropologist, Duijzings, stumbled upon a number of articles about a new ethnic minority in the former Yugoslavia: the Egyptians.[1] The previous year they had founded their own association and within no time at all they had received 6,000 applications for membership; they estimated their total number in Yugoslavia at 100,000. A similar organization had been set up in the Macedonian town of Ohrid ten years earlier. It had acquired 5,000 members and, during the Yugoslavian census of 1981, its members had campaigned in vain for official recognition as a 'nationality'.[2] The new association appears, in the interval, to have been remarkably successful at mobilizing support from various sides. It brought out a book featuring the folk tales, legends and customs of Egyptians in Macedonia and presented it to the Egyptian ambassador in Belgrade. Egyptian television devoted a documentary to the new countrymen and politicians, academics and journalists in Macedonia, and Serbia as well, supported their demand for recognition as a separate nationality.

Until a short while ago the members of this expanding group were known in their region as Gypsies. They have themselves adduced a number of arguments to demonstrate the fallacy of this label.[3] They maintain that they have lived for centuries in the historical heart of cities such as Ohrid and Bitola, whereas most Yugoslavian Gypsies inhabit separate and frequently impoverished peripheral neighbourhoods. They make a point of their relative prosperity and the absence of unemployment in their ranks and they allege that they have always constituted a specific group of artisans – smiths – and that they are currently active in modern, specialized vocations that require considerable schooling, a form of labour mobility said to be beyond the reach of Gypsies. According to their own statements, they are 'more developed' and 'more modern' than the Gypsies and the Albanians in Yugoslavia. Finally it is argued that their oral traditions indicate that they belong to the oldest inhabitants of the Balkans and that, in the fourth century before

Christ, they founded a region called Little Egypt in Greece. From here they later journeyed along trade routes to Macedonia where they were responsible for making the city of Ohrid flourish. In the course of their becoming integrated they are said to have adopted the language of the peoples among whom they lived and to have forgotten their native Egyptian.

In their attempts to provide the history of their own group with the desired ethnic-nationalistic foundation, the Yugo-Egyptians have received support from science.[4] Serbian doctors have claimed to be able to demonstrate through blood samples that the Egyptians are no Gypsies. An ambitious interdisciplinary research project by an ethnologist-archaeologist and an arabist has been approved with the goal of proving the thesis of Egyptian origin. They claim that archaeological finds in Macedonia point to similarities with the Copts, or Christian Egyptians, and also suggest similarities in religious aspects of popular culture. They consider it possible that the Copts first settled in Greece and subsequently dispersed to other parts of the Balkans. Only many centuries later would the first Gypsies have arrived in Little Egypt, to continue on from there to the north. That would explain why they, also on account of their rather swarthy skin, would have been called Gypsies (*Gitanos, Cigani*) by the indigenous population, a term which is derived from Egyptian.

Duijzings, in explaining why the Yugo-Egyptians themselves actively engaged in the process of nationalistic or ethnic labelling, refers to fluctuations in the socio-political circumstances in Yugoslavia.[5] In the 1981 census the majority of them had let themselves be registered as Albanians, with whom, they maintained, they shared a common language, religious observances, and a variety of customs. For their part the Albanians adamantly insisted on distinctions, and identified the others as Albanised Gypsies (*Askalije*). They were said to have been forced to assimilate during the Ottoman era, then to have migrated to cities where they always had lived separately from most Gypsies who usually enjoyed a lower social status and with whom they forged no marriage ties.[6] Notwithstanding this situation, the Yugo-Egyptians have been subjected to pressure to let themselves be registered as Albanians during population counts. The underlying motivation for such pressure derives from the use of census data to divide such social goods as jobs, housing and university entrance places proportionately among the different ethnic groups. Considering the fact that until the early 1980s, the Albanians were economically and politically the strongest party in Kosovo, many Gypsies, including today's Yugo-Egyptians, very pragmatically admitted to this Albanian identity. In the meantime the Albanians did not cease to discriminate against the Gypsies on various grounds.

When political relations shifted with the advent to power of the Serbs in Kosovo in the late 1980s, the Gypsies landed in an identity vacuum. Against this background, Duijzings portrays the decision of the Yugo-Egyptians to reach back and reclaim an old, alternative identity, hoping, meanwhile, to acquire in the near future the status of a recognized nationality (with Egypt as their motherland). In principle the Serbs harbour no objection whatsoever against the numerical decline of registered Albanians, although it is uncertain whether they will ever recognize the political claims of the Yugo-Egyptians.

Some leaders of Gypsy communities in Yugoslavia speak of a divide-and-rule policy involving manipulation of statistics – of which Gypsies are the dupes. They emphasize the communal identity of all 'Gypsy-groups', including the Yugo-Egyptians, and cite the massive cumulative figure as an argument for ethnic recognition. Duijzings remarks that while it might be true that only 168,000 Gypsies let themselves be marked down as such during the most recent census, the real number is likely to be four times as great.[7] Ethnic identities, however, are not permanently fixed and peoples and nations do not comprise closed entities in themselves.[8] Duijzings seems unwilling to take account of the notion that 'Gypsy' is a collective ethnic designation for all segments of a single people. He regards the Yugo-Egyptians' claim to an Egyptian origin as an emergency tactical manoeuvre, the historical justification of which needs to be called into doubt.[9]

ARE 'GYPSIES' ONE PEOPLE?

Contention about the proper label for Yugo-Egyptians in Kosovo and Macedonia illustrates the tension that can arise during the framing of ethnic definitions between the wishes of the members of the group in question and the wishes of other concerned parties. In the instance under consideration, the Yugo-Egyptians' emphasis on cultural and social differences from other 'Gypsies' and their claims to a history of their own did not win immediate acceptance. Yet it is important to note that this strategy for promoting their own emancipation and for acquiring more social status under contemporary circumstances did appear in advance to have a chance of succeeding. Such a process certainly also depends upon the interests of other parties concerned – in this case politicians, judicial authorities, academics, authorities from the Gypsy community or communities, Egyptian diplomats, and those represent-ing the interests of the Yugo-Egyptians themselves. What matters is how they all interpret the label 'Gypsies': as a collective term for diverse (ethnic) groups or as the designation of a single people living scattered in groups throughout the world.

In trying to analyse this process we find ourselves facing two questions that recur as a motif throughout the following study. Do all those designated as Gypsies constitute one people? And who ultimately determines who is a Gypsy? The first question is usually answered in the affirmative in the academic literature, as in Angus Fraser's historical handbook published in 1992. In keeping with the views of authoritative authors writing about Gypsies, Fraser posits, on grounds of linguistic correspondences between *Romani* (the 'Gypsy language') and *Hindi* (the language of north-eastern India), that they came originally from India, departing from that homeland somewhere after the ninth century for reasons about which there is still ongoing speculation. Like the Jews, they subsequently spread over the globe, arriving in west and central Europe at the turn of the fifteenth century. There, comparatively unharried, they lived for decades as nomads, later to be confronted with continuous stigmatization by government officials as the result of the inevitable burden to the sedentary population that they came to represent. The social exclusion and persecution of Gypsies may be explained in this perspective as the consequence of the incompatibility of settled (agrarian and/or industrial) and nomadic communities. A consensus appears to exist about the common language and origins of Gypsies and about their original itinerant way of life. The notion is also dominant that demonstrable physical and ethnic differences exist distinguishing Gypsies from non-Gypsies, such as physical traits, codes of purity, endogamy and tribal laws.[10] For those who subscribe to this ethnographic viewpoint, it is assumed that the Gypsies constitute a single people with a number of specific characteristics of their own. In other words, Gypsy studies are dominated by a primordial standpoint that interprets their ethnic identity as, in essence, an incontestable given.[11]

The extent to which this postulation is justified has seldom been the subject of study. It seems, rather, that the idea 'Gypsy' dominates, obscuring both the historical and ethnic variety which may be lurking behind the monolithic concept.[12] I will illustrate where this can lead by using the findings of the American anthropologist Miriam Lee Kaprow who did fieldwork in the late 1970s among the Gitanos in the Spanish city of Zaragoza.[13] Her observations ultimately culminated in confusion because these people lived normally among other Spaniards in a neighbourhood where they visited the same shops, hospitals, cafés and movie theatres. They were physically indistinguishable from the others, they spoke only Spanish, and they lived in houses. As far as work was concerned, moreover, there appeared to be no specific vocational specialization, although they were usually self-employed, they seldom worked for wages and, economically, they belonged to the lower or middle class. Kaprow had essentially found that there was a group of people who, it was true, were known as Gypsies – who even called themselves 'Gitanos' – but who did not possess any of the characteristics of Gypsies identified in the literature. The single stereotype that she thought she could recognize had to do with style. Having reached that point she thought she had penetrated to the essence of 'the Gypsy':

> The vitality, the zest – the sheer energy with which they embarked on anything, gossiped about anyone, ate, cleaned the house, met at the cafes – was remarkable. There was a dash, a vividness, a gusto, that has made me, along with others who have worked with Gypsies, miss them terribly when we are away. Their flair, their elan, intensified everything.[14]

According to Kaprow, her Gitanos had an anti-conservative attitude towards life. They observed no traditions of their own, had no specific moral code, customs or marriage rituals, no ideology or group laws, no special cuisine or stories.[15] Continuity was said to be alien to them; celebration of the moment was of central importance. None the less, she regarded them as a social group with internal cohesion arising from a rather loose structure. She had no doubts that these Gitanos were related to Gypsy groups elsewhere in the world. Indeed the loose structure – she even goes so far as to speak of the lack of structure – was in her opinion a characteristic of all Gypsy-like groups.[16]

She overlooks, however, the fact that other contemporary anthropologists have reached opposite conclusions and have encountered social structures such as purity codes among the Gypsy clans which they have studied in England and the United States.[17] With respect to the available evidence it is too bad that only a limited number of monographs concerning Gypsy communities have appeared and, in the last analysis, they offer insufficient grounds for making general statements about Gypsies and any possible characteristics they might have in common.

The term 'Gypsies' appears to embrace different ethnic groups with their own designations, such as *Gitanos*, *Sinti*, *Rom* and *Kalderas*, while in some countries, including England and Ireland, native travellers are also called 'Gypsies'. To what extent these groups share a common descent remains to be seen. There seem to be mutual ties on only a modest scale and the groups do not appear to feel united by any awareness of a common history.

This prompts the question of whether such unity may have existed a century or longer ago. It is not very likely. Although no publications are available to settle the matter, there are more than enough indications that make the idea of a single Gypsy people a dubious one. Thus the

Quaker philanthropist John Hoyland wrote a book in 1816 about 'Gypsies' in England and Scotland with the intention of goading the social conscience of prosperous citizens into their ameliorating the living conditions of these 'roaming heathens' and bringing about their religious conversion. He had lists of questions distributed among provincial authorities, who checked their data with the leaders of various itinerant groups. From the group portrait of 18,000 Gypsies that was put together in this way, it turned out that there was no internal community structure. The people had no idea where their ancestors came from, were not organized among themselves, and were not at all aware of Gypsy groups elsewhere in Europe. They had no concept of a shared past and there didn't appear to be any solidarity among the groups. Their sense of being part of a group stopped at the level of the clan. No one spoke at all about belonging to 'one people'.[18]

A questionnaire commissioned by the Hungarian Ministry of the Interior and administered among Gypsies in 1893 revealed similar results. The government wanted to tackle vigorously the problem of these 'groups on the move', which they regarded as an anachronism in a modern, centralized state. The results from the official survey, however, did not harmonize with existing ideas about Gypsies: 90 per cent did not appear to be itinerant but rather seemed to live sedentarily and only one third of all those questioned used *Romani* as their mother tongue. Coppersmiths and musicians, two leading occupational groups in the circles under scrutiny, earned a comfortable living; further proof that they were better integrated than the government had supposed. The actual implementation of the research also proved that the interviewers could not rely on objective criteria such as language, lifestyle, physical characteristics or self-definition to find out who was a member of the Gypsy population. It was presumed that they would differ from others with respect to racial characteristics, but what happened as a rule was simply that the people who were asked questions were known by others as 'Gypsies'.[19] The text does not mention what they called themselves.

What we know about the still scarcely written history of Gypsies obliges caution when considering the proposition that they make up a single people. What I mean to say here is that not everyone to whom the label of 'Gypsy' has been applied, by themselves or by others, leads an itinerant way of life, speaks *Romani* (or at any rate one of its variants), stands out through bodily characteristics from others in their surroundings, is conscious of being subject to strict, group-specific mores, or shares an awareness of common roots. This is not to contend, however, that Gypsies do not exist. The history of the persecution of persons and groups so labelled, continuing as it does in the present, is already in itself sufficient to establish the reality of their existence beyond denial. Interest groups such as the *International Romani Union* or the *Zentralrat Deutscher Sinti und Roma* (in Germany) also testify to the feeling that there is a need for group self-presentation along ethnic lines. It is merely that this has probably not always been true and it seems that the idea that all ethnic Gypsy groups belong to one people obscures, rather than clarifies, their complex history. In that context the second question which I previously posed becomes relevant: who defines who is a 'Gypsy'?

CATEGORIZING AND STIGMATIZING

Four parties are, in principle, involved in the process of arriving at a definition of Gypsies: those being defined, i.e. Gypsies, the authorities (church and state), academics, and – however vague it may sound – the population at large. We saw how in the case of the Yugo-Egyptians some groups that are known as Gypsies choose, in their reconstruction of their own history, to emphasize ethnic ties with non-Gypsies – in this instance Albanians. On the other hand there were special lobbying organizations and political parties in post-war Europe founded on a basis of the participants' Gypsy background. The problem is that it is not always clear who exactly they are representing or whether there is always a clear relation between the initiators and the stigmatized Gypsy groups that they say they represent. Thus, in her 1992 documentary account of Gypsies encountered during a journey in Rumania, the Dutch writer Mariët Meester reports on an elaborate cluster of groups, but Meester's contacts with all these people, called *tigan* or *Rom* by the Rumanians, bring her to the conclusion that the members she met of the different guild-like occupational groups, the majority of the poor without labour skills, the rich businessmen, and the intellectuals, have little in common. She even maintains that only the intellectuals are intent on creating an entity which, in her opinion, is without foundation.[20] In point of fact there is insufficient information from 'Gypsy circles' available concerning their self-definition to acquire a reliable picture of the history of their group formation. Nor does extant literature permit us to determine whether current fragmentation mirrors a pattern that is centuries old. Up until now it does not seem likely that Gypsy groups themselves have exercised much influence on the labelling process and we can assume with all propriety that they will seldom have recognized themselves in recurrent images of Gypsies as parasites, criminals and romantic outcasts.

Consequently I will not further pursue the subject of the Gypsies' own power to define themselves, deterred in part by the absence of trustworthy historical sources. The same holds true for the population, in the broadest sense of the word. We are remarkably better informed about the influence which governments, and especially their judiciaries, have exercised on the definition of groups such as Gypsies and about the concomitant development of negative image formation.[21] To help us acquire a deeper understanding of the role of officials in acting against groups with a (supposed) itinerant way of living, a stigmatizing perspective may render good service.[22] The point of departure here is that governments, in forging policy towards a distinctly categorized group, base their actions on a set of negative value judgments – a stigma. To comprehend the process it is important to investigate the way in which an individual is branded or labelled as a member of such a group. When a government deals with groups whose members are not always immediately recognizable as such, in order to carry out a consistent policy, it finds itself obliged to spell out regularly who, in its way of thinking, belongs to the group in question.

Relying on the literature about the European history of persons designated in the sources as Gypsies, we find that at the time of their appearance in the fifteenth century they presented themselves as pilgrims from a country called Little Egypt. They did this in order to acquire safe conducts from higher authorities, even kings and the Pope, who assured them of safe passage through the countries of Europe. In reality, however, it turned out that the petitioners were thieves in disguise, charlatans and beggars. In Fraser's recent handbook (1992), the chapter recounting the early period bears the title 'The Great Trick'. In Europe during these years, however, there was a lively trade in travel passes and many (false) pilgrims roamed about.[23] For that matter from historical studies of the poor and vagabonds we know that, since the fifteenth century, a generally criminalizing policy was enacted towards beggars, people who were not bound to a landlord or a skilled tradesman, vagrants and outlaws.[24] At the core of the emergent stigma that fixed on these so-called vagrants nestled the presupposition that they were people who refused to hold down a steady job, preferring an insecure way of life that featured begging and stealing. They had no permanent abode and no acceptable economic status, and were seen as the personification of the protest against the ruling economic system. Their behaviour, often depicted in strong moral language, generated anxiety because they could encourage others to follow their example and so undermine the social order.

It is possible to defend the assertion that a small segment of this general category of 'vagrants', more specifically those who were not practising Christians and who were associated with a foreign origin, had such labels slapped on them by higher governments as 'Egyptian', 'heathen', 'Gypsy'. Since it was not always possible, in practice, to draw a clear distinction between indigenous and foreign drifters, especially for lower levels of government, it was necessary, time and again, through the distribution of edicts and ordinances to emphasize that Gypsies made up a separate category.

It is probable that the church also made its contribution to this stigmatizing process, as was the case with the social ostracism of Jews in Europe.[25] In the wake of the theological stigma that the Jews were the killers of Christ, a series of prejudices subsequently developed, varying in function to suit changing social circumstances. According to the British historian Moore, some myth or other was continually being concocted about other undesirable groups, with or without any basis in reality, in order to identify these people as a source of social decay who deserved to be driven out of Christian society so that they then could be subjected to persecution including the appropriation of their property, their freedom, and at times even their lives.[26] Such persecution in the final analysis was an expression of the consolidation of power, with a European peak in the period between 1450 and 1650. The ongoing stigmatizing of Gypsies as heathens in West Europe (in combination with their foreign origin and – in part – mobile way of life) conforms admirably with the pattern of persecution just sketched, where victims were regarded as religious deviants.

This is also the reason why the labelling of socially rejected groups by institutions empowered with authority recurred over and over again. The process was propelled by the fear that the faith of the 'simple at heart' would be corrupted by Jews, Gypsies or heretics and their work ethic eroded by vagrants without home or hearth, especially if these vagrants were (or were believed to be) foreigners. It remains an open question, however, whether the 'Gypsy' category was actually the source of so much specific trouble and was felt to be unusually oppressive.[27] There are no empirical studies available to settle the matter and the publications which do exist are characterized by an almost exclusive reliance on official judicial sources. As a result a one-dimensional picture has come into being, presenting the view that, historically, Gypsies have only known persecution and marginalization. In contemporary socio-historical research, at any rate, they only make the scene in a context of penury, mendicity, vagabondage, marginality and criminality.[28] No one seems to doubt that the criminal or asocial behaviour of aimless vagrants impelled the authorities to take cruel suppressive measures. Publications dealing exclusively with Gypsies do not arrive at an essentially different interpretation, only here we encounter the practically obligatory observation that governments or chroniclers were afflicted with the prejudices of their time. Nevertheless authors put their trust in these texts and refer to the lack of tolerance towards Gypsies since the sixteenth century because the Gypsies, as (camouflaged) beggars and criminals, are purported to have been a nuisance to the population.

This one-sided selection of sources consistently ignores or plays down signs that point to the integration of Gypsies. The musical tradition that Gypsies in diverse lands were able to build up; the prosperity that some groups of horse traders achieved; their occasional absorption into the ranks of sedentary society; their marriages with indigenous peoples (which explain the 'mixed population' that we will come across regularly in this study) are all indications of social integration. The success of such an interactive process requires concessions from both sides – newcomers and long-standing inhabitants – which implies that Gypsy societies were less closed than is often assumed.

The most important cause for the failure of the historical picture to admit change is that most writers about Gypsies accept the premise that Gypsies constitute one people with a number of fixed characteristics.[29] It is said that the specific nature of the Gypsy people means that they always end up having difficulties and meet with rejection from others in the societies where they live. As a result of this point of view, few researchers have an eye for the socio-economic and ethnic-cultural variety that is incorporated in the history of these groups. This fact is important, above all, because authoritative scholarly texts in particular have played such a prominent role in the process of defining Gypsies and in the formation of ideas about their group character – certainly since the last quarter of the eighteenth century. Until then, writers about Gypsies followed for the most part in the footsteps of the government and considered Gypsies as one of many categories of vagrants. For a long time they were thus more followers than leaders. A change in this situation occurred when a number of German authors 'proved' that Gypsies are the descendants of an Indian caste of pariahs, with all the unfavorable traits that would belong to such ancestors. From then on governments and judicial authorities could legitimize their stigmatizing policy by invoking scientific arguments.

With the connection between science and policy as my point of departure in this study, I pose the question of how our knowledge has evolved since the idea that all Gypsies are members of an Eastern people gained hold in western Europe.[30] By this I mean that the ethnic category of a 'people' began to function as an overall concept, as an objectification of the characteristics which were said to unify all groups labelled as Gypsies so that categorizing them as beggars, vagrants, criminals and heathens was pushed into the background. At the same time a process of codification took place: everyone who belonged to the Gypsy people was presumed to possess all the traits of the group with respect to language, origin, and way of life. There were certainly shifts in ways of thinking about Gypsies, arising from social changes and fluctuations in scientific interest in the subject, and I will be tracing their development. I shall also consider why, at the same time, governmental and judicial stigmatization of these groups has carried on relentlessly.[31]

AUTHORITATIVE TEXTS ON GYPSIES

In order to determine the authors on whom most authority has been conferred, all standard works about Gypsies should have to be consulted – a virtually impossible undertaking! It is also impracticable to make a well-considered selection from all (popular) scientific publications which have appeared in this field. In George Black's *A Gypsy Bibliography*, which dates from 1914, there are 4,577 titles reported and it is hardly daring to imagine that the number must have doubled in the interim.[32] Moreover, Black provides no commentary on the quality of the research carried out, which increases the difficulty of assembling a corpus of the most authoritative texts, in part because there are practically no thoughtful analyses of the history of Gypsy studies.[33]

A reasonably objective method is to track through time the entries in encyclopedias, where, as we know from earlier research on Dutch materials, the most up-to-date information on the topic of Gypsies is to be located.[34] We are able to deduce the state of knowledge at any given time from these entries (although there will always be a slight time-lag) since authors seldom risk making a critical appraisal of the material that they have consulted. In a certain sense encyclopedias constitute a reflection of the thinking of a period, with or without prejudices, from which it is possible to draft a family tree of ideas, or a genealogy of our knowledge about Gypsies. At the same time we are able, by ascertaining the literature that the authors used, to discover which texts have exercised the most influence over time.

Thus I assembled a ranking list of writers who have dominated Gypsy studies since the earliest West-European encyclopedias appeared at the beginning of the 1700s until the 1980s, using the encyclopaedia articles from the Netherlands, England, Germany and France as my basis. Perhaps this compilation is not exhaustive, but it can claim to be representative.[35] It comprises 54 Dutch, 40 English (and American), 30 German (and Austrian) and 28 French lemmas. Not all these writers consistently cited their sources, however, so the number of lemmas on which the count of Gypsy specialists is based is somewhat lower.

Mention of the top ten will suffice here, with specification of the years in which the most important Gypsy studies of the writers concerned were published. This yields the following hierarchy for consideration: August Pott (1844–45), Heinrich Grellmann (1783), Franz von Miklosich (1872–81), George Borrow (1841, 1843, 1851, 1857, 1874), Charles Leland (1873, 1882, 1891), Michiel de Goeje (1875, 1903), Heinrich von Wlislocki (1880, 1890–92), Paul Bataillard (1843–49), Alex Paspati (1870), Bath Smart and Henry Crofton (1875). The rankings are distorted by a bias, for more recent authors will not yet have had as much of an opportunity to make an impression with their authority, but, this aside, the dominance of nineteenth-century writers is unmistakably evidence of the authority attributed to these texts over a long period of time. In this respect it says a lot that even an eighteenth-century writer such as Grellmann seems to have retained influence for hundreds of years, continuing to be quoted in post-World War II encyclopedias. This German historian is therefore generally recognized to have laid the foundation of the scientific study of Gypsies. His general survey work created a thematic framework to which nineteenth-century and some twentieth-century researchers, too, may perhaps have added refinements but whose basic assumptions they never challenged. He may consequently be considered as the father of what became known in the course of the nineteenth century as 'Gypsy studies'. For this reason he is central to the first part of this study.

When we scan the top ten, we see included the linguists Pott, Miklosich, and Smart and Crofton who further explored the linguistic theme introduced by Grellmann. The authority of Pott's two-volume standard work on the subject has remained unrivalled from the moment of its initial appearance up until the present. De Goeje, Bataillard and Paspati further elaborated hypotheses about the place of origin and the earliest history of Gypsies (in Europe and beyond). Leland and Wlislocki added depth to aspects of the ethnographic portrait of Gypsies which Grellmann first sketched. The latter pair represent the 'folkloristic' school of thought, that which arose in the second half of the nineteenth century in England and central Europe and which was destined to become an important tradition within Gypsy studies. The man who inspired this interest in the folkloristic side of Gypsy societies, through his travel accounts and his semi-autobiographical publications but certainly also through his historic, linguistic, ethnological and folkloristic observations about Gypsies in Spain, Russia and England, was the English writer George Borrow. His work would have a profound effect on later ideas formulated about Gypsies. Accordingly I devote the second part of this study to him, and briefly examine, in a separate chapter, his folkloristic heirs.

Even today, all these diverse research orientations within Gypsy studies can be confident of adherents. Moreover, new approaches entered the scene in the twentieth century. Thus, in the 1930s, publications appeared, in Germany in particular, which reflected a eugenic and criminal-biological way of thinking, deeply rooted in a criminological tradition dating from the early nineteenth century. Since this approach led to a shift in thinking about Gypsies, again especially in Germany, and gave a dramatic twist to the stigmatizing of this (these) group(s), the fourth part of this study is devoted to the most important representative of this branch of science, the German youth psychiatrist and eugenist, Robert Ritter. Finally, since 1945, a strong social-scientific interest in Gypsy groups has emerged, more particularly concerned with the discrimination against them and their response as a self-conscious minority. The consequences of this interest have only lately penetrated the columns of encyclopedias. For practical reasons I have chosen not to go into this recent trend, contenting myself with a reference to a study by the English historian David Mayall scheduled to appear presently.

THE EARLY HISTORY OF GYPSY STUDIES

In order to appreciate what an extraordinary role the German historian Grellmann has played in the process of defining Gypsies it is necessary to examine the publications that preceded him. Such an undertaking has been considerably simplified by the appearance in 1987 of a compilation of sources by Reimer Gronemeyer, who has printed the most important writings on the subject from the fifteenth century up to Grellmann in their entirety.[36] Down through the centuries the chronicle and the cosmograph (a kind of predecessor of the encyclopedia) appear to have been the genres of primary significance in shaping ideas about Gypsies. Closer reading of these sources reveals that the written tradition concerning the earliest identification of Gypsies in western Europe rests entirely on the testimony of two witnesses from that era: one passage from the year 1417 by the Dominican monk Cornerius of Leipzig and a fragment from the year 1424 by the canon Andreas of Regensburg. We can derive the following picture from what they reported. A group of some 300 people (30 according to Andreas) were involved, alien to German territory. They lived in tents outside the city walls: permission to live within the gates had been denied them on account of the thefts which it was assumed they would have committed. Designations for these people differed. According to Cornerius they were black as Tarters and called themselves *Secaner*; Andreas wrote of *Cigäwnär*.

They were said to come from Hungary and, by wandering about for seven years, to be acting out penance for sliding back into heathendom. They had with them an undated safe conduct from Sigismund (the King of Hungary and, since 1410, Emperor of the Roman Empire) in which it was written that the authorities should treat them humanely wherever they travelled. Andreas maintained that the people suspected them of being spies.

In his commentary on these first texts Gronemeyer points out that the descriptions of both authors have so much in common rhetorically – although they probably were unaware of each other's work[37] – that he imagines that they hark back to an oral tradition of imagery depicting this sort of group. The anxiety regarding spies was possibly part of a general fear of foreigners from the Ottoman Empire. In this connection it is too bad that the historical canon of texts about Gypsies has never been compared with texts in which other groups are depicted with a physical appearance, style of dress and manner of trade felt to be striking, if not threatening.[38] As a result it is difficult to determine which elements were group-specific and which, for example, might reflect general reactions in the face of any newcomers. The same holds true for the lack of attention to the functionality of certain images, such as the recorded accusation of spying.[39] Ruch explores its background in his analysis of the effects of diet ordinances in Germany after 1498 (in Freiburg) when such an accusation was first aired at the government level.[40] He discloses that during sittings of the Convention in the preceding years there was absolutely no talk of Gypsy spying, nor, in point of fact, was there any mention of stealing. To the extent that Gypsies came to official attention as an issue in the drafting of the regulations, they were included in the general disciplinary rules which applied to travelling musicians, beggars and categories of that ilk. Only once the German Emperor Maximilian (enthroned in 1493) needed extra tax revenue in the state treasury to finance his war against the Turks did it become functional to play on the fear of spies, and then Gypsies, as 'pagan orientals', made an ideal scapegoat. By the time of the Convention's decision of 1529 the accusation, according to Ruch, was no longer mentioned explicitly. As an element of the image which people had of Gypsies it had by then become common property.

When we look at sixteenth-century sources on Gypsies, of which the best known is probably the *Cosmography* of Münster of 1550,[41] we see that, above all, they reflect changes in the mentality of the times, with new emphasis on sedentariness, steady work and ties to the land. These later writers were no chroniclers, but rather the compilers of previous sources, giving rise as a consequence, to the reproduction of the Gypsy portrait sketched by Cornerius and Andreas. There seemed to be a shift in the definition of Gypsies, however. Whereas they were initially considered primarily as 'foreigners', in the sixteenth century emphasis came to fall on their 'heathen condition' and 'criminal way of life'.[42] In 1520 the theologian Krantz spoke of the scum of the nation, of Gypsies who lived 'like dogs', without religion and from day to day.[43] He did not describe them, however, as a closed (ethnic) group, but as a community of drifters, thieves and beggars from many countries. In that connection Gronemeyer refers to a division that developed during this century in the interpretation of Gypsy history, a split he designates as the 'two groups theory'. The origin of the split can be traced to the Swiss chronicler Stumpf who in 1538 had described the arrival in Zürich 120 years earlier of 14,000 Gypsies, driven out of Egypt as Christians and completing a seven-year-long pilgrimage. These people owned a lot of gold and silver, and they did not behave as thieves, as was the case with vagrant knaves in his time. Stumpf suggested that the original Gypsies had gone back to their land of origin after their pilgrimage and the contemporary 'mixed band of deceivers' had little to do with them or else had fallen to the depths, socially. This ambivalence of thinking is, in my opinion, the earliest expression in writing of what I call the search for 'the true Gypsy'. The idea was apparently that at the beginning of the fifteenth century 'real', 'good' Gypsies had been identified, while a century later only reprobates of diverse origin travelled about who would, however, indeed have called themselves Gypsies. These were said to live without God and his commandments, to disturb the social order (by their itinerant way of living), to speak their own language and, as heathens, to be a thorn in the eye of the literate classes. In the seventeenth century historical works of Camerarius (1602) and Toppeltin (1667) the idea that *Cingari* were of foreign origin was explicitly rejected and emphasis fell on their heathen state and their way of living as rootless mendicants and scoundrels from various regions.[44] Once again, the question is whether this negative image has not unjustly overshadowed the far richer and more complex reality of Gypsy life and Gypsy integration into diverse communities.[45] This remains to be proven by the detailed study of other kinds of sources.

The most authoritative published writing about Gypsies in the seventeenth century – at least in German-speaking areas – was by Jacobus Thomasius (1652) and Ahasverus Fritsch (1662).[46] For them, Gypsies formed a social category of outsiders, originating from various countries, who had mingled with indigenous beggars and scoundrels and who swarmed throughout Germany like a 'plague of tramps'.[47] They found, wholly in keeping with the spirit of the policy prevailing at that moment, that the entire category of low life and vagrants deserved to be combatted by vigorously repressive government action. This approach can also be seen in the *Steckbriefe* (lists of wanted persons) which were used by justice departments and police from the second half of the eighteenth century onwards to exchange information systematically about members of groups which they considered to be undesirable and criminal, numbering Gypsies among them.[48] The format of these lists was to arrange in alphabetical order the names of persons who had been arrested or taken into custody, annotating the entries with known facts about them, bringing the data up to date once every few years. The rudiment of a method which would be further and further refined and in some periods, as we will see in the fourth part of this study, grew into an extensive registration system in which all the information that it was possible to amass about Gypsies and their social context was incorporated.

One list of suspicious characters representative of the genre of the *Steckbriefe* in the last quarter of the eighteenth century was that compiled by Georg Jacob Schäffer, *Oberamtmann* of Sulz (in Württemberg) who distinguished himself as head of the police. His work is of such interest above all for a reversal can be detected in it coinciding with the appearance of Grellmann's book. Thus in his earliest work, from 1784, Gypsies were still included as just an ordinary component of what he regarded as a lump sum of all kinds of 'vagabond trash'. In Schäffer's second publication, however, in 1787, a 'Gypsy List' can be found and it seemed that the relation between vagabonds and Gypsies was closer than ever before.[49] For the compact typology of groups which Schäffer prefixed to his compilation of names of undesirables, he based his text primarily on Fritsch and Thomasius. This explains why many of their ideas about this subgroup are recognizable in his characterizations. Gypsies are said to have a secret language (*Rotwelsch*) of their own and possibly a foreign origin, but nevertheless they were Germans and as such a segment of the larger category of itinerants. It was the first time that the concept of 'Gypsies' as an umbrella term for 'vagrant filth' appears in a publication put out by judicial authorities. Schäffer, moreover, proposed measures for rehabilitating them, thereby putting into words the Enlightenment ideas about social elevation current in his time.[50]

THE CONSTRUCTION OF A GYPSY IDENTITY

In an afterword to his list of wanted persons, Schäffer referred to Grellmann's book about Gypsies which had reached him at the last moment and with which he was extraordinarily pleased. From those points to which he referred, it can be deduced that the most important effect of Grellmann's study upon its publication was that it gave fixed direction to the vague notions which, prior to this, had circulated about these people with – in the opinion of some – foreign antecedents who for centuries already were said to have mixed with Germans on the margins of society. Grellmann brought all these itinerant groups moving through different countries together under a single name, ventured an estimate of their number, and provided them with a collective history.

My short excursion into the early history of Gypsy studies illustrated that hardly any empirical sources exist on which to base justifiable assertions about a general history valid for all the groups of Gypsies that can be differentiated. At the same time I ascertained that a pronounced stigma had come into being against them, conceivably as a consequence of religious-political and socio-economic developments. Moreover, thinking about Gypsies seems to have been coloured by a tradition of imagery that depicted not only groups and 'heathens' as foreigners who were, as non-Christians, wild and uncivilized,[51] complemented by portrayals of Orientals inspired by wars with the Ottoman Empire and ideas about the representatives of an exotic, half-criminal beggar's guild (with its own language, administration and mores).[52] The early history of Gypsy studies entails so little originality because for centuries a limited number of scarcely reliable sources were continually reproduced.[53] As a consequence, so runs my hypothesis, our image of Gypsy identity and its underlying history has been shaped primarily by (pseudo-) scientific interpretations. Whether the identity that has been constructed in this way at all reflects historical reality is a very real question. In the next chapter we will look into the extent to which Grellmann with his historical study, recognized by many as the first scientific standard work in the field, may have altered the situation.

My suppositions about the influence of authoritative texts within the field of Gypsy studies on the defining of Gypsies will be tested in this study as follows. For each of the representative writers distinguished, I will sketch an intellectual portrait. To begin with I will probe more deeply into the importance of the authority in question, thereafter I will discuss his personal development and his social network. Scientific and socio-political thinking in his time will be considered in this context, with special attention to the direct surroundings. Analysis of the content of thinking about Gypsies in the publications of the authors portraited will be central to this study, with shifts in ideas with respect to their predecessors and innovative tendencies being contrasted repeatedly with what passed for generally accepted knowledge at that time. I will explore the influences to which each author has been exposed, the tradition(s) within which he belongs or sees himself as belonging, and the sources on which he has based his work. The origins of these sources or the identity of their authors are of importance as are the manner in which the knowledge expressed in them has been acquired and the reflections of later writers on this knowledge, because only in this way is it possible to trace the evolution of the ideas in which we are interested. Reviews of each work and other possible responses by contemporaries will be analysed with the goal in mind of discovering how a text has acquired its authority and what critical reservations may possibly have faded. Finally the influence of each author and/or his work over time will be examined.

By placing the lives, work and social context of these authors at the heart of this study, with special consideration of the way in which they acquired their knowledge, and by describing the consonance and dissonance of their preferred perspectives with those of their contemporaries, I hope to be able to trace both the most important shifts in thinking and the leading continuities in Gypsy studies. I am also interested in the similarities and differences in argumentation and imagery used by these authors and by the governments and judicial authorities of their time. A related question is whether, in the first instance, Gypsies have been studied with scientific purposes in mind or rather primarily as a social problem in need of a solution.

NOTES

1   See Duijzings (1992, pp. 24–38). An English version of this article, under the title 'The Making of Egyptians in Kosovo and Macedonia', will be published in Cora Govers and Hans Vermeulen, *The Politics of Ethnic Consciousness* (Basingstoke: Macmillan, 1997).

2   Duijzings (1992, p. 28) points out the official difference in the former Yugoslavia between *narodi* (a people aspiring to the recuperation of their former political autonomy), *narodnosti* (nationalities) and *etnicke grupe* (ethnic groups). Serbs and Croatians, with republics of their own, belonged to the first category. The Albanians and Hungarians, who had no right to their own republic because they belonged to a sovereign state outside Yugoslavia, to the second category. In the remaining category Gypsies (*Romi*) comprised by far the largest group.

3   Duijzings (1992, pp. 28–9).

4   Ibidem, pp. 30–1.

5   Ibidem, pp. 31–5.

6   In this context Duijzings alludes to a study by Tatomir Vukanović entitled *Rome (Cigani) u Jugoslaviji* (Vranje: Stamparija Nova Jugoslavija, 1983). This publication has not been translated, however, and I do not know to what extent it depends upon research into historical sources. In any event, Vukanović appears to have written (on page 138) that many of today's Yugo-Egyptians – who had not yet manifested themselves as such when he wrote his book – are related to the *Arlije*, that is to say to the Turkish, or, preferably, the turkified Gypsies who live in many of the cities and villages of the republics of Serbia and Macedonia and who have already been regarded as residents for a long time.

7   Duijzings (1992, p. 34, note 13). In this context he cites Vukanović in agreement; Vukanović estimates the total number of Gypsies in the former Yugoslavia at 600,000.

8   In this respect he says he follows Fredrik Barth who, in his anthology *Ethnic Groups and Boundaries* (1969), has shown that ethnic identities are not, as is often thought, immutable quantities but rather, they evolve dependent on external historical circumstances. This concept has since become known as the 'situational approach'.

9   Ibidem, p. 27, note 5.

10   Fraser (1992, pp. 10–32) is aware that the 'Gypsy people' manifest themselves in many guises but where language is concerned he writes that it is possible to go a long way in reconstructing a proto-language, a hypothetical ancestor of all Gypsy dialects. He also suggests that research into blood groups inspired by physical anthropology may prove able to establish the Gypsies' Indian origins.

11   For a more detailed exposition of this position, see Glazer and Moynihan (1975). See also the Dutch historian, Leo Lucassen (1990, pp. 12–14) for references to other relevant literature about the ethnographic perspective in Gypsy studies.

12   The historical study of Lucassen, in particular, enables us to see upon deeper consideration how in the Netherlands, during the past century-and-a-half, a number of (ethnic) groups have lurked behind the collective term 'Gypsies', groups which not only had disparate backgrounds and histories, but which – at least as far as some of them were concerned – did not even maintain any mutual ties.

13   See Kaprow (1991, pp. 218–31). Kaprow studied 47 households, a total of some 185 individuals.

14   Ibidem, p. 220.

15   Ibidem, p. 223.

16   Ibidem, p. 230, notes 1 and 2. In this context she refers to studies by Sharon Gmelch (1986) on indigenous Irish *travellers* (who, incidentally, have absolutely no ethnic or historical connection with Kaprow's Spanish Gitanos), by F. David Mulcahy (1989) about Spanish *Rom* (the self-chosen name of certain Gypsy groups who speak Romani) and by Matt and Sheila Salo (1977) on the *Kalderas* in eastern Canada.

17   The studies by Okely (1983) and Sutherland (1975) are of importance. See, too, Fraser (1991, pp. 336–7) for a number of titles of publications concerning purity codes among Gypsy groups.

18   For a more extensive discussion of John Hoyland's work, see the passage about him in the portion of this study which deals with George Borrow.

19   The findings of this Hungarian Gypsy survey will be discussed more extensively in the section of this study devoted to Austro-Hungarian folklore.

20   Meester (1992, p. 150). The groups she comments upon are the *Caldarari* (braziers in the *department* of Gorj), the *Romanizad* (the 'Romanized'), the *Arginteri* (silversmiths), the *Vatrari* (the *Romi* hearth), the *Cortorari* (a caste who once lived in tents), the *Gabor*-women (who have considerable contact with Hungary), the *Ursari* (prosperous bear trainers), the *Zidari* (still more prosperous masons), the *Lautari* (highly-respected musicians), the *Rudari* (who make wooden utensils) and the *Gunoieri* (the caste of waste collectors).

21   For reference to the government's stigmatizing role in the Netherlands see Lucassen (1990) and Cottaar (1996); in England, see Mayall (1988); and in Germany, see Fricke (1991).

22   See Lucassen (1990, pp. 15–17) and Willems and Lucassen (1990, pp. 19–20). The concept of 'stigmatizing' was introduced to the social sciences by the American sociologist Erving Goffman in his *Stigma. Notes on the Management of Spoiled Identity* (1964). It is a central concept in the model with which the Leiden University historian Van Arkel (1984, pp. 34–70) has historically explained the active discrimination against Jews. The stigmatizing perspective is in part based on his model.

23 See the fascinating study by the Polish historian Geremek (Dutch translation 1992, from an Italian translation of the original).

24 This point is worked out in more detail by Lucassen (1997, 'Eternal vagrants?'). He relates fluctuations in the stigmatizing of Gypsies in different European countries to specific variations in economic and political development, with special attention to the influence of the formation of nation states.

25 See Van Arkel (1984) for an empirically supported exposition of this statement.

26 See Moore (1987).

27 Take, for example, Germany – the classic setting for Gypsy studies. In the eighteenth century some 8 per cent of the population there still belonged to the so-called vagrant marginal classes. They survived through such diverse activities as catching rats, sweeping chimneys, selling books and almanacs to peasants. See Fertig (1997).

28 See Lucassen (1993, pp. 209–35) for an analysis of the perspectives (criminality, marginality, poverty) within which historical examinations of the socio-economic position of Gypsies are offered. Lucassen argues for an approach in which the economic function of itinerant groups is of central importance.

29 That studies based on an ethnographic perspective are inclined ultimately to explain the policy of persecution by pointing out that Gypsies were (conscious) outsiders, we observe as well in German post-war studies which have analysed the roots of such harassment during the Nazi regime. For a critical discussion of the consequences of this approach, see Lucassen (1995, pp. 82–100).

30 For exposition of this concept, see Hughes (1945, pp. 353–9).

31 In this context, I also refer the reader to Lucassen (1996, '*Zigeuner*').

32 See Black (1914). In addition McGrigor Phillips (1962) deserves mention if only because the catalogue refers to another, larger, collection. Recently Hohmann published a chronologically organized survey (1992).

33 Martins-Heuss (1983) is handy as surveillance of the field. More fundamental is Ruch's unpublished doctoral dissertation (1986), once more confined to German-speaking territory. Publications concerning the founders of the *Gypsy Lore Society* will be discussed later in this study.

34 See Willems and Lucassen (1990, pp. 31–50). Our findings were recently confirmed in an article about the German situation written by Rao and Casimir (1993, pp. 111–24).

35 The list derived from Dutch encyclopedias is practically a complete one. For foreign reference works I was forced to rely on Black who mentions in his bibliography a great many entries about Gypsies in German, English and French encyclopedias. It was not possible for me to determine how thorough he did his work. For the post-1910 period I have depended on the encyclopedias in the Royal Library in the Hague.

36 See Gronemeyer (1987). He deals with the largest part of the German and Latin sources on which Grellmann based his work.

37 Ibidem, p. 21. The manuscript of Cornerius (Hermann Korner) was only published officially in 1723, for that matter, and that of Andreas in 1763. It is, however, likely that the manuscripts were consulted at an earlier date by the writers of sixteenth-century chronicles.

38 In this respect our academic knowledge of the history of itinerant groups has not notably been enriched by the recent publication of source materials by Gilsenbach (1994). This compilation of printed passages which (presumably) are about 'Gypsies' simply confirms the existing ethnographic picture.

39 The persistence of the spy image is apparent, for example, from the fact that the Nazis still used it as an argument on the eve of the Second World War for deporting Gypsies from the east of Germany.

40 See Ruch (1986, pp. 49–53).

41 Ibidem, pp. 57–8. There have been many printings of the *Cosmography* of Münster which, translated into English and French, according to Ruch, popularized the emerging negative image of Gypsies.

42 Gronemeyer (1987, p. 25).

43 Ibidem, p. 26.

44 See Gronemeyer (1987, pp. 58–65, 69–71).

45 In the sources which Gronemeyer reproduces, we encounter different indications that suggest an accommodating attitude on the part of the (Christian) population towards Gypsies. See, for example, the theological work of Becanus from 1580. The persistent repetition of edicts issued by the diet in 1497, 1500, 1530, 1544, 1548 and 1551 (denying Gypsies the right of residence in German territories) also indicates, according to Gronemeyer (p. 90), that the proclamations had little effect and that the lower governments largely ignored these directives from above. From police regulations for the earldom of Palts in 1599, in which stress was placed on Gypsies' godlessness, it could also be inferred that the police authorities felt that the people gave the Gypsies far more support than they deemed desirable.

46 The lemma on Gypsies in Zedler's *Universal Lexicon* (1749), for example, is deeply indebted to their formulation of insights.

47 A. Fritsch *Historische und Politische Beschreibung der so genannten Zygeuner. Nebenst wahrer Anzeigunge ihres Uhrsprungs/Lebens/Wandels und Sitten* (1662, p. 9). Reproduced integrally in Gronemeyer (1987, p. 144).

48 See Lucassen (1996, *'Zigeuner'*) for an analysis of these wanted person lists and of other police circulars in which descriptive information for tracing persons were included.

49 For the complete description of the title of this *Zigeunerliste* (1787) by G.J. Schäffer from Sulz, cf. the references to this study.

50 See Schäffer (1787, p. 4). For the impact of his writings (many new editions of which appeared during the next decades) on the drafting of laws and regulations affecting Gypsies in Württemberg, see Fricke (1991, p. 39 *et seq.*).

51 In his doctoral dissertation (1990, p. 53) Peter Mason writes: 'Both European peasants and exotic, non-European Gypsies could serve as the internal negative self-definition of the European upperclasses. The term "heathen" could cover both European wild men (as well as peasants, Gypsies and beggars) and exotic races from abroad.' See also Vandenbroeck (1987) for an analysis of the iconographic tradition of the genre which included 'the wild man' and 'the beggar'. Vandenbroeck examines the portrayal of scenes with Gypsies in them in a series of tapestries which reveal the fascination with this exotic theme that reigned in European courts.

52 See Geremek (1992) who, especially in the chapter 'In the footsteps of the pilgrims', goes into detail about the socio-cultural and political structure of these *communitas* and *civitas* not only of vagabonds, beggars and criminals, but also of peripatetic tradesmen who made a secretive and suspect impression on many of their contemporaries and who were thought to be in command of perfectly developed secret languages. In his 'concluding remarks' Geremek draws attention to the pattern of the cosmography of this anti-society and emphasizes that it was literature, above all, which introduced the stereotypical image of the otherness of these groups into the social conscience of the period.

53 In his book on Orientalism, Edward Said (1978, p. 23) exposes a similarly centuries-old system of citing works and authors. Geremek (1992, p. 272) also points out that during both the Middle Ages and modern times it was normal procedure while gathering and publishing scientific data, to rely on assumptions, gossip and fictional accounts.

2

Heinrich Moritz Gottlieb Grellmann (1753–1804): an enlightened historian and his sources

INTRODUCTION

Die Zigeuner, ein historischer Versuch über die Lebensart und Verfassung, Sitten und Schicksahle dieses Volks in Europa, nebst ihrem Ursprunge is the title of the book with which Heinrich Grellmann made his debut as an academic in 1783. For detectives such as Schäffer the volume was an eye-opener, and it continued to have this effect among investigators, court officials and criminologists throughout the entire nineteenth century and part of the twentieth century although, in practice, they wrestled continuously with the problem of defining precisely who were 'Gypsies'.[1] Again and again, in popular criminological writing, we find Grellmann's vocabulary list of 'Gypsy words' recurring – to which every subsequent writer tried to add a number of words that he himself had noted down – printed together with an ethnographic portrait of the group, and with comments about the Gypsies' occupational activities and character. From the time of Grellmann's study, Gypsies emerged as the freedom-loving vagabonds about whom settled folk knew hardly anything at all. The following figures can be placed in this tradition: Ferdinand Bischoff (1827), Friedrich Christian Benedict Avé-Lallemant (1858), Richard Liebich (1863), Hans Gross (1894), Alfred Dillmann (1905) and Hermann Aichele (1912). They, in their turn, exercised considerable influence on criminological biologists during the Nazi regime. Nor did their notions disappear from criminology textbooks after the Second World War.[2]

In the second part of this study, where the writer George Borrow figures centrally, I will address the undeniable influence of Grellmann's book in English-speaking countries. In countries where German predominated, the continuity of his ideas is every bit as traceable, even if simply because many writers in their introductions frankly acknowledged their debt to him before, as a rule, launching into lengthy paraphrases of his work. In this context, aware that the following list is far from exhaustive, I wish to cite educational inspector Alfred Graffunder (1835), school director Theodor Tetzner (1835), the French work of Michel de

Kogalnitchan (originally dated 1837, appearing in German translation in 1840), the legal historical dissertation, written in Latin, by the Dutchman Franciscus Rudolphus Spengler (1839), the Prussian Major, Carl von Heister (1842), Carl Hopf (1870) and the ethnographer, J.H. Schwicker (1883). In his standard work on linguistics in 1844, August Pott also confirmed that Grellmann's work served as a model for many imitators:

> Da Grellmann's in vielen Beziehungen ausgezeichnetes Werk von den meisten späteren Schriftstellern über Zigeuner sowohl im Aus- als Inlande gekannt ist, und dasselbe oft blindlings benutzt und auf die unverschämteste Weise geplündert worden … ('Because Grellmann's book, in many regards an excellent work, was known to most later authors on Gypsies domestic and foreign, and they often made blind use of what he wrote and plundered it most shamelessly …')[3]

Black explicitly noted that dozens of titles in his Gypsy bibliography of 1914, were clearly derived from Grellmann's work. Later writers, including Martin Block (1936: 24), Hermann Arnold (1965: 253), Heinz Mode and Siegfried Wölffling (1968: 22) have similarly referred to the cultural historic importance of Grellmann's study. If we take yet another step closer to the present, we find that Grellmann is still considered to be a reliable source of historical ethnographic information about Gypsies in the eighteenth century.

The importance of his work is uncontested, even though contemporary researchers who reflect critically on the history of Gypsy studies no longer attribute much authority to it.[4] The only individual who has seriously occupied himself up until today with the way in which Grellmann collected his material and chose to present what he knew is the ethnographer Martin Ruch.[5] In his doctoral dissertation he reviewed German literature on Gypsies – excluding Austrian publications – from the fifteenth century down to circa 1900. In part his analysis has something in common with the design of this study, but he was not particularly interested in the relationship between scholarship and policy. Moreover, he only deals superficially with shifts in prevailing imagery and scarcely pauses to consider the historical context of the research material presented. These are, however, indispensable for a proper understanding of developments. It also strikes me as important to delve more deeply into the sources that form the foundation of Grellmann's work – an enterprise at which Ruch has made but a tentative, if worthy, beginning. The two major pillars of Ruch's study are his critical analyses of Grellmann and of the Hungarian folklorist Von Wlislocki, whom I examine at some length in the fourth part of this study. Wherever necessary I have indicated in the text where our work overlaps, yet it did not seem to me very useful to refer in a footnote to Ruch every time we arrived at (roughly) the same conclusion or, more seductive still, to engage in continual discussion of passages where our interpretations diverged. My critical comments concentrate on parts of Ruch's text which reveal, to my way of thinking, mistaken readings.

In what follows I describe concisely the principal subject matter of Grellmann's book and its underlying ideas. These ideas appear to derive from the intellectual heritage of the Enlightenment and they display a strong affinity with the reform politics of the Austro-Hungarian emperor, Joseph II, which is why I subsequently present a sketch of his policy and of the tension between theory and practice inherent in them. In the following section I make the transition to Göttingen where Grellmann studied and taught and which, in the 1780s, was considered to be the academic centre of the German Enlightenment. It is against this university background that I proceed to place the author of the authoritative text about the Gypsies, and then carry on to trace his scholarly career. Once my exposition of the social context of the writer and his work is complete, I return to the book itself, in particular to the generalizations about Gypsies which it contains. The reason for doing this so elaborately is that Grellmann sketched a kind of Gypsy archetype which held sway for centuries, admitting only slight variations without anyone ever challenging the portrait's historical merits. This strengthened my resolve to examine, as exhaustively as possible, how Grellmann acquired his expertise and to identify the sources on which he depended. At the same time, I try to clarify the reception of his work, noting both the huge success which it enjoyed in that era and the criticism which it evoked.

A COMPREHENSIVE HISTORY OF GYPSIES

Grellmann laid claim to writing the first comprehensive historical work about Gypsies, although in his foreword the reader comes across the qualifying remark that a lack of sources from other regions of the world has meant that the accent has come to fall on Europe.[6] At the time of publication, the autumn of 1783,[7] the author had just received his degree as an historian from the University of Jena, which accounts for his dedicating the book to Duke Carl August van Saksen. He wished to make a contribution to both history and to ethnography. It is uncertain what led him to write the book he chose to write. In Grellmann's correspondence with the publisher Friedrich Justin Bertuch of Weimar, who for decades served as his Maecenas, the first mention of work on the project is dated 18 December 1781.[8] At that time it was simply a matter of his being busy amassing material for an article about the origin of Gypsies in Hungary and Transylvania. During the summer of that year a certain Professor Bruns of the London Society of the Sciences had appeared in Göttingen to collect information on that subject.[9] This visit suggested to Grellmann that he himself devote a piece to the topic, whereupon one of his teachers, the linguist Christian Büttner, placed at his disposal all the sources on Gypsies in his possession. This gesture enabled him to explore the theme more elaborately than had originally been his intention.

On 29 December 1781, Grellmann wrote to Bertuch that Büttner had advised him to major in history because he was so enthusiastic about the manner in which Grellmann had analysed the sources that had been made available to him for his treatise on Gypsies. It was no longer a question, as it had been two weeks before, of his simply mapping Gypsy origin; now his task was to portray their way of life and distinguishing characteristics. He had read the piece to Büttner who had been unstinting in his praise.

What had brought about the burgeoning interest in this theme in England and Germany? It is possible there was a connection with the essay prize announced in August 1779 by the Swedish Royal Academy of Sciences (Stockholm) on the topic 'the origin of Gypsies'.[10] At the beginning of the 1780s no prize winner had been announced, although a silver medal was awarded to the Finnish chaplain Christfrid Ganander for the essay he had submitted on 27 November 1780.[11] The subject appealed to the imagination, at any rate, for between 1770 and 1790 a remarkable number of publications were devoted to it, among which Grellmann's can retrospectively be seen to have been one of the most interesting. We do not know whether he still wanted to be considered for the golden medal of the Swedish Academy, but his publication, scheduled initially for Easter of 1782, continued to expand throughout that year. In August he appeared to complete the finishing touches, yet the writing actually ended only a year later.[12]

The reason for expanding the essay into a broad, popularized study probably had to do with a current event which strongly fired the imagination: the accusation of cannibalism made against a group of Gypsies in the Hungarian district of Honth in the summer of 1782.[13] One-hundred-and-thirty-three persons were involved. They were arrested because they were said to have robbed travellers, then to have disfigured and eaten them. No one had been reported missing to the authorities, however, and there were no eyewitnesses. During their hearing 53 men and 31 women admitted that they were guilty as charged. The gruesome news received prominent attention in the newspapers and during the court sessions which followed rapidly on each other's heels the accusations assumed grotesque proportions. The fixation on cannibalism began to lead such a life of its own that the death penalty appeared a foregone conclusion. To portray the tenor of the punitive climate which prevailed I reprint below a passage from one of the convictions:

> The following year in the woods of Hodrus they murdered a peaceable, unsuspecting individual in their familiar, inhuman fashion. For this third murder Miklos Didys' domicile was used as a slaughtering house. The cloth and clothing tradesmen and an unknown farmer were killed. They were deprived of their lives and of their goods, too. In a manner unknown to Europeans they were boiled, divided up, cut into bits and pieces and wholly devoured. Bones were tossed to the dogs or into the fire to destroy any trace of evidence. The money of the victims was shared out among the band members.

On 8 November 1782, the Hungarian Governor, Josef Kelcz de Fületincz, received permission from the Royal Court in Vienna to carry out the sentence, although questions had arisen there in the meantime concerning the affair. The judicial verdict for 41 of the accused Gypsies was, however, irreversible. In the trial documents we read that anyone who was a Gypsy or Jew and who later retracted his voluntary confession could, according to law, expect harsher punishment. The judge found that taxpayers had a right to the strict maintenance of the public order and he furthermore believed that this would have an emancipatory effect on the Gypsy community. To his way of thinking Gypsies put to work escaped from the land or the workplace far too easily and he found that the regulation which granted them permission to marry only if they worked for a living needed to be revived with renewed vigour. He also wanted their moral situation to change in some way. Many of them, according to him, lived together unmarried and everyone slept around freely which accounted for the spate of bastard children. He also pointed out that, during the winter, families slept in small huts together with their relatives by marriage and that they copulated like monkeys. The judge considered this incestuous behaviour as an undesirable practice for a civilized country. He also ruled that the children of the condemned should be taken from their parents and brought under the care of small farmers. These surrogates would receive three crowns a day for which they obligated themselves to raise their wards to become hard-working citizens. Of the 84 suspects, in the end, 41 were executed; a number were beheaded with a sword, others were broken on the wheel and hanged, yet others were crucified and quartered. The carrying out of the death sentences of the rest was stayed at the end of 1782 when an imperial commissioner from Vienna eventually turned up to investigate the matter more closely. He discovered that none of the corpses which allegedly had been eaten were actually missing, whereupon the Gypsies still in prison were caned for the robberies they had perpetrated and were subsequently released.

In 1974 the Dutch advocate in Gypsy affairs, Lau Mazirel, wrote that news of the imputed murder had spread through Europe like wildfire and had trailed a broad wake of lynch parties behind it. Reports of the exoneration of the accused will have diffused far less rapidly.[14] Mazirel, in turn, fails to cite sources and since the historical background of the cannibalism affair is difficult to analyse, her hypothesis remains for the time being unproven. None the less, it seems scarcely debatable that public curiosity was dominated for some time by bulletins concerning this lugubrious event and, as a result, Grellmann's book filled a demand.

The author dealt with the subject of 'cannibalism' in a chapter devoted to the food and drink of Gypsies. He himself says that the reason he only devoted six pages to it in the first edition of his book was that he did not yet have documents from the trial and this meant that he had to rely on reports that appeared in four newspapers.[15] After a summary of these (brief) news items, Grellmann wrote that he would have preferred to ignore the subject but that he felt obliged to warn governments to keep alert since incidents of cannibalism had manifested themselves down through the centuries in diverse places. According to him, this 'hideous trait' belonged to the morals and behaviour of the Gypsies' country of origin and therefore it was not unlikely that they still practised the custom of partaking of human flesh. He even had an explanation for why accusations of cannibalism did not appear in older sources. Because Gypsies were nomadic and lived outside of normal society – and what's more their victims were often their relatives – the victims in question would not be missed by the authorities.

The 13 pages that Grellmann spends on this topic in the second edition of his book were identical to the text that appeared in the first up to the point at which he began to discuss the accused persons' confessions. Then he explained, referring to an historical parallel,[16] that these were extracted on the rack. In addition to intimidation, he thought that the Gypsies' inclination to act in a tough and garrulous manner had played a role. From the court's records, however, it was evident that no *corpora delicti* had been discovered, and thus that the judge had reached his verdict merely on hearsay. That the rack had wrought its influence on the rash talkativeness of the Gypsies was something called to Grellmann's attention by a Hungarian letter writer, not specified by name.[17] A further source that he cited in this context was 'someone who asked questions afterwards of the court official'. The person so indicated had also not seen the report of the imperial commissioner, but he knew enough to state that the commissioner had removed the judge who had passed sentence on the convicted Gypsies from the bench. From a written communication to the author – once more anonymous – Grellmann learned that the final judgment had been restricted to the crime of robbery. Thus, in his treatment of this subject, Grellmann had to rely on rather unaccountable sources. He ultimately deflates the accusation too, but without altogether eradicating the suggestion that something was amiss.

He was much more explicit in describing his attitude towards policy regarding Gypsies. In various places he acknowledged that he was ideologically indebted to the thinking of the Enlightenment, especially to the political ideas of the Austro-Hungarian sovereigns, Maria Theresa and Joseph II. He was extremely open about how he regarded the group(s) that he studied: he thought of them as the scum of humanity. What he considered to be the most remarkable thing about them was that for 450 years already they had roamed the earth without ever being influenced by their surroundings but forever remaining vagabond thieves: 'Afrika macht sie nicht schwärzer, Europa nicht weisser; in Spanien lernen sie nicht faul, in Teutschland nicht fleissig seyn; unter Türken nicht Mohammed, unter Christen nicht Christum verehren.' ('Africa does not make them blacker, Europe not more white; in Spain they do not learn to be dishonest, in Germany not to be diligent; among the Turks not to worship Mohammed, among Christians not Christ.')[18] In this context he drew a parallel with the Jews who, by virtue of their religion, but in his perspective primarily because of their Eastern origin, always clung fast to their own ways in foreign places. Such a deep attachment to traditions was in his opinion characteristic of uncivilized people in general and of orientals in particular. New ideas and customs would seldom take root among them, unless introduced deceptively or by force. In other words it was their Eastern origin which made Gypsies immune to change. They stuck to their traditions and inborn instincts and so remained 'unenlightened' and their history in Europe bore testimony to this. In support of this position he presented the story cited in my introduction about the way in which Gypsies as pilgrims played on the devout gullibility of those in higher places and by so doing secured official passes which guaranteed them freedom of movement. For a long time no one paid heed to their begging, deceit and theft until their atrocities increased excessively and complaints from people resounded too loudly to ignore. Only once things had reached such a state did governments and courts exercise stricter control. Banishing Gypsies or hanging them was, however, not an adequate policy either, for such a keep-them-moving tactic at the European level only culminated in a vicious circle and led to inhumane persecution.

From Grellmann's perspective the process of exclusion turned out to be two-sided. On the one hand there were the Gypsies, who had always demonstrated their preference for a segregated existence and so remained outside civilized society because their inclinations, customs and oriental minds stood fundamentally in the way of their assimilation. On the other hand society on all sides had also constantly reacted to them with rejection and left them to their fate. The banishment that this process had caused in different countries was, to Grellmann's way of thinking, a path to disaster. First, expulsion only temporarily warded off the evil since there was always another state burdened with the undesirable group(s) and not all governments everywhere were equally strong at the same point in time. In addition the means were said to be too hasty. Removal solved nothing. Not enough effort was expended to see whether there was some decent way to bring about their improvement. Finally he considered the means superfluous and the drift of the process, to his way of thinking, could only be changed through strong state interference. In Grellmann's thinking his partisanship for emancipation was prominently reflected:

> Und nun denke man sich den Zigeuner, wenn er aufgehört hat, Zigeuner zu seyn; denke sich ihm mit seiner Fruchtbarkeit und seinen zahlreichen Nachkommen, die alle zu brauchbaren Bürgern umgeschaffen sind; und man wird fühlen, wie wenig wirthschaftlich es war, ihn als Schlacke weg zu werfen. ('Just imagine the Gypsy ceased to be a Gypsy; with his fertility and his numerous offspring, all transformed into useful citizens; then one is able to feel how economically wasteful it would be to throw them away like snails.')[19]

With New Testament rhetoric, Grellmann goes on to say that missionaries are dispatched to the East and West but no one troubles himself with those roaming about right in front of his own door. He found that they should be taught religion and virtue with conviction, for they did not learn by example. Only through compulsory means, together with education and instruction, did he believe it possible to bring some light into the minds of mature Gypsies and some improvement into their hearts. The energy of the government, however, should concentrate on how Gypsies raised and interacted with their children, for, according to the author, this was the only path by which one could nourish positive expectations for the third and fourth generation. He thus regarded the Gypsy people as not totally unsusceptible to change, despite their coming from the East. Nurture would, he believed, in the long run prevail over nature.

The ideas presented here meshed flawlessly with the basic principles of the 'civilizing attempts' of Maria Theresa and Joseph II. The regulations which had been undertaken during their reign to convert

Gypsies into industrious and useful citizens,[20] must, as far as he was concerned, be forcefully prolonged. He observed that, in Hungary, ordinances had been enacted since 1768 with the aim of 'winning this poor and unfortunate people for virtue and the state'. There had simply not been a good reaction at the local level and many initiatives therefore never took hold and few results were achieved. This accounts for the repetition of the ordinances in 1773, this time in more trenchant wording. When that failed to help, the empress prescribed that a Gypsy might not marry until such time that he could afford to support a wife and children properly, and that the children of married Gypsies must be taken from their parents to receive a better upbringing elsewhere. These, for Grellmann, were hard but necessary measures and he regretted that so few authorities actually carried them out and that the policy remained restricted to Hungary.

Next he deals with the ordinances of Joseph II which he claims to have copied from the imperial-royal decrees.[21] In brief, the following directives were the heart of the matter. Gypsies were required to let themselves be tutored in religion and to send their children to school. They had to ensure that their offspring did not run around naked to prevent annoyance and disgust in others. Children of the opposite sex would no longer sleep with each other in their homes. They had to attend church regularly, certainly on Sundays and holidays, submit to spiritual advisers, and live according to their instructions. In diet, apparel and language were required to follow national usage, eat no dead cattle, sport no multi-coloured garments, and refrain from speaking their own tongue. They should no longer let themselves be seen in mantles whose only purpose was to cloak stolen goods. Only Gypsies who panned for gold were permitted to keep horses but they had to refrain from horse dealing at yearly markets. The government would see to it that Gypsies didn't waste their days in idleness. They had to work, for themselves or for a land owner, or else accept a job for wages, and also be set to work in agriculture with an allotment of land on which to grow crops. It was, moreover, up to the government to see to it that they performed these tasks befittingly. Whoever neglected his work on the land deserved corporal punishment. Music and other forms of diversion were only permitted during free time. Grellmann was profuse in his praise of Joseph II for such, in his eyes, wise policy intentions. According to him the emperor's approach was a new pearl in his crown about which descendants in later times would speak in extolling terms:

> ... dass er über achzig Tausend solcher Elenden, die unbekannt mit Gott und Tugend, tief in Laster und Wildheit versunken, als Halbmenschen in der Irre liefen, aus ihrem Unrath herausgezogen,

und sie zu Menschen und guten Bürgern gemacht habe. ('… that he has pulled more than eighty thousand of these poor wretches, who live in wickedness and barbarity, ignorant of God and decency, only half human in their bewilderment, out of their filth and has turned them into human beings and worthy citizens.')[22]

The author of the first comprehensive history of Gypsies was thus strongly influenced by the notion of civilization as Maria Theresa and, especially, Joseph II conceived of it, although he did not place the measures enacted with respect to Gypsies within the context of the emperor's general (social) reforms and policy of combatting poverty. There were, however, a legion of parallels.

JOSEPH II: ENLIGHTENED ABSOLUTISM

A vast body of historical work exists concerning the reign of Joseph II. He was co-regent of the Habsburg Empire at his mother Maria Theresa's side from 1765. From 1780 until his death in 1790 he was the solitary ruler of the Austro-Hungarian monarchy. Here I will discuss a number of aspects of his reform policy that were designed to decrease the power of the church and nobility and to enlarge the rights of farmers and tradesmen. As patron of freemasonry, although he himself never became a member, he rallied behind the ideals of the enlightened period during which he grew up. His politics have moreover been interpreted as a practically all-inclusive attempt to defuse the social tensions in his realm through a series of preventive measures.[23] In this way he resolved to curtail the seemingly unassailable political and economic power of the propertied classes and its abuse, inherent from ages past. In Austria, the centre of his own might, his efforts achieved positive results but in Hungary, a part of his kingdom with independent institutions, his reforms met with so much resistance that the most important measures were soon retracted after his death in 1790.

His reforms pertained to three spheres of influence. First of all there were ordinances affecting the church that were intended to reduce the worldly influence of religious orders. Within the walls of church and monastery, greater equality was to prevail; outside those walls tolerance was to be promoted towards people with different beliefs. Joseph II deprived the nobility of various privileges, whereas the burghers acquired more rights. He thus abolished serfdom and limited the violence that would be meted out to subordinates as punishment. He also carried out a series of measures that were meant to eliminate social evils. Among other things these were directed at improving educational facilities, regulating relief for the poor, ameliorating care of the sick, codifying inheritance law (in particular strengthening the position of children born out of wedlock), prohibiting the labour of children under the age of nine in factories, bettering the legal position of servants, and simplifying the procedures through which artisans became masters. Joseph II's reforms effectively laid a foundation and created conditions to sustain a unified, modern state with strong, central authority and far-reaching administrative competency. Under his sway, the number of government employees increased appreciably.

I would like to consider Joseph II's social reforms, especially his measures for countering poverty.[24] Until well into the eighteenth century the poor were invariably dependent on the favours of the church and nobility. Care for the sick and poorhouses were available in some parts of the empire but elsewhere they were not, while at the time half the people in the Austro-Hungarian Empire were living at or below the poverty level.[25] Unattached workers, day hands and seasonal labourers, pedlars, and others who tried to support themselves through an itinerant occupation, comprised an important segment of these indigents. The situation was seldom rosier financially, moreover, for salaried factory hands and servants. Some 10% of the population was made up of *Randexistenzen* (marginal figures), many of whom struggled for survival as thieves, criminals, beggars and prostitutes.[26] Only with the government campaign of Joseph II was a systematic attempt made for the first time to improve the circumstances of their lives, initially through the establishment of a national network of facilities for the poor, the organization of which was entrusted to the parishes, with an eye to uniformity. Each parish enumerated its poor, in co-operation with the local government, and on Sundays provided alms in the church, so that church and social policy became tightly interwoven. Together with the introduction of this social reform a more authoritarian measure was put into effect as well: as of 11 October 1783, loafing and begging were forbidden by law and greater emphasis came to be placed on the distinction between 'well-disposed' and 'recalcitrant' poor, a difference that had indeed been increasing in importance in European consciousness since the sixteenth century.[27] Social behaviour could thenceforth, as it were, be compelled, even if in practice this seldom happened.

Another important reform provided for the care of children neglected by their parents. Already in 1773 a measure was enacted to interest people, in return for an annual remuneration paid by the national government, to serve as foster parents for the offspring of soldiers. As a sequel to this arrangement, a later ordinance followed intended to guarantee these same children a Christian (formal) education. The transfer of the care (involving payment) of foundlings to foster parents in rural areas was conceived of in the same spirit. Just as with gifts of charity, supervision of the realization of this policy was put into the hands of the clergy who were to receive the support of local authorities and district civil servants.[28]

The social policy of Joseph II was certainly inspired by concepts of the Enlightenment, but his reforms, ordinances, decrees and acts were carried out with an iron hand and all lands belonging to the monarchy were admonished to pursue common tactics. Given the great differences between national, regional and local government, the process of actually putting the government's policies into practice ran into constant difficulties, opposition and lack of co-ordination. The general goal being pursued might well be the betterment of life's circumstances for all state citizens, yet it entailed that groups that were in any way different were expected to submit to the ideal of uniformity. True enough different edicts were issued with respect to the toleration of Jews, but these involved provisions that they must bear a German family name, must speak and write German, and, certainly in public, abandon Yiddish. The same held true for other (sub-)groups within society. The aim was equality and conformity. The ideal was that of a monolithic state exercising central authority and adhering to the utility principle as the foundation of its ideology, with a core position destined for agrarians. That is why many land reforms were passed, but a major colonization of Hungary by Austrians and Germans also took place between 1763 and 1787 (19,000 families consisting of 80,000 persons relocated, especially in the Banat).[29] These families settled down on the public domain and modernized old, deserted villages.

One area in which the discrepancy between theory and practice led to (partial) loss of contact with social reality was that of begging.[30] Even during Maria Theresa's reign, a losing battle was being waged against the large number of beggars in both towns and countryside. Regulations prohibiting begging on the street culminated in frequent arrests and foreigners among those charged were systematically taken to the border and literally kicked out of the country. This notorious clean-up (*Schub*) did not, on the whole, produce the desired results, for most of those expelled were back inside the borders again a few weeks later. Maria Theresa treated indigenous beggars much more mildly. Joseph II's regime saw a visible stiffening of the policy; hawkers and pedlars also had a hard time of it under his reign. Itinerancy and lack of a steady job were both, in principle, punishable. The first imperial initiative on this front, a partial solution, was to round up male beggars and send them off as recruits to the army. In reality this measure proved totally ineffective, not only because most beggars were not cut out to be soldiers, but primarily because the majority of the ranks of beggars consisted of women. Another, more juridical regulation prescribed that every person found guilty of begging would receive a prison sentence of at least three months, but in no time at all this led to overflowing jails. Finally the emperor decided that everyone held for begging would be put on a diet of bread and water for three days and then given such a beating that they would be cured forever of their wish to beg. Although under the rule of Joseph II torture and barbarous methods of execution, such as breaking a man on the wheel, had been abolished, from Grellmann's perspective a beggar, the embodiment of uselessness, did deserve harsh physical punishment.

It is important to note the extent to which the social-political spirit of the times had repercussions for the academic climate, especially in the university world of Göttingen where Grellmann taught for some decades. What interests me in particular is the nature of the image of man which dominated the disciplines of history and ethnography in those days, both fields to which Grellmann claimed to be making a contribution with his book.

THE INTELLECTUAL CLIMATE IN GÖTTINGEN AT THE END OF THE EIGHTEENTH CENTURY

An enlightened university

Even though Göttingen was rather a young university, it still occupied a prominent place in the German academic debate of the second half of the eighteenth century.[31] The university, founded in 1734, was named after Georg August II, Elector of Hannover (Braunschweig-Lüneburg) and King of England, who also, in title, was rector of the university.[32] Its spiritual father and curator for forty years was Gerlach Adolph Freiherr von Münchhausen who later became Minister of State. He modelled the Georgia Augusta – the colloquial name for the university – after the example of the Protestant University of Halle, with the difference that Halle was known as the centre of pietism and Göttingen would become the hearth of the German Enlightenment. To attain this end, Von Münchhausen introduced *Lehrfreiheit*: the (pre-)censor was abolished so that instructors were no longer subservient to the Theology Department and – within certain limits – they were free to teach and publish whatever they chose. The university privileges that the Georgia Augusta secured in 1736 are acknowledged as a milestone in the history of academic freedom.[33]

This arrangement spawned a wealth of new subjects, such as political science and political history, and Von Münchhausen tried to lure the (well-heeled) nobility into pursuing legal or political academic training. He also hoped, in this way, to entice the middle classes, from whose number the future officials of the Hannover Electorate were enlisted, to Göttingen. To judge by the status that the University enjoyed during the closing decades of the eighteenth century, he was extraordinarily successful at his undertaking. The appeal of the faculties was reinforced by a hiring policy that sought excellence, with the fame which a candidate may have won through his publications proving to be of decisive importance. Von Münchhausen was skilled at winning the loyalty of established names by offering them exceptional working conditions: better salaries than elsewhere,[34] the title of *Hofrath* for professors[35] and greater social security such as a widows' fund for professors' wives. In addition Göttingen's resources were looked after better than at other universities. There was, for example, its famous library which, in 1787, contained some 120,000 bound volumes, including a rich supply of travel descriptions and maps and a treasure trove of manuscripts.[36] The unique thing about this library was how acquisitions were co-ordinated with ongoing and planned research. Both information and documentation were at the direct disposal of professors and students alike. In this manner the library grew into a scholarly source in its own right. It owned an enormous collection of English language books which attracted learned readers from all points of the compass to Göttingen. The same held true for the manuscripts and books which had to do with Russia, many of which could not even be consulted in Russia itself. With this research library, Von Münchhausen was far ahead of his time.[37]

The establishment in 1752 of the *Königliche Gesellschaft der Wissenschaften* in Göttingen also provided an important stimulus. This academy rapidly expanded as a research institute and a platform for interdisciplinary discussion. It did not belong, as elsewhere, to any princely residence with all the controversies and polarizing effects such an arrangement commonly brought with it.[38] The academy functioned rather as an institutional setting for research, the impulse behind which was provided by the university. As a rule professors prided themselves on becoming members and knew that they were encouraged to bring out a publication every year on some scholarly discovery of theirs. This also laid the basis for the scientific periodicals and reviews that arose at this time, such as the *Göttingische gelehrte Anzeigen*, published under the aegis of the academy. Completely in the spirit of the Enlightenment, the editors repeatedly attempted to make their expertise accessible to an interested and educated public. By virtue of the originality encouraged in this way, Georgia Augusta reached beyond her territorial boundaries and acquired an international appeal. Year by year the number of foreign students increased; ties with Hungary, England and

Russia were of great importance.[39] That tolerance was practised as it was preached can be deduced from, among other evidence, the acceptance of Catholic students at a university where the professors appointed were exclusively Protestant. All these factors meant that Göttingen, which was only the fourth largest of German universities measured by number of students (after Halle, Jena and Leipzig) in 1750, had risen to first place 20 years later and in 1781, with 947 students, booked the highest enrollment recorded for the century.

Pragmatic history

In this liberal university climate subjects could develop that reflected, as it were, the enlightened spirit of the times by taking a close, critical look at various political systems, paying special attention to the power of the state and its misuse. The institution of the state formed one of the most important objects of study in the Philosophy Department and the rational criticism of sources grew into a method by which political scientists and, subsequently, the new scholarly type of historian presented themselves as representatives of the ideas of the Enlightenment.[40] They declared their indebtedness to the great *amateur historians* as personified by Montesquieu, Voltaire and Hume, but asserted their difference from these towering figures' successors who, they felt, lost themselves in the straightforward presentation of innumerable historical facts without ever discussing their context. Göttingen wanted to study phenomena in their interconnectedness and promoted a pragmatic brand of history that dared to relate the interpretation of historical processes to the problems of the contemporary era. Thus current notions of people and the world were historicized and within the humanities the idea won a following that can only be understood today through a study of the dynamics of antecedent events. To distinguish between important and irrelevant happenings in the past, an historian needed to have a strong *intuitive understanding*: a combination of understanding, memory and imagination. Only through creative reconstruction could he reach a certain level of 'clarity', to put it in the terms of that time. Montesquieu's message was that the order of things required study, for only through an analysis of the material and cultural environment and man's interaction with his surroundings was it possible, to his way of thinking, to penetrate to the 'popular spirit' of a period.[41]

The idea began to win ground that language expressed the mentality of a people and that implied a yoking of philology and historical analysis. It was felt that written sources should also be examined in their historical context. This was the only way for academics to arrive at an appreciation of the spirit of a time or people and the only way, through comparison and analogy, to detect congruences. The idea was that when the deep structures of languages, but also of literature, fairy tales, myths and other narratives were similar, then the speakers and writers of these must be kindred as well. This prompted a tidal wave of publications about national literatures. The notion flourished that language, like people and societies, developed in stages, in a manner analogous to the laws of nature. This entailed that each stage of development must also have an expressive form or character of its own. It was a dynamic model of elucidation thus, in which the writer was considered to be the representative of the spirit of his times or of the public mind, as a kind of channel. The method of the analogy infiltrated every discipline and, around 1780, had come to dominate scientific thinking to a marked degree:

> In allen Wissenschaften sind die grössten Erfindungen nur durch Analogien gemacht worden: man dachte sich mehrere ähnliche Fälle und machte Versuche (...) und führte sie auf allgemeine Begriffe, zuletzt auf ein Hauptprincipium zurück; und wenn dies auf jeden der gegebnen Fälle passte: so war *die* Wissenschaft erfunden. ('In all branches of science the most important discoveries are only reached by means of analogy: one considers a number of similar cases and tries to trace them back to general concepts, and in the end to one leading principle; and if this covers all the given cases, thus *this* bit of knowledge has been established.')[42]

Not simply this historical method, but the very discipline of history itself had become institutionalized within a period of 20 years, from 1760 to 1780. The approach was steadily more professional and the number of students swelled every year. One of the most prominent representatives of the Göttingen research trend as described here was August Ludwig Schlözer (1735–1809), professor of history, political science and statistics. He is of particular interest to me because Grellmann was strongly influenced by him. They worked together for years.[43] Schlözer is known as an original exponent of the eighteenth-century Enlightenment. His many journeys were intended to make him more knowledgeable. He had fixed in his mind's eye a *Universal History*. Applicability and utility were concepts at the heart of scientific debate in Göttingen in his day, which explains the keen interest in such subjects as constitutional law, political science, economics, international law, commercial law and statistics, all oriented to the comparative study of internal relations in European nations. Social, economic, constitutional and cultural relations were of central interest. In a certain sense statistics was an all-encompassing and even an emancipatory discipline that highlighted the administrative failings of the state and enabled governments to see, through empirically supported studies, how the welfare of a country could be improved and the contentment of its subjects promoted. Schlözer formulated four principles for the proper use of statistics towards such ends: reliability (through the critical analysis of sources), precision (quantitatively, but also qualitatively), the use of many kinds of sources, and the capability of combining these sources. He had in mind documents, deeds, chronicles, travel accounts and newspapers, exactly those sources upon which Grellmann based his work on Gypsies. Schlözer was an extraordinarily active publicist, who also edited various periodicals that were much talked about at the time, including the *Briefwechsel* (1776–82) and the *Staatsanzeigen* (1782–93) which acquired reputations as sounding boards for public complaint.[44] In their pages he vigorously criticized the administrative evils of the day, but also assailed the misery of serfdom, religious intolerance, superstition, the suppression of freedom of opinion and the press, the privileges of the nobility and the burdens heaped on its citizens by corrupt systems of government. In his journalistic sallies, Schlözer could count on the partisanship of 'enlightened' sovereigns such as Maria Theresa[45] and Joseph II, although he was not always able to evade the grip of the censor. In his turn he was, for years, a fervent admirer of the reform measures that they had carried out, bearing witness to his feelings on paper and during his classes until, late in the 1780s, he began to devote himself to studying the drawbacks of their policy.

As teacher, Schlözer inspired many students, among whom one was Grellmann, although we do not know how many courses he took from Schlözer.[46] We do know that Schlözer took him as a student under his wing and even gave him the notes from his journeys to Italy so that Grellmann could arrange for their appearance in a printed edition.[47] They were indeed published as *Staatsanzeigen von Italien* in Göttingen (1785–86), even before the revised second edition of Grellmann's book on Gypsies. In 1770 Schlözer had also conceived of the plan to make a critical compilation of all German language chronicles since Charlemagne, a project for which he later recruited Grellmann owing to his familiarity with German history. In this instance, however, no publication was ever realized. As far as the historical chapters in Grellmann's Gypsy tome are concerned, reading them reveals that he worked wholly in the spirit of Schlözer.

Nature or nurture: a centuries-old debate

We now turn to the ethnographic part of Grellmann's work and in this context we must address the question of whether here, too, his ideas reflected the ethnographical debate of his era. In his foreword he wrote emphatically that he wanted to make a contribution to ethnography. One similarity between his approach and the bulk of published writing in the field was a marked dependency on the genre of travel literature so popular at the time.[48] Schlözer, to be sure, had also praised such work as indispensable for the writing of history. At the time whoever wanted to know something about other peoples and cultures would resort first of all to consulting this source of information. An important dichotomy in the perspective of Europeans who published accounts of their travels differentiated the *civilized* from the *savage*. It was assumed that both East and West had exotic groups on the fringe of their own civilized society. The heart of the matter was determining what place all these peoples occupied in nature's *great chain of being*. Had the savage peoples become bogged down in an early phase of development? If so, then the task at hand was to find out what could be done to help them along until they became civilized. Ethnographers and natural scientists developed the scientific methods of comparison and classification necessary to impose order on their observations. These interpretations, however, were coloured by classical notions of beauty, middle-class virtues (moderation, honour and hard work), and by national myths and symbols, all of which paved the way for conceptions about superior and inferior peoples.[49] Enlightened thought in terms of moderation and order, it must be said, tended to reject everything that was considered to be primitive. Only within the Romantic literary tradition would the idea of the *noble savage* create a stir.

This paradox can be clearly detected in the development of physical anthropology. Whoever categorizes must sooner or later confront the question of how differences between people are to be explained. For those with the monogenetic vision of the Bible as a point of departure, environmental factors such as climate and diet, along with inherited traits, would be seen as having led to the noted differences. That perspective justified the thought that people could perhaps be civilized through emancipatory measures. The point was that science sought for objective methods to grasp the differences among groups of people and, in the first instance, somatic characteristics seemed suitable. That explains why phrenology (skull measurement) and physiognomy (the reading of faces) soared to such prominence. Through the calibration of people's external traits, and classification by measurement, some semblance of order could be brought to the muddle of human diversity. These classifications did not always manage to remain free from prevailing value judgments, however. Thus in the work of the Dutchman Camper, who introduced the facial angle as an indicator, and Lavater, the father of physiognomy, we find representations of ideal types in which Greek standards of what is beautiful are recognizable. Their observations of (a people's) character agreed with the idea of a unique *Volksgeist* as propounded by Johann Gottfried Herder. Herder, though, did not combine this concept with any hierarchy of a human sort. Others, such as the Göttingen professor Christoph Meiners, did.[50] He attributed diversity among peoples to structural inequality, the consequence of multiple lines of descent; that is to say, descent from divergent 'ancestors'. To this way of thinking environmental factors were but of negligible importance and the characteristics of a people (or race) were ultimately hereditary. The extreme consequence of this vision was that people were regarded as essentially unchangeable, an idea which clashed with Enlightenment precepts regarding the possible emancipation of 'uncivilized man'. The clash generated debate at the time and we encounter this in Grellmann's book on Gypsies. The immutability of uncivilized peoples was explained by their nature, but the culturally inspired vision of the Enlightenment wished to lift them up morally through emancipation, which implied a belief they could become different.

A fashionable Göttingen scholar who figured in this discussion and who knew Grellmann, was Johann Friedrich Blumenbach (1752–1840), an anatomist and natural scientist who merits brief mention here because of his publication on the skulls of Gypsies. Blumenbach's starting point was the unity of the human species and he attributed differences among groups of people to such processes as migration, climate and food. By comparing characteristics including the skin, hair and skull (while acknowledging the importance of language and morals), he devised a typology of human races with which he believed himself able to reconstruct the history of different varieties within mankind as a whole. He reached a total of five basic *ideal types*, distinguishing many further internal variations within them. The Caucasian type, to which he himself belonged and which according to him was characterized by a perfectly spherical skull, he considered to be, physically, the most attractive – which indicates that he too was unable in his research to wrestle free from traditionally determined aesthetic judgments. In making his classifications, however, he relied simply on physical characteristics without as a rule venturing out onto the thin ice of correlations with the supposed mental or cultural traits of a people – in theory. In practice, however, he did sometimes make such speculations, as may be seen from the little which he wrote about Gypsies.[51] In his collection of skulls of foreign people, which now is housed in the Anatomy Institute of Göttingen University, there was, at the time, an example included of a 'true Gypsy'. This skull was, according to Blumenbach, so characteristic that visitors from Transylvania easily picked it out as that of a Gypsy from among the 65 skulls of non-German origin on view.[52] He did not restrict himself to an anatomical analysis of this skull, but also drew a connection to traits of the Gypsies themselves. He maintained that it was possible to encounter original specimens of that race only in Transylvania. He believed that wandering was their way of life, that they lived in forests, and that they sought protection as drifters and vagabonds. It was also said to be established that they lured children away cunningly and that their own offspring were the product of diverse combinations of parents. For these reasons Blumenbach did not find it strange that their bodies at birth assumed all kinds of unusual postures. From where or from whom he garnered this last observation, he fails to say. What is interesting is his claim to have discovered staggering similarities between his 'true Gypsy' skull and head bones and the head of an Egyptian mummy in his collection. This find, as far as he was concerned, only appeared to contradict Grellmann's theory about the Gypsies' coming from Hindustan, for Meiners, in his study of comparative ethnography, had specifically pointed out the resemblance between the Hindus from India and the ancient Egyptians.[53] In this way Blumenbach implied that although it was true linguistics suggested Hindustani roots for Gypsies, physiognomy exposed their more ancient origins.

GRELLMANN: UNFULFILLED PROMISE

From this sketch of the world of Göttingen University in the second half of the eighteenth century, Grellmann emerges as typical of his time: the author of a book that received a great deal of notice and was translated into many languages and brought him a professor's post at an early age. He was well connected and had an appealing personality, so nothing apparently stood in the way of a successful career. Yet, from the scarce details we know about his life, in the end he did not live up to Göttingen's high expectations. He was well known, true enough, but fell short of fame. That it would be his book on Gypsies which would make his name, albeit in the small circle of Gypsy studies experts, was something he surely never suspected.

Heinrich Moritz Gottlieb Grellmann first saw the light of day on 7 December 1753 in Jena.[54] He was the son of Paul Christian Grellmann, the head of a baker's guild and apparently of Russian descent.[55] In Weimar, Heinrich attended the William Ernst Gymnasium where he caught the attention of Johann Michael Heinze, rector of the school from 1770 to 1790. At the time he was friends with the later playwright, August von Kotzebue[56] and, according to his friend Bühle, he achieved study results that were so much better than everyone else's that he became Heinze's pet pupil. The rector, a classicist and a deeply religious man, also received him in his home and on 25 April 1791 gave him his daughter, the widow Anna Christina Carolina Heinze, in marriage. They were married in church by the renowned Herder,[57] an intimate friend of father-in-law Heinze.[58] Four children were born of this union and from the names in the baptism register it can be inferred that Grellmann, presumably thanks to his in-laws, was welcomed into the better circles of Weimar and Göttingen and established a relationship with the illustrious publishing house of Ruprecht.[59] His choice of what to study also betrays Heinze's influence. He studied theology at the University of Jena between 1776 and 1781 where the close reading of texts particularly captured his interest. He also preached regularly in the churches of Jena, Weimar and the surrounding area; one of these sermons, delivered in the church of the University of Jena, appeared in print in 1780 and thus became his first published work. In that year, moreover, his interests appear to have taken a new turn. What began to fascinate him increasingly was the relationship between religious services and the position of the church, together with that between the position of burghers and the national administration. In order to increase his understanding of such processes, he began to follow lectures in history, statistics and politics.

The move to Göttingen, where he enrolled on 2 May 1781, was an obvious one at the time, although he was awarded his master's degree from the Department of Philosophy at Jena on 25 October 1783.[60] At around this time he had already found his academic stride at Göttingen, where in that same year, 1783, thanks to the intercession of his Maecenas, Friedrich Bertuch from Weimar, he managed to have his book on the Gypsies published.[61] This attracted publicity which, wholly in keeping with the spirit of Göttingen University, earned him extremely high regard.[62] The successful reception of his work, which also owed a debt to Bertuch's influence,[63] the translations into English and French which followed, and other writings which he had published in the following years led, in 1787, to his being named to the Philosophy Faculty as professor extraordinary. In 1794 his appointment as full professor ensued.

With the appearance of his concise survey of German statescraft, Grellmann seemed to be climbing the career ladder apace.[64] Thus Grellmann let it be known to the *Geheimrath* in Hannover, on which the trustees of the Georgia Augusta sat, that the University of Jena had offered him a post with the salary of 500 rixdollars.[65] His heart might lie in Göttingen, yet anxiety about his insecure income obliged him to weigh the offer seriously, all the more so because in 1791, at the age of 37 he had resolved to marry. The request resulted in his remuneration being increased a short while thereafter to 300 rixdollars. He chose to continue his Göttingen ties despite the appreciably better financial prospects at Jena, in the expectation that his merits would in time be compensated according to their worth. Göttingen, however, demanded that the talented constantly perform to the full extent of their capabilities and whoever failed to distinguish himself year in year out faded into the grey host of the diligent who would have a long wait for their reward.

The documents concerning Grellmann that have been preserved in the University Archives tell a tale primarily of frustration with appointments and salary increments. Thus in August 1793 he petitioned the university for a loan of 1,000 rixdollars from the university treasury with which to buy a house. He added that for years he had been led to expect promotion to a full professorship and he was therefore of the opinion that he could lay claim to an advance which, finally, was granted to him. In the internal letter of authorization, Heyne remarked: 'Die Stelle eines Professoris ordinarii wurde ihm vor mehreren Jahren vorbehalten, was *nicht ohne Kränkung* abgegangen ist.' ('The post of a full professor was dangled in front of him years ago already, which did not fail to give some offence.')[66] Even with his installation as full professor in 1794, however, these wrongs failed to come to an end. In 1801 he complained to Heyne that the chair in statistics had gone to a younger colleague which he took to be a motion of non-confidence in him. He found that one couldn't rebuke him for a lack of industry simply because for a number of years nothing from his hand had been published, especially since various important writings of his were about to appear. Heyne at once closed ranks with him, emphasizing Grellmann's prodigious capacity for hard work. In exoneration he wrote: 'Er leide durch die Zeit umstände, die ihn hindern, gefertigte Arbeiten ins Licht zu setzen.' ('During this time he had to contend with circumstances which interfered with his producing finished works.') What these circumstances were remained unspecified. Heyne advocated that the board of trustees in Hannover offer Grellmann a chair in history, even if this had to be newly created for him. This happened in May of that year. Grellmann might be on record as a diligent and painstaking scholar, his productivity clearly proved disappointing. Only guesswork can answer why. In eulogizing Grellmann, in 1805, his friend Bühle had the following to say:

If only this good man had continued along the path on which he had embarked with such favorable portents! That was the dearest wish of his friends and colleagues. Often they even pleaded with him to do so! The elite of Hannover wanted to encourage him in this direction. His statistical descriptions primarily concerned the German states, difficult material, true,but they constituted the most useful and most eagerly anticipated portion of the entire work. Yet, Grellmann let the project lag for twelve years. This delay cost him the fruits of his good reputation, as long as he kept the book to himself. (...) Therefore I asked him what the reason was that he did not sooner complete the work which he had started on with the highest of praise. At first he replied that he had grown disgusted with the continuation of such a work. Later that he had become totally obsessed with the political turbulence in France and how it would turn out. He also said that the situation of the German states, as long as they waged war against France, remained so unstable and insecure that he asked himself whether there was any point to venturing an historical-statistical description. That there would be time for that later, when the book could harmonize with reality. That is why he found it necessary to await the restoration of peace.

The reason why Grellmann's handbook on Germany finally did come out in 1804 had to do with a far-reaching alteration in his circumstances. In that year he was approached, together with many other German scholars, and offered a post as professor of universal history and statistics at the University of Moscow, an opportunity which he seized with both hands.[67] Indeed the prospects were extremely enticing: a salary of 2,000 roubles, the title and rank of imperial *Hofrath*, elevation to the hereditary nobility, a handsome domicile, free firewood throughout the year, and generous provision for widows and orphans.[68] In May 1804, probably with his wife and children, he undertook the journey to Moscow by way of St Petersburg and there, on 31 August, he delivered his inaugural oration. The tide seemed to have turned. Tragedy would have it, however, that a month later, on 1 October, he died from a nervous fever.[69]

In Grellmann's Moscow oration, he expressed his views in strong terms.[70] We can hear in it the voice of an historian tempered in the intellectual climate of Göttingen. He calls history the 'Light of Truth', 'Mistress of Life', and he conceives of scholarship as a part of human history. Both should make a contribution to the progress of the middle classes and lend support to the state, while reason must serve the common good and by probing after the causes of prosperity and adversity exercise an influence on the form of government. In the context of the discipline of statistics, he cited Seneca who wrote that the way of precepts is long, but it is shorter than that of examples. By revealing where circumstances were advantageous or else indeed hurtful, how errors could be avoided, and which examples merited follow-up, statistics, to Grellmann's way of thinking, could prove exceptionally salutary and useful. His speech offered several variations on this theme:

> Just as in medicine it is of major importance, and contributes most of all to the easing and cure of illnesses, to understand their cause and symptoms, so in combatting diseases of state advice is sought from those who are familiar with the source of the affliction, and with its nature.[71]

He illustrated his point with reference to the abolition of the slave status of serfs in Europe by emphasizing the advantage to all concerned of this historical development. Next he warned, however, that this emancipation must proceed in phases because, so he reasoned, people who are rough and of primitive mind, avaricious and not capable of restraining themselves once they have heard the voice of freedom, readily resort to the use of violence to get their way, whereby unintentionally a wise decision can deteriorate into a general disaster. People, in his view, should be trained for true freedom in small stages.

These were the fundamental principles upon which Grellmann's book on Gypsies, which appeared 21 years previously, was based. It was a form of enlightened absolutism totally in keeping with the way in which great sovereigns of the era attempted to rule. Only when Grellmann wrote the book he was a historian who had just completed his studies and certainly not an experienced scholar. He might refer to the enlightened emancipation policy of Maria Theresa and Joseph II, but he made no attempt to place the policy with respect to Gypsies within the broader context of the rulers' general reforms. In his work references to academic debates concerning the nature and essence of foreign peoples are also missing. The author limits himself to those groups that his sources designate as Gypsies. It is doubtful whether, after 20 years further study, he would have written very differently on the subject. Whoever scans Grellmann's complete works can only come away with the realization that he certainly cannot be counted among the original thinkers of his time. In his scholarly approach and choice of subjects he followed paths that his teachers had cleared away. Comparison with his contemporaries also brings to light that he was certainly not remarkably erudite and he trailed far behind others in productivity.[72] Whoever examines the list of his publications, sees that he prepared many editions of source materials. Perusal of the tables of contents of his other writings discloses that he primarily brought into print descriptive surveys of political-scientific topics. In this respect, his book on Gypsies is unique within his total production, especially by virtue of its combination of ethnographic, historical and linguistic themes. A predeliction for ethnological subjects also appears in later publications, it is true, but these were consistently minor, self-contained contributions. The greatest part of his work, however, had to do with affairs of state. It is consequently time to turn back to his great 1783 publication on Gypsies.

GRELLMANN'S GYPSY IMAGES

Grellmann's book set a basic pattern for ideas about Gypsies which during the following centuries we recognize recurring constantly in publications whenever the subject arises. I will bestow ample attention here on the archetypal image of Gypsies that he constructed because it has left such a deep and virtually unavoidable imprint. In scholarly literature about Gypsies we still repeatedly come across many of his themes, motifs and even his very sentences. It is necessary to provide a comprehensive overall view of Grellmann's initial portraiture in order to be able to determine to what extent later writers were anchored in his tradition, whether they may have changed elements of his images or made additions – to be in a position, in short, to point out modifications of the Gypsy image. In the process I differentiate a number of subjects areas where Grellmann set standards for later writers: communal history, an ethnographic portrait (morals and customs, vocational activities, general character sketch) and, finally, language and descent.[73]

A communal history

To start with let me recapitulate how many Gypsies or gypsy-like groups there actually were according to Grellmann in about 1780 and in which countries they lived. He only dared to make assertions with confidence for the countries surrounding Austria, where some 100,000 Gypsies were said to reside. For Asia and Africa all he reported was that countless groups remained. As for America, no exact figures were on hand. Consequently he confined himself to Europe, but that was a part of the world which they indeed covered, he stated, like grasshoppers. As regards the distribution of Gypsies within Europe he was able to report that they still lived in northern countries and in Russia but no exact data were available. England was *terra incognita*; roughly 40,000 Gypsies lived in Spain and not many less in Italy, although how many was not known. He was equally vague about the kingdom of Turkey where tens of thousands apparently lived, and in France, the Netherlands, Switzerland and Germany Gypsies were found, as far as he knew, but only sporadically. As a result of the shortage of reliable sources, the accent, as Grellmann himself wrote, came to fall on central Europe; this I confirmed by an analysis of the literature on which, judging by his footnotes, he based his work.[74]

With his expatiation on the various names by which Gypsies were known, Grellmann also set a trend and opened a realm for fanciful etymological speculation. He lumped together diverse groups of people who, as far as their way of life, appearance and occupations were concerned, displayed traits consonant with the image of the Gypsy that he envisioned; he brought them under one heading in order to provide a foundation for his hypothesis about Gypsies as a people in diaspora, along the lines of the history of the Jews. Historical sources were lacking to prove whether all these groups really had anything more in common than a supposedly itinerant way of life and a shared stigmatization by the government. In his eagerness to demonstrate that these were the descendants of a single people, during his summary of the disparate names for Gypsies used in different countries, Grellmann indulged himself in linguistic exercises variations of which can be detected in many publications after him. Encyclopedia entries provide a representative sample of this phenomenon. It is rather pointless, however, to follow in the footsteps of all these authors, however keen their fascination for morphological parallels may have been.

Another area of extensive speculation prior to Grellmann, but also after him, concerns the time of the first appearance of Gypsies in Europe. On the grounds of the image that the author had compiled from old annuals, and on the premise that Gypsies were foreigners from the East, he launched into a mission of detection backwards in time. As I already indicated in the introduction, at the outset of the fifteenth century it was believed that these were people who, out of religious conviction, had gone on a pilgrimage. According to Grellmann these were mere stories swallowed in their entirety because they harmonized with the spirit of pilgrimages during the era of Latin Christiandom and because the time of the Gypsies' arrival coincided with the return home of groups of crusaders. These accounts, however, to his way of thinking, belonged to the realm of fables, and Gypsies simply yearned to be taken for pilgrims. In this context he pointed out the gullibility of the population at that time, for Gypsies won acceptance, effortlessly, as holy people. The notion is said to have circulated that whoever insulted them threw away his chances for happiness. In addition lower levels of government behaved on occasion rather ambivalently towards them so that Gypsies, according to Grellmann's reconstruction, could roam about for a long time unpunished.

That they also had possession of official letters of protection and safe conducts surprised him exceedingly. The way in which he handled the topic is typical of how he worked when dealing with controversial aspects of Gypsy history, which is why I am so closely following his process of reasoning here. He began by alluding to the fact that different annuals devoted attention to this phenomenon and some even claimed to have laid eyes on copies of the sealed letters. Immediately afterwards he undercuts such testimony by citing a source that mentions how Gypsies numbered forgers in their ranks who could falsify seals. Another had written that they couldn't always produce these documents for inspection and that they were written in a style that had little currency. In other words, there must have been deception involved to a certain extent. Once Grellmann has dropped this hint, he eases up slightly. For there was a chronicler who had seen such a safe conduct which – a hundred years after the inscribed date – contained the information that the bearers were on a pilgrimage lasting seven years.[75] The Gypsies carried it with them like an heirloom. If it had been counterfeit, Grellmann continued, then surely they would have been clever enough to change the date to their advantage in order to convince contemporaries. In the sixteenth-century state there were also ordinances that, in certain regions, the roving of Gypsies under safe conduct was no longer permitted and complaints were raised against rulers for issuing such documents. For Grellmann, this was yet another proof that these actually had once existed. After confusing the reader with contradictory statements, Grellmann at last offers two examples of such safe conducts as evidence confirming their existence. These were said to have been included in the chronicle of Andreas from Regensburg.[76] His transcription was made from the copy that Gypsies carried with them in 1424 when they passed through his city.

In Grellmann's eyes the Gypsies' 'golden age' lasted a surprisingly long time. Only after half a century of leniency did former prejudice – as he oddly enough referred to it, thus suggesting that they had already been known in Europe – surface again and, scorned as the dregs of society, Gypsies were targeted for acts of banishment. Subsequently he turned to the controversy explicit in his sources about the supposed difference between those who asserted in the fifteenth century that they were on pilgrimage and the Gypsies of later centuries. He discarded sources that alluded to that distinction with the argument that the earliest group would still have had to support itself and had thus resorted to stealing. How it could happen that, despite such a way of life, they repeatedly and over a longer period of time went on acquiring safe conducts from high-placed officials is a question that at this stage in his discussion Grellmann simply drops. According to him the later Gypsies were simply the descendants of the first scum – to adopt once more his use of language. Only in this way could he clarify that, as well as being similar in appearance to their predecessors, they were also distinguished by an oriental mentality and way of life. This did not prevent him from holding the view that all sorts of riff-raff had in addition mixed in with the Gypsies in the course of time.

The ethnography of a people

APPEARANCE, MORES AND CUSTOMS

In Grellmann's ethnographical portrait of Gypsies, he raises topics which return again in studies after him as more or less standard fare, often using the same wording. His first fascination was with how Gypsies looked, a subject that has set the lyrical strings of many writers vibrating. Grellmann started by remarking that in the earliest chronicles, Gypsies were portrayed as black and hideous beings but that in the following centuries their appearance was described in primarily positive terms. He ascribes their good health to the Spartan living conditions to which they were exposed. From an early age children, too, lived on the road, enduring all kinds of weather, which hardened them. Characteristic of the thinking of the time was the explanation offered by the author for the colour of their skin. This was said to be a brownish yellow because they grew up in the midst of smoke and filth.[77] It wasn't a question of skin pigmentation inherited at birth, but rather the way they were raised and lived that had left its mark. Grellmann believed he could prove his point by calling attention to Gypsies in Hungary who performed music or who served as soldiers in the imperial army. According to him they were cleaner and you could not tell anything about their origins from their colour, even though they had been raised by their parents until the age of 14. To this he added that a black had to live many centuries in the land of the whites before his blackness faded.[78] In his eyes this was one of the many proofs that argued in favour of allowing the emancipation of Gypsies to proceed through their retraining. Appearance and character could, he maintained, ultimately be 'washed white'.

He had little positive to say about their eating habits: a grimy cuisine, eating and drinking whatever was available whenever it was convenient, with a particular preference for dead livestock. He did not go along with the accusations, however, that they fetched carrion from the knackery or ate horse meat. On the other hand they would not turn up their noses at animals who perished in a fire or from disease, nor would they reject the corpses of cattle that others thought unfit for consumption. In the description of their preference for raw, uncooked food we detect an intimation of the cannibalism of which they were accused. They only drank water and beer, he maintains, if they could get it free; wine was too expensive and they appeared not to like it much anyhow. They did eagerly pursue the expansive high that came from knocking back brandy wine. Another characteristic of both men and women was said to be their longing for tobacco, which they preferred to smoke in a pipe. He describes their nibbling and sucking on the stem as an activity that took precedence over everything else, as if it were an addiction. That their apparel was shabby looking didn't amaze Grellmann, given that he considered them to be members of the beggar class. Their whole style of dress and preference for bright colours, for red especially, he considered a manifestation of a misplaced wish to show off. The flair with which Gypsy women decked themselves out he found void of any vestige of taste.

From their manner of homemaking he also believed it was obvious that they stood on the bottom step of civilized society. Even the sedentary among them were said to own no more than a decrepit hut. In any event 'true Gypsies' were nomadic and brutish, living like wild animals in tents, caves and subterranean holes. They were said to live by nature's clock and react instinctively to external impulses. Sedentary Gypsies, like those in Spain, had, to Grellmann's way of thinking, climbed to a somewhat higher step of culture. They came closer to usual middle class norms, although they were often destined to endure poverty and want. In this context he also discussed the burning desire that both sedentary and nomadic Gypsies were said to nurture for fine gold and silverwork. According to him they would sooner spend their money on such 'superfluities' than on necessities, and this had been true since the distant past. He added to this that such precious objects could have the function of being passed on as heirlooms. By later burying them, beneath the hearthstone of a house, for example, they thought it was possible to guard them from theft.

Gypsy marriage provoked Grellmann's amazement and his response to it set the tone for other commentators – a tone that lasted for centuries after him. In his opinion, you could scarcely describe this as a ceremony. It hardly involved any discussion beforehand. By virtue of the fact that Gypsies usually lived outside the field of vision of the authorities, there was no control of marriage on the part of officialdom. Grellmann noted that Gypsies were not altogether indifferent towards the marriage rite, the author went on to note, only this was not because they wanted to act in keeping with the rules, but rather out of an arrogant desire to emulate. Addressing themselves to a clergyman was too troublesome, so one of their own number acted as priest. Grellmann wound the topic up by observing – and here too echoes would continue to resound down into the twentieth century – that Gypsies only married among each other. As far as their children were concerned, according to him they always looked good despite their swarthiness and parental neglect, only it irked him that from early youth they were taught to dance and to steal so that they never went to school for an education. Like other uncivilized peoples, the author continued, Gypsies spoiled their children by being too lenient. They never resorted to the rod and responded to all kinds of mischief with flattery and affection, with the consequence that parents were repaid with ingratitude. As long as the way they brought their children up didn't change, the Gypsy, according to Grellmann, would never cease to be a thief and 'moral monster'.

Since their initial appearance in Europe Gypsies were said to have travelled about in bands under the leadership of chiefs. Down through the years these headmen were referred to in annuals by such titles as *woiwoden* (a Polish term for governor or leader), knights, counts, dukes and kings. Grellmann derided these designations as the ridiculous aping of titles that Gypsies encountered in 'the civilized world'. An advantage of the title *woiwoden* that he acknowledged, however, was that in time of war the state could call upon these 'leaders' to supply fighting men. The leader's actual power was, according to Grellmann, slight and he was said merely to serve as an intermediary between his own followers and the government. Still, Grellmann added, perhaps one thing he may well have done in their own interest was to administer justice. That was also, to his mind, the reason why Gypsies preferred to settle their own affairs, because then everybody – at least in their own circle – fared better.

The prevailing idea about their religion was that they brought none with them from their homeland and accommodated to the tradition of the country in which they stayed. Raised without discipline and schooling, they were supposed to remain unreceptive to higher thoughts. Grellmann insisted that even the Turks were convinced that Gypsies were never true believers and, in contrast to converted Jews, Gypsies had to go on paying poll tax (*Charadsch*) in the Ottoman Empire, even if their ancestors were known to have been Islamic for centuries.[79] Only the right to wear a white turban after visiting Mecca appears to have been granted to them. The author also stressed yet again the idea that Gypsies in the Christian world gladly let their children be baptized several times in order to go on receiving gifts from godparents (from other than Gypsy circles). The curious thing about this remark is that elsewhere Grellmann had written that Gypsies habitually sought godparents from their own number.

VOCATIONAL ACTIVITIES

All the sources that Grellmann consulted agreed, according to him, that the root cause of Gypsies' poverty lay in their laziness and love of ease. What we can conclude from his analysis of the vocations that they practised, however, is that they fulfilled a function in disparate economic sectors. He apparently understood this as well – even went on about it at length – but time and again he played down the value of their labour because the notion of their parasitical nature dominated his thinking. Here I will briefly review those occupations that received the most attention in his summary.

Gypsies had long been known as smiths. Grellmann trivializes their work, however, by talking about the forging of thin horseshoes and other objects of little importance. According to him they used poor material in their work, such as rusty iron, and they moved about with only a stone for an anvil, a few bellows, and a smattering of other portable tools. In spite of their simple equipment they were generally praised for their drive, to which Grellmann added the qualification that the task at hand should not be one requiring perseverance, for they couldn't summon up the patience. They had also acquired a reputation for horse trading and in Hungary they even earned a good living raising and selling horses. Grellmann added, however, that this did not hold true for them all and some of them carried on a trade in blind and broken horses. When they purchased a horse they emphasized its faults and when the horse wasn't worth anything any more they sold the hide to a flayer. To conceal the shortcomings of an animal, Grellmann maintains, they employed numerous tricks. He attributed the fact that people continued to do business with these traders to the nature of the enterprise of trade, drawing a parallel with the Jews, at whose hands, he believed, customers also expected to be cheated but still went ahead and took the risk, lured by low prices.

In Hungary and Transylvania, Gypsies were reported working as executioners and hangmen and they also at times filled a demand for flayers. Through this association with what are known in modern literature as 'infamous callings',[80] it is as if Grellmann offered a partial explanation for the social aversion with which Gypsies have been confronted throughout history. Even in contemporary studies we come across allusions to vocations that are somehow connected with death as a clarification for why Gypsies came to be stigmatized as outcasts.[81] Without going into the backgrounds of these jobs, Grellmann quotes an author who adduced the cruelty of Gypsies as a general characteristic that would explain why they were so well suited for such vocations.[82]

A number of things are striking about how Grellmann wrote on the subject of the occupations that groups of Gypsies without a doubt actually practised. First of all he presented each occupation as if only Gypsies performed the kind of work in question, not failing to mention, however, that they inevitably, at the very least, practised deceptions or delivered goods of inferior quality. He thus made the economic services of the Gypsies by definition suspect and denied the successful aspects of their existence. His bias stands out very clearly when he turns to consider the soothsaying with which for ages Gypsy women had created a stir from which they earned handsomely. We see how belief and disbelief, awe and a compulsion to find an explanation for things contend for priority but, in the end, disgust prevails. Grellmann introduced his discussion by expressing his amazement that the women of such a 'filthy folk' should be the very ones with eyes sharp enough to read the dark secrets of someone's future in the lines of his hand. Next he mocked the Gypsies for their superstition – in his eyes the typical product of the benighted Middle Ages. Grellmann pointed out that, in the Middle Ages, the divine art of palmistry (reading hands) was said to have been practised by wise and learned minds who even gave public lessons. According to him, their erudite knowledge, which lay buried in the treasury of the past, had enabled them easily to surpass the Gypsies. Gypsies had seen to it, however, that such forms of deception – as in the following phase of his argument palmistry has suddenly again become – remained alive. The same held true, he maintained, for the belief in the wonderful powers of healing that Gypsies were said to have and which they applied, for example, by selling amulets. Just more forms of fraud, he appended, otherwise they would make themselves truly happy. He was willing to acknowledge that simple people in towns and villages were all too willing to spend a few pennies on such chicanery, artifice, and sleights of hand but it offended him that such practices still went on in late eighteenth-century Germany where religion and scholarship had brought the Enlightenment. In his rejection of superstition Grellmann was aligning himself with the spirit of Joseph II, although he laid the blame for its persistence entirely on the Gypsies.

Only when he is describing Gypsies' musical qualities do straight-forward positive phrases flow from Grellmann's pen. Here, too, he launched a trend which carried on for centuries. With the violin above all they had, according to him, acquired fame. They were regularly appointed to play even in the chapels of counts and earls, and promoted as bandmasters. Young, talented Gypsy women were said to be great favourites among the Hungarian nobility and were often summoned from far away to display their gifts at a ball. On their heels, so Grellmann added, there also came bunglers, however, who wandered about and tried to find engagements at country weddings.

Another activity from which thousands of Gypsies earned their living, according to Grellmann, was panning for gold, especially in central Europe. Special permission was needed from higher up to engage in this work. Thus in Wallachia and Moldavia only those who served the rulers directly were entitled to pan for gold. Grellmann goes on for many pages about how Gypsies didn't earn uniformly impressive sums everywhere, providing details of incomes per group. At a certain moment, however, he confessed his surprise that Gypsies in the Banat made such modest profits despite the abundance of gold ore in the regional streams – a result which he attributed to their indolence. He then illustrated his point with a lengthy passage about the slovenly way they performed their work. Immediately thereafter he produced a report from another source which seemed to make it clear that Gypsies were indeed highly energetic when it came to panning for gold and that was why it was also so easy for them to find employment doing such work. With Grellmann's pointed grumbling about *dolce far niente* in the background there was little chance that his readers would form a positive, overall impression of hard-working men.

At the end of Grellmann's long account of Gypsy occupations, his pervasive negativity became highly explicit when he began to explain in detail that idleness and laziness *nevertheless* dominated Gypsy behaviour and that begging and stealing were how they usually managed to keep themselves going. According to him, Gypsies could only be kept in the harness like soldiers under the discipline of a corporal. In addition, in Grellmann's opinion only the Transylvanian Gypsies who panned for gold and some musicians had become familiarized with the concept of bourgeois honour and shame. Not even a nail would be safe from the rapacity of the rest. He considered their work to be a smokescreen that made it easier for them to be able to steal things. Gypsy women especially knew precisely how to go about their business: sales talk at the front door and children breaking in at the back. That was why, he insists, they were so eager to visit annual markets. They joined forces then in gangs; men and women began to disport themselves scandalously to divert tradespeople while others meanwhile picked unattended stalls clean. Other sources would have it that Gypsies only stole trifles and avoided violence. Grellmann concurred in general, but argued there were exceptions. Gypsies were by nature quick to fear which meant, as he saw it, that they were never keen to commit theft if there was any danger involved. Once more a stereotype that held sway well into the Nazi era.

GENERAL CHARACTER SKETCH

At the end of the ethnographic part of his book, Grellmann produced a character sketch of the 'Gypsy people'. They were said to be distinguished by a childlike way of thinking and a soul that was crude and uncivilized. Moreover, they were sooner governed by sensuality than reason and only used their minds to satisfy their basic, animal drives. Furthermore he portrayed them as quick, garrulous and capricious, not to be trusted (even by other Gypsies) and incapable of gratitude, as well as fearful and fawning towards people in high places. How vicious they were could be seen according to him in the behaviour of some mothers who in their anger picked up one of their children by the leg to swing and use to batter someone with who had insulted them. That they were also arrogant baffled Grellmann, considering that their shallowness stood in the way of their developing any feelings of honour or shame. They never contemplated the causes of their behaviour, according to him, and what had been taken for arrogance he was far more prone to see as a variant of their childishness. They were fond of showing off with splendid clothes and squabbling and quarrelling with their fellows in public places, even going as far as to roar and simulate fury. All were given to debauchery, wrote Grellmann – especially the women who knew no shame and gave free rein to their lust. That they had no bread on the shelf and resorted to thievery and conning operations he attributed to their laziness, forever after an ineradicable element of the Gypsy image. Sources that passed on a more positive judgment of Gypsies, had relied, the author felt sure, on mistaken reports about these masquerading 'Egyptian pilgrims'.

One character trait described as favourable to a certain extent was Gypsy affability. They accepted their lot in life, an attitude which, according to Grellmann, derived from an excess of improvidence – thus it was difficult to call it a true virtue. None the less they were said to possess some real talents; this was apparent above all in the slyness and cunning with which they set to work in the world of fraud and larceny. In this context he also cited a Hungarian author who had written that Gypsies were agile and clever, did excellent work with their hands, and were extremely eloquent in their own defense when the situation demanded it. Be that as it may, they had not yet made any progress in, for example, education, owing, most of all, to how easily they fell back into their carefree way of life. To Grellmann's way of thinking, the Gypsies thus did have aptitudes but their inconstancy and fickleness nipped any burgeoning proficiency in the bud. This lack of will power kept them from becoming the useful citizens that they otherwise could be.

When we investigate how Grellmann filled in his proposals for ways to improve the Gypsies, we observe that his vision floundered under the weight of his pessimism. Thus, for example, he reported that Gypsies were valuable as soldiers, referring to their historical ties with military action and to their physical attributes which made them exceedingly suitable for the army. Immediately afterwards he wrote that they were primarily mobilised to plunder, set fires, steal and spread destruction in the land of the enemy. It was in such roles as these, according to him, that they really came into their own. Wholly in keeping with the tradition of the centuries before him he asserted that Gypsies lent themselves readily to become the agents of treason in wartime, which would explain their reputation as spies for the Turks. He added that, although he found this a far-reaching accusation, he didn't consider it to be altogether beside the point. Their indigent circumstances, in his opinion, prompted the taking of bribes. They badly wanted to be thought of as important, moreover, and enemies played on these feelings. Their happy-go-lucky character would ultimately enable them to flirt with danger undetected, a view that Grellmann elaborated with a number of historical anecdotes about Gypsy treachery since 1468. Thus what started out as a short discussion of the Gypsies' potential utility for the state concluded with the assertion that you could only expect the worst of them.

Language and origins

A third terrain where Grellmann established a pattern for a great many Gypsy studies after him consists of the thematic combination of their language and origins. Indeed there had been ample speculation on these subjects before him, and Grellmann first lets all these theories pass one more time in review, leading up to an entirely novel interpretation. Here I want to follow him up to that point.

He considered most of the ideas raised in the past on this subject to be eminently disposable. This held true in the first place for all those authors who thought they could determine the Gypsies' origins on grounds of their name or way of life but who, he thought, were really relying too much on guesswork. That would also be his criticism of Wagenseil's hypothesis,[83] for a long time so fashionable, which looked upon Gypsies as German Jews who, accused in the fourteenth century of having caused the plague, hid out in woods, deserts and subterranean caves to escape persecution. After 50 years, when the tide had turned, they dared to reappear. To justify their own, deviant religious observances, they then spread word of their Egyptian origins. The same was also true for their language which was said to be derived from Hebrew, and for their palmistry, something for which, it appeared, they found a ready demand among the people. Grellmann expended eight full pages on this theory, dismissing it ultimately with the remark that Wagenseil's powers of imagination had prevailed over his sober skill at argument.

Grellmann devoted a separate section to ideas pertaining to Egyptian origins; these, he stated, rested exclusively on oral tradition until the end of the seventeenth century. Later authors, such as Vulcanius, Thomasius and Salmon,[84] found themselves on the trail to Egypt through clues of linguistic similarity or historical interpretation. Griselini was the one, however, who, several years previously, had mustered the most evidence in support of the Egyptian hypothesis.[85] Grellmann filled no less than 11 pages retelling of Griselini's points, only to end by stating that he found it unnecessary to refute his arguments because no evidence had been presented and his predecessor had therefore shown himself to be a poor scholar in the fields of history and ethnography. He found many of the so-called correspondences between Gypsy and Egyptian character traits erroneously evaluated, which said a great deal about his image of Egyptians. Thus he commented that Gypsies were not at all sad by nature, did not superstitiously cling to religious rites, and definitely consumed beans and onions. Typical of Grellmann's method is the manner in which he continued after making this rebuttal. He went on to say that he found it a pity that Egyptian origins could not be proven for then the magicians whom the Egyptian pharaoh had installed as overseers of 'the children of Israel' would have been the forefathers of contemporary Gypsies. These magicians were the later killers of the children of Bethlehem who, after the exodus of the Israelites from Egypt, had gone on preying on society for some time before taking their leave to fend for themselves with trickery and deceit in foreign lands. Grellmann thus rejected the thoughts of others concerning the Egyptian roots of Gypsies in order thereafter to suggest himself that their supposed forefathers were the parasitical cheats who elsewhere in the world roamed about as Gypsies. And while he was at it he also made them out to be the murderers of children.

With the hypotheses that Grellmann handled in mind, I can venture to say that his idea of detecting the homeland of the Gypsies through comparisons of language was nothing new. He did lay claim in his work to the honour of being the first to have identified the actual country of origin through systematic linguistic cross-referencing. An article in an Austro-Hungarian periodical put him on the trail to Hindustan.[86] The piece in question was a third-hand story that is still today eagerly regarded as the cradle of Gypsy studies.[87] The historical account was first written up in Latin and based on a manuscript in the possession of the Hungarian collector of handwritten documents, Captain Szekely van Doba. Thirteen years earlier, on 6 November 1763, he had been visited by a book printer named Stephan Pap Szathmar Nemethi and their conversation had turned to the language of the Gypsies. Nemethi told him an anecdote about a reformed preacher, Stephanus Vali, in Almasch in the district of Comorn in Hungary, who had studied in Leiden and who came in contact with three youths from the Malabar coast, also studying there. Vali thought he detected similarities between the language these fellow students spoke and that of the Gypsies from Raabe in his motherland. The youths also informed him that on their peninsula in India there was a province called 'Czigania', a remark which elicits the comment from Grellmann that he had looked for this province on the map in vain. Actually on James Rennell's 'Map of India' (1782) the Province 'Cingana' does appear![88] Together with the three students, Vali had compiled a list of 1,000 words, with meanings. When he returned home, he had visited the Gypsies who were able effortlessly to give the meaning of a major portion of the words from Malabar which he read to them aloud. For Grellmann the problem was that Malabar, where at the time there was a Dutch trading post, was situated deep in south-west India where a different Indian language was spoken from the language of the north-east. To make his line of reasoning sound, he turned the students from Malabar into the sons of Brahmins who read Sanskrit, the ur-form of all Indian languages. In this way he believed that he had made his hypothesis about the relationship between the Gypsy and Hindustani languages plausible.

It is only possible to appraise the historical reliability of this anecdote indirectly. Vali's vocabulary list has never been found, nor was it used as a source in studying Gypsy languages.[89] In the seventeenth and eighteenth centuries hundreds of Hungarians did study theology at the Dutch universities of Leiden, Utrecht, Franeker and Groningen; this was not possible in their Catholic homeland and many could count on financial support from their hosts in the Netherlands.[90] By skimming the *Alba Studiosorum* of the universities, the registers signed by foreign students upon arrival, it is in theory possible to find out if a certain person studied in the Netherlands. With Stephanus Vali this indeed proved to be true, although he enrolled not in Leiden but in Utrecht in 1753, where the rector noted down Waali instead of Vali.[91] The three youths from Malabar could have run into Vali during visits to Leiden, except that Malabar, a prominent VOC trading post in those days, did not offer the schooling necessary to prepare for further study in the Netherlands. Such preparation was certainly available in the Dutch trade colony of Ceylon, situated nearby, where European education was offered both in Jaffna and Colombo.[92] Which brings us to the question of whether there were Ceylonese studying in Leiden around 1750. The enrolment registers provide an affirmative answer. Three theology students, Joh. Jacobus Meyer, Petrus Cornelissen and Antonius Moyaars registered in 1750, 1752 and 1754 respectively.[93] It also is possible to conclude from secondary literature that the first two were *castiezen*, that is children born in the Orient of European parentage.[94] They were also certainly fluent in Sinhalese, which, like Hindi, is considered a modern Indian language. There thus does exist historical material that encourages us to accept, with the necessary corrections, the story of Stephanus Vali as providing the first impulse to locate the birthplace of the Gypsies somewhere in the Indian subcontinent. In the second, enlarged edition of his book, Grellmann had added that both the linguists Büttner and Rüdiger, without, according to him, any knowledge of the article in the Austro-Hungarian periodical, had reached a similar conclusion that the language of the Gypsies must be east Indian. The reason that he had not paid Rüdiger's publication from 1782 any attention previously was his disappointment about its appearance just at the moment when his own manuscript was in such an advanced stage. In a letter to his patron Bertuch (22 September 1782), he spoke in highly conceited terms about this rival who had suddenly popped up out of nowhere:

> Rüdigers Schrift wird nichts weniger, als der Meinigen Schaden thun. Dafür hat schon die Göttingische Zeitung gesorgt. Er hat in einer dörren Untersuchung auf anderthalb Bogen den Ursprung der Zigeuner obgleich richtig, doch zu einseitig und mangelhaft bewiesen. Etliche sechzig Indostanische Wörter vergleicht er mit ebenso viel zigeunerischen, und schliesst nun aus der Aehnlichkeit dieser zwey Sprachen, dass die Zigeuner Indianischen Ursprungs seyn. Aber dabey zeigt er nicht, ob diese beiden Sprachen auch in ihren Flexionen und Abänderungen einerley sind, welches etwas beweisen will. Von der Geschichte ihrer Auswanderung gesteht er selbst, gar nichts zu wissen. ('Rüdiger's piece of writing will injure mine. The Göttingen newspaper has already seen to that. In a dry argument of one and a half quire he has traced the origins of Gypsies. Although what he writes is true the account is one-sided and poorly argued. He compares no less than sixty Hindustani words with just as many Gypsy words and concludes, solely on a basis of the comparison of these two languages, that the Gypsies are of Indian origin. He does not show, however, if the two languages are common in their declensions and inflections, which would really prove something. He even freely admits that he knows nothing about the history of their migration.')

To meet this competition, Grellmann decided to disregard Rüdiger's publication. All he did in the foreword of his first edition was to mention that Büttner had provided him with his word lists – including material from Rüdiger! – without discussing the two scholars in his chapter about comparison of languages. Only after he had won universal respect with his own work did he, in the second edition, finally do so, also citing Pallas and Marsden,[95] who during the 1780s had also pinpointed India on grounds of language comparison as the Gypsies' place of origin. All these sources in combination strengthened Grellmann in his conviction that adequate evidence had been marshalled in support of his assertion that the Gypsies came from India. He had 20 pages added with words from the 'Gypsy language' and Hindustani (a collective designation for languages spoken in the north of India) and gave their definitions in German. According to the author more than every third Gypsy word was Hindustani, or 12 or 13 out of every 30. Afterwards, to put the matter in perspective, he remarked that the comparisons presented were simply a small beginning. He had not been able to examine all the languages that the Gypsies wandering in diverse lands spoke, only the language of a number of them. Furthermore they were known, according to him, for wanting to keep their own language secret, and thus they had perhaps, out of distrust, carelessness, or ignorance, given words that weren't authentic. In other words Grellmann was advocating the undertaking of more comparisons.

Once, with the help of the language he had hit upon in Hindustan, he set out in search of similarities between the population there and Gypsies. To start with he analysed traits that he found to be charac-teristic of Indians and, so he went on to say, of all Eastern peoples. The picture he drew looked as follows: dusky pigmentation, slight bodies, apprehensiveness and cowardice, children scrambling about naked, living in tents, a preference for red clothing, secretiveness with respect to their language, work as smiths, exuberant dancers, soothsaying, eloquence, well endowed with natural abilities, a fondness for saffron, and marrying only among their own kind (because of the caste system). After this resume Grellmann arrived at what he called the *real goal of his disquisition*. What he wanted to show was that Gypsies were descended from the lowest class of Indians, the pariahs (as they were designated on the Malabar peninsula and in Hindustan), also known as Sudras. He thought that he could draw a host of analogies from travel accounts. In the process, now and again, he revealed his understanding that the caste involved was, to be sure, a despised one, which indubitably had social-economic consequences and to a large extent determined caste members' position in society. In the elaboration of his arguments, however, Grellmann left this out altogether and only had eyes for similarities in the character of both peoples.

Towards the end of his book, Grellmann devotes a few more pages to the reasons why these Gypsy/Sudras left their homeland when they did. The most plausible explanation seems to him that they took flight during the war of conquest waged in 1408/9 by Timur, who was bent on introducing the Islamic faith into India by fire and sword. That only the Sudras moved away at the time he explains as follows. The three highest castes considered their land as sacred and themselves as elect, thus, on principle, they did not abandon their place of birth. To flee along with the Sudras would have been humiliating, for the higher castes considered them to be inferior creatures. This was the source of their mutual hatred, Grellmann added in a note. What happened to the Sudras afterwards, remained unclear. The author did not consider himself capable of a reliable reconstruction of their journey to Europe. The most likely route seemed to him to pass through Arabia, Egypt and Turkey, but because there was no factual evidence, another pattern of emigration was, for him, every bit as possible.

GRELLMANN'S SOURCES

An ethnographic blueprint

In the foreword to the first printing of his book, Grellmann wrote that he had compiled his text from fragments of other people's industry. This was true for all three parts, the *ethnographic*, the *historical*, and the *linguistic*. In assembling his book he knew himself to be dependent on the usual sources of the period for an historian, such as travel descriptions and chronicles, and also on information from learned connections, some of whom he names in his pages, others of whom he leaves anonymous. Thus he acknowledged his intense gratitude to *Hofrath* Büttner, who had steered him onto the track of linguistic comparison between Hindi and the Gypsy language, the core of the second part of his book. He also makes special mention of Bauer from Hannover in appreciation of the unique linguistic material which Bauer put at his disposal.[96] In the second printing the names were added of Dániel Cornides, professor at Pest, and Penzel, professor at Kraków. He did not specify what information they provided him with, however; nor do we encounter any of their publications among the literature to which Grellmann refers in his footnotes.[97]

The author laid claim in his foreword to being the first to publish a comprehensive book about Gypsies. Only the writer of an essay in the *Wiener Anzeigen* concerning the situation in Hungary was said to have attempted to proceed in that direction before him. He alludes to this source in a subordinate clause which is rather startling when we later discover that it crops up in his footnotes on no less than 103 occasions, 97 times in the ethnographic part of his book, and six times in the second part about the origin of Gypsies. Indeed this turned out to be no arbitrary fragment on which Grellmann depended, but a series of magazine pieces from 1775/76 which, cumulatively, occupied 131 double-column pages.[98] Together, the subjects which are discussed in the series take up 183 pages, including footnotes, in the first edition of Grellmann's book. He thus borrowed an estimated 75 per cent of this portion of his text – at times entire passages word for word – from articles which had come out seven or eight years before.[99] As far as the structure of his book is concerned, he faithfully adhered to the chapter divisions appearing in the *Anzeigen*. All 43 publications to which the author of the articles referred we find again in Grellmann's footnotes. But we may assume he also consulted the greater part of the sources himself, for his phrasing at times differs just ever so slightly from that found in the *Anzeigen*. This might, however, also be a matter of paraphrasing. In this connection it should also be mentioned that the series only dealt with the situation of Gypsies in Hungary and Transylvania, while Grellmann also gathered sources concerning Gypsies in Spain, Italy, Russia, Turkey, England, France and other countries or parts of the world, even though these were comparatively few in number. This explains why, among subjects which for the rest all were derived from the *Anzeigen* articles, certain extra sections stood out, borrowed from travel impressions featuring Gypsies in, for example, Spain and Turkey.

We also recognize such an international orientation in the historical part of Grellmann's work, in particular in the chapter where he reviews governmental action towards Gypsies over time. Grellmann, certainly in his second edition, was also rather comprehensive in his summary of passages from German chronicles dealing with the initial appearance of Gypsies in west and central Europe.[100] In this context the work of Grellmann's teacher Schlözer springs to mind, about whom I reported earlier that he had been busy already since the 1760s acquiring a collection of German language chronicles and records (from Charlemagne on) with the intention of publishing a critical compilation. Perhaps Grellmann was granted access to a body of texts about Gypsies from this collection. If we recall his early collaboration with Schlözer, this would indeed seem highly probable.

But let me turn back to the magazine that Grellmann calls the *Wiener Anzeigen*. This was in fact the *(Kaiserlich-Königlich allergnädigst privilegierte) Anzeigen aus sämmtlich-kaiserlich-königlichen Erbländern*, published from 1771 to 1776 in Vienna,[101] a leading periodical in those years.[102] Its spiritual father was presumably Adám Kollár, since 1772 Director of the Court Library in Vienna. Already for ten years he had been nurturing a plan to found a society of academics whose goal would be to stimulate the study of Hungary. Despite his network of contacts and voluminous correspondence, however, he failed to assemble enough competent scholars, so that he found himself obliged to modify his ambitions. In the early 1770s he succeeded in motivating the Hungarian legal expert Dániel Tersztyánszky to accept the post of editor-in-chief of the journal. For copy, in addition to a number of major names such as Ignaz von Born and Karl Gottlieb Windisch, he could draw on a multitude of Protestant intellectuals from the entire region where Hungarian was spoken. Although the articles published appeared without attribution, it is possible nevertheless to learn from partially preserved correspondence with the publisher the names of a number of contributors, such as József Benczur, Jonás Andreas Czirbesz, Samuel Augustini ab Hortis, János Kriebel, Johann Seifert and István Weszprémi.[103] The journal contained pieces on diverse topics: analyses of the trade and economy of the states of Austro-Hungary, news about the school system, essays in the natural sciences, descriptions of coins, articles about matters of constitutional law which above all concerned Hungary (but never with any political dimension) and reviews of a predominantly informative sort.

The periodical's mode of operation was wholly in the spirit of the Enlightenment; it aspired to print articles that were of general use and in this way to be of service to the fatherland and to help morally elevate society. To these ends the magazine conformed with the political line of the imperial court in Vienna and proved itself to be an impassioned proponent of the reform policies of Maria Theresa and Joseph II. The publishers seized every opportunity, however, to make it clear that they were especially committed to promoting the spread of information about the nation of Hungary, to strengthening the position that it occupied within the Habsburg monarchy, and to disseminating the culture of that country in German-speaking areas through (popular-) scientific articles.

It appears impossible, given the tradition of withholding authors' identities, to puzzle out which articles in the *Anzeigen* were from whose hand. Even Ruch, after dealing at length with parallels between Grellmann and the periodical series, simply puts on record that an unknown author was responsible for the articles on Gypsies in Hungary and Transylvania.[104] Wrongly so – for at the bottom of the last instalment devoted to the Gypsies, in a tiny and unobtrusive letter face, the initials 'ab H' are printed. This, which occurred at the end of more concluding articles, is the only hint to authorship which, now and then, the journal dropped. A quick glance at the earlier-mentioned contributors yields the name of Samuel Augustini ab Hortis as 'ab H'.

Little is known about the life and work of this Protestant scholar of Hungarian descent. He was born on 5 August 1729 in Nagylomnic (Gross-Lomnitz in German) in the district of Szepes (Zips) and died on 5 August 1792 in Szepesszombathely (Georgenberg).[105] From 1761 on, he was a clergyman there for the evangelical-Lutheran community, after completing his training at a number of German universities, including Wittenberg. He wrote various pieces for the *Anzeigen* on the natural history of Hungary. That he was also the author of the series on Gypsies is not recorded anywhere in so many words. During his life he published four books; after his death a fifth one appeared.[106] Besides his initials, I have found a second indication which makes it extremely likely that Ab Hortis was the author of the series in which we are interested.[107] I have already mentioned that some of the letters exchanged between contributors to the journal and the publisher survive in the Hungarian National Library and the Library of the Hungarian Academy of Sciences, both located in Budapest. In the indeed limited number of letters still remaining there, not once is anything at all said about the series on Gypsies and none of Ab Hortis' manuscripts appear to have been preserved. What the archive does contain is a letter from András Jónás Czirbesz, both one of the editors of the journal and employed as a cleric in the province of Szepes, which includes a passage which reinforces the plausibility of my deductions:

> Einer meiner Freunde, ein fleissiger Mitarbeiter an den gelehrten Anzeigen, bewogen durch die Allerhöhste Sorgfalt, unserer gnädigsten Landesmutter, für die Regierung des armen Zigeuner- volks, arbeitet an einen Versuch, die Geschichte dieser Nation betreffend, ihren Ursprung, Sitten, Gewohnheiten, Lebensart, Kleidung, Krankheiten, Laster und Ausschweifungen, Sprache und dergleichen betreffend. ('One of my friends, a diligent con- tributor to learned journals, moved by the utmost concern, just as the merciful Mother of our country [the Empress – WW], for the governing of the poor Gypsy people, is working on an essay about the history of this nation, dealing with their origins, manners, customs, way of life, clothing, illnesses, vices and excesses, speech and suchlike.')[108]

After this biographical digression, the task which concerns us involves investigating the similarities between Ab Hortis' approach and Grellmann's. In various passages, Ruch stressed that Grellmann completely missed the nuances of the author of the series of articles in the *Anzeigen* and, mistakenly, generalized observations which were applicable to one region.[109] It strikes me that in Ruch's eagerness to ridicule Grellmann's Gypsy book, he has constructed a false contrast here. Neither the aim nor the work method of Ab Hortis, at any rate, differed in principle from Grellmann's. In part the two men made use of the same sources, although Grellmann blindly followed the course Ab Hortis had set. The question is how Ab Hortis came to know so much? From personal observation, which seems true for many topics, or from the observations of others, an alternative for which there are also indications? Only by examining his notes would it be possible to settle the matter with any confidence. Furthermore Ab Hortis, too, clearly aspired to study the character of the Gypsy people with the intention of resolving the question of whether they could be considered as useful citizens. He demonstrated his acquaintance with the work of his predecessors, commenting that as a rule these were of foreign origin and not conversant with local relations within Hungary and Transylvania. His intention was indeed to accentuate the situation of Gypsies in these countries, bringing out the differences among them. Despite his sensitivity to distinctions, he felt that he could not deny that similarities among Gypsy groups were so significant that one had to speak of a general Gypsy character. His initial subtlety thus served to enable him to justify why he was publishing a series of articles about the morals and customs of *'unseren Landeszigeunern'* ('the Gypsies of our country'). The reason for his doing so was simple: others, as non-residents, were not competent enough to do it in a responsible way. As a native scholar, however, he thought he possessed the capabilities to describe and explain the culturally determined differences among groups of Gypsies. His thinking about the nature of these people nevertheless ran along the same lines as both his predecessors' had and, later, Grellmann's would: '... um sowohl der Nachwelt zu zeigen, was dieses gesegnetes Land, für ein schädliches und unnützes Gesindel, mehrere Jahrhunderte hindurch, in seinem Schoosse ernähret, und erhalten habe' ('... and also to show future generations, what harmful and useless riffraff this blessed country, through the ages, has nourished and welcomed to her bosom').[110]

He also praised Maria Theresa's uncompromisingly implemented emancipatory regulations and expressed a hope that his articles would help advance this national policy. In so doing he was acting wholly in the spirit of Göttingen University and its Statistics Department and following in the footsteps of Schlözer and other ethnographically-oriented historians. The provisional conclusion is thus justified that Ab Hortis provided a detailed blueprint for the ethnographic part of Grellmann's book on the Gypsies.

A linguistic blueprint

Research reveals that the linguistic portion of Grellmann's book on the Gypsies was also handed to him on a plate, this time by *Christian Wilhelm Büttner*. As a student in Göttingen, from 1781 to 1783, Grellmann lived in this eccentric linguist's house. A relation of mutual trust grew up between them which would prove advantageous to them both. Apparently the student's scholarly debt to his landlord was a secret for no one, for it is referred to in both Büttner's obituaries and in reviews of Grellmann's work. Indeed Büttner had been the first, in 1771, to point to the East as the place from which the Gypsies originally came.[111] According to him they were the descendants of a Hindustani-Afghanistani tribe and he was convinced that further comparative linguistic research among the peoples in this frontier region would more narrowly identify their place of origin. The question then arises why a scholar who had scented this trail at such an early date never himself published anything about it? Perhaps a short biographical sketch will help us understand.[112]

Büttner lived from 1716 until 1801. He was born in Wolfenbüttel as the son of a court pharmacist, a vocation that he learned in his youth. To become more highly qualified at this trade, which was already at an early age, he undertook various journeys through Germany, but also made his way to Hungary, Poland and, later, to Copenhagen. On the threshold of adulthood, he turned his back on the apothecary's life, a decision related to his growing aversion to freemasonry which exercised great control over the professional network in Braunschweig. Whoever did not comply with the rules which the free masons imposed had a hard time holding his own. The young Büttner preferred to keep his expertise to himself and the result of his obstinacy was that he had to withdraw from his work as a pharmaceutical druggist. He set forth on new travels throughout Europe, to increase his knowledge of natural history, of nations, peoples and languages, subjects which would prove to capture his interest for good. In 1737 he studied for half a year in Leiden, with Boerhaave among others, while he shared a room with the famous Swedish natural historian, Carl Linnaeus.[113] Back in Wolfenbüttel he spent many years imposing order on the material that he had collected. In this respect he was carrying on a family tradition, for his father had taken over a seventeenth-century collection of natural scientific curiosities from his father. Over time the collection had continued to grow and in this grandson of its founder it found a worthy curator. Thus he inherited, as it were, his interest in natural sciences. In 1773 he donated this unique collection to Göttingen University, in return for an annuity. The natural scientist Blumenbach, his student and friend, had the opportunity to install the collection in an academic museum.

Ethnography and comparative linguistics were the sciences which, along with natural history, began to absorb Büttner more and more in the course of his life. This led to his acquiring a formidable private library (of 10,000 volumes in 1783)[114] consisting of rare works and manuscripts. He collected manuscripts and vocabulary lists from all the languages of the world and diligently set about comparing them at the levels of sound, word and grammar, subsequently developing hypotheses about the descent of peoples and their peregrinations and variations. Operating altogether in the academic spirit of *intuitive understanding*, he believed that, through comparison and analogy, he could penetrate to the character of peoples. His journey to Göttingen, the centre of the German Enlightenment, in 1748, was entirely in keeping with this interest. Although he himself had not completed any formal degree (his knowledge of natural history being acquired through practical experience) he commanded so much respect that he was soon being asked to deliver lectures. He did this using texts which he himself compiled and which he illustrated with pieces from his own cabinet – which in those days seems to have been an exceptional approach. In 1758 he became a professor extraordinary on the Philosophy Faculty, an appointment converted to an ordinary professorship in 1763. What earned him his position – and this too was a departure from usual policy in Göttingen – was not his written publications, for Büttner published remarkably little.[115] According to the writer of his obituary this was owing to the inadequate schooling he had enjoyed during the years of his youth; as an autodidact he continued to struggle with a lack of fluency in writing. He had learned what he knew in 'the school of life' and during his countless journeys. His compulsion to collect had culminated in unique compilations of sources which he then put in order and described. He was conscientious in the copying of data, comprehensive in bringing together information – the papers he left behind must comprise a rich source for historians – but when it came to writing up his analyses and syntheses, he was a failure. Among his multiple talents, the ability to select was missing. He was certainly a child of his times, but in a certain sense also a victim of them as well. His hypotheses based on analogies, in particular, missed the discipline of limitation. This induced a contemporary, Professor Lichtenberg of Göttingen, to write about him:

> Der Mann hat vieles gelesen, versteht aber fast alles falsch. In Hypothesen ist er unerschöpflich, weil bey ihm nur flüchtige Aehnlichkeit nöthig ist auf eine zu verfallen. (…) denn er ist sehr geneigt die Lücken mit Erdichtungen auszufüllen. Aus seinem Sprachwerck wird nie viel sonderliches heraus kommen. Ein guter Kopf, der sich die Daten bekannt machte, würde vieles falsch, gewagt und läppisch finden. ('The man has read a lot, but understands almost everything wrongly. He is inexhaustible in formulating hypotheses since he only needs the merest similarity to formulate one (…) for he is highly inclined to fill in the gaps with his own inventions. From his linguistic work nothing special should ever be expected. A good mind, familiar with the data, would find a lot that was false, unfounded and silly.')[116]

Carried away by universalistic ideas, he wished to show the inter-relatedness of all the languages that he knew. He formulated a common genesis for languages as well as peoples, believing thus that all forms could be traced back to an ur-form or race, a thought which had also inspired Blumenbach to make his classifications.[117] Büttner, however, did not manage to work out his hypotheses in concise theories. On the theoretical plane the services he rendered were accordingly not impressive. On which plane then were they? His first contribution consisted of the transfer of his valuable collections contained in the natural history cabinet mentioned above. Second, in 1783 he donated his library of many rare works to Duke Carl August van Sachsen-Weimar, the same man to whom Grellmann dedicated his Gypsy book. At first the Duke had the library housed in his palace but later it would constitute part of the university library in Jena. In exchange Büttner acquired the title of *Hofrath*, was granted an annuity of 300 half crowns, and, for the last 18 years of his life, as librarian, administered his own collection. It is Büttner's merits as book collector that we have to thank for our being able to unearth more summary information about the man.[118] It was no less a person than the court librarian, Goethe, to whom his friend the Duke from Weimar entrusted the task of arranging for the transfer of Büttner's library. In preparation he had sought contact with the Göttingen orientalist Eichhorn but, and here all our *dramatis personae* converge, it was Grellmann who shortly thereafter would act as intermediary between Büttner and Goethe.[119] In June 1781 Grellmann had offered his landlord his help in preparing the catalogue that would serve as the basis for Goethe's librarian's labours, and the offer was gratefully accepted.[120] In one of his letters Goethe called Büttner an *'alte lebendige Encyklopädische Dicktionair'* (venerable, living dictionary). A polymath, but the prototype of a collector without principles for imposing order. Someone mad about books rather than someone who loves them. Goethe learned at first hand what all this could lead to when he had to look after Büttner's legacy. He was not overjoyed.[121]

Back to the ways in which Büttner was of service. What dignified him in the eyes of his contemporaries was that he made his not inconsiderable accumulation of sources accessible to his academic friends and colleagues upon request. They were, however, obliged to address an appeal to him in writing for literature or material of another sort on a particular topic, but then they could as a rule rest assured that Büttner would spend hours or even days of his time pulling together all of the relevant books and manuscripts in his possession and jotting down on paper his own knowledge of the subject.[122] In this way he exercised an enormous influence, acknowledged by many, on the emergence and progress of a great deal of research at that time. His well-attended lectures in disparate fields, such as natural history, ethnography and linguistics, also enhanced this influence.

Büttner's third contribution was narrowly allied with the one just described, for not only did he assist many people as a peripatetic library: he also launched people on research topics that especially interested him. Even Goethe conceded, in his botanical studies, that he had benefited from Büttner's knowledge and perceptions.[123] In part out of his own incapacity, but certainly also out of generosity, he was easy about placing his classified material at others' disposal so that the recipients of this favour need only, in a manner of speaking, pick up their pens and write. This certainly held true for the linguistic sources that comprised the foundation of the language-related portion of Grellmann's Gypsy book and for which, in his foreword, he elaborately thanks the great teacher. Certainly, Grellmann, with his theological and historical training, knew some philology but he was still very much of a layman in the field of linguistics and accordingly hardly the most obvious candidate for working on Büttner's vocabulary lists. Perhaps the extreme indifference of this autodidact towards academic specialization accounts for why he made these sources available to his lodger. Only after the lengthy insistence of a friend, who had undertaken to publish his work in the future, did he proceed to pass on his notes and manuscripts related to comparative linguistics[124] to Rüdiger, professor in Halle in this field.[125] His publications about Gypsies are, by the way, also of importance, as well as his criticism of Grellmann, but more about that later.

THE RECEPTION OF GRELLMANN

After this analysis of Grellmann's indebtedness to others, it is important to determine how his work was judged by his contemporaries. That a second, expanded edition appeared, and that a comparatively short while afterwards translations into English, French and Dutch were for sale indicates that it certainly did not go unnoticed internationally. What interests me primarily is which aspects of the book met with exceptional appreciation and also whether parts of the work encountered criticism, not only in reviews but also in the articles of colleagues who wrote about Gypsies. It goes without saying that it was not possible to do an exhaustive study of the reviews that appeared after the first and second editions and the translations. My bibliographic research was necessarily of a limited nature.[126]

Reviews

The reviewers I traced all agreed that, from the standpoint of scholarship, Grellmann's book was of great value for historians, linguists and philosophers, that it testified to much diligence, perseverance and critical acumen, and that, moreover, it was absorbingly written. They were also unanimous that it was an original piece of work. A unique compilation of all extant knowledge in the field, pieced together from the most diverse sources, sifted with scientific precision, aptly distinguishing sense from nonsense. They praised the author for his erudition. True enough all German notices referred to the notes which Büttner had made available – by virtue of which asset Grellmann undoubtedly will have been taken all the more seriously – but the reviewers did not fail to emphasize what they saw as Grellmann's own achievement: that he was the first to have painstakingly worked out the comparisons of languages. The line of reasoning that led to placing the Gypsies' point of origin in Hindustan and, subsequently, to singling out the Sudra caste in India as their antecedents convinced many, if not all reviewers.

The most elaborate criticism of this last hypothesis came from an anonymous reviewer for the *Allgemeine Literatur-Zeitung* (1787), who indeed began his piece by praising the author for his thorough treatment of the comparison of languages, which came across as extremely persuasive. In important concrete ways, however, he turned out to be far less satisfied. The word lists and columns of grammatical declensions came, according to him, from Büttner and he had therefore expected that they would have been worked out more conscientiously. He was convinced that, in the form in which they appeared, they contained too many downright mistakes. Thus there were said to be many 'Gypsy words' included which were really compounds for which certainly there were no equivalents in the original Indian. Moreover, he found many words erroneously defined and Grellmann, according to him, had also been extremely careless in his treatment of the grammatical structure of the language. Finally, from the vocabulary lists and other resources at hand it was his conviction that many more points of agreement between the Gypsy language and Hindi could be demonstrated. He appreciated the author's dedication, but denigrated his nonchalance, and he commented that it did not strike him as probable that the Sudras had emigrated after the invasion of the Mongolian Timur in 1407. With the nomenclature for Gypsies in various lands in mind, he thought they had lived for some time in Egypt and, taking this transitional period into consideration, it was accordingly hardly feasible that they would then already be appearing in Germany in 1417. He sooner fixed on the time that Ghengis Khan waged his wars of conquest, counting on Arabian sources to furnish the truth in the future.

He shared this last suggestion with various other reviewers, according to whom it would be worthwhile having orientalists test Grellmann's hypotheses by delving into manuscript collections in the Escorial, the Vatican, and in London and Oxford – a rallying cry which, as far as I can tell, went largely unheeded during the following two centuries. The sole reviewer to voice criticism of Grellmann's deductions from the first mention of Gypsies in European historical sources wrote for the *Critical Review* (1788). He commented that of course they were only written about at the moment when they had attracted the attention of government employees, the police in particular. For him the dating of such reports provided an inadequate basis for the conclusion that Gypsies only then appeared for the first time in West Europe. This was a cautionary note that we can label as extraordinary, not only for the circle of the reviewers being discussed here but also for later writers about Gypsies.

A second critic of the linguistic but also of the moral comparisons which Grellmann drew was the reviewer for the *Monthly Review* (1787); part of his objections were shared by a colleague in a piece in the *Critical Review* (1788). In the first-mentioned review of the English translation of Grellmann (1787), the reviewer, after first expressing his deep admiration for the ethnographic part of the book, expressed his dissatisfaction with the hypothetical second part. He found that the material presented did not establish proof of the assumed relationship between the two languages compared. Many words might be, more or less, the same, but others were to his way of thinking different. He regarded the way in which comparisons were made with the Sudras as even more egregious. He spoke of a frivolous work method and of evidence that proved little. To claim similarities between groups of people because both love horses even betrayed, he felt, scholarly naivete. This surprised him above all because he had genuine esteem for the lifelike sketch Grellmann offered of the Gypsy community, culled, he presumed, from personal observations.

Prompted by linguist M. le Baron de Bock's paraphrastic French translation, a reviewer in the *Journal Encyclopédique* (1788) had one or two things to say about Grellmann's work. De Bock had embarked on his translation out of a fascination with the way in which this nomadic people held fast, as he saw it, to the customs and language of their country of origin. He brought this into connection with their emigration which was said to have preserved aspects of their culture that had not been found in India itself for a long time. He believed that Grellmann was blind to the linguistic consequences of the processes at work, and this provided a reason for De Bock to wedge extra observations on the subject into his translation. He believed he could differentiate three layers within the 'Gypsy language': words which, in 1788, were still part of the daily speech of people on the Malabar coast; words from Hungary, Moldavia and other countries where Gypsies had settled for protracted stays; words that were no longer current in any language whatsoever, and thus which possibly belonged to Sanskrit, the mother of all Indian languages (and the oldest of the family of Indo-European languages to which Western languages also belong).[127] It was the study of this last branch that especially preoccupied him.

Among reviewers there was a consensus of praise for the ethnographic part of Grellmann's book owing to its comprehensiveness and also because, until then, the history of Gypsies had been shrouded in darkness. They were especially lavish with compliments for the chapters about the character of the Gypsy people and their special abilities. The reception of Grellmann's vision of how Gypsies were assimilated into settled society was highly favourable too. Instructive for the public, invaluable for historians, and highly useful for governments in diverse countries where Gypsies lived. Reviewers could also condone the purpose of the book, namely to determine whether Gypsies might be considered useful citizens or could be rehabilitated as such. In the *Allgemeine Deutsche Bibliothek* (1791) the reviewer, after underlining the public's enthusiasm for the book, even spoke of its creating a real sensation in 'Gypsy countries' and expressed his hope that so much concentrated attention would also actually reduce the gap between Gypsies and civilization. It was certainly no easy matter to raise *nomadic peoples* – the dominant designation for Gypsies in the reviews – to the cultural heights of bourgeois society. He agreed with Grellmann that expulsion, branding and hanging were not appropriate measures, since persecution merely intensified how people clung to their past. Maria Theresa and Joseph II had understood that principle well, and this explained their hope that their emancipatory ordinances would, in the long run, bear fruit. Moreover, to have patience was essential, for the changing of *Völkerracen* could not, according to the thinking of the reviewer, be accomplished by force, but rather could only come about gradually.

The cunning that the Gypsies were said to have developed was, according to reviewers, born of necessity and, in that context, reference was made to the physical causes which were fundamental to such adaptation. If you change the circumstances, so ran their message, the Gypsy changes as well. In some reviews, notably in the *Göttingische Anzeigen von gelehrten Sachen* (1784), a proposal was made to arrange regular earnings for them and to entice them with the prospect of owning property. The writer of this review, the renowned Göttingen scholar Heyne, explained the circumstances in which Gypsies lived at the time by referring to their nomadic past. This had obliged them to live in poverty and want in the midst of more-or-less cultivated peoples. The reviewer for the *Historische Litteratur* (1784) went one step further by pointing out the intolerance of Christian society towards civilized peoples, for he considered Gypsies to belong to this category. To his way of thinking they were abandoned to their fate simply because they did not want to conform to the hegemony of Christiandom. It is not improbable, he went on, that it was because of their recalcitrant disposition that these 'pure, civilized and honest folk' had become nomads, with all the consequences of such a way of life. Several times he drew parallels with the Jews, about whom the most nonsensical lies were always spread, springing from Christian society's lack of toleration towards people who think differently. This reviewer had an eye – and this was exceptional for his time – for what at present we call the processes of stigmatization and minority formation and for their social repercussions. The reviewer for the *Journal Encyclopédique* (1788) also wrote that, through lack of education and property, Gypsies had not had a real chance to integrate anywhere. In this connection he alluded to the translator De Bock's pronouncement that Joseph II should put his recently acquired Polish territories at the Gypsies' disposal. Only in this way could the situation possibly take a turn for the better.

A pair of English reviews make us aware that the tenets of 'Enlightened absolutism' could not count on the same support in all countries. First of all a reviewer in *The Monthly Review* commented, without pursuing the matter further, that German Gypsies differed in appearance and eating habits rather markedly from the Gypsies one came across in England. After his discussion of the chapter about reform measures, for which he had high esteem and which he considered feasible – at any rate as far as the civilizing of German Gypsies was concerned – he expressed his doubts about the efficacy of such policies in other countries. He rejected the idea of physical punishment above all because, according to him, a 'savage' should be tamed by exposure to good examples. Only through friendly treatment would he be persuaded to adopt more civilized behaviour. His idea was that you had to invite someone to take shelter under your roof without any strings attached. By the placement of a stick in the reformer's hand, civilization and barbarity became intertwined, a combination from which, he found, little good could come. In the *Critical Review* scepticism about attempts at reform arose primarily from the thought that they couldn't be implemented since Gypsies were notorious for clinging to their own customs and were impervious to the civilizing influence of religion.

According to this critic, social change could not simply be imposed from above compulsorily. Nature, to be sure, was stronger than nurture!

One last aspect of the reviews worth commenting upon here concerns the remarks that they contained about the reputed cannibalism of Gypsies. In the *Gothaische gelehrte Zeitungen* (1784) the reviewer found Gypsies an interesting subject because every child had heard of them and knew of their existence, but also because Europeans had recently been astonished by their consumption of human flesh, referring in this fashion to the Hungarian cannibalism case of 1782. The ambivalent stance which Grellmann took on this accusation is matched by the reviewers who broach the subject – and no foreign reviewer failed to do so. Surprise, denial and credulity went hand in hand. The review in the *Critical Quarterly* reported that Grellmann had not proven that Gypsies were cannibals, so the charge will have been groundless. On the other hand, the review continued, the opposite had not been established: 'We know not what a gipsey urged by hunger, secure of concealment, with little feeling, and no religion to interpose, might be induced to do.' What Grellmann had intended to do was to save Gypsies from the shame that accrued to them from the suspicion that, now and then, or even frequently, they stooped to such practices. In the *Journal Encyclopédique* there wasn't even the shadow of a doubt any more: both the translator (who worked freely) and the reviewer averred that the Gypsies had a special taste for human flesh and their appetite sometimes gnawed so insistently that children even killed their parents to make a meal of them: 'L'appétit qu'ils ont pour la chair humaine va si loin, qu'il n'est pas rare de voir des enfants égorger leurs pères, afin de les dévorer.' ('They are so fond of human flesh, that it is no rare event to see children slaughtering their fathers, in order to devour them.')

All in all it appears from reviews that the ethnographic part of Grellmann's book made a convincing and authentic impression. At the time everyone already had a picture of Gypsies in his mind, but people groped in the darkness as far as Gypsy history and daily life were concerned. The descriptions that Grellmann offered probably matched so well with the contemporary image of an 'uncivilized' and 'nomadic' people – the passages about settled Gypsies did not affect that image in the least – that the general impressions that he put down on paper were accepted as accurate. The public knew no better and saw existing prejudices confirmed and reinforced by the authority of the sources cited in support. In addition Grellmann seems to have succeeded in making his ethnographic portrait of Gypsy groups so lifelike that he created the impression that he was speaking from personal observation. These factors account for his book's being so favourably received and its profound influence on public opinion for a long time. The critical voices which might have led to more subtle appraisals were simply ignored.

Criticism in later years

In the decades after the appearance of Grellmann's work, little of any substance was written in German-speaking countries about the Gypsies.[128] If the subject cropped up in a book or article and Grellmann was cited as a source, it usually happened without commentary. To the extent that criticism was formulated, it did not demonstrably reach the writers of later studies or intrude into the entries on Gypsies in encyclopedias.[129] There are three causes for this development: the admiration of Grellmann's work among his contemporaries; its wide distribution, also in translation; and the form in which it was published, namely a survey. Once in a while one part or another may have been derogated, as in the reviews discussed above, but this in no way detracted from the tenor of the reception of the work as a whole.

JOHANN ERICH BIESTER

The same holds true for the most elaborate criticism of Grellmann's approach and main conclusions; this appeared, spread over two articles, in the *Berlinische Monatschrift* and was written by the publisher and editor of the monthly, the librarian Johann Erich Biester.[130] He had all kinds of reservations about the book. He fiercely attacked the ethnographic approach, the linguistic and ethnographic comparisons, the bias-ridden use of language and even the scientific vision that underpinned Grellmann's perceptions.[131] For my purposes, Biester is primarily important because he was the only one to oppose the *communis opinio* of his time and so grants us a glimpse of the historical German Gypsy underneath the reigning stereotypical image.

The empirical part of Biester's narrative contains a summary of the notes that two scholars, friends of his, had provided him with. One manuscript recounted the ups and downs of 40 Gypsies from Königsberg who were imprisoned there in 1784. It was written by Chr. Jakob Krause who had been able to observe them at length and who often spoke to them at the time.[132] The second manuscript, which contained similar notes plus a dictionary and grammar of the Gypsies' language, had been prepared by the clergyman Zippel who, from 1787 onwards, had observed a group of Gypsies in Prussian Lithuania.[133] This material, unique according to Biester and based on first-hand observation, had almost been consigned to oblivion when he gained permission to edit it for publication. He cast the work into two parts: a detailed critique of Grellmann's work prefaced by a long ethnographical description, based on both the Krause and Zippel manuscripts, of the Gypsy groups concerned. What was special about Biester's approach was the way he consistently drew parallels with other groups of Germans. An example: 'Die Mannspersonen unter den hiesigen Zigeunern kleiden sich gerade so, wie die hiesigen Deutschen an den Sonntagen.' ('Gypsy men in this region dress exactly like the local Germans do on Sundays.')[134] As a result of this work method a much more differentiated picture emerges of the way of life, morals, and customs of Gypsies than in Grellmann's work. Let me add at once that the authors of the source manuscripts also applauded Joseph II's reform measures and considered strict government control indispensable to turn these 'lice in the pelt of the state' into honourable citizens, in the long run.[135] To take children from their parents and to raise them properly elsewhere was in total conformity with this view. That was the far from positive overall picture with which the summary ended.

The tone changes only once the voice of Biester himself takes over. Then empiricism is no longer the crux of the matter, but a detailed critique of Grellmann. True, he began with words of respect for Grellmann's wide reading and the erudition of his work, but immediately afterwards he distanced himself from those who acclaimed Grellmann's book without qualification. For him the enthusiasts lacked real involvement in the subject so they were insensitive to the many contradictions in Grellmann's book. These, Biester felt, stemmed from Grellmann's irresistible compulsion to generalize everything. For, so he continued, how can you portray Gypsies as born vagabonds and at the same time discuss diverse sedentary Gypsy groups under the heading of 'occupations'? In a similar vein Biester singled out countless exaggerations in the text, especially where Grellmann was exposing negative facets of Gypsy communities. Biester was noticeably disturbed by the many jibes and sallies of false wit that were part of Grellmann's description of the inhuman circumstances in which Gypsies live; indeed they provoked him to remark: '… hier, wie an mehrern Orten, mögte man zweifeln, ob Hr. Grellmann je Zigeuner gesehen hat, beobachtet und untersucht kann er Sie wenigstens nicht haben.' ('… from this passage, as from many others, one may well harbour doubts whether Mr Grellmann has ever even laid eyes on a Gypsy. In any event he cannot have observed and studied them.')[136]

Biester was not only indisposed to pardon Grellmann the sneering tone of his armchair expertise – he was convinced many of Grellmann's observations couldn't be taken seriously. To attribute dark skin colour to people's sitting for a long time in the smoke of fires revealed, as far as he was concerned, profound anthropological innocence. He found Grellmann's speaking of Gypsies as *oriental souls* even more serious, as if people would ever stay the same for 400 years under entirely different natural and cultural circumstances from in their land of origin. Biester rejected such almost mystical determinism with the words: 'Im Orient ist der Orientaler freilich Orientaler, aber anderswo wird er, wie jeder andere Mensch, das, wozu ihn die Summe seiner Erfahrungen macht.' ('In the Orient the oriental is oriental of course, but anywhere else he becomes, just as anybody else, that which the sum of his experiences makes him.')[137]

What had irritated him as well was the way Grellmann specifically ascribed a fearful character to Gypsies. After all, wasn't their very survival constantly menaced by society and, in particular, by the government, so that they had to constantly be on guard for danger in their surroundings? That Grellmann went on further to rebuke Gypsies because they cut themselves off from others and were only interested in themselves constituted for Biester yet another proof of his shortsightedness, not only because all peoples in a certain sense are self-interested and speak ill of others (think of the animosity between the French and Germans, he added) but, above all, because no one took the slightest notice of Gypsies so that by definition their sphere of interaction remained restricted to their own circle. To label that a Gypsy trait, Biester felt, was evidence of malicious intent. Grellmann's total lack of empathy, the absence of any sympathy for the people about whom he wrote, surprised Biester. It struck him as odd as well that Grellmann had such a poor eye for similarities among different population groups. In fact he cast doubts on the empirical basis of practically the whole ethnographic part of Grellmann's study:

> Was Hr. Grellmann sonst von ihren schlechten Gesinnungen, als Charakterzüge, anführt und ziemlich stark ausmalt: ihre Undank-barkeit, ihr Kleiderstolz, Hang zum Putz, und Geschmäck an rother Farber, ihre Lust an Tabak und Branntewein, ihre Wollust, Faulheit, diebische und betrügerische Neigung, ist den Zigeunern theils nicht mehr, als allen andern Menschen, eigen, theils natürliche Folge ihrer ganzen Lage. ('The rest of what Mr Grellmann has to remark about their bad traits and characteristics: their ingratitude, their vanity in how they dress, their fondness for ornament and bright colours, and taste for tobacco and brandy, their lechery, sloth, inclination to steal and defraud – these in part are no more typical of Gypsies than of other people, and in part are the natural result of their living conditions.')[138]

Time and again Biester emphasized that circumstances induce people to behave in a certain way and not their 'natural character'. He therefore found it absurd to impute to Gypsies an aversion to hard labour and to a sedentary life, seeing as how everyone who instinctively rejected these only grew accustomed to them of their own accord through their upbringing. Consider the Gypsies in Transylvania who pan for gold! To leave the cultural tradition and social circumstances of a group out of consideration and categorize people on grounds of assumed group characteristics, and then to attribute a barbaric character to them had, according to Biester, nothing whatsoever to do with scholarship.

In his second article, also based on Zippel's and Krause's manuscripts, Biester aims his critical barbs at the linguistic part of Grellmann's work and at what he considered to be Grellmann's erroneous equation of Gypsies with the pariahs or Sudras in Hindustan. In these sections, too, he notes many methodological shortcomings, perhaps the most important of which was Grellmann's recurring reductiveness in the way he one-sidedly fixed on Gypsy group dynamics and left other causes of the exclusion process out of consideration. For Biester it wouldn't do to attribute how little we knew of Gypsy languages to the secretiveness of the oriental soul, and then subsequently to allude to a parallel trait exhibited by pariahs. The experience of Biester's authorities indicated otherwise, which brought him to the conclusion – an extraordinarily apt one to my mind – that those who studied Gypsies at that time had never taken the trouble to bridge the distance separating them from these people on the edge of society. Of course it was true, he continued, that as the consequence of centuries of social rejection some Gypsy groups were not inclined to share their language readily with outsiders, but to explain this development in terms of Gypsy character instead of offering social analysis demonstrated, he found, scant historical understanding. He equally failed to understand why Grellmann paid such little attention in the linguistic chapter to the question of how the groups concerned referred to themselves. In this context Biester introduced such terms as *Rom*, *Sinte*, *Manusch*, but even *Gajo* seems at the time to have been current among Prussian Gypsies. Not moral traits, but rather these names and their inflexions, according to him, pointed the way to their land of origin. Biester made it out to be the Indus River, which in India was said to be known as the Sinde and where, as recounted in eighteenth-century travel descriptions, the people called themselves *Siganer* or *Singaner*.

At this point Biester went more deeply into Grellmann's linguistic comparisons. His first point of criticism was that Grellmann had shown too little awareness of the linguistic diversity of Hindustan, a country some 70,000 square miles in area, where people spoke Sanskrit and Persian as well as Hindi. The latter was the *lingua franca* in the eighteenth century. Furthermore careful comparison of Hindi and the 'Gypsy language' would reveal, besides similarities, many grammatical and morphological differences as well. In his linguistic essay, Biester thought he could show that Hindi had a shorter history than the language spoken by (Prussian) Gypsies. According to him theirs was an earlier tribal tongue, considering the fact that comparisons at every linguistic level brought out that what Gypsies spoke – stripped of all words borrowed from a European language – was more primitive, or rather less of a linguistic mix. On the basis of his comparisons he concluded that the Gypsies must have emigrated even before Hindi came into existence. If we are mindful of the Islamic influences which Hindi exhibits, that must have taken place during the era of the great religious conquests. Research into the languages which Hindus spoke before that period could, in his opinion, disclose when the Gypsies had departed.

The final aspect of Grellmann's book which Biester called into question was his association, based on analogies, of Gypsies with the Sudra caste. Here Grellmann, he felt, had made things all too easy for himself. The argument depended entirely on comparison of lists of words, so he began, while as yet we knew so little about Hindi and, moreover, who was to say that the sources accurately reproduced the spoken language. True enough, Grellmann conceded that his grasp of word and sentence structure and grammar was imperfect, but he failed to draw the conclusion that this therefore constituted a shaky basis for undertaking a linguistic comparison which would lead him to such far-reaching assertions. In addition Biester asked himself why these Sudras, who were assumed to belong to the most despised caste of all, had packed up and left their fatherland at the time of a foreign invasion. He argued, just as contemporary researchers investigating migration do,[139] that social elements capable of self-defense will far sooner move away than those at the foot of the social ladder. He also rejected Grellmann's representing Sudras as on a par with pariahs, for whereas Sudras belonged to the fourth class, that of manual labourers and agriculturists, pariah was a collective term for all kinds of groups on the periphery of society. He found Grellmann's simply lumping the Sudras in Hindustan together with the pariahs in Malabar equally as unjustifiable, as was his fusing together of various data from travel accounts about regions which were situated some 500 miles apart. In point of truth Biester rejected all the components of Grellmann's ethnographic endeavour. The only finding which he endorsed was that India was the place from which the Gypsies studied by his authorities originally came. For the rest he emerged as a conspicuous critic and an advocate of further linguistic research.

JOHANN CHRISTIAN CHRISTOPH RÜDIGER

To facilitate such linguistic research, so Biester wrote at the end of his second article, he had already forwarded his manuscripts on the subject to the linguist Johann Rüdiger (1751–1822) with a request to work out the contents further. This Rüdiger actually did in 1793, as we can infer from a brief comment in one of his writings.[140] Rüdiger was professor of political economy in Halle and an authority in the field of comparative linguistics. Büttner, too, left some of his annotated manuscripts to him. In the small volumes about the world's diverse languages which Rüdiger published, beginning in 1782, he included a long article wherein, on grounds of some linguistic comparisons, he believed he was able to show that Gypsies originally came from India.[141] Thus already before Grell-mann, but some years after Büttner (1771) and also after Ab Hortis (1775/76). In his long article he wrote that he had arrived at this finding by way of linguistic comparisons based on his own material.[142] This material was a series of sentences and words which Rüdiger presented to a German Gypsy woman who translated them orally into Romani. In 1777 he had shown these results to his friend Bacmeister in St Petersburg who in turn reported the connection to Pallas – one of the figures whom Grellmann thanks in the foreword to his second edition – who had referred to it in a published travel description from 1781. A year after Rüdiger had imparted the news of his discovery to Bacmeister, he read about Büttner's parallel observation which, in his eyes, detracted from his own finding, but did not keep him from publishing his own material anyhow. Retroactively it is scarcely possible, and also hardly meaningful with such thin and anything but reliable sources, to hazard a decision about who should have the credit for being first.[143] The development of comparative linguistics during the second half of the eighteenth century pointed naturally to the East, the cradle, to be sure, of all European languages.

In Rüdiger's single substantial article about Gypsies, he revealed that he was of the romantic school which would come to maturity only decades later and then especially in England.[144] From the romantic perspective, Gypsies are the last free men, renouncing private property and refusing to recognize the laws of the state. Thus theft is actually justified, since they are only availing themselves of what is common property. Even so the consequence of this way of life is said to be that society regards them as aliens and as enemies. Their marginalization culminated in Gypsies' only managing to survive as *'herumziehende Räuberbanden, Wahrsager- und Bettlertrupen'* ('wandering gangs of thieves, and bands of fortune-tellers and beggars'). In this respect, according to Rüdiger, the law of the strongest nevertheless ultimately won out. This humanitarian loss of face, as he characterized the process of exclusion, could only be set right, he felt, by acknowledging that all people were essentially equal. Thus he developed into an advocate prepared to dedicate himself to put an end to discrimination against

Gypsies. It could be that his personal contacts with them – to which he calls the reader's attention on various occasions – induced him to take their side in writing, arguing for more humane treatment for these 'children of nature'. In contrast to the 'enlightened historian' Grellmann, his pleas on their behalf did not entail any compulsory measures to civilize them.

Rüdiger held nothing back in his linguistic critique of the work of his predecessors. He considered Wagenseil's hypothesis about the Jewish origins of Gypsies to be a blunder. He could understand the mistake, to be sure, since in his time the two groups were often confused with each other. All that he himself had wanted to show, based on linguistic comparison, was that Gypsies were a people who had lived originally in north-eastern India. He didn't consider himself in a position to say anything more specific about their descent, singling out a caste, for example, or a tribe. That was sooner terrain, he found, for historical researchers to explore. All he had wanted to do was break the seal. The only speculation that he permitted himself was that Gypsies, because of their itineracy, were also looked upon as a group of outsiders during their residence in India. For this reason, he thought, they had been a nomadic people since ancient times.

After 1782 Rüdiger only raised the subject of Gypsies occasionally in his work. In 1784 he referred to Grellmann's book which had been published a little while previously, mentioning its merits although he was discontent with the linguistic part of the text. According to him many of the words included simply did not belong to the Gypsies' language. A statement to which he added: '… worin aber die Aehnlichkeit noch grösser seyn würde, wenn nicht manches blindlings zusammen geraffet wäre' ('… greater similarity would have become apparent if not so much had been blindly lumped together'). When, nine years later, he gained access to Biester's two manuscripts, in Part 5 of his works he wrote that he planned to return to the subject still one more time and work it out thoroughly, for his suspicions about the weak aspects of Grellmann's book had only been confirmed by the new material. In 1796 he repeated this promise. He was then more specific in his criticism, remarking that he had documents to prove that the Gypsies lived in Europe prior to Timur's sweep into India and that it was highly improbable that they were the descendants of a low caste. His thoughts ran instead to an uncultured '*Nebenstamm*'. Through analysis of the linguistic collections in his possession he would seek the definitive answer, an exercise which he was saving for an anthology with historical contributions by Indian scholars. In the last 26 years of his life, however, Rüdiger didn't publish anything more. A biographical entry about him in a reference work informs us that he was a mine inspector, thus there is a good chance that he cut his academic career prematurely short.[145] The manuscripts of Krause and Zippel which he had in his hands – and perhaps those of Büttner as well – continued drifting about in any event, coming to rest with August Pott who, half a century later, used them as the basis for his standard work in the field of Gypsy language.[146]

LANGUAGE AS A CONTINUOUS FACTOR

For centuries after him no one challenged Grellmann's assertion that language disclosed where Gypsies came from. The first comprehensive linguistic study of Gypsies, as mentioned previously, was by the German Sanskritist Pott who, in his bipartite treatise of 1844–45, making use of all available written sources, constructed an annotated vocabulary of Romani. In his study, acknowledged as a masterpiece, he arrived at three conclusions: all the Gypsy languages which he had collected were in essence the same; as a vernacular they had nothing to do with any thieves' language; the language, which originated in the north of British India, was obviously related to Sanskrit, the '*vollendetste aller Sprachen*' ('the most perfect of all languages').[147]

In his work published a few decades later, the Austrian Slavist Franz Ritter von Miklosich differentiated 13 Gypsy dialects and tried to reconstruct how the Gypsies had fanned out from India across the world by ascertaining which words they had borrowed where along their migration routes.[148] He concluded not only that they probably had already left home in the early ninth century,[149] but also that they had remained in Greece for a long time in the fourteenth century before continuing on to West Europe.[150] In addition to these two extensive studies, Ralph Turner made a name for himself with an article in 1926.[151] He maintained, after comparing Romani characteristics with Indian inscriptions, that the Gypsies' language had originally belonged to the central Indian group, just as Hindi had, but that those who spoke it emigrated around 250 B.C. to north-west India where they settled for a long time.[152] His linguistic research brought him to the conclusion that Gypsies had left India in groups somewhere between the eighth and tenth century – without his venturing to establish the reasons why – a standpoint which continues to win supporters even today.[153] There has been an ongoing interest in the study of Gypsy language, with the idea of an umbrella parent language as a continuous thread, even though social reality presents the more differentiated picture of many dialects and mixed languages – with a Romani vocabulary, true, but the grammar of another language.[154] As to how or when these mixed languages emerged, linguistics is still groping in the dark.[155] What has been noted recently is that some Gypsy groups adapt their core vocabulary to the grammar of the country in which they are living so that to outsiders it appears as if they are listening to their own language without their being able to follow the words actually spoken.[156]

Evidently there is an idiom which children are taught at a somewhat advanced age. In this context a statement made by Professor Beekes of Leiden University in his recent historical recapitulation of comparative linguistics becomes relevant. He was discussing among other things the results of linguistic and archaeological studies of Indo-European languages and their speakers in the past and pointed out that archaeologists today exercise considerable restraint when it comes to reconstructing the migration routes which Indo-Europeans might have followed on their way from the East to the West. It is also possible, to their way of thinking, that linguistic influence made itself felt through trading outposts or cultural transmission and that thus the speakers of an Indo-European language in Europe did not migrate in the remote past from Central Asia but perhaps made the language of others their own.[157] Research into these matters has still not generated conclusive answers, which prompts the question whether in the case of so many diverse Gypsy groups a similar process may not have taken place, i.e. that certain groups between the eighth and eighteenth centuries came, as a kind of group ritual, to adopt a dialect of the Indian Romani. That we may not equate 'language' with 'people', and that different ethnic groups can speak a dialect of the same language, or have learned to do so in the course of passing centuries, are indeed things that the fascinating study of the linguistic roots and original home of speakers of Indo-European languages have made clear, speakers who we already now for a long time no longer believe, as scholars in the nineteenth century still did, emigrated from India before the birth of Christ.[158]

This does not mean that in nineteenth-century scientific, literary and criminological circles fascination with the subject was anything less than overwhelming. For George Borrow, who is the central figure of my next chapter, it was one of the inducements which led him to become involved in the lives of Gypsies. For my purposes in this study, Borrow is also important because analysing his network of contacts enables me to appraise the influence which Grellmann's book on Gypsies had in English-speaking countries.

NOTES

1   See Lucassen (1996, '*Zigeuner*') for the tracing and labelling of Gypsies in Germany between 1700 and 1945.
2   See Berbüsse (1992, pp. 151–71) for an analysis of Germany criminology textbooks from 1949 onwards.

3   Pott (1844, pp. 14–15).
4   See, for example, Martins-Heuss (1983, pp. 84–5).
5   As far as I was able to discover, Ruch (1986) has never issued an official publication with his findings about Grellmann. By chance I stumbled on his work while engaged in my research in 1991 in Göttingen. Only in recent years has the contents of his unpublished doctoral dissertation penetrated into German publications.
6   Grellmann (1783, p. 18).
7   The author dated his preface 4 September 1783; the first review appeared in December of the same year.
8   Grellmann's seventy letters to F.J. Bertuch span the period 1780 to 1800. See *Goethe- und Schiller-Archiv* in Weimar.
9   Cf. Grellmann's letter to Bertuch dated 24 February 1783.
10 This reference to the Academy of Stockholm's essay competition is from Rüdiger (1782, p. 63) who wrote that in 1782 the winner of the prize was not yet known. According to him there was still time to bring the truth of the matter to light.
11 Derived from Etzler (1944, pp. 117–24, 177–84) who consulted Ganander's manuscript *Undersökning onde s.k. Tattare eller Zigeuner* (40 pages, containing a list of 150 Finnish Gypsy-words) in the Archives of the Swedish Royal Academy of Sciences (*Kungl. Vitterhets Akademie*) in Stockholm. My thanks to Peter Bakker, a linguist from the University of Amsterdam, who, after reading my dissertation, called Etzler's publication to my attention.
12 See Grellmann's letter to Bertuch dated August 31, 1782 in which he wrote: '… another 12 days and my work will be completed!'
13 For published sources concerning this affair, see Karoly (1907, pp. 251–95 (in Hungarian) and 479–97 (in Latin)). The articles contain such a confusing argument that the translations yield information that is scarcely coherent. Doubtless this is connected to the insufficient number of sources upon which the publications were based.
14 Cf. RIOD, box 6, 'Gypsy persecution', Lau Mazirel's comments on Jos van Loenen's thesis (Oct/Nov. 1974).
15 Grellmann specified the following papers: *Beyträge zum Reichspostreuzer* (Aug. 21, 1782, St. 71; must be Sept. 12, 1782 – W.W.); *Hamburgische Neue Zeitung* (Sept. 4, 1782, St. 151); *Hamburgische Unpartheiische Correspondent* (Sept. 22, 1782, no. 1590); *Frankfurter Staats-Ristretto* (Sept. 29, 1782, no. 157 and Dec. 24, 1782, no. 207).
16 Grellmann referred to a case in 1534 when Gypsies were suspected by the Hungarians of letting themselves be used as the instruments of the upstart Joh. Zapolya. On the rack they confessed to having committed arson and murder. Later they took back what they admitted and their testimony indeed did not appear to be accurate.
17 That the figure in question was probably Baron Von Jessenak can be deduced from Grellmann's letter to Bertuch dated 22 September 1782.
18 Grellmann (1783, p. 1).
19 Ibidem, p. 40.
20 For a concise account of the most important decrees that Maria Theresa and Joseph II promulgated in sharper terms on 9 October 1783, see Szabó (1991, pp. 69–76).
21 Circular no. 6525, dated 12 September 1782. Grellmann himself says that a copy of this was provided to him by the *Registratur Kayserl. Königl. Befehle* (1783, pp. 147–57).
22 Grellmann (1783, p. 151).
23 For a succinct survey of these measures, see Gutkas (1989, pp. 84–7).
24 See Gutkas (1980, pp. 77–85), as well as Lis et al. (1985) about the disciplining of the lower classes through social politics. The authors point out that churches and

governments, despite frequently having opposed interests, as a rule developed a tight consensus with respect to the goals of such an agenda.

25 According to Lis et al. (1985, p. 49), the number of poor who begged permanently in most west European countries during the first quarter of the nineteenth century amounted to roughly 10 to 15 per cent of the national population.

26 Küther (1976) arrives at the same percentage for Germany, although his critics lean more heavily towards a figure of 4 to 5 per cent. For a review of the discussion about poverty at that time, see Lucassen (1993, pp. 209–35).

27 For changing attitudes towards beggars after the sixteenth century, see Geremek (1992, pp. 297–305).

28 The top-heavy workloads of the clergy who were implicated in carrying them out have been singled out to account for why the reforms were not put into practice in all places and at all times with equivalent dispatch. With passing years opposition provoked by the *josephinischen Aktionen* grew (Gutkas 1980, p. 83).

29 From Gutkas (1989, pp. 105–7). See also Király (1969, pp. 5–11) who sketches the most important changes in the history of Hungary in the eighteenth century.

30 The observation is Bernard's (1979, p. 65), from whom I have borrowed my data concerning policy towards begging.

31 Cf. *250 Jahre Vorlesungen* (1985); Lewin (1971); Rollmann (1988).

32 For an explanation of how the university was run, see *Die Königlichen Commis-sarien, Prorectoren und Rektoren der Georg-August-Universität zu Göttingen 1734 to 1957*. With commentary by Ernst Gundelach, Göttingen (no date).

33 See Rollmann (1988, p. 38).

34 Salaries were individually determined. Ordinary professors usually earned between 300 and 500 rixdollars, famous names between 1,000 and 1,500, with exceptions commanding even more. Fertile literary productivity could boost this amount appreciably, and this was true in Göttingen for quite some number of professors. See Rollmann (1988, pp. 57–66). Von Münchhausen also eagerly recruited young, unknown scholars who had distinguished themselves in some way or other. They accepted a low salary and, when they failed to live up to their promise, they were denied promotion. As a result of this policy Grellmann, too, became a professor at Göttingen at a relatively young age.

35 Through securing titles such as *Rat, Hofrat, Geheimer Regierungs-* and *Justizrat* or *Konsistorialrat*, professors acquired entry into the hierarchy of state officials which was a manifestation of their attachment to their sovereign. See Streich (1977, p. 248).

36 Ibidem, p. 251.

37 See Fabian (1977, pp. 209–39).

38 The standard work on the nature and function of academies is McClellan III (1985). For Göttingen, cf. pp. 114–16.

39 Of 701 students enrolled in 1801, 465 were foreigners as reported by Wischnitzer (1907, reprint Vaduz, 1965, p. 25). The influence of an academic education in Göttingen on the intellectual climate of the upper crust in Hungary forms the subject of an historical-philosophical thesis by Pettrits (1984). I only came across Grellmann's name twice in this thesis; the passages contained no relevant information for this study. For relations with England, see the essay by Wellenreuther (1985, pp. 30–63). For Russian ties, see, e.g., Keller (1987, pp. 184–260) and Wischnitzer's work. A large number of Dutch students also enrolled in this period; cf. Frijhoff (1981, pp. 112–13).

40 For more on this topic, see Reill (1985) and also Bödeker (1985).

41 See Reill (1985, p. 178).

42 Ibidem, pp. 190–1.

43 See Saage (1987) and Kern (1987). References to Schlözer's collaboration with Grellmann can be found in Frensdorff (1909, pp. 90, 91, 103, 104).

44 Cf. Frensdorff (comment I), p. 583 *et passim*. Cited by Saage (1987, p. 16).

45 Of whom it was reported that she rejected a decision by one of her councillors with the words: 'What would Schlözer say to that?' (Saage 1987, p. 14).

46 See Frensdorff (1909, p. 90).

47 This can be deduced from a letter from Grellmann to Bertuch dated 26 February 1785.

48 An extensive literature deals with the nature, function and effect of this genre. A recent, convenient survey of the material, with an elaborate bibliography is Breuner (1989).

49 For this view of things, see Mosse (1978, pp. 1–35) and Poliakov (1974, pp. 155–82).

50 A fascinating article about the methodological conflict (mono- versus polygenesis) within eighteenth-century anthropology has been written by the Blumenbach expert, Dougherty (1990, pp. 89–111).

51 See Blumenbach (1793, pp. 3–5, plate II).

52 The skull was that of a Gypsy who, having been struck down by farmers after his committing a robbery, later died in the prison of Klausenburg. It had been forwarded to Blumenbach by Dr Patacki. Remarkably, the Gypsy involved was a *sedentary* one (Ruch 1986, pp. 162–3).

53 Blumenbach had severely attacked the working methods of this same Meiners, during a dispute, however. Meiners was a historian of religion but didn't shrink from entering onto other academic terrain as well. Thus, since 1775, he had published a whole series of writings devoted to the history of mankind. His approach was primarily that of a cultural historian and certainly not an anatomist. He relied heavily, like most scholars at the time, on travel literature. According to Poliakov (1974, pp. 180–2), the Nazis considered Meiners to be the founder of race theory.

54 Grellmann's date of birth is reported as 7 December *1756* in practically all biographical sources. In the baptismal register of Jena, volume 6, p. 481, however, as reported in writing to me on 17 June 1992 by the *Evangelisch-Lutherische Kirchgemeinde Jena*, it states that he was born on 7 December 1753. To compound the confusion: I have come up with yet another year of birth. In 1805 in his eulogy for Grellmann, Johannes Theophilus Bühle wrote that his friend was born in 1758.

55 On page 29, note 38 of the second printing of his book on Gypsies, Grellmann remarks: '… and I myself was the child of native Russians.'

56 Kotzebue was to write the play, 'Die kleine Zigeunerin', in *Neue Schauspiele* no. 16 (Leipzig, 1810).

57 See the 'Traubuch der Hofkirche Weimar', 1762–1800, year 1791, p. 422. With thanks to Roswitha Otto of the *Evang.-Luth. Kirchgemeinde Weimar*, who sent me this information on 15 April 1991 in reply to my written request.

58 For the mutual influence which the two men had on each other (in 1776 Herder became the top man of the Weimar school system), see Walter's article (1908, pp. 36–59).

59 My gratitude to Mrs Pyras of the church archives in Göttingen for her assistance in searching for data about the Grellmann family.

60 See the relevant documentation from the University Archives at Jena, File M, no. 180, Philosophy Dept, 1783/84. It is thus not true as Ruch (1986, p. 98) asserts that in 1781 Grellmann left for Göttingen with his master's title in his pocket.

61 Concluded from Gellmann's letters to Bertuch dated 27 January and 16 March 1782: 'To say thanks for Your support, which I enjoy on behalf of my first literary fabrication. That my little essay will be published by a house that as a rule only produces the work of great men, came as such a surprise to me that I really was astonished and filled with anxiety that I would fare as a dwarf who stands next to a giant.'

62 In his eulogy Bühle (1805, p. 8) even goes as far as to say that the work made him 'celebrated'.

63 In his letter to Bertuch of 13 March 1784, Grellmann wrote: 'A thousand thanks for sending on my reviews to Hamburg and Gotha. Until now I always thought I would stumble on them unexpectedly in the world of journals and magazines; but I haven't found anything yet. I fear that they will fail to appear completely. If you are able to relieve my anxieties and really can accomplish the publication of these reviews, I appeal to your goodness and beg you to do so.' When the second printing appeared Grellmann appealed to his patron to see to it that a favourable review was placed in the *Allgemeine Literatur-Zeitung* – and it was. See his letter dated 18 March 1787.

64 For a listing of Grellmann's publications, see Annex I.

65 Once more it was Bertuch who flaunted this offer from Jena in order to force Göttingen to give Grellmann a raise. This can be deduced from a letter which Grellmann addressed to him on 10 March 1790.

66 See p. 12 (12/8/1793) in Dossier KA 4Vb 55 of the University Archives in Göttingen.

67 At other Russian universities German professors were also appointed at this time, as in Kazan. See Wilson (1988, p. 39): 'Of the 7 professors most were German' (period 1804–10). With thanks for this reference to André Köbben.

68 This data is borrowed from a piece by Meiners in the *Göttingsche gelehrte Anzeigen*, Part I (1804, pp. 689–91) about recruitment of professors for the University of Moscow in collaboration with *Geheimrath* Muravjeff in St Petersburg.

69 His widow received a pension of 500 roubles and his oldest son was given a post in a state institute where he was trained at the emperor's expense (GGA, 1805, pp. 973–6). How they fared later has proven impossible for me to discover. According to Nikita Kolpinskij no information about the Grellmanns is to be found in the central state archives of the Soviet Union, neither under reference number 359 (Moscow universities) nor 17 (scholarship, literature and art). Reported in a letter from Kolpinskij to Jan Lucassen (IISG, Amsterdam) on 29 April 1991.

70 See Annex I.

71 Grellmann (1804, p. 5).

72 From a survey in Rollmann (1988, pp. 165–73), Grellmann appears, as far as number of publications is concerned, to have been one of the least productive scholars in Göttingen. As a reviewer he was also considerably less active than his colleagues.

73 This section on Grellmann's portrayal of the Gypsy is based on both the first (1783) and second editions (1787) of his book. I have chosen not to refer repeatedly to the pages where his comments can be traced back. The table of contents of his book reveals at a glance in which chapter the subject at hand is dealt with.

74 On a basis of the text or descriptive title of each source, I investigated which countries were concerned – something that did not prove possible to determine for them all. Grellmann referred 234 times to Hungary/Transylvania and 73 times to Germany. Spain, India, Turkey and Italy received mention, respectively, 44, 41, 38 and 29 times. Seventy per cent of the sources Grellmann consulted were written in German.

75 The figure meant here was Sebastian Münster, author of *Cosmographie* (Basel: Henrichus Petri, 1550, see the edition of 1628, p. 603 *et passim*). Münster also reports an 'interview' with Gypsies in Eberbach. For the integral text, see Gronemeyer (1987, pp. 34–6).

76 The person in question here is the chronicler Andreas from Regensburg who included an eyewitness account of *Cigäwnär* in his *Diarium Sexennale* covering the year 1424 (printed in Andreas Felix Oefelius *Rerum Boicarum Scriptores* (Augsburg, 1763) pp. 21, 26). See Gronemeyer (1987, pp. 18–25).

77 Grellmann (1783, pp. 30–1).

78 For the diverse explanations which circulated during the eighteenth century for the black colour of the skin of negroes, see Mazzolini (1990, pp. 169–87).

79 For these tax regulations and the comparative freedom which Gypsies enjoyed in

the Ottoman Empire, see Fraser (1992, pp. 173–8).

80 See, for example, Blok (1981, pp. 104–28).

81 See especially Heymowski (1969, pp. 40–1) who in the course of his genealogical research on the ancestors of Swedish *tattare* and Gypsies, came across families of executioners, flayers and other vocations that ordinary Swedes would have looked down on.

82 For the continuity of the image of 'the cruel Gypsy', see Willems and Lucassen (1990, p. 35).

83 See Johann Christoph Wagenseil, *De civitate Noribergensi commentatio* (Altdorf, 1697) pp. 435–50.

84 The figures meant here are the learned Dutchman Bonaventura Vulcanius who wrote *De literis ἐt lingua Getarum sive Gothorum* (Lugduni Batavorum, 1597, pp. 100–5), Jacobus Thomasius *Dissertatio philosophica de Cingaris* (Leipzig: Johann Ericus Hahn, 1652) and S. Salmon *Staat aller Nationen in Europa* – translated from English by Elias Caspar Reichard (Altona and Leipzig, 1752). For the first two authors, see Gronemeyer (1987, pp. 113–16, 122–34).

85 Francesco Griselini 'Etwas von den Zigeunern überhaupt, und insbesondere von den Zigeunern im Temeswarer Banat', in *Neueste Mannigfaltigkeiten* (1781), week 157, pp. 3–13; week 158, pp. 17–25 (the articles appeared unattributed). Grellmann himself referred to Griselini's *Versuch einer politischen und natürlichen Geschichte des Temeswarer Banats* (Vienna, 1780) pp. 199–212.

86 *Wiener Anzeigen* (1776, pp. 87–8).

87 Fraser (1992, p. 193) also devotes extensive attention to the story, although he comments that no sources have been passed down to confirm the contents. He does not commit himself as to the historical authenticity of the account.

88 See Goss (1993, section on Rennell). On later maps of India, however, one searches for *Cingana* in vain.

89 We do not find a reference to this source in the mid-nineteenth-century standard work on linguistics by Pott (1844), for example.

90 These findings I have taken from Eekhof (1923, pp. 151–71). See, too, the article by Tantö (1920, pp. 120–9, 161–81, 376–89, 441–50). With thanks for these literary references to the historian of Leiden University, Willem Otterspeer.

91 For the period 1750 to 1763 the *Volumina inscriptionum* and the *Recensielijsten* in Leiden and Franeker contain no Vali, Wali or Valyi. In 1753, however, a Stephanus Waali (Hungarus) registered with the rector of Utrecht. See *Album Studiosorum, Academiae Rheno-Traiectinae* (1636–1886), *Accedunt Nomina Curatorum Professoru. Per Eadem Secula* (Utrecht, 1886) p. 152.

92 See Van Goor (1978).

93 The examination registers of Staten College, kept in the Dousa room of the University Library in Leiden, include the names of this trio who enrolled, respectively, on 14 September 1750, 7 October 1752 and 23 September 1754.

94 See Van Goor (1978, p. 78, 82, 89, 90, 99, 153) where it can be read that Meyer especially made a remarkable career for himself in the East after receiving his doctorate from Leiden. To no avail I searched for the name of Moyaars in Van Goor's lists of pupils who, during the eighteenth century in Ceylon, completed preparation in Jaffna and Colombo for higher learning elsewhere.

95 Pallas (1781–96, p. 96) and Marsden (1785, pp. 382–6). Both claimed, mistakenly, to be the first to have pointed to India as the place where the language of the Gypsies came from. See Wolf (1987, pp. 16–19) for what he calls the controversies which coloured the early years of *Romaniphilologie*.

96 In his notes Grellmann referred on various occasions to Bauer's publication *Memoires sur la Valachie* (Frankfurt and Leipzig, 1778) pp. 24, 48, 86.

97 A total of 131 publications are named in the footnotes to the first edition of the Gypsy book, a number which rose to 183 in the second. Publishing data provided

together with the titles was, as usual for the times, generally anything but complete. Time and place of publication, for example, were seldom noted. About the nature of the works cited, it can be noted that descriptions of travel and chronicles dominate, although articles in periodicals and historical surveys were also consulted.

98 The articles in question were (see also note 107):
a) *1775*: 159–60, 165–8, 175–6, 180–2, 187–91, 196–200, 204–8, 215–16, 222–4, 229–32, 236–40, 286–8, 293–6, 302–4, 309–12, 318–20, 327–8, 334–6, 342–4, 349–52, 358–60, 373–6, 406–8, 414–16.
b) *1776*: 1–2, 7–8, 13–16, 19–24, 32, 37–40, 46–8, 56, 63–4, 71–2, 85–8, 93–6, 102–4, 119–20, 127–8, 134–6, 150–2, 157–60, 162–4, 166–8.

99 This finding is based on close reading of both editions of Grellmann and all the relevant numbers of the *Wiener Anzeigen*. Ruch arrived at the same conclusion in his own dissertation (1986, pp. 104–10).

100 Gronemeyer (1987) reproduces Grellmann's sources and discusses them critically. See, too, my introduction where this protohistory is examined.

101 I studied the six volumes of this weekly magazine on microfiche in the National Library of Austria in Vienna.

102 The most extensive information about the world of German-language magazines in the eighteenth century is to be found in Seidler and Seidler (1988, pp. 38–9). Bibliographic reference books about Viennese journals in the eighteenth century in which something is said about the *Anzeigen*, include: Winckler (1875, p. 35), Richter (1875, pp. 283–4); Zenker (1892, pp. 58–9); Feest (1945, pp. 171–2); Kirchner (1966, p. 61).

103 Entries about most of them can be found in Von Wurzbach (1856–1923, 58 parts; reprinted 1966); De Luca (1776–78); Gräffer (1833).

104 Ruch (1986, p. 104).

105 At present this city is called Spišská Sobota and is situated in current-day Slovakia. The information here about Ab Hortis comes from two Hungarian biographical dictionaries: the *Nevri Nagy lexikon*, Part 2 (1811, p. 299), under 'Augustini ab Hortis, Samuel' and the *Magyar életovjti lexikon*, Part 1 (1881, p. 62), under 'Augustini Sámuel, ab Hortis'. In addition I consulted two German dictionaries. In the first, Von Wurzbach (1856–1923, p. 311), under 'ab Hortis, Samuel', I found 26 August 1729 given as date of birth and the date of death was listed as unknown. The same was true for the entry in De Luca, Part 1, 2nd, expanded edition (1777, p. 255).

106 See the short biographical introduction by Rudolph Weber written for Ab Hortis' last, posthumously published work, *Topographische Beschreibung des Flusses Poprad oder Popper in der Zips aus dem Jahre 1782* (Kesmark, 1900).

107 The Hungarian ethnologist Dr Viera Urbancová recently arrived at the same conclusion, first of all on grounds of the initials but also through consulting local Hungarian sources. She has also prepared a complete dual language (Hungarian/German) edition of the series of articles on Gypsies: Samuel Augustini ab Hortis *Cigáni v Uhorsku/ Zigeuner in Ungarn (1775)* (Bratislava: Studio Bratislava, 1994). See, too, her introduction and afterword in which she urges the restoration of this 'forgotten monograph' to the respect it deserves. My thanks to Han F. Vermeulen, an anthropologist from Leiden University, who, after reading my dissertation, called my attention to Urbancová's publication.

108 This letter, dated 3 Febuary 1775, was addressed to Dániel Cornides, the 'professor in Pest' whom Grellmann thanked in the second edition of his book for the materials which Cornides had put at his disposal. According to a letter from László Ottovay of the Hungarian National Library (11 June 1991), the letter from Czirbesz is in the manuscript collection of the Hungarian Academy of Sciences, the *Ungarische Literaturkorrespondenz* section (Magyar irodalmi levelezés), 4r.60, no. 81. Ottovay

added that he too considers it probable that Sámuel Augustini Ab Hortis was the writer of the series about Gypsies.

109   See Ruch (1986, pp. 104–16).
110   *Wiener Anzeigen* (1776, p. 167).
111   See Büttner (1771, p. 4).
112   My material on Büttner's life comes from Ebel (1962, rubric Ph.1, no. 28, p. 104) and, especially, from Schlichtegroll (1802, pp. 211–40). A portrait of Büttner by Konrad Westermayr hangs in the aula of Göttingen University.
113   With his much talked about *Système de la Nature* (Brussels, 1793), Linnaeus left his mark on the anthropological classification of humanity into four (coloured) varieties, namely the European, the American, the Asian, and the African. Nor did he forgo linking judgments about character to these classifications.
114   See Streich (1977, p. 287).
115   See Schlichtegroll (1802, pp. 217–18).
116   This characterization appears in *Lichtenbergs Briefe*, published by Albert Leitzmann and Carl Schüddekopf. Part 1 1766–81 (Leipzig, 1901) pp. 403–4.
117   Cf. *Neue Deutsche Biographie*. Part 3 (Berlin, 1957) p. 6.
118   See in particular Paunel (July/August 1949, pp. 235–69). Also Bogeng (1922, pp. 299–302); Milkau (1957, p. 26); Lerche (1929, pp. 59–64). For the original passages from Goethe's work, see his *Sämtliche Werke*, Jubilee edition (1902–7; part 25, p. 246; part 30, p. 101; part 38, p. 238; part 39, pp. 304–5; part 40, pp. 310–11).
119   See Paunel (1949, pp. 242–3).
120   This Grellmann reports in a letter to Bertuch dated 15 July 1781. From a letter of 25 March 1783 we can deduce that crates with books stood in readiness for conveyance to Jena.
121   Goethe's *Sämtliche Werke*, part 30, p. 101.
122   Büttner lived on a comfortable inheritance from his father, never married, scarcely maintained any family relations and led a rather unconventional domestic life.
123   Thus Milkau (1957, p. 26).
124   For the last ten years of his life Büttner appears to have worked exclusively on his never-published *Prodromus linguarum*. At the time copies of this work circulated among all those who were interested. Thus a manuscript in his writing, with unnumerable notes, must also have been presented to his friend Blumenbach. Cf. Schlichtegroll (1802, pp. 222–3).
125   Also from Schlichtegroll's obituary (1802, p. 222).
126   For this part of my study I had the good fortune during my stay in Göttingen, to be able to appeal for help to the experience of Klaus Schmidt, co-ordinator of a work group occupied with preparing indices of German language periodicals from the period of 1750 to 1815. Together with him I compiled a list of reference works to be consulted. I also submitted request slips for armloads of leading German language periodicals at the State Library in Göttingen. This hunt turned up a total of 15 reviews, some of which, such as the Italian and Dutch ones, on closer examination proved not to contain any judgmental remarks about the book. (See Annex 2.) In his dissertation Ruch (1986, pp. 123–7) discussed four of these 15 reviews.
127   For a concise explanation of the basic principles of the Indo-European family of languages, see the recent standard work by Beekes (1990, pp. 33–53).
128   My research into such writing remained limited to German-language publications in the reference works that I have summarized in the footnote to Annex 2. In addition I consulted the chronological bibliography included by Ruch in his dissertation (1986, pp. 475–6).
129   Among other works, see the *Österreichische National Enzyklopädie*, Part 6 (1839) pp. 246–8; and the *Staats- und Gesellschaftslexikon*, Part 23 (1867) pp. 13–24.

130 Zippel and Biester (1793).

131 Ruch (1986, pp. 127–31) allies himself with this critical contemporary of Grellmann's but puts on record that Biester's comments only targeted the ethnographic part of Grellmann's book. Biester is said to have hardly voiced any objections to Grellmann's treatment of linguistic comparison. This is wrong. Indeed, in his second article, Biester went into detail about the linguistic flaws in Grellmann's book, and the related dubious deductions.

132 Biester himself does not reveal the name of this learned friend in his articles. Ruch (1986, p. 130) writes of 'Krause aus Königsberg' without disclosing how he came to know his identity. The full name of Biester's source is mentioned in the work of the linguist A. Pott (1844/45, p. 17).

133 Biester refers to him simply as the 'Littauischen Pfarrer, Hrn Z - 1'. Ruch, like the *'Index deutschsprachiger Zeitschriften'*, speaks of Zippel.

134 Biester (1793, p. 128).

135 Ibidem, p. 148.

136 Ibidem, p. 151.

137 Ibidem, p. 156.

138 Ibidem, p. 162.

139 See, for example, Moch (1992).

140 Rüdiger, Part 5 (1793, p. 236).

141 See the following: Rüdiger (1782, p. 88, paragraphs 180 and 181) in which he mentions – but does no more than that – that the Gypsies' language is the same as Hindi; Rüdiger (1782, pp. 37–84), where he discussed the language and origins of Gypsies from India in detail; Rüdiger (1783, pp. 151–2), where he defends himself against an attack from Göttingen on a comparison he appears to have made between Gypsies and Jews; Rüdiger (1784, pp. 130–2); Rüdiger (1785, p. 222) in which he cites a number of publications where information about Gypsy languages could be found, for instance Marsden; Rüdiger (1796, p. 134), partial reprinting of No. 2.

142 Rüdiger (1782, p. 62).

143 In the introduction to his survey (1987, pp. 16–19) Wolf rejects the 'birthright' claims of linguists from both Hungary (based on the articles in the *Anzeigen*) and England (based on Marsden's findings from 1785); he awards primacy to Rüdiger for his conclusions based on systematic comparisons. For Ruch (1986, pp. 119–23), however, there is no doubt that Büttner deserves recognition for being the first to demonstrate where Gypsies came from by linguistic means.

144 Ruch (1986, pp. 134–41) waxes almost lyrical when he comes to write about Rüdiger's article. He speaks of Rüdiger's honesty and modesty, his openness towards Gypsies, and of his moral and scholarly integrity. He takes Rüdiger's call for social *Wiedergutmachung* more than seriously. He hardly mentions that Rüdiger none the less also reaffirmed countless prejudices and painted an extremely naive picture of Gypsies.

145 The *Allgemeine Deutsche Bibliographie*, p. 468. According to the article about him printed here he was *Kammer- und Thalsecretar, Assessor des Salzamtes*.

146 See Pott (1844, pp. 17-19) who writes that the unpublished collections of Prof. Chr. Jak. Kraus and the cleric Zippel from Niebudzen had been handed over to him by his learned friend Peter von Bohlen on his death bed, a true gift which left him duty bound to complete their analysis.

147 Ibidem, p. xv. His teacher, to whom he also dedicated his book, was the famous linguist Franz Bopp. According to Wolf (1987, p. 19, note 39), with his two part study in 1846 Pott won the intensely coveted Prix Volney.

148 Miklosich (1872–81). He discussed the numbers, history (in brief) and the linguistic influences of Greek, Romanian, Hungarian, Moravian-Bohemian, German, Polish-Lithuanian, Russian, Finnish, Scandinavian, Italian, Basque, English-Scotch and

Spanish Gypsies. He also included several fairy tales and songs in 'Gypsy language'. The greater part of his work, even so, is linguistic.

149   Ibidem, Part 6, p. 63.
150   Ibidem, Part 3, p. 7. That is why, according to Miklosich, Greek elements can be identified in all European Gypsy languages.
151   Turner (1975, pp. 251–90). Appeared earlier in the *Journal of the Gypsy Lore Society*, 3rd series, Part V, no. 4 (1926, pp. 145–89).
152   Ibidem, p. 276.
153   See, for example, Heinschink's recent survey (1994, pp. 110–28) and Holzinger (1993, pp. 1–2).
154   See the collection of essays by Bakker and Cortiade (1991) for a resumé of how things stand linguistically.
155   Ibidem, pp. 39–40.
156   Ibidem, p. 41.
157   Beekes (1990, p. 73).
158   Two recent studies in this area that have been the subject of much discussion are Renfrew's (1987) and Mallory's (1989).

3

George Borrow (1803–81), the walking lord of Gypsy lore

INTRODUCTION

Dora Yates, honorary secretary of the English Gypsy Lore Society for more than 20 years, drew from her own experience when she wrote in her memoirs of 1953:

> The first question asked of every Romano Rai and every Romani Rawnie is always what turned his or her interests to the Gypsies. And in five cases out of six the invariable reply is: 'Reading the works of George Borrow'.[1]

Her position within the exclusive society in the field of Gypsy studies validated such an estimate. Whoever pages through the many volumes of the periodical which, with some interruptions, the society has issued for more than a century,[2] will, to be sure, reach the conclusion that George Borrow has served as an inspiration to many generations interested in the world of the Gypsies. Strictly speaking his works are not scholarly but comprise a mix of genres: philological excursions, spiritual autobiography, romantic travel journalism, picaresque missionary tales. In his books there are encounters with Russian, Spanish and English Gypsies, and there are also lists of words from the languages that these groups spoke, translations of their songs and poetry, ideas concerning their origins and customs, and pronouncements about their nature as a people and their vocations. Many historical, ethnographic, linguistic and literary aspects of Gypsy life are examined in such diverse works as *The Zincali, or, An Account of the Gypsies of Spain* (1841), *The Bible in Spain* (1843), *Lavengro* (1851), *The Romany Rye* (1857) and *Romano Lavo-Lil: Word-Book of the Romany* (1874).[3]

The approach of Borrow's first book was very similar to Grellmann's broad study. After a summary treatment of a number of aspects of Gypsy communities in Russia, Hungary, Wallachia, Moldavia, England and Turkey, Borrow deals at length with their history in Spain. Names, occupations, morals and customs, way of life and legislation passed against the Gypsies all pass in review, as does the Gypsy language, in England as well as in Spain. The writer also takes time to consider Gypsy fortune telling and the variety of frauds practised by Gypsy women whose appearance and behaviour fascinated him. He also deals with all kinds of rumours and debunked theories concerning their origin and examines the way in which, down through the years, they charmed segments of Spanish society with their exotic aura. Borrow devotes some sections to his first-hand contacts with Gypsies in that country. The only thing that is new is the taste he gives of Gypsy verse. His next book, *The Bible in Spain*, was without historical, linguistic or ethnological pretensions; he merely related his adventures in Spain as colporteur in the employ of the English Bible Society. He presented the volume not as the report of an arbitrary traveller, but as the story of a pilgrimage that was necessary to dispel 'Papal superstition'. During his extensive wanderings through Spain he met up with Gypsies from time to time, alone or in a band, recording these often mysterious encounters in both a romantic and a documentary fashion. If we go by the anecdotes that he writes down as testimony, the Spanish Gypsies readily trusted him although, at least judging from Borrow's writings, they were usually marginal social figures, if not criminals.

Borrow's two novels, *Lavengro* and *The Romany Rye*, are of a different character altogether. They form a two-part semi-autobiographical account of the first 22 years of the life of his alter ego, Lavengro, in whom the reader recognizes from earlier works many of Borrow's own traits and preoccupations, such as his love of philology, horses, boxing and an unencumbered life. In Lavengro's detailed reconstruction of the most important phase of his young life, his run-ins with Gypsies (*Romany Chal*) play a leading role, even if they all involve only a single clan, that of his romantic bosom-companion Jasper Petulengro, the proud, freedom-loving horse trader, who is also no slouch with his fists. From Jasper, Lavengro learns the Romany language, even asking him later to set down the history of his people in writing, a request which deeply displeases Petulengro's mother-in-law, Herne, who develops into a veritable witch bent on murdering the initiated *Romany Rye*. When Lavengro, after abortive attempts to earn a literary living, temporarily chooses a rover's existence as a smith, a number of classic scenes unfold in Mumper's Dingle where he fights with the Flaming Tinman, falls in love with the young traveller, Isopel Berners, and seems to become part of the small clan of Petulengro, his wife, and his enchanting sister.

The *Romano Lavo-Lil*, last of Borrow's books, contains a compilation of texts from English Gypsies: lists of words, sayings, verses and songs. Borrow also discusses Gypsy names and again portrays many tricks of deception which he maintains are specifically Gypsy. In addition the book contains reports of meetings he had over the years with diverse travellers, often only partially of Gypsy descent. In a blend of journalism and memoir writing he tells about his excursions to wayfarers' camps in Wandsworth, the Potteries and Kirk Yetholm (in Scotland), especially emphasizing his friendship over the years with some of these Gypsies and the social distinctions between the different groups of travellers and Gypsies. Borrow presents the book as a collection of anecdotes and things worth knowing, passed on by an intimate of the Gypsies who is convinced that the days of gypsydom are numbered and who therefore looks back one last time to share his personal knowledge of this disappearing people with the reading public.

George Borrow wrote so vividly about the life of Gypsies that he was described in a contemporary poem as 'the walking lord of Gypsy lore'. The major difference with his continental predecessor, Grellmann, was that Borrow's readers knew that he had encountered Gypsies in various countries, including Russia, Spain, and Hungary as well as England and that when he wrote about them he was in part writing from his own experiences. He already accentuated this fact in the introduction to *The Zincali*. As a result, for a long time, many took him extremely seriously as philologist, folklorist and ethnologist. This image of Borrow as an anthropologist *avant la lettre* continues to colour the way he is looked upon even today. Some, without any evidence, assume that in his youth, just as he described in *Lavengro*, Borrow regularly frequented Gypsies and picked up their language, which is said to be an indication of his great ability to win people over, for these tent dwellers were not thought to be inclined to impart the secrets of their speech so easily to non-Gypsies.

What also has made Borrow such an influential figure is that he operated along the interface of various disciplines that concerned themselves with Gypsies. He carried on the linguistic tradition that was launched by Grellmann and his contemporaries, brought to the attention of a wider public current initiatives of socially or religiously inspired philanthropy aimed at improving the Gypsies' lot in life, and was more or less the founder of the folkloristic study of the culture of the 'pure Romani' which, he believed, was rapidly vanishing. Added to this were the power of his literary imaginings and the veneer of mystery attached to many of his adventures. With this combination of talents, he was able not only to captivate readers but also to goad intellectuals, adventurers, and writers from the Romantic school into imitating him. This turned him into the best-known nineteenth-century English writer on Gypsies.[4]

Later I will speak more extensively about Borrow's ties with those who came before him, and those who followed after. For the moment I will confine myself to filling out the picture of his position as the man who devised the society which had the strongest influence on determining the image of the Gypsy that has prevailed in Western Europe during the past century: the Gypsy Lore Society (subsequently GLS).[5] The society's perspective, certainly in the early years after it was founded in 1888, was almost exclusively ethnographic. It was out '[to] garner the thousand and one stray scraps of curious Gypsy lore now lying scattered ...'[6] While a debate was going on in the Lower House of Parliament about the introduction of a system of registration for caravan and tent dwellers, a proposition raised by the philanthropist George Smith from Coalville, members of the GLS delved into the degree of racial purity of a people who were at risk, they believed, of dying out – a prospect that George Borrow, their mentor, had warned against almost half a century earlier. This prompts the question of how he had arrived at his standpoint and why it evoked such a strong response among his readers and his followers.

In the interests of finding answers, I will first examine the base on which Borrow's reputation actually rested and see how much contact he really had with Gypsies, to the extent, that is, that we can find that out retrospectively. Indeed, his literary creations in the two 'Lavengro' volumes acquired added depth for readers because the writer was himself known to be a half-Gypsy.[7] The same held true for his meetings with Gypsies in the documentary account of his travels, *The Bible in Spain*, based on his personal adventures while dispersing Bibles there. Publications with more scholarly pretensions, such as *The Zincali* at the outset of his career, and the *Romano Lavo-Lil* at the end, seem just as credible, once more thanks to his personal touch. But was he truly the friend of the Gypsies that he claimed to be? And from what source precisely sprang the heralded bonding of their souls which he felt so keenly? Rumours circulated about Borrow's Gypsy background and his nomadic way of living in the company of Gypsy clans. During which period in his life we should place these experiences?

In this context it is necessary to raise the issue of the complex relation between *Wahrheit* and *Dichtung* in Borrow's writing career. In so doing we come across the creation of diverse Gypsy characters in various genres. For a better grasp of what Borrow was doing, it will help to trace the influence that linguistic, evangelical and literary circles exercised upon him. Only in this way does it become comprehensible why he created the figure of the *Romany Rye* which enabled him to explore the theme of 'the Gypsy' in a unique way. The very fact that when he wrote about Gypsies he did so in different capacities meant that, through Borrow, for the first time, an unprecedented broad public came to read about them. In contrast to the image of Gypsies presented by other experts, Borrow's, owing to his authorial versatility, dispensed with strict uniformity. I will therefore pause to consider inconsistencies in his portraiture, subsequently to indicate the ways in which Borrow with his work recast the way people had come to regard Gypsies since Grellmann.

BIOGRAPHICAL SKETCH OF THE FIRST 'ROMANY RYE'

The life and works of George Borrow have always enjoyed a host of admirers; as a consequence, in the intervening years, nearly 20 biographies of him have appeared, the first of them in 1899, the most recent, for now, in 1982.[8] The number of publications featuring remembrances of the writer or reflections on some aspect of his work is rapidly approaching the 200 mark, not counting more than 100 reviews of his books. As is not unusual in the realm of biographies, many have devoted their efforts primarily to laying bare the reality behind the facade of Borrow's semi-autobiographical writings, with, it must be said, only moderate success. This is connected in the first place to the circumstance that few personal documents survive from the period preceding Borrow's emergence as a public figure. In addition a great deal may have been written about him but that is not to say that much new has been added. Furthermore there is a dearth of published sources and Borrow's correspondence with his contemporaries, for example, has only been brought out in fragmentary form.[9] We know a good deal more about him than about Grellmann but, nevertheless, the literature that exists provides no conclusive material on the subjects that are of importance to this study. Indeed, little is yet known about the nature and frequency of Borrow's personal contacts with Gypsies and the sources of his information about them have remained virtually unexamined. Before venturing an attempt to shed more light on these matters, I shall first provide a biographical sketch.[10]

The formative years

George Henry Borrow came into the world on 5 July 1803 while Napoleon and his marauding armies were trying to bring the world to its knees. He would grow into a tall, muscular figure with energy to spare, hair that turned white at an early age, and penetrating, brown eyes. Many found his appearance imposing: a giant of a man, free from anxiety, capable of supreme physical effort. Beneath this virile surface, however, there lurked a person plagued by lifelong fits of depression, or, as he himself put it, both in his work and in his personal correspondence, 'the horrors'.[11] According to his biographer Collie, as the result of Borrow's unusual appearance and depressive nature, from his youth on he became something of a social misfit and, to compensate, withdrew into a world of books. The family life of the youthful George may have figured in his painful, personal development. His father, Thomas Borrow, son of a farmer from Cornwall, was in danger of going wrong as a young man and ultimately sought his salvation in the army where he climbed to the rank of captain. At the age of 34 he married the 21-year-old Ann Perfrement, the daughter of a tenant farmer in East Dereham, Norfolk. The story which recurs regularly of her being an actress in a road company who won the heart of the hard-bitten army officer during a performance will have sprouted from the fantasy of later biographers who wanted to provide their hero with suitably romantic parentage. We don't know the facts about what happened. We simply know that Thomas Borrow's regiment moved from place to place. Borrow's boyhood years were lived in the shadow of the Napoleonic Wars, which in practice meant that his father's regiment, which never saw battle, was stationed in many locations in England, Scotland and Ireland. An adventurous but also restive life for George, which entailed a rather fragmentary upbringing that afforded him little chance to forge close social bonds. Only in 1816 did the family return to Norwich (Norfolk) where, three years later, Captain Thomas Borrow became a pensioner.

For a reconstruction of the first decades of George Borrow we must rely almost entirely on what he himself has written about them in his linked novels *Lavengro* and *The Romany Rye*. In these books he expresses his preference for independent characters, confined to their own isolated world of ideas, and for men who, like himself, delight in physical activity: long foot journeys, swimming, horseriding and 'the noble sport of boxing'. Through his fascination with books he also discovered, as a youth, that he had a gift for languages. In the different areas of Great Britain where the Borrow family lived, he had picked up Welsh and Irish and at school he had mastered Latin with remarkable ease. Upon reaching secondary school in Norwich, between 1816 and 1819, he learned French and Italian from an immigrant priest. From grammar texts in the library he acquired some fluency not only in Spanish but also in Greek and Hebrew; he would develop a lifelong interest in some of these languages. He was practically 16 years old when his father managed to place him as an apprentice in the successful legal firm of William Simpson and Rackhan where he would remain in service for five years, living with his employer's family. If, once more, we go by *Lavengro*, then Captain Borrow had little confidence in the career of his youngest son, who hardly expended any effort as a juridical worker to improve his father's disparaging opinion of him. He spent all his spare time, even during office hours, on expanding his repertoire of languages. With a Jew he developed his command of Hebrew further and also succeeded in arranging German lessons with the Germanist William Taylor, whose home served an important function in the intellectual life of Norwich and who quickly regarded his talented pupil as one of his favourites. In the meantime George had grown interested in other, more exotic languages, such as Danish and Romani, the language of the Gypsies. Above all he grew passionate about old Danish literature, the epics and ancient sagas, and throughout his adolescent years he worked indefatigably on translations of medieval Danish ballads which brought him into contact with a lost world of heroic poets whom he took as his role models and whose grandeur he would strive to evoke for the rest of his life through the power of his imagination. For a time he even signed his letters George *Olaus* Borrow, after the Danish poet Olaus Wormius whom he revered.

Shortly after the death of his father in 1824, Borrow's training period in the law office expired and the 21-year-old man, who had already earlier resolved to follow the calling of poet, girded himself to try his luck in London. With great bravura he wrote to his friend at that time Roger Kerrison: 'I intend to live in London, write plays, poetry and abuse religion and get myself prosecuted, for I would not for an ocean of gold remain any longer than I am forced in this dull and gloomy town.'[12] These and other letters of the period reflect the melancholic mood of an adolescent who swung back and forth between excessive expectations of himself and depressive insecurity about a future on which, lacking adequate means for survival, he had but a tenuous hold.[13] Thanks to a letter of recommendation from William Taylor, Borrow managed to find an opening in the small, once-celebrated publishing house of Sir Richard Phillips, which may have declined to publish his translations of poetry but entrusted him with the editorship of a series of famous law cases, *Celebrated Trials and Remarkable Cases of Criminal Jurisprudence, from the Earliest Records to the Year 1825*.[14] This project not only increased his interest in social outsiders, people condemned by law to take recourse in an adventurous life, but it also taught him, in his own words, how to tell a story: clearly and directly, without frills. What's more Phillips gave him the opportunity to publish translations of (Danish) poetry in *The Monthly Magazine* and reviews in *The Universal Review*. Reviewing was something that Borrow did with the greatest reluctance.[15] He thought books could speak for themselves. In this period, however, his own work hardly generated enough money for him to live on and only after he succeeded in having a story published was he able, financially, to leave London and seek his fortune elsewhere.

The history of that first published story merits more consideration.

He described it himself at length in *Lavengro* in a manner which has sown confusion about its authenticity among his biographers. Collie's investigations brought to light the story behind the story: a publication of Borrow's from 1825, the *Life and Adventures of the Famous Colonel Blood*. The core of the story was a narrative that Borrow had polished for Phillips' anthology of famous law cases. That could explain why he never later referred to this youthful specimen of 'literary plagiarism'.[16] In any event, his earnings from the story made it possible for him to ship his belongings to Norwich where his mother lived, and to spend a few months roaming as an adventurer through the English countryside. His experiences on the road became the nucleus of his novels, *Lavengro* and *The Romany Rye*. In accounts which have contributed to Borrow's image, this period regularly becomes blown up into years of living among vagrants and Gypsies where, as a tinker, he was the cynosure of a romantic universe, discovering fresh adventure around every bend in the road. If we accept the time span presented in his semi-autobiographical fiction, however, then it adds up to no more than about three months during which he possibly had a taste of how road folk lived. Afterwards he returned to Norwich where, except for a few short periods, he sheltered under his mother's wings for seven years, leading a marginal existence as translator/writer. Something like a myth has arisen about this less-than-spectacular phase of his life, which ever since Knapp's biography has been known as the veiled period, for Borrow was ever after reticent to speak about it, perhaps because so little occurred that fits his image of a writer, which was created retroactively. Some say he made trips to Europe and Asia in these years, and that he even made a stop in India, meeting with groups of Gypsies all over the globe. What we know for sure is conducive to a more prosaic interpretation. His precarious financial situation will have left him with little cash to spare for travelling. His vain attempts to land work, including as a member of English or foreign armed forces,[17] together with the vast scope of his translations from this period – without his succeeding in publishing anything more than a single anthology – make it more than likely that the radius of his mobility extended no further than England itself.[18]

Employee of the Bible Society

In 1833 Borrow was offered a position with the British and Foreign Bible Society (BFBS) where he had been introduced as a young man without university training, highly productive and capable of reading the Bible in 13 different languages.[19] This last qualification proved decisive. The BFBS, a product of the Victorian evangelical revival, was one of the most important religious institutions of the nineteenth century. It was founded in 1804 by a group of men who belonged to the expanding nineteenth-century bourgeoisie. The secret of its success lay apparently in the combination of a religious-social goal and a commercial approach.[20] The set-up was, in essence, simple: Christ's word should be spread among the people. This could only be achieved by translating and printing the Bible in every conceivable language and then spreading it, at a modest price, among all the poor, the heathen, and the Catholics of the world. The underlying conviction was that Bible reading and charity would of themselves lead to social reforms based on Christian principles. By choosing the Bible without commentary as text, one could work in every country with the version that was authorized there and so steer clear of controversies between those of different religious persuasions. There was, moreover, utter belief in the convincing power of God's word, which, certainly as far as the New Testament was concerned, would speak for itself. By establishing a network of field offices in as many places in the world as possible, and by deploying a corps of volunteer salesmen, the society assured itself of maximum coverage. And the formula worked. In the year Borrow entered its service, the BFBS had grown into a rich organization with an annual budget of £80,000. The executive secretary of the London head office was an important figure, an intermediary between the board and the 'representatives in the field'. As a rule this was a cleric. It was Joseph Jowett during the two years when Borrow co-ordinated the translation of a Manchu Bible in St Petersburg (for dissemination in China), and Andrew Brandram during the four years when he was responsible for spreading Bibles throughout Catholic Spain. These were the tasks for which the society hired him and which, as its foreign representative, he carried out with great flair.

The job signified more than an easing of Borrow's financial straits; it was also the first time his special gift for languages was taken seriously socially. This motivated him to learn the fundamentals of first Manchu and then Russian within several months so that, with the requisite letters of recommendation in his pocket, he could build up a social network in St Petersburg that made it possible for him to supervise the entire production process of the translation. Distribution of the Bibles in China never was realized, although Borrow, once he had completed his assignment to all parties' satisfaction, would gladly have undertaken the trek eastwards and continued to dream of such a journey for a long while to come. In his work as cosmopolitan philologist and as an organizational jack-of-all-trades his personality flowered abundantly. Russia and St Petersburg, moreover, had stolen his heart. He made important friends and found the time to translate a large number of poems which, this time, also were actually published.[21]

Between 1835 and 1840 the BFBS sent its most linguistically gifted employee to Portugal and Spain on various occasions where, with increasing determination, he persevered in the distribution of Bibles to the farthest corners of the Catholic peninsula which, in those years, was engaged in a bloody civil war. In the course of events he found the spiritual and the secular authorities ever more emphatically opposed to him, despite the fact that the Bible Society had guidelines preventing its representatives from becoming involved in politically sensitive affairs. His fraternizing with Gypsies, moreover, first in Badajoz, and later in Madrid and Seville, roused the suspicions of many, especially when he translated the Gospel according to Luke into Spanish Gypsy dialect and in 1837, with the permission of the BFBS, had an edition of 500 copies printed. Accusations that he was a spy, a provocateur and a wizard grew louder over the years. They even led to Borrow being imprisoned in Madrid in May 1838 for a few days after a conflict with the police authorities; an incident which, in his literary travel journal, *The Bible in Spain*, he transformed into a deed of religious heroism as part of a series of terrors with which he had to contend in his efforts to bring the scripture to the Spaniards.[22] Socially, we can deduce from Borrow's correspondence that he never felt truly at ease in either Portugal or Spain. Most population groups had to pay the price of his displeasure. He found the Jews in Lisbon primitive and dull, the Portuguese backward and superstitious, the Spaniards arrogant, reserved, cruel, badly raised and hostile to foreigners. The country was a wilderness and a chaos, the people an uncivilized horde. During his early days there, he wrote to his mother that he never went out in the streets by night because: '... then the people walk about by hundreds, cutting and murdering one another on account of their being split into different factions (...) for every Spaniard is by nature a cruel, cowardly tiger.'[23]

In this same letter he wrote that he had spent some time in Estremadura with Gypsies who were extremely nice and for whom he felt sorry because the Spaniards were said to misuse them and keep them on the run like wolves. Yet it does not seem tenable to me to maintain, as Collie and many others with him do, that Borrow did feel at ease in the company of mule drivers, riff-raff, or above all Gypsies because he was alleged to have such a perfect understanding of their way of life.[24] At any rate few things he writes in his work lead one to believe so.

Career as a writer

In the last year of his stay in Spain, Borrow invited the widow Mary Clarke with her daughter Henrietta to come to spend some time with him in Seville. When still in Norwich he had made friends with her; later they had corresponded and she, as a 43 year old woman with modest property in Oulton (and a 21 year old daughter), notwithstanding her firm Christian principles, apparently had no objection to coming to live for a few months with this adventurous Bible distributor in Spain as a first step towards a marriage which, indeed, actually took place on 23 April 1840. The marriage provided Borrow with the financial independence that he needed, once back in England, to enable him to devote himself to writing. He had also imagined that, owing to his position as husband, he would automatically be accorded some honorary function among the local notables. In that expectation, however, he proved to be deceived. He might take the gentleman's code of honour seriously, but the gentlemen themselves knew better and therefore he failed to penetrate their ranks, no matter how hard he tried to win recognition as a respectable resident. Seen in this light, his frequent attacks in writing on the gentility become very comprehensible.

Fortunately he still had his writer's talent in which his wife perhaps believed still more devoutly than he himself did. And she lent him her support, with the full force of her personality, copying his manuscripts meticulously, penning letters and looking after his finances. She was a life companion about whom he always expressed himself in tender terms, despite the fact that his biographers rather stressed the absence of passion between them, spoke of an 'unconsummated' union, and speculated about the intimate bond between Borrow and his step-daughter, Henrietta.[25] However that may be, once back in England and wed, Borrow settled down in his garden house in Oulton to work out the material on Spanish Gitanos which he had collected while attending to all his other responsibilities. What began as a collector's hobby originating from his interest in philology grew into a broadly conceived work on their poetry, morals, customs and history down through the centuries. The publisher John Murray appeared prepared to publish the manuscript, after exacting an opinion from the hispanist Richard Ford. *The Zincali* was decidedly not an overnight best seller, unlike *The Bible in Spain* two years later, in which Borrow, in part acting on Ford's advice, put down on paper all of the adventures he had lived through in Spain, with great feeling for the grotesque and the dramatic. His mission as a Bible salesman provided continuity to the framework of stories which were also actually based in part on the letters and reports that Borrow had written to the secretary general to justify his actions during the years he worked for the BFBS.[26] This book, thick as a fist, catapulted him instantly into the front ranks of England's leading writers: Murray brought out one edition after another; an inexpensive edition reached tens of thousands of readers, and in America pirated editions met with just as voracious a reception. *The Bible in Spain* became one of the best selling books in Great Britain in the middle of the previous century.

The later works, especially *Lavengro* and *The Romany Rye*, which were realized with such difficulty, and in which Borrow portrays unforgettably his encounters with the Gypsy family Petulengro, were judged by the reading public first of all by the veracity of their contents. For an autobiography, this makes sense. Much later critics also came to distinguish Borrow's literary intentions in his spiritual semi-autobiography. The core of the conflict with Borrow's contemporary public was that publisher Murray had promoted the book for years as the life story of the author of the successful travel book about Spain. Borrow may once have set to work with this in mind, but during the drawn-out, arduous creative process his imagination had the upper hand and a work emerged which resembled autobiography in format but was meant to be more of a dream, a poem, a philological journey, to put it in Borrow's own words. He had wanted to reveal the spiritual truth of his life and not the bare facts, but these were what the public was expecting. The result was confusion on both sides, which instilled in Borrow the feeling that he was not understood.[27] In the soon-to-become-notorious appendix to *The Romany Rye*, the sequel to *Lavengro*, he would vent his frustrations in virulent terms in a lengthy complaint against critics who accused him of only having eyes for Gypsies and other 'low life', against what he saw as the pernicious power of the Catholic church, and against the so-called refinement of people from well-to-do circles, 'the evangelical, moralistic and Philistine attitudes of part of its middle class'.[28] He drifted still deeper into isolation as a result, or, as Collie writes, he became yet more defensive, closed, suspicious and more paranoid.[29] Sound of body until old age, he led an ever more lonely life, certainly after the death of his wife in 1869. In the 1850s and 1860s he had made a number of long journeys on foot to various remote corners of the British Isles, but only an account of his visit to Wales, one which included but a single Gypsy scene, would ever appear in book form.[30]

In Borrow's swan song from 1874, the *Romano Lavo-Lil Word-Book of the Romany*, he returned for yet one last time to a Gypsy theme. He had felt himself more-or-less obliged to assert his authority in this field anew and emphatically once he noticed that an ambitious generation of young gypsiologists were growing impatient for him to pass on the torch. The crucial figure in this change of the guard was the American Charles Godfrey Leland who had settled in England in 1869. He wrote to Borrow telling him that his books had kindled in him an interest in the language and the folklore of the Gypsies and he asked permission to dedicate to the great teacher his own work in progress, *The English Gipsies and their Language*, which would be published in 1873. Borrow reacted with little generosity, scraping together in great haste all the notes he had accumulated over the years and bringing out his own linguistic study on English Gypsies. While Leland reaped high praise for his work, establishing himself in one blow as an expert in Gypsy studies, critics branded Borrow's book as dated, spelling the end of his monopoly as England's foremost gypsiologist.[31] The same fate attended Borrow's career as a writer, and during the last decade of his life, he was consigned to obscurity. Only after his death on 26 July 1881 did interest in him gradually revive, peaking during the first decade of the twentieth century.

HOW *ROMANY* WAS THE *RYE*?

Those who become involved with Gypsies always seem constrained to justify their interest in these social outsiders. Since Borrow a number of the arguments have typically become common property, such as (partial) Gypsy descent, a love relationship with a Gypsy, kindred spirits and a shared preference for an itinerant way of life. We constantly come across these self-justifications, above all in folklorist circles. The underlying premise seems to be that unless we belong to the other's group or are related to it, we can't understand him. For the other the same is said to hold true, which is why the phrase about recognition keeps recurring.

A supposed Gypsy past

We encounter all these aspects in relation to Borrow, both in his work and in stories about him as, for example, in the remembrances of a clergyman who, in his youth at home, had heard the general secretary of the Bible Society say at the family table that Borrow had told him the first time they met in London that as a boy he had been stolen away by Gypsies. For years he was said to have been forced to remain in their company and there he acquired his secret knowledge of them until, at a market in Norfolk, an uncle recognized him and straightaway returned him to his parents' house.[32] In 1953 Vesey-FitzGerald went much further than introducing a rumour into the world with a book in which he wanted to demonstrate that Borrow was of Gypsy origin.[33] FitzGerald had himself brought out various publications about Gypsies and had written that at the age of 13, he had fallen in love with a Gypsy girl. He then came to know many Gypsy families with whom he had always remained in touch. Only a person like him, who knew what he was talking about, could judge the truthfulness of Borrow's observations. He based the idea that the writer he admired was a full-blooded Gypsy, brought up in a non-Gypsy environment,[34] primarily on Borrow's appearance, especially his piercing glance, and on his personality traits. Thus his work was said to express a superstitious respect for names, a remarkable memory for distances, people, and place names, an absence of historical understanding, an elastic memory, and a strongly developed capacity to tell lies. In a sober article from 1972 Angus Fraser wrote that with such argumentation we would be able to provide many people with 'improper ancestors'.[35]

We do not know whether Borrow actually ever referred to his abduction by Gypsies, but he might well pride himself on his command of Romani and in the 'Foreword' to *The Zincali* he wrote that in a previous life his soul had belonged to this people. To this he added that Gypsies, as exiles from India and disciples of Buddha, believed in reincarnation and thus recognized him as one of them. In 1838 he added an element of mystification to this picture of his intimate relationship with Gypsies by having an article appear in the Spanish–English newspaper *The Morning Herald* for which he himself delivered the text.[36] This article dealt primarily with the power that George Borrow was said to exercise over the Gitanos, but also over Gypsy groups elsewhere in the world. From a confidential source, so wrote the journalist, he had learned that a group of Gypsies: '… crowned him their King near the ruins of Merida in Estremadura, at a barbaric festival, where they strewed the ground with sweetmeats, and danced upon them, performing at the same time other wild and uncouth ceremonies.'

The article went on to describe the concern that had arisen among the Spanish clergy about Borrow's translation of the Gospel according to Luke into Gypsy dialect. Every Gypsy woman in Madrid was said to carry a copy in the pocket where she concealed her stolen wares. They are unable to read the book, true, added the journalist, but they regard it as a talisman that protects them from harm. For most of the year Borrow was said to ride through Spain on his horse alone to spread the word of God, and despite the state of plundering that prevailed in the land, he never came to any grief, probably in part owing to his ties with the Gypsies. This mystifying self-portrait was a foreshadowing of the figure with which Borrow would cast a spell over the readers of his books on Spain.

Actual contacts with Gypsies

How much contact did Borrow indeed have with Gypsies during his lifetime? This is not an easy question to answer, for on whose testimony are we to rely? We might rely on the writer's own, his semi-autobiographical writings about the years of his youth provoked a discussion about *Wahrheit* and *Dichtung* the last word of which has not yet been heard in 'Borrowian' circles. We might also go by the recollections of contemporaries who reported on a meeting between Borrow and the Gypsies, by the statements of those who heard talk of the 'Romany Rye' straight from the mouths of Gypsies themselves, or we might restrict ourselves to documents in which the writer's relation to the people who figure in so much of his work is raised as an issue far more directly. In principle such documentary sources would be the most convincing, for the evocative scenes in Borrow's literary production are less reliable as reports of his actual encounters with Gypsies.[37] In these books the writer is not documenting experience but, first of all, displaying his gifts as a romantic.

Outside the literary world that Borrow created with his books there are no indications that, prior to his departure for St Petersburg, he maintained any deep contacts with English Gypsies. Every comment on this score rests on indirect interpretation or supposition as, for example, in a newspaper piece from 1900[38] in which the author maintains that the young George learned his Romani words in the company of a Gypsy band which, at the time, frequently stood along Green Lane, a mile from Dereham Church, the writer's birthplace. There they held markets and pitched camp, so he recalled from his own boyhood, before the time, according to him, Gypsy children dared to beg. This is not simply a rather flimsy historical interpretation, but, given how Borrow moved about in his young days, the chance that it is accurate is very slim.

Other writers have done their best to discover the historical persons on whom Jasper Petulengro and his family are based. From indications in early Borrow manuscripts, they arrived at an identification of Ambrose Smith and his relatives.[39] A successful man, twice married, he roamed throughout England and Ireland and took off in 1860 for Scotland where he made his fortune as a horse dealer. In the summer of 1878 he camped with his family a mile outside of Dunbar. There Queen Victoria is said to have honoured him with a visit. It was in the same year that he died, after which his widow received a condolence letter from Her Majesty. We can deduce at the very least from this factual reconstruction that, at that time, not all English Gypsies were looked on as outsiders. The family subsequently migrated to America; nothing is known about the rest of their fate. About the nature of the bond which George Borrow and Ambrose Smith had we are unsure. It has been suggested that they only got to know each other when Borrow lived in Norwich, which would mean that his descriptions of his youth would be purely fictional.[40] The only indication we have to suggest that

Borrow had already come into contact with Gypsies before entering the service of the Bible Society is a passage from a letter that he wrote at the end of December 1832 to Reverend Francis Cunningham, the man who had introduced him to the society. What led to Borrow's remark was a conversation he had with Secretary Brandram on that subject:

> ... for, many years ago, hearing that they had a language which they themselves are alone acquainted with, I went amongst them, and having discovered the truth of the report, I was at some pains to learn *a portion of it* [italics mine – W.W.].[41]

On this occasion Brandram had also asked him, upon his return to Norwich, to draw up a vocabulary list of this Gypsy language. Considering Borrow's full work schedule for the coming months, it is questionable whether he actually went out and moved among Gypsies to compile such a list, although there is indeed a reference in his legacy to a list with words which were supposedly transcribed from the mouths of Gypsies who camped in the neighbourhood of Norwich.[42]

The first account that Borrow ever wrote about Gypsies and whose authenticity is beyond doubt dates from September 1835. It consists of passages from a report to his employer at the time, the *British and Foreign Bible Society*. He wrote it, however, only after he had already left St Petersburg and was back in England. It would later be included, almost without any changes, in *The Zincali*.[43] He wrote in it about the Gypsy women in Moscow who sang so well, and about his encounters with them in a camp outside the city where the young men from better families came to enjoy themselves with music and dancing, and where Borrow, upon uttering a few Gypsy words, was said to have been welcomed by the women as one of them. That his contacts with English Gypsies at that moment could not yet have been very intensive, he himself implied with the remark: 'I addressed them in a loud voice in the dialect of the English Gypsies, *with which I have some slight acquaintance* [italics mine – W.W.].'[44] Borrow sent a second report about a meeting with Gypsies to his employer from Madrid on 19 July 1836 and this constituted the basis for later chapters in both *The Zincali* and *The Bible in Spain*.[45] In his report he described how on 6 January of that year he reached Badajoz just over the border between Portugal and Spain, where he made the acquaintance of a small group of Spanish Gypsies. Since he, as he himself says, had a rather good command of Spanish Gypsy dialect, he could communicate with them easily. While after returning from St Petersburg he wrote that he had a limited knowledge of English Gypsy dialect, some four months later he claims suddenly to have just about mastered the Spanish variant. Where, we're driven to ask, had he learned it? If we assume he was never in Spain before – and there is good reason to believe so – he can only have studied the language in books. Which books these were, I will come back to presently. That the Gypsies he met in Badajoz were his first in Spain we can already conclude from the deep impression which they made on him. A number of encounters with them prompted him in his report to the Bible Society to make a crushing judgment of their character, prefaced by the sentence: '... the Spanish Gitanos are the most vile, degraded and wretched people upon the earth.'[46] His general view of Gypsies was probably so strongly influenced by these first impressions, that they set the tone for his book about them that appeared five years later. In subsequent letters to the Bible Society he still referred on several occasions to meetings with Gypsies in, among other places, Seville and San Lucar,[47] but never again at such length as in the reports about Gypsy women in Moscow and Gypsy families in Badajoz.

The eyewitnesses

Eyewitness accounts of the way Borrow conducted himself with Gypsies are scarce. The most well-known one is from the diary that Colonel Napier kept during his journey through Spain. The diary entry for 5 May 1839 concerns a visit Napier paid to the ruins of Italica accompanied by a man with whom he had become acquainted a short while before in Seville but whose nationality he was at a loss to guess since the fellow could express himself in every conceivable language.[48] The travelling companion had suddenly begun to recite a poem and while he was declaiming, a pretty, young Gypsy woman had walked up to them. When the noise ended, she had asked for alms. Napier began at once to grope in his purse but Borrow objected and said that she should renounce such behaviour. He addressed her in Romani, but she was unable to answer him back properly. She did bring him to the members of her 'tribe', however, who reacted with mistrust until Borrow came out with a certain word in their language. At once the ice was broken: '... but that word had the effect of magic; she prostrated herself at his feet, and in an instant from an object of suspicion, he became one of worship to the whole family.' When Napier later asked him where he had learned their speech, Borrow replied that many years back he had come into contact with Gypsies in Moultan (India). He was reluctant to reveal more. In any event, a Borrow untruth has infiltrated Napier's narrative, for no evidence whatsoever exists to suggest he was ever in south-east Asia.

It is similarly impossible to say anything with confidence about the nature and intensity of his contacts with Gypsies elsewhere in the world.

In the year 1844 Borrow made a journey that lasted seven months and took him through east Europe as far as Constantinople. He left no record of these travels.[49] He did alter several passages about Hungarian Gypsies in later editions of *The Zincali*[50] and vocabulary lists that he drew up in part that year were published more than a century later by the Gypsy expert Winstedt.[51] On grounds of the surviving wordlist manuscript, Winstedt maintained that Borrow had lived among east-European Gypsies for months. To all appearances the trip was undertaken to search them out and to collect material for the autobiography that he was working on. If, instead, we base our analysis on the letters that he wrote at that time, a number of which have been retrieved, we note that in only one is there mention of any encounter with Gypsies.[52] Given Borrow's itinerary, moreover, it does not seem very likely that he actually spent a number of months with them. It is far more feasible that the vocabulary lists were the product of years of collection.

We are rather better informed about what took place on his property in England. Thus it is confirmed from various sides that Borrow allowed small groups of Gypsies to camp on his land in Oulton. A female acquaintance of his wrote that he sought them out there to sing songs with them in their language and to swap ghost stories, to which he was said to be addicted.[53] The picture that emerges of such encounters, however, is not wholly consistent, judging by the recollections of another friend. He wrote that once, after dinner, they went together to visit a group of Gypsies who had pitched their tents on the land of the Borrow family. The 'Romany Rye' then began to render a song which he himself had composed in Gypsy language and in which he summed up their deceptions and dastardly deeds. The Gypsies became terribly agitated:

> ... then they began to kick their property about, such as barrels and tin cans; then the men began to fight and the women to part them; an uproar of shouts and recriminations set in, and the quarrel became so serious that it was thought prudent to quit the scene.[54]

George Borrow's attitude towards Gypsies was characterized, at the very least, by ambivalence – that is the lesson of this incident. That he had a certain name among English and perhaps even Spanish Gypsies[55] is none the less a credible proposition based on eyewitness accounts which have reached us. In the archive of the Hispanic Society, for example, there is a piece from 1889 by J.M. Menzies which never was published, entitled *George Borrow and the English Gipsies*,[56] in which the author tells about his own visits to Gypsies in the suburbs of North and South London. Menzies already knew many words of the language of their companion group in Hampshire and was eager to compare his results with the dialect which they spoke. When he approached their tents, they were on the point of going to work: hawking and soothsaying in Woolwich, Greenwich and other villages. They told him that at first they had thought he was their friend George Borrow, the 'Romany Rye', coming to visit their camp. According to Menzies Borrow was a hero to them and they could tell all kinds of romantic stories about his life. They also confided to him that at times, in Gypsy circles, Borrow was regarded as a *gentile* (a denigrating term for a non-Gypsy) and that he was then asked for money or to have his fortune told. On such occasions he flared up so that some had fled to their tents while for hours he had maintained an icy silence in the presence of their women. At other times he had been generosity itself, even presenting them, for example, with a gold coin. They had always honoured him, based on such experiences, as a father. They had also treated Menzies, according to his own words, with extreme courtesy and without reticence had provided him with the linguistic information that he had come after. Menzies simply never published the results of his study, nor did Knapp, in his biography of Borrow, refer to Menzies' account. It is not, however, the sole indication of contacts between Borrow and English Gypsies that we possess.[57]

How Borrow could make a brief encounter into a scene consistent with his own self-image as the great 'Romany Rye', I will demonstrate with reference to the solitary Gypsy passage in his travel book *Wild Wales* from 1862. We have two sources that confirm that he actually crossed paths during this trip with a small group of Gypsies. The more reliable one is a passage from a letter that he wrote to his wife in November 1857: 'On the side of the Black Mountains I met a cart load of real Gypies. They were in a dreadful rage, and were abusing the country right and left.'[58] The notation in his journal already contains an immediate romantic touch: 'Gypsy Caravan – discourse Are you one of the ingrins I am the *Romany Rye* [my italics – W.W.]. Well my gal said you were one of us.'[59] This family Ingram (ingrins) was, according to Fraser, a well-known Gypsy family from Wales and Borrow was describing here the manner in which English Gypsies greeted those from Wales. If we turn to the encounter as recorded in the travel book *Wild Wales*, we observe that the hasty meeting has been expanded into a scene of three pages in which Borrow on foot sees Captain Bosvile coming down the hill with his wife and children in a caravan. The 'Romany Rye' strikes up a conversation with them and together they dredge up a memory from 30 years back, from a time when the 'Rye' himself was a rover.[60] In this text Borrow not only puts a Hungarian Romani verse in Bosvile's mouth while they reflect briefly on the past, but he also has him refer to the protagonist of *Lavengro*, a rhetorical device by means of which the mirror images of the writer and his character stand side by side: 'The last time I think I saw you was near Brummagem, when you were travelling about with Jasper Petulengro and – I say, what's become of the young woman you used to keep company with?'[61] Fraser speculates in his article on the origin of this Captain Bosvile and concludes, rightly to my mind, that Borrow took the name from a figure in a pamphlet written in 1822 by an anonymous clergyman and reproduced in a book dated 1832 by James Crabb, about whom I will have more to say shortly.[62]

DIRECT GYPSY SOURCES

There is good reason to quibble with the image of Borrow as an intimate of Gypsy groups all over the world. Undeniably there were contacts made, but less frequently and probably also more superficially than is often accepted in the literature. That he came and went among Gypsy friends as a youth is even hardly defensible. It appears that the writer Borrow, in his zeal to justify his choice of Gypsies as a subject, extravagantly accentuated his personal experiences with them. After the fact he pretended that as a gentleman adventurer – a 'Romany Rye' – he had mingled among them in order to penetrate more deeply into their secrets. Just like Grellmann's book on Gypsies, his first work, *The Zincali*, is set up as an historical, linguistic and ethnographic study of Spanish Gitanos and is supposed to be the result of his infiltration. But was Borrow truly the participant observer he made himself out to be rather than one of the behind-the-desk scholars whom he claimed to despise? Was his first offspring exclusively the result of his own experience or did he also exploit other sources? Questions which concern the essential originality of his work and its reliability as an historical source on Gypsies.

Paid informants

In 1841 Borrow wrote to Lord Clarendon, the count to whom he dedicated his first work, informing him that collecting the vocabulary of the Spanish Gypsies alone had cost him £300.[63] Already, when entering into the employment of the Bible Society, he had, to be sure, written to the secretary telling him that a Gypsy translation of one of the gospels was possible if only money were set aside for paying a number of informants. Later, in St Petersburg, he had seen how missionaries there also made use of native speakers to teach them languages they didn't know, at least when there was no, or hardly any, academic opportunity for studying them.[64] This was a common method then and now, and one which Borrow would fruitfully adopt in Spain. About the Gypsy women in Badajoz, Madrid and Seville who had assisted him with the preparation of the *Gypsy Luke*, he himself, moreover, had written that he had filled their glasses with madeira and fed them, when required. His story doesn't mention the extent to which money changed hands.

That Borrow's informants were compensated for their efforts can also be concluded from an account written by the grandson of the Gypsy Wester Boswell (1811–90), said to have been one of Borrow's important informants.[65] This Wester was a cultivated figure, the first Gypsy to become a churchwarden. He traversed Norfolk, Essex and Lincolnshire where the 'Romany Rye' came to visit him many times with a pouch of roll-tobacco in hopes of prising loose information about Romani and other Gypsy matters. According to Gordon Boswell, his grandfather was Borrow's leading informant for a long time, for he was said to have pronounced and spelled the Gypsy language most correctly. When it turned out that Borrow had written down in a book all that he had heard about the way of life, the soothsaying, and the horse dealing of Gypsies, without acknowledging who had provided him so extensively with this information, the elderly Wester felt betrayed and the relationship cooled: 'He crippled the hand that fed him.'[66] From Gordon Boswell's narrative it is not easy to identify the book in question or in what period the contact between Borrow and his grandfather was at its height. Presumably that would have been around the middle of the nineteenth century when Wester had reached an age at which his experiences would have been interesting enough to an outsider to cash in on them. In that case it could have been the book *The Romany Rye* from 1857 which he laid eyes on, where passages about Gypsies are in greater abundance than in the first part of Borrow's autobiographical cycle. After his dismaying experience, old Wester would have demanded payment (a guinea – a pound and a shilling – per hour) for further information on English Gypsies. Borrow also seems to have asked Wester to comment on his texts, for he was afraid other Gypsies might have been deceiving him – and not infrequently: '… for Mr. Borrow was not always told the truth in return for his half-ounces of twist, and there was many a good laugh at his expense after he had left a Gypsy family seated around a stick fire.'[67]

At that time Wester's relatives were said to have asked Borrow, and later other 'Romany Ryes',[68] why they didn't admit their indebtedness to their important informants more readily. One also wondered, moreover, why he didn't do more, as he had promised, to improve the social circumstances of the Gypsies, which in the years between 1860 and 1870 grew progressively worse owing to the harsh measures of local authorities. Borrow himself appears to have taken little of such criticism to heart; others did, to the extent at least that they arranged for old Wester to be awarded a medal of honour with the inscription: 'Sylvester Boswell/ Grammarian/ of the/ Ancient Gypsy Language/ New Year's Day/ 1875.'[69] That he gave away the secrets of Gypsy vocabulary, his grandson tells us, is something others of his group blamed him for, since by so doing he had weakened their defences which consisted of their ability, when persecuted, to communicate with each other without outsiders understanding them. To be sure it is not certain whether we should take the testimony of Gordon Boswell from 1955, based on accounts handed down by word of mouth, seriously. Yet the possibility cannot be excluded that Borrow's knowledge of the language of English Gypsies (Romani) was much patchier than he leads us to believe in his writings if, even in the years immediately preceding the appearance of *Romano Lavo-Lil*, he was still constantly depending on his principal informant for additional material. We are also able to deduce from Boswell's account that Gypsies didn't unequivocally recognize Borrow – as he himself and many gypsylorists after him were eager to maintain – as one of them and provide him with unbridled information but that, as a rule, for what they gave they received compensation in return. On grounds of his reference to the three hundred pounds (more than his annual Bible Society salary) that compiling a word list of the Spanish Gypsy language had cost him, the practice of paying for information will not have differed very much in Spain from England. A perfectly legitimate way of working, certainly that, but disillusioning for anyone who believed in the romantic image of the Gypsy Lord who, as soulmate of the Gypsies, had access to their secrets.

Spanish assistants

The collectors of Gypsy songs and language provided Borrow, certainly in Spain, with material, at a price, but not always with the credit which they had expected in return.[70] This was the case with Juan Antonio Bailly, who during Borrow's stay in Seville in 1839, had worked assiduously to assist in the compilation of wordlists and Gypsy(-like) poetry. As the child of an English mother and French father Bailly had ended up in Spain in the early 1820s and had taken a Spanish bride. He earned his living as a tourist guide, delighting his clients with his countless anecdotes. In the 1840s he complained to a traveller that his predecessors had cut a fine figure with his stories in their memoirs without any written acknowledgement of his role, whereas it often had cost him a great deal of trouble to lay his hands on the material that they were after. On this occasion he is also said to have claimed to have been extremely well-versed in Gypsy language and poetry,[71] which prompts us to wonder whether Borrow might have been one of the ungrateful predecessors accused. From those of Bailly's letters that have been preserved,[72] it can be seen that, in any event, a few weeks after Borrow's departure from Seville for Madrid, he had sent him a packet of verses collected by the lottery ticket vendor, Manuel, one of the *Maestros del Caló* with which Andalucía was so richly endowed in those days.[73] The term denoted figures who had conceived a passion for the *caló* and themselves composed Gypsy verses. Manuel was one such devotee and he supplied Borrow with considerable material, a reason for Borrow to mention him with praise various times in his books.[74]

It is too bad that the biographer Knapp never completed the article he once spoke of writing on the sources of the *caló* literature in Borrow's first book.[75] It is, however, possible, using manuscript material from the Knapp-collection at the Hispanic Society,[76] in combination with references to literature that Borrow himself included in his book,[77] to make a list of sources consulted for *The Zincali*. It would have been going too far to call up all these Spanish and Latin sources and to compare them systematically with Borrow's text (see Annex 3). The Knapp collection does indeed contain a number of manuscripts, one in Borrow's hand and two in a handwriting with which I am not familiar, with passages copied verbatim from the works of such seventeenth-century authors as Quinones and Torreblanca, and the laws passed in Spain against Gypsies down through the centuries.[78] Comparison of what Borrow has written on these subjects in *The Zincali* reveals that, at the factual level, he was satisfied with summarizing the original sources. It has every semblance of being true that only the meetings which he describes with Gypsies in Moscow and Badajoz, which also appear in his letters to the Bible Society, together with a single memory of his childhood in England, are based on personal experience, for his encounters with Wester Boswell were of a later date.

All the Spanish and Latin sources about which I have just spoken are currently available in the National Library in Madrid and were probably also there in Borrow's time.[79] While occupied with collecting previously published literature about Gypsies, he was, in all likelihood, assisted by the English-oriented Pascual de Gayangos, the librarian of the institution at that time, later a professor of Arabic studies, who also supervised the transcription of texts for Borrow.[80] Of yet greater importance was the help of the later Hebrew specialist Luis de Usoz y Río (1805–65) who during Borrow's days in Madrid, was editor of the prestigious newspaper *El Español*. He assisted Borrow with his work for the Bible Society and helped him with his research on the Gypsies. From time to time they also wrote to each other in *caló*, which raises the question of whether

Borrow was indebted linguistically to Usoz.[81] The latter, moreover, wrote a review of the *Gypsy Luke* and gave extensive publicity to Borrow's first publication. From their correspondence it is clear that the Englishman had a high opinion of the Spaniard and wished to dedicate his pending publication to him, a prospect that delighted Usoz. Borrow would, however, end up dedicating the book to Lord Clarendon, a clear indication that, by then, their friendship had cooled. In Usoz's copy of *The Zincali* in Madrid a number of omissions and careless errors are noted which primarily amounted to Borrow's neglecting to mention for certain parts of the book that others, including Usoz, had written or copied them for him. He did not bring this oversight to the author's attention in vain, for in the second edition Borrow did add a number of acknowledgements and in *The Bible in Spain* he devoted many words of thanks to his great friend Usoz. Fraser even has suggested that Borrow's sharp condemnation of Spain and the Spaniards was kept out of the introduction to this second book through Usoz's defense of his countrymen in their correspondence and his attack on Borrow's lack of subtle powers of discrimination. Although Fraser continues to praise the merits of his subject, he none the less ends his article on Borrow's closest colleagues in Spain with the sentence: 'One wonders how much of Borrow himself there may have been in his story in *Lavengro* of the gentleman author who suffers from a conviction that he will be unable to write an original book and that he will be exposed as a plagiarist.'[82]

Borrow's first work on Spanish Gypsies, apart from the extent of its originality, merits attention for the way it is presented. The book may have come into the world as a work of popular scholarship, the author's intention in the first place was to captivate the reading public with his story – which meant that he conjured up a picture not always in conformity with reality. This can be vividly illustrated by an analysis of the story, 'The Bookseller of Logroño', which fulfills a key function in the first part of *The Zincali*.[83] The tale concerns the history of the bookseller Francisco Alvarez who managed with difficulty to prevent Gypsies from sacking the city of Logroño in the middle of the sixteenth century. In a footnote at the end of his narrative Borrow said that much of the contents had sprung from his fantasy but that the core rested on historical sources. Now he can very easily have picked the story up, from Bailly, for example, but that does not hold true for the historical reference in it to Fernández de Córdoba.[84] His discussion of Gypsies, it is true, included the Logroño story, but this author had in turn referred to two older sources: Albert Krantzius and Sebastian Münster.[85] In neither of these two texts, however, does a bookseller appear, or Logroño, or a plundered city. The theme of the utter wickedness of

Gypsies is, by way of contrast, very much present in seventeenth-century texts by Spanish authors who had proposed the banishment of this group from Spain and who, in their turn, had referred to Córdoba as the source of the story about the sacking of Logroño.[86] Only the Gypsies' use of poison (the *drao*) in the city's water supply to break its resistance is said to have been added by Borrow himself. Even for a nineteenth-century reader his descriptions of the symptoms of this poisoning must have bordered on the incredible. On the other hand it will not have been unusual to make the transition from the realistic to the magic-dramatic world of the Gypsies as known from the literature. In short Borrow produced a composite narrative with conscious use of archaic language and historic references to heighten the illusion of authenticity. This playfullness, wholly in the spirit of Cervantes, keeps the reader fascinated. True, there was an historical source in which the history of Logroño was recorded and which spoke of the heroic resistance of the inhabitants against the French in 1521, but in this account Gypsies played no active part.[87] Borrow merely implanted events in an historical context to make his rendition of the absolute wickedness of Gypsies in the past more believable.

RICHARD BRIGHT

Finally there is a source which has already been referred to from different sides: Richard Bright's *Travels from Vienna through Lower Hungary; with some remarks on the state of Vienna during the Congress* (from 1818).[88] Bright was an Englishman who travelled through Hungary in 1814 and published a book about his journey four years later which featured descriptions of his encounters with Gypsies. He also included in it a reworking of a manuscript by an unnamed friend about the living conditions of Spanish Gypsies. After reading this work, the GLS-expert Groome felt the need well up in him to unmask his great teacher as a fraud:

> On my return home, I found Bright's *Hungary* come from the library for me (...). Borrow has quietly appropriated Bright's Spanish Gypsy words for his own work, mistakes and all, without one word of recognition. I think one has the ancient impostor there. Bright is the origin of all.[89]

Bright had encountered the subject of Gypsies through reading the first edition of Grellmann and during his travels through Hungary he decided to study their customs and circumstances more closely. Once back in England, he wanted to devote himself to those who shared their lot there, but then the work of the English Quaker John Hoyland appeared (in 1816) and he felt temporarily relieved of the task. This accounts for why he concentrated in his book on the experiences that he had in Hungary and included an annex on the Gitanos based on the manuscript of a friend who had written it during his stay in Spain during the years 1816 and 1817. Owing to the kinship which, according to Bright, existed between *Bohemien*, *Zigeuner*, *Cygany*, *Tschingenes*, *Gitanos* and *Gypsey* he had decided to append this Spanish annex to his historical Hungarian study.[90]

Bright's account reveals that there were diverse Gypsy communities in Hungary. We read of a village where they engaged in such vocations as smith, carpenter, courier and seasonal labourer and performed all kinds of haphazard work. Here they lived in poverty, hardly caring at all for their bodies, easy to distinguish from others by their appearance.[91] Only few managed to rise above the station of peasant to become a horse dealer or tobacco trader, while others earned handsomely with their musical abilities. According to Bright they were not cold-shouldered by other Hungarians. Later he stopped in a village in the heart of Hungary where six Gypsy families had already lived for generations.[92] They all turned out to be skilled artisans and excellent traders and were obviously better off than peasants in the village. One of the families had even hired a number of peasants to process the harvest of tobacco into snuff. They welcomed Bright hospitably and everyone was curious about the English stranger, for whom they staged an elaborate musical performance. In another village in Croatia he again ran into much poorer Gypsies who had scarcely any regular work. They would build houses, repair wagons or serve as messengers on demand. Their leader, who had some five villages and a total of 120 people under him, served as their intermediary with the landowner. Bright was unable to induce people to teach him many words in their Gypsy language.

What all these personal observations have to teach us is first of all that Gypsy groups living in Hungary lived in different socio-economic circumstances, and more important still, that their vocations indicate that they led sedentary lives in the midst of other Hungarians. Bright based himself in large measure on his general historical and ethnological overview of Grellmann. He only deviated from his source of inspiration in that he discovered little baseness among Gypsies, except among those who married a Gypsy within their own group. These were supposed to exercise a bad influence on others. According to him the fortunate condition in which Gypsies usually found themselves was not sufficiently appreciated by those who wrote about them. Their life out in the open, with all the freedoms they enjoyed, was to his mind in many ways much to be preferred to the existence of the urban poor who wasted away in their cramped houses.[93] In the general way Bright characterizes things, he is no less of a romantic than Borrow would later prove to be in certain passages of his two-part *Lavengro* saga.

Bright followed wholly in the tradition of Grellmann with his interest in Gypsy language and descent. He was aware of not reporting anything new by pointing out the remarkable similarity of speech among diverse Gypsy groups in the world, but was keen on adding material of his own to existing publications.[94] He collected a number of words in Hungary which he showed to a Gypsy family in Norwood who seemed to understand a good number of them. Comparison with the language spoken by Spanish Gitanos was, however, far less satisfying. The report on the condition of the Gypsies in all the known provinces and places of Spain which Bright included as an annex dealt with a large number of topics that we also find in Borrow's work; he is even more thorough about the vocations Gypsies followed than his successor. Thus he referred to the trade in scrap iron and to the smithery by means of which some managed to achieve a substantial level of prosperity. Itinerant traders in secondhand goods were mentioned, as were horse dealers, although they were portrayed as cheats. Gypsies in Spain appear to have won much respect as matadors and toreros, as dancers, at times even as private teachers of the *bolero* and the *fandango*, and as singers and musicians, with guitars and castanets. The detailed descriptions of the skill of horse dressers is highly reminiscent of Borrow, but Bright's friend of unknown identity also pointed out – uniquely, I believe – that in some regions Gypsies held a monopoly position as butchers enabling them, not infrequently, to acquire wealth. None the less he concluded that, in all these lines of work, they were known to be charlatans and imposters.[95] In that context there followed a series of negative stereotypical characteristics, with as their common denominator that Gypsies were just such devil-may-care folk as most Spaniards and only married each other, upon which he described their wedding ceremonies in detail, with various elements recognizable from Borrow's later descriptions.[96] Thus Bright had touched on a major portion of the themes that figure in *The Zincali* already, decades before, although not always so extensively. He also reported that, as a general rule, the Spanish population wanted little to do with Gypsies, but that in certain better circles people amused themselves with Gypsy affairs and also imitated their language and expressions. To this he added that both the Gitanos and the Spaniards maintained that Egypt was their country of origin. Another point of agreement with Borrow was Bright's review of anti-Gypsy legislation down through the centuries and an emphasis on the rights that they were granted under Carl III. Finally comparative wordlists were included from English, Hungarian and Spanish Gypsies, with the conclusion that the first two language variants showed

many resemblances but that they differed markedly from the Gitano-
words.[97]

AN AMBIVALENT GYPSY IMAGE

While Grellmann concluded, exclusively on a basis of the sources that
he studied, that Gypsies all over the world were similar, Borrow argued
the same thing from his personal experiences with them in England,
Russia, Spain and Hungary. These contacts were also said to have
established that Gypsies, owing to their common morals and customs,
language and appearance, belonged to a single people (sect, caste or
race).[98] Yet we have seen that in reality these contacts were more
superficial than he wanted people to believe. Moreover, analysis of the
informants on whom he depended, the assistants who collected material
for him in Spain and the written sources from which he derived an
important part of his knowledge, leave little room over for the
flamboyant 'Romany Rye' whose pen merely jots down what he himself
has experienced. Just as Grellmann, in his reconstruction of the history
and way of life of the Gypsies, Borrow had relied heavily on earlier
writings. In contrast to his German predecessor, he wrote works of
different genres to bring the Gypsies to life. As a result of this versatility,
his portrayals of Gypsies are lacking in uniformity and embody
remarkably conflicting feelings which can be pointed out. Nevertheless
I want to venture to attempt to distinguish a number of characteristics
and at the same time to identify modifications that Borrow brought
about through his work of the earlier image of the Gypsy that Grellmann
had introduced in Europe.

God's degenerate creations

Borrow found one of the most striking characteristics of Gypsies to be
that everywhere they displayed the same inclinations, as if they were
not humans but rather an animal species.[99] As God's most degenerate
creations, they therefore had need of the pity of the Christian philanthropists of the time, which is why Borrow wrote about them. Except
his dilemma, just as Grellmann's, was that on the one hand he regarded
them as incapable of change, and on the other he attributed a soul to
them and so the ability as well to adopt Christian morality. To all
appearances, certainly in his two books on Spain, Borrow preferred to
paint the historical vicissitudes of the Gypsies as grimly as possible in
order to achieve the maximum contrast with nineteenth-century efforts
to civilize them.

At any rate he did not have much positive to say about their past. He argued that nowhere did they work the soil or labour in the service of a master and in all countries they were known as swindlers, thieves and frauds. For him it was above all the stubborn way in which they clung to their uncivilized behaviour that indicated the great age of their (in his eyes) antiquated way of life. He devoted a long historical discussion to this point of view, one in which he relied entirely on the texts of ancient Spanish authors. Remarkably, it is especially in these passages, derived from others, that he allows himself to express the most uninhibited negativity about Gypsies and to generalize unreservedly. In this vein he attributes the circumstance that until the nineteenth century they were able to maintain their corrupt character, at least in Spain, to the state of immorality which prevailed in that land. Spanish law was said to have always protected the rich and promoted corruption and in such a climate the cruel and criminal nature of Gypsies flourished, according to him, exceedingly well.[100] He then goes on by observing that social circumstances had not made them who they were, but that they already possessed criminal natures when they came to the West. In a linguistic discourse on the languages spoken by criminals, such as Germania, Argot and Rotwelsch, and the influence exerted on these languages by Gypsy speech, Borrow even came to the conclusion that Gypsies had introduced the calling of thieves into Europe. Other groups were said to have adopted such behaviour subsequently, as the result of which differentiation emerged among criminal groupings. This analysis led him to the lamentation: '... words originally introduced into Europe by objects too miserable to occupy for a moment his lettered attention – the despised denizens of the tents of Roma.'[101]

True, Borrow continually admitted that his texts on the history of Gypsy bands were based on older sources, but this did not apparently induce him to attempt any subtleties of analysis. This leads me to believe that the sources were consistent with his ideas about the unavoidably criminal nature of Gypsies. He wrote: '... their presence was an evil and a curse in whatever quarter they directed their steps.'[102] After this he sketched a picture of the working class – the most honest of souls no matter where in the world – who were forever the victims of Gypsy tricks. Their mules and horses were stolen and sold in distant markets, and their sheep and goats extorted by Gypsy bands. Borrow depicted them as swarms of grasshoppers who swooped down in the vicinity of a village and wasted everything bare. Robbery and murder, that was the historic pattern.[103] To which he added that as highwaymen they really couldn't measure up to the great bandits, for they avoided putting their lives in danger: the image of Gypsies as cowards that had held sway since Grellmann. Those who morally or physically weren't up to criminal exploits, also worked as smiths making small utensils or tried to find buyers for stolen animals at horse markets.

Besides this starkly negative characterization of Gypsies as horse thieves, robbers, cheats, and smugglers, that is to say hardened criminals, traces of which we can note lasting until Borrow's final book, we also come across totally contradictory observations about their economic activities. These provide the reader with a chance to distinguish shades of meaning in Borrow's text, however far from his intentions the introduction of nuances might have been. His earliest impressions of Gypsies, for example, in Moscow and in St Petersburg, were still of a romantic and practically idealizing nature. Only once he was confronted with impecunious Gypsies in the Spanish Badajoz in 1836 who, if we can accept his version of things, boasted about the half-criminal activities by means of which they tried to keep themselves afloat, did the picture emerge of the figure who in a twilight zone took care of his 'affairs of Egypt', a romantic-mysterious euphemism for smuggling.[104] Still Baltasar, the son of his landlady in Madrid, later told him that the professional bullfighters of Andalucía all spoke Gitano and had primarily Gypsy blood. And when in his last book about English Gypsies he reported on a visit to Wandsworth (in 1864) he told of men who, seated in front of their tent or wagon, were busy with all kinds of activities such as the cutting of meat skewers, the making of clothes-pegs and baskets, the patching of kettles or other copper repair work.[105] He had, to be sure, already written earlier about how English Gypsies fixed tin and copper objects for farmers.[106] For Seville he was able to mention that Gypsy women roasted chestnuts for sale, a prized delicacy.[107]

Borrow wrote most of all, however, about the relationship between Gypsies and horses, doubtless in the first place because he himself loved horses and in addition to his interest knew something about them, but also because the Petulengro family, which he described in his semi-autobiographical works, consisted of horse dealers and thus he is likely to have had the most to do with this vocational group. He devotes various scenes to the magical power that Gypsies were said to exercise over horses; he himself appropriated a number of their tricks, such as special words to calm a horse down. He even relates the story that also appears somewhere in Grellmann about how to make an old jade lively, by forcing an eel down his throat so that it lands in the horse's stomach with foreseeable results.[108] Borrow was unstinting in his praise, on the other hand, for the capabilities of Gypsies in Córdoba as horsedressers (*esquilador*). These skilful figures always had a box of instruments with them; the small scissors (the *cachas*) and the *acial*, two small sticks joined by a string of gut. With these they worked on the lower lip of an unruly horse to subdue it and with the small scissors they removed hairs from places where it grew superfluously, by the back hooves, for example. Such a *cachas* was a delicate instrument, made only in Madrid and was thus a real investment.[109]

Whoever reads carefully will get a good overview of all the vocational activities of Gypsies, for in Borrow's work we even meet them as innkeepers in Spain, horse doctors in Russia, as prizefighters in England and as experienced smiths in Hungary. Only his fascination with deception and swindling, smuggling and black magic was so great that actual observations had little influence when he came to typify their general way of living. In this respect Borrow's vision matched closely with the traditional image of Gypsies' illegal ways which left no place for subtle distinctions when considering their social-economic position, since this by definition was held to be marginal and asocial.

The mystery of the Gypsy woman

Borrow emerges, from his letters, as someone who related rather eccentrically to women all his life. The way in which he wrote about Gypsy women betrays in any event both his wariness of their seductiveness, and fear of their power. Furthermore they dominate his extensive description of Gypsies' deceptive practices and he calls them the greatest swindlers on earth.[110] Already in his first book he referred to the fortune telling practices of English Gypsy women which he claimed to have observed for himself and which were said to indicate that their behaviour had gone unchanged for centuries.[111] Mankind's spiritual enlightenment turned out to be, to his way of thinking, an illusion; a truth that, time and time again, Gypsy practices and their superstitious victims demonstrated. The women had many tricks at their disposal, if we can accept Borrow's associative treatment of this subject. Thus he wrote about a trick still in use in his time in England, which had also been described in a Spanish source, and which a band of women criminals in India also, according to him, practised. He meant the 'false treasure in the ground' hoax – to have someone bury money in the earth with a promise that it will multiply – which was said to work lucratively above all with rich widows who were out for easy gains. Borrow presented a number of variants of this con operation.[112] He also included a number of anecdotes about thefts based on changing money, the sale of herbs and roots to women 'who are desirous of producing a certain result', and predictions of the future, above all by reading the lines in someone's palm. There was a well-stocked arsenal to complement the frauds which men were supposed to perpetrate with horses.

In this context Borrow went so far as to refer to past days when Gypsy women, quite rightly he felt, were condemned and punished for such practices as witches. According to him there was still always an element of witchcraft at work in the tricks which they executed. In his fascination with woman as sorceress he went far, and his ambivalent feelings rose very conspicuously to the surface. First of all in *The Zincali* he already admitted to finding the words 'Gypsy sorceress' romantic and exciting. He had often seen such women in Spain, mothers of two or three children, in the ripeness of their years and able to perform satanic arts:

> … she is a prophetess, though she believes not in prophecy; she is a physician, though she will not taste her own philtres; she is a procuress, though she is not to be procured; she is a singer of obscene songs, though she will suffer no obscene hand to touch her; and though no one is more tenacious of the little she possesses, she is a cutpurse and a shoplifter whenever opportunity shall offer.[113]

These women, so he went on, often look wild and beautiful like sibyls (prophetesses from Antiquity) but they come from the East with hatred in their hearts. They regard Spanish or English women as their prey; friendly as can be to the eye, but in the end loyal only to their own and primed to kill if they fail to gain their prize. They also pretended, according to him, to be able to cure sick animals supernaturally, but these they first made ill a short while before. In earlier times they went still one step further by poisoning animals, after which they bought them for a pittance.[114] The scene in *Lavengro* in which Jasper Petulengro's mother-in-law tries to do away with the protagonist by having her granddaughter offer him a poisoned cake and, when that misfires, stalks him to beat in his skull presents a character that is wholly in keeping with Borrow's portrayal of the female Gypsy.[115] During this scene the power of Borrow's romantic imagination operates at full tilt as the old woman Herne sits down beside the unconscious Lavengro and involuntarily notices the lines in his palm where she detects his future written. Many journeys await him and he shall win fame and fortune, we read. It is as if her clairvoyance here is stronger than she is and she is overcome by these signs of his destiny at the very moment she is trying to kill him. When her murderous attempts go wrong she is full of spite and takes her own life.

The reader had already seen a foreshadowing of this portrait of the Egyptian sorceress and mixer of poisons, as she is called in *Lavengro*, in *The Bible in Spain*.[116] There the principal character had come into contact in Badajoz with a Gypsy woman, typically portrayed as a witch, who had unfolded to him the story of her life in which all the romantic, adventurous elements appropriate to such a history pass in review (murder as vengeance, flight to the land of the Moors, a life of thievery, deceit and soothsaying among a foreign tribe). She also turns out to be a sorceress with secret knowledge of how to brew poisons and love potions which she acquired from the Moors. Now she tries to pair off her fortune-telling granddaughter with the first person narrator, flaunting as 'dowry', the girl's ability to use her tricks all over the world to make him rich. The Bible colporteur trips over his own words as he declines the offer. The failure of a similar effort to ensnare another of Borrow's protagonists in a union with a Gypsy woman takes place in the second part of Lavengro's adventures when Jasper Petulengro proposes to his friend that he make his sister Ursula his wife. Considering his indirect guilt in Mother Herne's death and that he has grown fond of his solitary existence as a wandering apprentice smith, Lavengro rejects the proposition, although when the two young people later talk they still carefully sound each other out to see whether perhaps the desire for such a match might not nevertheless be alive in them both. The adolescent Lavengro, however, turns into a bumbling suitor, only interested, according to Jasper, in old words and strange tales, thereby spoiling his chances with the mysterious Ursula who has fallen for him.[117]

With his portraits of Gypsy women as materialistic, false by nature, and enchantingly lovely, Borrow placed himself in the tradition of Cervantes. That holds true for the only positive traits that he believed distinguished Gypsy women from other women: their purity and marital fidelity. In line with Grellmann he had written that Gypsy women in Turkey danced sensuously to the sound of all kinds of instruments but had no dishonorable intentions in doing so.[118] A Gypsy woman was said to protect her virginity at any price. She might behave obscenely – her glance, her gestures, her speech – but she regarded her physical inviolateness as a precious commodity. Once she became engaged to a youth, any meeting between them without a chaperone was out of the question. She might, however, go on seeing other men, especially non-Gypsies, for sexual contact with 'the white blood' was inconceivable. Deceive and hate, that's what you did to people who weren't of your own kind. Tempt them and set their heads spinning but as soon as they dishonour a Gypsy woman, take revenge. That is the general picture which Borrow sketched, particularly where Spanish Gypsy women were concerned.[119] All these ideas recur in the talk that Lavengro and the breathtakingly beautiful Ursula Petulengro have in the valley called Mumper's Dingle in Borrow's English novel. She maintains that a Gypsy woman does not have to be guarded by her father and uncles because she is by nature indifferent to the charms of any non-Gypsy. Nor, to be sure, was her body for sale. The only engagements contracted with non-Gypsies in the past had, according to Ursula, always taken place under the pressure of circumstances, for as a rule the consequence was banishment from one's own group. Years previously a Gypsy girl had even been buried alive for such a trespass, she comments in closing.[120]

To enter marriage as a virgin, that was the law, and Borrow, who mentions it many times, apparently found this ideal of chastity admirable. About the ways in which Gypsies thought to celebrate a marriage in splendour, he once again had his doubts. Already in *The Zincali* he told of the wild and barbaric side of a wedding feast which he himself attended: of the uninhibited singing, drinking and dancing, and the gigantic portions of sweets that were heaped on the table at night, and the *yemas*, egg yolks with a sugar coating, that were tossed on to the floor to be danced on first by the bridal couple and then by the rest of the guests. Without a break the men began to leap into the air, to neigh, bray and caw. By now the women were dancing, snapping their fingers, assuming salacious postures and shrieking horrible words. A guitarist, mad with passion, accompanied the scene with demonic sounds. There were three days' long unrestrained, extravagant celebration, with everybody welcome, even the hated non-Gypsies, plunging people into debt sometimes for the rest of their lives.[121] The modest standard of living that they occasionally achieved, they thus annihilated utterly, according to Borrow, at a single go. Vanity and prodigality, two Gypsy characteristics which we have met with already in Grellmann.

A vanishing identity

When we trace the development of Borrow's linguistic interest in Gypsies, with respect to his predecessors we detect a distinct shift with which he set a trend for gypsiologists who, with their linguistic-folkloristic orientation, followed in his footsteps. Borrow, unlike Grellmann, was convinced that Gypsies, just like every people in the world, had their own original poetry. He thought that by studying their songs and ballads he would be able to penetrate their character. We run into a striking example of this in *Romano Lavo-Lil* where Borrow reconstructs the life history of Ryley Bosvil on a basis of the contents of his compositions.[122] This Ryley (the 'Flying Tinker') was a rich man who wanted to be king of all the Gypsies. He had two wives, Lura and Shuri, who brought in a lot of money – especially Shuri who was of the Petulengro clan. During the horse racing season, she earned £100 a month telling fortunes. The group travelled widely through England and Scotland, living extravagantly. The 'Flying Tinker' occasionally went hunting with non-Gypsies, wrapped in a fur cloak stitched with gold. One day his luck turned because he seems to have made too many enemies. Then he decided to send Lura away and to move on with Shuri, whose jaw he had first broken in fury. Consumed by homesickness, however, he never managed to escape from Lura's curse, which hounded him to death. Beside his grave his wife and children loudly keened, and afterwards they burned his possessions. Here Borrow interjects tellingly: '... not to divide his property amongst them, and to quarrel about the division, according to Christian practice.'[123]

Regarding the Gypsy poetry that had been handed down, Borrow distinguished between original compositions of the Gypsies' own making – which had, according to him, scarcely any poetic value – and pretentious pseudo-Gypsy compositions which primarily extolled their freedom and independence.[124] This latter genre was said to have originated in Andalucía, particularly in Seville, where, from the distant past, people had cultivated the songs and dances of Gypsies – above all Gypsy women. The Andalucíans, according to Borrow, had a special fondness for obscenities and for the life of *picardías* because they themselves relished indolence and frivolity.[125] In Spanish Catholic circles an entire imitation Gypsy literature was created, springing from the creators' own fantasy but larded with words from the Gypsy language. The *coplas* that he collected were, to Borrow's way of thinking, more authentic: four line verses that were said primarily to reflect the obsessive criminal mentality of Gypsies and their age-old strife with non-Gypsies. What Borrow believed he detected in their poetry was thus confirmation of their nature as a people, with fraudulence and hatred towards people not of their tribe dominant: 'The themes of this poetry are the various incidents of Gitano life – cattle-stealing, prison adventures, assassination, revenge, with allusions to the peculiar customs of the race of Roma.'[126]

Borrow did not think highly of the intrinsic literary merits of what he and others transcribed straight from Gypsy lips. In fact the only thing that interested him was the antiquarian value of what their culture produced. That held true as well for his interest in their language, which in the beginning was entirely instrumental, because, with the help of paid native speakers, he wanted to achieve a translation of part of the New Testament into the Gypsy language. Once that project was completed, he decided to systematize the words and meanings that had been compiled and to publish them in the form of an alphabetized vocabulary list. Borrow described his motives for doing this as follows:

> ... a speech which, if this memento preserve it not, must speedily be lost, and consigned to entire oblivion – a speech which we have collected in its last stage of decay, at the expense of much labour and peril, during five years spent in unhappy Spain.[127]

Study of the language of Gitanos had taught him that, as far as morphology and syntax were concerned, it had been turned on the same lathe as Spanish; only their choice of words still made him think of their having an original language of their own. According to him, most Spanish Gypsies had a core vocabulary that did not exceed 1,500 words with which, among their own kind, they were able to make themselves reasonably well understood. Above all, the older Gypsies in Madrid still spoke their language, Borrow found, rather well. Precisely because their language was said to be dying out there was every reason, he felt, to register as many words as possible, like the fossils of an extraordinary past. This philological-antiquarian point of view led to the paradoxical situation that, at the end of his life, Borrow came to use language as a criterion for differentiating true Gypsies from false ones, using his own vocabulary as a standard. From a researcher of the Gypsy language he had thus changed into a kind of judge. Already in *The Bible in Spain* he had described an encounter with two Gypsies who wanted a copy of the *Gypsy Luke* from him, but who were not themselves fluent in the Gypsy language.[128] A similar episode is recounted in the *Romano Lavo-Lil* where he tries to strike up a conversation with a devilishly pretty Gypsy whom he'd noticed already a few times standing with her small, neat caravan at the edge of the terrain in Wandsworth. But she had not understood what he said.[129] In that same book he reports on his going to Kirk Yetholm in Scotland, remarking when a woman he assumes to be a Gypsy doesn't understand him: 'She is *not true Gypsy* [italics mine – W.W.], after all.'[130]

What it comes down to is that, towards the end of his life, Borrow seldom, as he himself tells us, met anyone who was as conversant with the Gypsy language as he was. He interpreted the declining ability of people to express themselves in that language as an important indication that the Gypsy identity was vanishing. In other areas he also believed he saw signs that their culture and way of life were withering. The decreasing importance of the so-called Gypsy laws pointed, according to him, in the same direction. I consider the way in which Borrow had already treated this subject in *The Zincali*[131] as typical of his way of thinking. There, namely, he observed that during the entire eighteenth century Gypsies in England had led a peaceful, nomadic existence, abiding completely by the laws of their own group. He distinguished three of these, the most important ones, which were said to obtain for Spanish Gitanos and other Gypsies as well. First of all Gypsies were supposed to live among their own kind and not with *gorgio*'s, *gentiles* or *Busné*'s, diverse terms for non-Gypsies. One should live in a tent and not in a house, because the group's traditions prescribe a travelling way of life. A Gypsy mingled with non-Gypsies only to spread lies and practise deceit. The second law was said to apply first and foremost to Gypsy women: they were to be true to their husbands and not consort with others. According to Borrow they indeed hadn't consorted with others for centuries, which was why Gypsies could easily be picked out in a crowd by their appearance. The third law was primarily supposed to regulate how they behaved towards each other. Gypsies saw to their own maintenance on a family basis and were quick to help each other out. Such debts had to be quickly repaid, however, at risk of being banished from the group. Everyone was expected to adhere to this code of honour.

This interpretation of Gypsy laws was based on knowledge that had been handed down from generation to generation. Borrow's personal experiences in England and Spain had taught him that this form of gypsyism, as he called it, was on the wane. The laws of the countries where they lived were constantly being more rigidly applied, which had led above all to strict police control and had meant that the Gypsies' ambulatory way of life was subject to restrictions. Affluence and pressure to assimilate in the countries they inhabited had also, he felt, meant that they were becoming increasingly integrated with the dominant population. An important revision of the Gypsy image was inherent in this view. Borrow arrived at his ideas about Gypsies on the basis of materials that he had read, but the reality with which he was confronted was much less uniform. England was far too cultivated, in Borrow's opinion, for people to go trekking about there, yet Gypsy life there was said to conform totally to the notion of the Gypsy who wanders through the world like Cain, lingering nowhere for longer than three days.[132] Borrow's choice of this Biblical simile reveals that he too saw Gypsies in the first place as 'cursed vagabonds', except he had learned from his sojourn in Spain that most Gitanos were (semi-)sedentary and often had been for generations already. Such observations, however, did not lead him to change his general view. The same was true as well for other aspects of Gypsy life that were indicative of both economic and social integration, such as certain occupations that they followed and their intermarrying with non-Gypsies, without which it is difficult to explain how a mixed population arose. We find traces of an awareness of such things in his work, but this did not bring Borrow to place any question marks beside the idea that the Gypsies inherited a hatred for everyone who was not one of them.

Study of Gypsy history had instilled in Borrow a static idea of their culture against which he measured his own experiences, prompting him to conclude that the days of the Gypsy people, in England as well as in Spain, were numbered. As early as 1841 he wrote that their ties to each other had to a significant extent dissolved. They no longer shifted camp from place to place in Spain, for a long time already not everyone spoke the language, and he predicted that, within a generation, they would be absorbed by the Spanish population. To which he added that this was surely a good thing for no Christian or philanthropic soul would want such a group to survive, considering that their guiding principle was to hate and to deceive the rest of mankind.[133] At the end of his life, however, Borrow turned sombre about this anticipated social emancipation of the Gypsies, for he saw little in the way of favourable results and the only two virtues that, according to him, the group had possessed – the chastity of the women and sobriety of the men – had both been lost. Along with these losses, their self-respect was also said to have been damaged:

> The Gypsy salt has not altogether lost its savour, but that essential quality is every day becoming fainter, so that there is every reason to suppose that within a few years the English Gypsy caste will have disappeared, merged in the dregs of the English population.[134]

Thus we note that in the course of Borrow's life, 'the Gypsy', as the result of naive ethnography, uncritical use of sources, selective perceptions and romantic conservatism, developed into a kind of hybrid. Actually his philological-antiquarian interest focused ever more narrowly on the Gypsy as a mythical character, the relic of a bygone era, a dream in a dream, as he wrote in *Lavengro*.

The half-caste as a new category

An important consequence of Borrow's search for the remnants of the 'true Gypsy' as sketched above was the distinction that became constantly more pronounced for him between those who manifested most strongly the traits of the 'ancient race' and those whose behaviour was said to betray the dilution of their Gypsy purity. In his ideas about half-castes we can see the merging of philological ideas, social assessment and racial connotations. Above all he derived his idea of racial integrity from notions of tradition and purity and linguistic theories about how civilization had a corrupting influence on originality. As the hero of *The Romany Rye* sits by his wood fire and meditates at the end of the day, he mulls over the astonishing virtue of the chastity of Gypsy women who call to mind the Roman matrons of old, also so chaste and ready to steal for their husbands. He wonders whether the Romans weren't a Gypsy tribe, given the similarities of their language and behaviour. His thinking about the Gypsy people only then begins to gather momentum and he tries to imagine what it would have been like to live among them centuries ago when their language was still pure and they shared a larger number of secrets. He wonders where the Gypsy dream would have led to.[135]

Borrow was at his best as a novelist when drawing individual sketches of the practically mythical Gypsy. Thus Lavengro and Jasper Petulengro, after a joint visit to church with the family, strike up a conversation about the usefulness of Gypsies. The protagonist would like to see his friend learn to read so he can save his soul and lead a better life. During the virtuoso dialogue that follows, Jasper compares the *Romany Chal* (the Gypsy) to the cuckoo, a bird without any nest of its own and a bad reputation. Yet, he argues, the cuckoo is at the same time a happy creature, part of nature, and why should it change its way of life? Why debase the cuckoo into a chicken, scratching in the earth, or the *Chals* into a weaver or factory girl? He formulates what the two, Gypsy and cuckoo, have in common as follows: 'Everybody speaks ill of us both, and everybody is glad to see both of us again.'[136] Lavengro demurs that there really is a big difference, because people have a soul, whereupon Jasper wants to know if he has ever seen one? That, to be sure, he can only deny, which for Jasper casts a different light on the matter of his lost soul. It is typical of Borrow the novelist that only in this fictional world does he allow the Gypsy to grow into the pure symbol of an anti-world, one in which his existence is every bit as self-evident as that of the non-Gypsy is in his. In the world outside of literature, however, there was no place for such a figure. The Gypsy's right to exist was, in fact, denied him.

Above all in his last book, *Romano Lavo-Lil*,[137] but also in the *Lavengro* cycle, it is apparent that Borrow's observations on the world of the ambulant English scarcely agreed any longer with his stereotypical ideal of 'the Gypsy'. What struck him primarily was how many groups there were of indigenous itinerants and mixed-bloods. And they held no historical interest for him, but simply provoked his social disapproval. In this context he also alluded to laws enacted in the past against people who pretended to be Gypsies, the counterfeit Egyptians, who used this assumed identity as a cloak for indulging in asocial behaviour. Many of the accusations hurled in the face of Gypsies down through the ages, such as kidnapping, whoremongering and other forms of banditry, were said to have been the work of these impostors. When Borrow sets their position down on paper around the middle of the century, it suddenly appears that, compared to them, real Gypsies are half-noble. In this vein he speaks of the *Chorodies*, the descendants of robbers and outcasts who pillaged the English countryside before the Gypsies had set foot on British soil. They were low folk, noxious in appearance and behaviour, mostly small pedlars, coppersmiths and basket weavers but first and foremost thieves. Borrow's comparisons between Gypsies and these domestic groups made clear the enormity of his distaste for people with itinerant vocations who, ultimately, were dismissed as beggars and thieves in disguise. A yet lower sort of hawker was distinguished by Borrow as *Kora-mengre*. The lowest of all were said to be packs of Irish vagabonds, the *Hindity-mengre* who, as tinkers and tin and coppersmiths, tried to eke out living. To justify their social stigma, Borrow referred to the bad repute that they enjoyed, even with the Gypsies. Their asocial behaviour was said to stem from their intermarrying with other groups. Borrow introduced such biological argumentation, all the fashion during the nineteenth century, into Gypsy studies. Half a century later it would be further elaborated by eugenists with disastrous effects.

An additional point that would continue to crop up again in the discussion as late as the twentieth century was, as we have seen, that 'true Gypsies' also snubbed mixed bloods. Thus Borrow in *The Romany Rye* had let the beautiful Ursula Petulengro, talking to Lavengro, say: 'As for the half and halfs, they are a bad set.'[138] Through the pressure of circumstances such a race of half-castes had emerged, true, but, according to Ursula, Gypsies in practice did their best to keep away from vagabonds and basket weavers who rattled around the countryside in their caravans. To this she added that caravan dwellers and other drifters were even hated by the *Romany Chal*.[139] For Borrow and his successors a clear-cut dichotomy separated the 'real Gypsy-race' from 'impure travellers', a category where all the vices could be recognized that, prior to Borrow, had been attributed to Gypsies. By the second half of the nineteenth century Gypsies themselves had grown into the guardians of a lost culture and were, according to experts, worth studying in all the guises in which they appeared. The Gypsy figure whom Borrow had described in the *Romano Lavo-Lil* served them as a standard:

> These were *tatchey Romany*, real Gypsies, of the old sacred black race, who never slept in a house, never entered a church, and who, on their death-beds, used to threaten their children with a curse, provided they buried them in a churchyard.[140]

DIVERSE INFLUENCES

The network of a philological traveller

After this overview of George Borrow's ambivalent image of the Gypsy, we need to take another look at the way in which his books came into being. In this connection the question arises how someone who essentially thought so negatively about Gypsies could have a name, even today, as their friend. During discussion of his actual contacts with them it was clear that we needed to see through the myth. He certainly didn't visit their tents out of any kind of early ethnological curiosity. If we keep to the concrete evidence, it appears that his first contact with Gypsies of any significance took place in 1835 when Borrow was in Russia. There are indeed various indications that suggest that, at that time, he was not unacquainted with Gypsy language and that perhaps linguistic interest was the foundation of his involvement with Gypsies. What was the root of this fascination?

If we accept the accuracy of Ann Ridler's comparative analysis of texts, George Borrow read 51 languages, spoke 20 of them, made trans-lations in 47 and came into contact with native speakers of at least 76 mother tongues.[141] Perhaps it would be advisable to qualify these findings somewhat, since it is difficult to reconstruct retrospectively the degree to which he mastered certain languages, but there is no denying that his work reflected a linguistic cosmopolitanism. In many respects he was a dilettante, in the classical sense of the word – one who should be seen against the background of the cultural life of Norwich and the literary life of London in the 1820s, Borrow's formative years. Ridler, who presents his social-intellectual network with a rich sensitivity for detail, reaches the conclusion that we should see Borrow first of all as someone on a philological quest – an image which, she maintains, Borrow would have had no difficulty accepting.

Borrow spent his adolescent years in Norwich, which, in the period after the Napoleonic Wars, was past its prime since the local elite had left for London. It was Borrow's good fortune, however, to be taken under the wing of a number of good teachers, men for the most part with an immigrant background.[142] At the time religious life in Norwich was dominated by dissenters, a generic name for Protestant sects that did not belong to the Church of England, including such denominations as the Unitarians, Quakers, Baptists and Methodists. Bible study flourished there, certainly since the founding in 1811 of a division of the British and Foreign Bible Society, with the Quaker banker Joseph John Gurney as one of its leading spokesmen. The Society's policy of Bible translations and global evangelism led, during the first half of the nineteenth century, to a greater interest in languages. This was connected to the fact that dissenters, with no access to Oxford or Cambridge, felt themselves obliged to develop their potential through extra-university activities. In Norwich this sparked a flourishing intel-lectual life among the establishment, with pronounced emphasis on scholarship, literature and linguistics. Borrow benefited greatly from the stimulating, auto-didactic sphere. The city indeed boasted well-stocked libraries, book stores that sold many foreign titles, book clubs, and literary societies. Borrow's familiarity with the Greek testament and his life-long interest in Hebrew stem from the climate created by the dissenters' community in Norwich where the study of biblical languages was of dominant importance.[143]

Just as the universal linguist Büttner aroused Grellmann's interest in the Gypsy language, it is possible that the no less eccentric clergyman Walter Whiter, Rector of Hardingham (Norfolk), played an analogous role in Borrow's life.[144] The importance of Whiter in his life can be inferred from a letter that Borrow sent to his publisher, Murray, on 1 December 1842, where he mentions him early on as a character in his projected autobiography, although in the end only a modest part of that text is devoted to him.[145] We don't really know how well he knew him.[146] That Whiter's influence was considerable we note especially when we consider Whiter's linguistic theories. He earned his reputation above all with his *Etymologicon Universale* which came out in 1820, the elaboration of an earlier study from 1800 in which he had expressed himself enthusiastically about the importance of the language of itinerant Gypsies: '... with them only is preserved a faithful record of Primaeval Speech.'[147] He had already compiled the Gypsy vocabulary, on the basis of which he arrived at this insight, before 1800. This was partially the product of his own fieldwork, but the influence of Grellmann – a writer with whom Whiter was familiar in English translation, even if he dismissed Grellmann's book as an easy-going compilation – was unmistakable as well.[148] Because his interest in the subject turned out not to be a lasting one, his manuscript remained in rough form, to be lost sight of after his death until a century later a reconstruction of it was published as *Whiter's Lingua Cingariana* (by Lady Grosvenor).

Whiter considered his philological work to be an excavation of the secret history of mankind. He set his sights on pinning down the mystery of language which he regarded as the expression of the emotions of primitive man. These ideas bore a close affinity with those of Borrow's German teacher, William Taylor, for whom words were fossils that should be carefully examined. In this way, according to him, the different layers of civilization that comprised the history of man's progress could be laid bare – an activity that should lead to the revelation of the pure, elementary form of language. A logical extension of this thought was Whiter's idea about the regularity of language phenomena, with laws that would hold true regardless of time and place. This accounts for his efforts to produce a universal etymological dictionary.[149] Just as in Büttner's case, Whiter was anything but non-controversial: 'I pity Whiter. A great etymologist, perhaps the greatest that ever lived. A genius certainly, but it seems, like most eminent artists, dissolute.'[150] While he still lived both his character and his thinking met with stiff criticism. In 1801 commentators immediately ridiculed his theory that there was a connection between Gypsies and the origin of Rome, a notion we also encounter in Borrow's work.[151] Such responses did not deter him from spending a great deal of his life formulating theories about the common origin of languages, while the critics carried on repeating that he lacked the most rudimentary knowledge required for comparative and historical linguistics. Borrow nevertheless felt so drawn to his ideas that he, in turn, began to conceive of etymological research as a linguistic search for the original, primitive world language. In their work both speculated whether Celtic or Romani might be the lost ur-language. Borrow also developed a lifelong passion for the origin and meaning of place names. He worked compulsively to uncover the history of words that he looked upon as fossils loaded with significance. In his day toponymy (the study of place names) indeed enjoyed a great vogue. Determining the etymologies of family names, place names and popular sayings became a kind of parlour game. Borrow couldn't resist the temptation in his work of offering countless proofs of his skill in such pursuits.

To put things in proper perspective, let me say that much of this set of ideas belonged to the standard philological paradigm of the time, and thus need not merely reflect Whiter's (and Taylor's) influence. That Borrow was part of the cosmopolitan-oriented intellectual network of Norwich is also indicated by his membership of various libraries and of the Foreign Book Society, which devoted a great deal of attention to works in French and Italian. In London he was registered with the British Museum, but the circle of his acquaintances in the capital was never very large. He did read a great many current literary periodicals which provided him with intellectual baggage for the rest of his life. These were the years during which he expanded his activities as a translator, providing a reason for Ridler to propose calling him a traveller of the mind rather than one in the flesh. She considered him as one of a transitional generation of glorified amateurs with literary-linguistic interests who, during their lifetimes, experienced how linguistics took root in the English academic world.[152]

This increasingly linguistic orientation cannot be viewed separately from the burgeoning interest in archaeology, Romanticism and folklore at that time. Far more than Grellmann, whose fascination with the Gypsy language arose from historical curiosity about their origins, Borrow was actually interested in the peculiarities of folk cultures. His enthusiasm for tales about the awesome and the wild was closely connected to his passion for the historical layers of civilization to be deciphered from the etymology of a language and for the 'archaeological' fossils in folk cultures. This taste placed him in a Romantic tradition that put such concepts as 'savagery' and 'nature' in opposition to the refinements and artificiality of civilization. In the language of Gypsies (and their way of living) he combined these interests, which also explains his persistent search for '*the deep Romanes*', the purest form of this language, which he tried to find in vain. The idea that language was related to descent, as we met with in Grellmann and his followers, also gained ground increasingly in the nineteenth century,[153] and the interest in movements of migration led to the linking of languages with the 'race' of their speakers and with geographical location. Borrow's fascination with Gypsies also possibly had to do with their being people whose language could be related directly to their 'race' and yet who had lost the region of their origin.

In the England where Borrow grew up, the ideas of Johann Gotfried Herder, the first in the eighteenth century to point out the connection between poetry (in the broadest sense of the word) and the national character of a people, became ever more influential. He stressed the value of folk songs as a form of expression for national individuality and pointed out the importance of the translator's role in making the voice of other nations accessible. According to Ridler, William Taylor introduced his favourite pupil in Norwich to Herder's ideas. His compilations of translations from a large number of folk cultures also followed the same pattern as the work of the great pioneer,[154] and Herder's thoughts about the language of poetry demonstrably pushed Borrow's thoughts on the subject in the same direction. He was also particularly interested in the language of the 'lower classes' of society. He concentrated on thieves' slang, and the dialect of servants and other segments of the 'common people'. With his interest for the language of marginal groups and his linguistic slumming, Borrow fell in with a long tradition.[155] As far as Gypsy language was concerned, he already asked himself in *The Zincali* what it would have been like to study it in its purest form. A general tenet of nineteenth-century linguistics was that language evolved, passing through stages of growth, maturity and decline. This was connected to the nostalgic notion of an imaginary golden age in the distant past. Poetry translations of the classics were especially helpful to philological archaeologists wishing to penetrate to the origins of other cultures. At the same time it was believed that language in its original state became corrupted in the long run by the use that speakers made of it, and that it could only be preserved in part through 'archaeological' efforts at conservation.[156]

The institutionalization of this past-oriented movement was embodied in all kinds of societies and clubs – located for the most part in London – which, for example, arranged the publication of old texts and stimulated the making of dictionaries. In any event Borrow was a member of the *British and Foreign Institute* and the *Ossianic Society of Dublin*.[157] We don't know exactly what Borrow may have read in the fields mentioned above. His library was broken up after his death. He borrowed many books, moreover, not only in Norwich but also from the Bible Society and from the National Library in Madrid. Thus he was highly dependent on the chance availability of texts or editions.

What this network of a philological traveller teaches us is that Borrow considered language to be a treasury of words and poems which led him to people, to Gypsies in particular – instead of the other way around. Just as, in the spirit of Lavater, he thought he could read character from someone's facial expression,[158] he similarly believed that by studying linguistic phenomena he could penetrate to the essence of peoples or of nations. Chance had it that his path led primarily to Gypsies. The initial impulse in that direction was provided by the British and Foreign Bible Society which offered him the opportunity, analogous to the heroes of the poetry that he translated, to embark on a holy mission. It was specifically the Spanish Gitanos who determined the direction of this enterprise, but to be able to understand this connection we need to return momentarily to Borrow's great role model: Walter Whiter.

In the footsteps of evangelists

In a letter that Goddard Johnson wrote to George Borrow early in 1843, he reported on his fruitless efforts to locate the manuscript on the history of the Gypsies that a certain Dr Myers was said to have left behind him after his death.[159] He followed his account with some entertaining anecdotes about the famous clergyman, Walter Whiter, who even in old age took a dip in his pond every morning, and went for a long walk daily – thus displaying through his behaviour character traits similar to Borrow's own. At the moment that Johnson came to visit him, he had just sat down to answer a list of questions about Gypsies at the request of a young woman from a charitable evangelical institute dedicated to saving the souls of the poor. This one letter provides us with various concepts that help broaden our understanding of Borrow: a clergyman interested in linguistics, evangelically inspired charity, and Gypsies as the object of social concern.

The British and Foreign Bible Society fulfilled an important function in the revival of religious life during the first half of the nineteenth century and the Norwich branch was highly active.[160] An influential figure at this local level was the Quaker banker Joseph Gurney, whose son-in-law Francis Cunningham was an inspirational clergyman whom Borrow came to respect deeply and who ensured that he saw the inside of a church once again. In addition he introduced his new acquaintance to the head office of the Bible Society in London, where he recommended him as a man cut from the right cloth to take on the job of a linguistically-grounded missionary.[161] In one of his first letters to Joseph Jowett, Secretary of the Bible Society, Borrow referred to a talk that he had with the second Secretary, Andrew Brandram, about the conversion and uplifting of the Gypsies.[162] It was his idea that this could best be accomplished by translating a portion of the Bible into their language. Borrow proposed the Gospel according to John, although he would later opt for Luke, and believed it would prove possible for him to accomplish, at least if he should have the co-operation of one or two older Gypsies, for whom remuneration would need to be arranged, since 'the Gypsies are more mercenary than Jews'. He also wished Jowett to thank Brandram for the book that he had given him, *The Gypsies' Advocate* by Reverend James Crabb (from 1830). He was so impressed by the book that he very much wanted to become a member of the Southampton Committee for the Amelioration of the Condition of the Gypsies, which Crabb had founded in 1827. A letter of recommendation from the banker, Gurney, would in his opinion be a valuable help towards realizing this aim.

It was not Borrow himself who came up with the idea of a Bible translation into Romani, but rather Brandram. This is particularly important when we realize that it is an assumption of the biographical literature that Borrow's lifelong interest in Gypsies also appears as clear as day from this suggestion,[163] whereas the causal influence in point of fact worked completely the other way round. Borrow was not ignorant of the Romani dialect of English Gypsies, but his latent interest was only stirred to life by this impulse from evangelical circles. His natural talent for languages now, perhaps for the first time in his life, worked to his pragmatic advantage and the goal with which he could justify his translation activities was that of religious reform. It would prove to be in this very role that, during his years in Spain, Borrow tried to live up to his ideal of the heroic adventurer and later discovered the literary form he used to present his alter ego to the world.

SAMUEL ROBERTS

Although it was Brandram, as Secretary of the Bible Society, who gave Borrow the idea to make a Romani translation, this is not the complete story for there is good reason to suppose that he, in his turn, had been alerted to the call for such an enterprise by another. To trace the matter all the way to its source we must shine the spotlight on the work of Samuel Roberts (1763–1848), a socially concerned silver manufacturer and philanthropist from Sheffield who also regularly campaigned in print against social evils and, as a member of the Poor Board, had worked in support of innumerable groups in need.[164] In 1816 Roberts had delivered a plea on the behalf of Gypsies, a theme to which he returned at somewhat greater length in a publication from 1830.[165] This elaborated version he dedicated to *The Committee and Members of the British and Foreign Bible Society* to draw their notice to the situation of the – to him so extraordinary – Gypsy race which was said to constitute a human paradox.[166] They had never, he said, in all the centuries that they had spent in Christian countries, come to Christ. And there wasn't a single piece of writing translated into their mother tongue – not even the Bible. According to Roberts the time had come to lead them out of darkness. With his book he hoped to motivate Christian philanthropists to take an interest in them.

Roberts had a vision inspired by the Bible of the Gypsies' origin in Egypt, but their language was his primary concern, for he believed that through their language their secret could be revealed. It was his conviction that the Bible Society should take to heart the destiny of this long-neglected people, for had not God promised, 'They shall be brought to know the Lord'? He proposed that the Society translate part of the Holy Book into the language of the English Gypsies.[167] Their language was as old as the world after the Deluge and a publication of God's word in the Romani could work wonders. His idea was that something that was written in their own language would arouse their curiosity and create a desire in them to hear it read aloud or to learn to read it themselves. According to Roberts, if after careful deliberation, the society decided to publish a translation, the Gypsies would also assist such an enterprise. One side-effect of such an approach could be that, after conversion, they would set out as missionaries bent on civilizing their kin elsewhere in the world.[168] He reasoned further that, without doubt, God must have intended Gypsies to turn to Christianity for protection and support. That they had for centuries withstood the persecutions of the government made this divine intention all the more profound. God had given them their own place in the sun, in the open country, and they had clung fast to their way of life. In their simplicity they were a Christian example and should be left in peace. Only God's word was said to be able to lead them to the Light.[169]

This evangelical rhetoric was congruous with the vocabulary of the social reformers of the day. The Bible Society recognized its own strivings in Roberts' words and elected to act on his suggestion. In addition, however, Borrow was also more directly affected by Roberts' work, although he didn't wish to acknowledge this openly. The reverse appears to have been much less problematic, for in the foreword to the fifth edition of *The Gypsies* (1842) Roberts wrote that he had heard that the Gospel according to Luke had been translated into the Gypsy language and that the author of that work, one George Borrow, had also written a book about Gypsies. Roberts had immediately acquired both publications and openly expressed his extraordinary enthusiasm for the books and their author whom he qualified as the best equipped person in the world to write about the Gypsies. In the new printing of his own book he therefore had included excerpts from *The Zincali*, with an attribution. Borrow had made such a deep impression on him that he speculated about his possible Gypsy descent: '… whom any one that has read his interesting work would almost be ready to suspect had some of the royal blood of the Pharaoh's flowing in his veins.'[170] While reading Borrow, Roberts had indeed noticed that Borrow in his turn had read his work because he had discussed Roberts' assertion, in order subsequently to reject it, that Egypt was the Gypsies' original homeland, commenting that it was a position that a number of writers favoured. Roberts became curious to know what arguments his unexpected supporters advanced and wrote a letter to Borrow requesting clarification. On 14 June 1841 Borrow answered him from Oulton, saying that ten years previously Andrew Brandram had handed him Roberts' book to read.[171] He had found the theory about Egyptian descent intriguing and ingenious. While working on *The Zincali* the theory had again sprung to mind although the author and title of the book where he had seen it had long since slipped his mind. He offered his excuses for this, for of course he should have written '*a* most ingenious writer' instead of using the plural form. It is worth quoting why he said he had nevertheless done so: 'Pray excuse the inaccuracy; but it is my common practice in composition, when speaking of myself, to use the plural number.' The catch is simply that in reproducing the Egypt hypothesis he was not giving his own ideas but those of another. The account doesn't say what Roberts thought of this pretext.[172]

Moreover, Borrow had indeed already cited him in a note to an article from 1836,[173] thus the question is whether he had not consciously ignored this comparatively well-known figure in evangelical circles, as he did, in fact, all authors writing in English about Gypsies. We know, in any event, that he was familiar with the work of both Samuel Roberts and James Crabb and was susceptible to their influence. My attempts to find out about possible contact between Borrow and the Southampton Committee led nowhere, for no documents from the period have been preserved.[174] We can easily deduce from the work of both the authors mentioned that they were indebted to Grillmann, as he is called in Roberts, or Grellman, the Crabb variant, for their general knowledge about Gypsies. As for the image that they had formed of, specifically, English Gypsies, this they owed first of all to John Hoyland who, in part because of his ideas about the social reformation of Gypsies along religious lines, may be considered as the founder of British interest in this population group. The study of his work, moreover, discloses that he actually constituted the *trait-d'union* between Grellmann and Borrow.

JOHN HOYLAND

Not much is known about John Hoyland (1750–1831).[175] He, too, lived in Sheffield and only began to do research on Gypsies at a later age, primarily in Northampton, Bedford and Hertford. He was a Quaker and a piquant detail in the story of his life is that he was banned from the church for a time, probably because he fell for a black-eyed Gypsy girl, with whom, rumour has it, he even married.[176] However that might be, during a yearly meeting of his church in 1815 the proposal was made to improve the religious and social conditions of Gypsies in Great Britain, but first, before acting towards this end, to acquire more information. Hoyland, who had earned something of a name as a writer, was thought to be the appropriate person to carry out the job. In order to find out about the situation of the English Gypsies, he decided to send a list of questions to all district magistrates. A year later he published a report on the results from the questionnaire in book form.[177]

For the historical survey that Hoyland offers in this book, he had relied, as he himself admitted, above all on the 'learned Grellmann', whose book he knew in Matthew Raper's translation of 1787. It has been argued that Hoyland's book is no more than a summary of Grellmann,[178] but such an interpretation misses the innovativeness of his work which is contained above all in the passages on English Gypsies. He was the first to have tried, with the help of questionnaires, to collect contemporary information about this group on their own soil. What he found out about them has been considered for a long time as the standard information about English Gypsies. Sufficient reason thus to pay attention to his findings.

The outcome of his inquiries enables us to deduce the opinion of Gypsies held at that time by provincial governments. Hoyland's findings were further based on personal experience and on the opinions of leaders of itinerants.[179] The most important conclusions included the following: the number of Gypsies in England was unknown (estimates placed the figure at 18,000 to 20,000); they all said they came originally from Egypt, although they had no idea when their ancestors came to England; they had no inkling what genealogy is; they had no internal organization but they did know each other's sharply regionally-bound trek routes; half of all Gypsy families practised no vocation, the others worked in capacities known from the literature; they did not permit outsiders to study their language, which they themselves called 'jibber-jabber'; they observed their own morals and customs, which Hoyland fails to specify further; they had no religious observances of their own and for the most part knew only the Lord's Prayer; they married without ceremony as a rule, festivities being reserved for the more prosperous; they passed the largest part of the year under the open skies, sheltering in cheap hotels only in the winter, in London, for example, and Cambridge.

In addition to this portrait of the English Gypsy community, based on questionnaire responses, Hoyland also reported on his own experiences with Gypsies, many of whom he had visited during the period he was at work on his book. What is so striking is that in these passages he is almost exclusively positive about them, whereas in his general chapters based on Grellmann he does not shy away from the most negative interpretations. This discrepancy between the ease with which the most far-reaching generalizations of others are repeated and the subtlety that appears as soon as personal impressions are being recounted, characterizes more studies than Hoyland's alone. As we have seen, the same mechanism is operative in the accounts of many governments and writers, including the above-mentioned Crabb and Roberts. George Borrow's writings are no different in this regard.

Hoyland wrote that he noticed that the farmers and burghers of Northamptonshire had no complaints whatsoever to make about the Gypsies except that, every once in a while, they took some wood from their fences.[180] Most people said that their trust in the Gypsies was seldom abused and that, contrary to what the authorities apparently believed, there were advantages to letting them spend the night on your land or in your shed because they immediately kept an eye on things. The principle of reciprocity was at work here. During a visit to an annual market Hoyland struck up a conversation with a small group of Gypsies – he had learned a few words of their language from Grellmann – and he was impressed by how intelligent and communicative they were.[181] He writes many pages on his pleasant meetings with Gypsies, whom he experienced as honest, courteous and inspiring confidence. According to him the stipulations of the amended Vagrancy Act were especially crippling for their way of life. As a result they had brushes with the police more frequently than ever, not because they committed so many crimes, but through the strict application of regulations.[182] In particular the vagrancy law was meant to prevent people from appealing for welfare benefits in more than one community, so that those with no fixed abode, including many Gypsies, were viewed with suspicion by the authorities and regularly rounded up. In this context Hoyland reports that Gypsies hardly ever applied for poor relief and it had also become apparent to him that, in London, they constituted not the slightest nuisance as beggars.[183] To this he added that they didn't move from place to place as a form of opposition to law and order, as the authorities all too readily imagined, but to earn their living in the traditional way.[184] It was thus his opinion that they were treated with unnecessary severity, with the result that it was more difficult for them to earn a respectable income. It should be mentioned that he wrote occasionally about their vocational activities – for example, that they circled about London at a radial distance of some 20 to 30 kilometres with their wares packed on donkeys, taking on all kinds of jobs along the way, such as harvesting hops and bringing in the hay. A flexible work pattern, in other words.

Perusal of historical documents had taught Hoyland that there had already always existed a certain tension between the actual socio-economic functioning of Gypsies and the attitude of governments towards them. In the sixteenth and seventeenth centuries, for instance, they had provided entertainment as acrobats, jugglers, and as fortune tellers, drawing many spectators. Crowds were attracted by their mystic arts and talents, which people took to be Egyptian.[185] Their popularity, according to Hoyland, also appears from the fact that they were brought over from the continent until, for the first time in the middle of the sixteenth century, the king took measures to prevent them from coming. From that moment on there was a fine of £40 for importing Gypsies to England, which must apparently have been common practice until then.[186] Hoyland's interpretation of the fifteenth-century pilgrim's tale was also remarkably matter-of-fact. While Grellmann, following the lead of his predecessors, had construed it as a form of fraud, Hoyland took it to be telling evidence of Gypsies' ability to adapt themselves rapidly to the most disparate ways of life. He emphasized their developed sense of social distinctions, and not their 'deceptive nature'.

In addition to the survey in England, George Miller, a friend of Hoyland's from Edinburgh, had sent questionnaires to the bailiffs of every county in Scotland. Thirteen replied that within their jurisdiction no Gypsies travelled about, others that Gypsies only passed through now and then. There are two reasons which impel me to linger over these responses. First of all they introduced a new concept in Gypsy studies. According to these bailiff informants, Gypsy colonies residing in Scotland, especially the one in Kirk Yetholm, consisted of a mixed population of Gypsies and indigenous travellers. The illustrious novelist Sir Walter Scott was bailiff of Selkirkshire at the time and he responded that the population with which he was familiar did not belong to the Oriental-Egyptian race, but had undergone extensive intermarriage with native outlaws and vagabonds. Some were blondes, others redheads, although the tan-coloured complexion of the Gypsies was said to be dominant. With Scott's observations, the idea of 'mixed-bloods' or 'half-castes' made its way into the literature. The development of this concept is of importance, for it produced a split in thinking about Gypsies that had far-reaching ramifications.

A second reason Kirk Yetholm merits further consideration is that, in his passages about this colony, Hoyland disclosed that he didn't occupy himself with Gypsies solely from religious or philanthropic motives. What was special about the Gypsy colony in Kirk Yetholm was its long history; throughout the entirety of the nineteenth century it remained known as a phenomenon owing to its famous 'Gypsy kings' and to the countless attempts at reform that were undertaken there.[187] The Gypsies had always leased the land where they stood from the owner who resided in the region, a man who generously granted them many favours in the eighteenth century, appointed them to be his bodyguards and regularly gave them money. Relations only grew troubled in the early nineteenth century once a new owner assumed control of the former's holdings. This figure decided that Gypsies had a harmful effect on the work ethics of the vicinity. That they refused steady work also bothered Hoyland. This forms a clear parallel with Grellmann's ideas (and those of Maria Theresa and Joseph II), they had also extolled 'the hard-working citizen'.

The question was simply how a change could be wrought in the Gypsies' attitude and behaviour. The rational-economic approach of Enlightenment thinking had turned out to be inhumane and ineffective. According to Hoyland it was a good idea to try to turn Gypsies into useful burghers but there was a key element missing – Christian brotherly love. He had more faith in the exemplary effect of God's word and a Christian education than in the application of force. In this respect he wanted to align himself with previously formulated proposals for amelioration and was merely recapitulating thoughts that had been expressed in articles submitted by readers to the *Christian Observer*.[188] It was his idea that children should receive the most attention, for older persons no longer had the flexibility needed for change, and he felt that the best approach would be to place the children in charity schools in the mould of the British and Foreign School Society, a few of which were in operation in every part of the country. Their financing would have to be provided by the state, otherwise provincial budgets would be burdened too heavily. In a later phase boys could be apprenticed as artisans to masters, with some financial leeway for the purchase of tools, and girls could work as maids in a family home. This was a strategy that aspired above all to prevent children from following in their parents' footsteps. The crux of what Hoyland had to say was that Gypsies should settle down and change their work habits. Christian education would serve to pave the way.

JAMES CRABB

Hoyland's ideas inspired many evangelical charitable institutions after him to concern themselves with the situation of the Gypsies in a similar way, although with variable, and seldom spectacular results.[189] The initiatives of the Southampton Committee[190] were exemplary. For various reasons I am particularly interested in the founder of the committee, James Crabb because his book *The Gipsies' Advocate* (1830; 3rd edition 1832) was so popular that successive editions of it appeared,[191] but above all because Borrow set eyes on it at a moment when his interest in Gypsies was aroused in earnest. Analysis of Crabb's work also reveals that Borrow was influenced by both the spirit and letter of this charismatic clergyman's ideas. James Crabb (1774–1851) was a Methodist preacher in Southampton.[192] Like Roberts, he championed the more vulnerable social groups in society, among whose number were also Gypsies, particularly in the New Forest. His friends and his conscience had pressed him to put something on paper about them. He wrote that 'Grellman' (sic) and Hoyland had already extensively described this neglected branch of the human family but since the respectable Christian reading public was perhaps not aware of their publications he ventured his sketch, adding what he had learned about Gypsies over the years.

He, like Hoyland, had a great deal to say about them that was positive. They were always on time paying off their debts, for example, as countless shopkeepers who did business with them let him know.[193] What Crabb wrote about the busy traffic of letters among Gypsies, despite the fact that few could read or write, is also extraordinary. They were said to exchange many letters above all with relatives transported to the colony of New South Wales (Australia). According to him they went regularly to the post office to claim packages and he had never once heard complaints that they weren't prepared to pay the postal charges, even though these were often high.[194] He also eulogized their commemoration of deceased relatives. At Christmas they usually visited the graves of their loved ones, which for the most part were impeccably maintained. The grave-digger was paid well to look after them and expensive headstones, according to Crabb, were certainly not exceptional. The Gypsies' strong internal ties were also evident from the attachment between husbands and wives. As for their children, they had them baptized at birth in the closest church, in part because they thought it was the right thing to do, but especially because the child would be registered with a municipality. On such an occasion they would usually ask the official in question for some support for the child. 'Settling the baby', was their name for it according to Crabb. The godparents at such a baptismal rite almost always belonged to the same branch of the family and were highly respected.[195]

In this context I wish to point out a mechanism which, in my opinion, has become characteristic of society's attitude towards Gypsies. What I mean here is the practice that on the one hand social reformers such as Crabb kept trying to encourage Gypsies to settle somewhere and lead regular lives, while on the other the stance of local governments diametrically opposed this aim. Municipal civil servants were afraid that if these Gypsies would come to stay they would raise the total of 'work-shy poor' within community boundaries, and thus they did everything they could to deter them from any such move. Crabb reports in this context that some Gypsy families played on the officials' anxieties by asking for a sum of money, threatening that if they did not receive it they would settle in the place where their names were registered. What Crabb feared most of all was idleness and moral decay. It bothered him, for example, that music-making Gypsies saw themselves obliged to play in houses of ill repute.

That brings me to a second contradiction which, since Crabb, has become a commonplace. Whereas Grellmann found the laziness of Gypsies remarkable, Crabb stresses that the work they did, such activities as caning chairs, sharpening scissors, repairing kettles, weaving baskets, rat catching and peddling, took quite a bit of time and kept them busy from early in the morning until late at night. This observation, however, did not imply that he regarded the way they earned their livings as full-fledged work. His negative assessment of the Gypsies' work ethic and the apparently economically useful function of their activities will undoubtedly have been connected to the fact that women went out selling, too, so that they often had to leave their children alone in camp and took inadequate care of them. Furthermore morality, in the eyes of people like Crabb, was undermined by the kind of work with which these mothers were said to have supplemented the family income: fraudulent tricks and soothsaying.[196] Once he broached this topic, the methodist proved unable to stop. He described a repertoire of deceptions and ploys to separate fools from their money which, for the most part, we come across again in Borrows' books, especially in the ones about Spain. While Grellmann opposed these practices strenuously because, to his mind, they constituted evidence that even though the Enlightenment had dawned, superstition still persisted in the world, Crabb felt above all that his religious integrity was offended. He cited the words of Moses in Deuteronomy (xxix: 29): 'Secret things belong to the Lord our God' to condemn the actions of people who indulged in letting their futures be predicted. It upset him extraordinarily that members of society's upper circles, who should be the ones setting an example for the rest, paid dearly for these services. He acknowledged that many Gypsy women were rather good at it, cleverly exploiting the vanity, circumstances and expectations of those whose palms they read. People seemed eager to be fooled and since afterwards they were unwilling to make their embarrassment public, fearing ridicule, such practices could continue uninterrupted. He had heard of cases where people had spent no less than £400 to be deluded with visions of the man of their dreams and a whole range of other trickery. Crabb goes on for pages about these practices, so un-Christian in his eyes.

Like Hoyland, Crabb discovered that English Gypsy families – he was familiar in particular with the 200 members of the Stanley family – knew hardly anything about their fellow Gypsies in other countries and were largely interested in their own affairs.[197] He also wrote that many people pretended to be Gypsies. These were figures who for one reason or another had been excluded from society, married into a Gypsy clan and then *led them to commit crimes which they would never have thought of by themselves*.[198] Crabb thus added a component of social degeneration to what Hoyland designated as the 'mixed population'. For the first time in his work a distinction was drawn between 'true Gypsies', who did not behave asocially, and 'false Gypsies', a sort that was capable of anything. Appearances, because of biological intermingling, no longer betrayed which was which, nor did their way of life, since all, more or less, were incessantly on the move. Thus only a single criterion remained: that of language. As we noted with Borrow, during the nineteenth century command of deep Romani became the indicator of choice for determining if someone belonged to the 'pure Gypsy race', at least where judgement was being passed by non-Gypsies.

Crabb's consideration of English Gypsies indeed led him to the conclusion that they bore no resemblance at all to the monstrous figures Grellmann had described in his book on continental Gypsies.[199] They stole no sheep or poultry, staged no robberies or burglaries, certainly abducted no children, to pass over in silence still more serious crimes attributed to them. That they were so often accused of committing such violations occurred, according to him, because they made such convenient scapegoats.[200] As far as he knew they also seldom poached because this would turn the villagers in the vicinity of where they lived against them. They took care to prevent this from happening. At times they would remove some willow wands from farmers' stacks of firewood with which to weave their baskets. Usually they abided by the saying: '... despise those who risk their necks for their bellies.'[201] Yet they had no hesitation, he believed, about feasting on a dead sheep found along the wayside, which accounts for the common accusation that they intentionally poisoned such animals.[202] The only charge that he seconded was that they were famous horse thieves.

His own interest in Gypsies was awakened in the spring of 1827, in a courtroom where two horse thieves were sentenced to the death penalty. The judge had added that for one of the pair, a Gypsy, there was no hope for clemency, since by his very origin he was destined for the gallows. Once outside Crabb engaged in conversation with the Gypsy's wife, soon to be a widow. She and her small child had made a deep impression on him. A short while later, he read Hoyland's book which made him decide to take action. In November of that same year he founded the Southampton Committee, but he had also assumed custody of one of the children of the hanged Gypsy, soon to be followed by a second one. By the time he started writing his book, 23 converted Gypsies were then living in Southampton.[203] If we accept his descriptions, they all behaved in model fashion and worshipped him as their beloved reformer who had brought them in touch with God's word. Compulsion and instruction were, according to Crabb who cited the frustrating experiences of Emperor Joseph II, out of the question. Nor was he a proponent of encouraging Gypsies to settle in the city, for if the experiment proved to be a disappointment that only made the move back more difficult. Helping them out was the issue, and supporting them in their attempts to lead another life by visiting them in their camps, doing good, and spreading the holy word.[204] Crabb made examples out of people who went out as Christ himself had and through their deeds of brotherly love for others served as light buoys. He envisioned a network of philanthropic societies with a Christian foundation, clearly a goal in which the approach of the kindred Bible Society can be recognized, except he had less success, for he received few responses to the circulars and questionnaires that he had sent to all kinds of people (clerics, philanthropists and other Christians) requesting information about Gypsies and urging them not to falter in performing their Christian duty to this category of their fellow citizens.

This theme of personal involvement is one I wish to probe more deeply because the strategy that Crabb propagated was so similar to the way in which Borrow would later approach Gypsies. Above all the heroic role of the man who brought enlightenment to the human misery of the tent dwellers must have appealed to him greatly. Crabb set out each summer to visit Gypsies in the districts of Kent, Sussex and Surrey where they found work picking hops. For days at a time he kept them company and in the evenings he talked to them at length about the gospels. He also tried to allay their fears that their children would be shut up in the nursery school in Southampton and at a certain moment be transported away. During winter he went from city to city, including London and Bristol; this was the ideal time to persuade them to send their children to school. He also went to see them during the Ascot and Epsom Races, or at markets surrounding London, where he could count on finding them.[205] On such occasions those who knew him introduced him as the Gypsy's friend from Southampton, and this won him great respect and visibly flattered him. He himself says that during such calls they invariably asked him to read aloud from 'that little book' and tales from the New Testament made their eyes glow. Practically none of them was able to read, but they all wished to have a Bible or a prayer book so that they could request other visitors to read to them. In this picture we recognize a prototypical 'Romany Rye', the honorary title which Borrow later appropriated for himself and with which he set a trend for succeeding generations of Gypsy experts.

Another initiative through which Crabb distinguished himself was the holding of an annual assembly at his home to which all converted Gypsies were welcome. These gatherings could amount to more than 150 people who camped with their tents, horses and wagons on his property. On such a day he read out texts from the Bible and referred to the sin of soothsaying, for he believed this to be the greatest evil of the Gypsy community.[206] To all Christians present who were not of Gypsy descent he pointed out their duty to concern themselves with the fate of these wretched of the earth. In 1847 Crabb's failing health compelled him to put an end to the yearly meetings. Another activist organized the event for one more year, but with the death of the Gypsies' advocate, his initiative died as well. His work had no structural consequences elsewhere in the country either. In practice it turned out that most clergymen were not really prepared to perform missionary work in their own back yard.

IMITATIO CHRISTI

Wholly in Crabb's spirit, George Borrow believed that, with his sermons, he could mitigate the lot of the sinners and he hoped that he would be repaid by their childlike gratitude. It was the religious inspiration behind his books, especially those about Spain, which lent them an heroic cachét that appealed to his reading public. A later critic wrote that Borrow brought to mind '… one of the heroes of the old stories of Christian Chivalry, half saint, half knight, riding through wild moors and desolate haunted forests on some holy mission or quest.'[207] In 1983 Ridler wrote that contemporary 'Borrowians' found it difficult to accept an image of Borrow as a religious polemicist, a preacher intent on conversions.[208] She points out, correctly, that in St Petersburg he translated no less than 226 pages of English sermons into Manchu and he had described his attempts to convert 'the simple of spirit' in Portugal and Spain with great verve.[209] If, in other words, it was already a role that he was playing, then it was one into which he had thrown himself completely. That he behaved too much like an evangelist was reason for even the board of the Bible Society to admonish him, complaining that he had been sent to the Iberian peninsula for other tasks. Yet Borrow's plan to translate the Gospel according to Luke into Romani was certainly not only intended to be a linguistic feat that would impress his employer. It was founded on pragmatic reasons as well. In his letters home, but also later in *The Bible in Spain*, we see how he emerged as more and more of an evangelist. During his years in Spain he became enamoured with his self-image as an adventurer on a holy quest. For him Gypsies were the people most deserving of being raised up from their fallen state: 'That I was an associate of Gypsies and fortunetellers I do not deny. Why should I be ashamed of their company when my Master mingled with publicans and thieves?'[210] Gypsies, he believed, were degenerate creatures of God, so they especially merited attention. He demonstrated his New Testament zeal to save souls with the conviction of a person who first saw the Light himself rather late in life. Whereas during adolescence he was still writing to his friend Kerrison that he was off to London to take the (literary) world there by storm and to insult the Church, in the 1830s he felt a new compulsion.[211] Whether it was empathy, overcompensation or fanaticism plain and simple, the fact remains that he began to concern himself with the lot of the Gypsies to the extent that he wanted to spread the Word among them. The more resistance he encountered from the Spanish clergy against his work as Bible salesman, the greater his motivation, as if some personal chord were struck that gave direction to his ambition.[212] Thus in *The Bible in Spain* he wrote how small groups of Gypsies, almost all of them women, called on him in Madrid or Seville to listen to him read aloud from the Bible. If they hungered, he fed them and he slaked their thirst. Through such imagery he turned himself into the Redeemer, a common enough experience for evangelists in England. In such an account the Gypsies fulfilled a very functional role, for they were the flock that longed for a shepherd.[213] His rhetoric makes it seem that his visitors yearned for the comfort of Christian reconciliation, although this did not keep him from finally admitting that he did not succeed in having a profound religious influence on the women. What all of them did want was a copy of the Romani translation of the Gospel according to Luke, which they regarded as a talisman to shield them from bad luck.[214]

A mosaic of literature

The attempts Borrow made to spread the Bible throughout the Iberian peninsula had provided him with material for an adventurous travel book. Part of the popularity of *The Bible in Spain* has at any rate been ascribed to its supposed religious character which meant that it came to stand in the bookcase among other edifying works. Its title and subject matter accounted for why Christian parents had few objections to their children picking it up to read. They then discovered, to their surprise, that the story concerned the sales representative of the Bible Society, but he had such bizarre adventures that they made a deep impression on children who on Sundays, as a rule, read such books as John Bunyan's *The Pilgrim's Progress* (1678).[215]

Borrow's book may be read in the first place as an account of an actual trip through Portugal and Spain, yet now and then the reader finds himself in a fantasy world where the main character undertakes a heroic journey through surroundings that are hostile to him. It is indeed the power of the imagination that, retrospectively, came to be recognized as the essential characteristic of the literary movement that would go down in history as Romanticism. This holds true, too, for the widely prevailing idea of freedom in which the exaltation of feeling and imagination were said to have their origin. These elements have yielded a battery of typical romantic, literary motifs that we encounter in all of Borrow's work. Thus in *Lavengro*, the first part of Borrow's literary autobiography, we come across passages in which the natural simplicity of the itinerant life is glorified in a lyrical manner. When the protagonist has fled from worldly London, he meets up with a poor tinker, Jack Slingsby, and his wife who, no longer able to make ends meet, are driven from their home territory by Jack's rival, the 'Flaming Tinman', a Gypsy half-caste. Talking to Jack, the young Lavengro delivers an ode to the free life, without a boss and in the midst of beneficent nature:

> Would you compare such a dog's life as that with your own – the happiest under heaven – true Eden life, as the Germans would say, – pitching your tent under the pleasant hedge-row, listening to the song of the feathered tribes, collecting all the leaky kettles in the neighbourhood, soldering and joining, earning your honest bread by the wholesome sweat of your brow.[216]

The romantic fascination with life at the bottom or on the edge of society was certainly not new. In European literature vagabonds, outcasts, clever rogues, romantic rebels and comic recalcitrants have always scored heavily. Consider Tijl Uilenspiegel, Falstaff, Robin Hood or the head of the robbers in Schiller's *Die Räuber*. From the fifteenth century,

Gypsies, too, figured in that literary universe, as Bronislaw Geremek has convincingly shown in his standard work on the subject.[217] Interest in this category of exotic outsiders, however, reached a peak during the Romantic period.[218] The appearance of Grellmann's book, with its many literarily interesting themes placed in social context, proved a strong stimulation in Germany.[219] Considering the wealth of literature on this topic, I will content myself here with mentioning the most popular patterns.

The literary Gypsy character with the longest tradition is the social outsider: the beggar, vagabond, robber and pariah. Until late in the eighteenth century robber chieftains with their bands were dominant, menacing but also slightly heroic; in the nineteenth century the individual outsider assumed centre stage, and his anti-bourgeois inclinations were either idealized or rigorously repudiated. A second literary stereotype was that of the Gypsy woman as a magic or occult figure. In this personification Gypsies had created excitement before Romanticism and would do so after it as well. Gypsies, in part because of their supposed Egyptian origins – a country known since antiquity as a 'sorcerer's paradise' – were invariably associated with superstition and sorcery. Through appearances as witches or prophets predicting peoples' fates their position as representatives of an almost magical universe was underscored. Every age has its references to Gypsies as soothsayers with power over the future. Often they were ideal characters for fables because they served as intermediaries between the supernatural and the daily world. Finally there are the purely romantic symbols: the Gypsy as the European equivalent of the 'noble savage', the man of nature whose craving for freedom leads him to choose to live on the edge of society, knowing himself to be untrammelled, abiding by his own laws, never betraying his feelings. Their self-aware drive to be free is embodied, for example, in *Lavengro* by the Gypsy Jasper Petulengro, who celebrates life in contrast to his friend, the book's leading character, who is indeed consumed by existential doubts.

In his work Borrow, depending on the genre in which he happened to be working at the moment, drew freely from the familiar stock of literary and social Gypsy stereotypes. Sometimes his Gypsies are devilish murderers or bandits, at other times they are mysterious representatives of a counterworld; they are also the iconographic heroes of a dying race or even the finest specimens of mankind. They are the same, Borrow wrote, always and everywhere, but his own books contradict the generalization. Apart from the rest, there is no evidence that Borrow's interest in the Gypsy as a literary theme predates his arrival in St Petersburg in 1833. Thus this interest must have been aroused in Russia, predominantly through his reading the work of Alexander Pushkin.[220]

PUSHKIN'S ROMANTICISM

In 1835 George Borrow published his anthologies containing poems translated from Russian in which he explored, for the first time, the theme of 'the Gypsy'. The collection *Talisman* included various translations of Pushkin. Borrow also worked on Pushkin's poem *Zigáni*[221] at this time although during his lifetime the translation was never published.[222] Gypsies were all the vogue in better Russian circles at that time and distinctive literary stereotypes emerged, such as the beautiful, proud Gypsy woman; the wise, old Gypsy; and the impulsive, untamable Gypsy youth. Society's interest was connected to the popularity, then at its height, of Russian Gypsy choruses.[223] The first of these famous choruses was formed at the behest of Count Aleksey Orlov in 1774. Chorus members were serfs from the village of Poesjkino, close to Moscow, who performed after dinner on Orlov's estate. The fame of this Sokolov choir spread rapidly and once the Moscow elite had discovered them, they received invitations to sing elsewhere as well. At this point, in 1807, the count decided to free them from serfdom. The lead singer was Stepanida Sidorovna Soldatova, better known as Stesja, a legend in those days, to whom Borrow also referred.[224] Napoleon Bonaparte had cherished the hope of hearing her sing, but when he took Moscow in 1812 she had already fled and the male members of the chorus were serving as hussars in the army. The renowned Stesja died in 1822, but during Borrow's Russian sojourn (1833 to 1835) Gypsy choruses were enjoying their heyday. They were in demand with aristocrats and merchants alike in both Moscow and St Petersburg, even though they were not permitted to set their tents up within city limits. Undoubtedly Borrow would have attended a performance by one of the Gypsy choruses, despite his failure to mention them in his work. What he does refer to is a visit he paid to less-gifted Gypsy women in an encampment far from Moscow.[225]

Many of these choruses rented imposing houses in St Petersburg as well as in Moscow; these had vast halls where they entertained their guests and camped, more or less, themselves. Borrow was also familiar with these houses and wrote about them enthusiastically. The women who sang in these choruses might be celebrated for their song and dance, but marriages between them and Russian nobles were less common than Borrow would have us believe. These unions were usually not sanctioned by the church and even in the event of 'legalization' people remained scandalized by them. The Gypsy diva in Borrow's day was Tania Demianova, who counted Pushkin and later Franz Liszt among her admirers. Like other poets, Pushkin, too, dedicated verses to her, but his interest in the Gypsy theme had already been sparked earlier. The story goes that during his banishment in Moldavia he had travelled together for a time with Gypsies.[226] He was said to have fallen in love with a young Gypsy, Zemfira, whom he later made into the heroine of *Zigáni*, his poem in eleven scenes.[227]

Once back in Russia Pushkin acted as the patron of various Gypsy choruses, which he often mentioned in his work. When Borrow came to St Petersburg, Pushkin's Gypsy poems were already classics. The poet was also said to have recorded a number of poems straight from the lips of the Moldavian Gypsies among whom he had lived. Their Gypsy women, he maintained, were distinguished from those in North Russia by their extreme moral purity. Not only Pushkin, but the Russian intelligentsia in those days had thus a romantic-idealistic idea of Gypsies, seeing them as a people who loved freedom and opposed every form of tyranny. Above all they cultivated the image of the Gypsy woman as a *femme fatale*, and she was immortalized in this role by Prosper Merimée in 1846 in his *Carmen*. Many of these romantic literary stereotypes appear in Borrow's writing, even in such late work as the *Romano Lavo-Lil* of 1874 in which he expresses his fascination with an English Gypsy woman, a typical specimen of the *beauté idéale*: swarthy, mysterious, beautiful and terrifying, an almost Faustian portrayal of a woman who drives every man mad and eventually brings him to ruin:

> She is considerably above the middle height, powerfully but gracefully made, and about thirty-seven years of age. Her face is oval, and of a dark olive. The nose is Grecian, the cheek-bones rather high; the eyes somewhat sunk, but of a lustrous black; the mouth small, and the teeth exactly like ivory. Upon the whole the face is exceedingly beautiful, but the expression is evil – evil to a degree.[228]

THE PRECIOSA AND PICARESQUE OF CERVANTES

George Borrow claimed that once every nine years he read *Don Quijote* (First Part 1605) by Miguel de Cervantes Saavedra. He was also familiar, however, with Cervantes' *Las novelas ejemplares* (1613), of which *La Gitanilla*, set in a Gypsy milieu, is probably the most famous. As a play, *La Gitanilla*, caused a sensation into the nineteenth century.[229] With this exemplary novella Cervantes actually introduced the Preciosa-motif into European literature. The adventures of this idealized Spanish Gypsy woman who turned out not to be a Gypsy became a traditional theme in literature. Countless versions of the story recur in all western European countries.[230]

There has been extensive speculation about how authentic Cervantes' portrayal of Gypsies is, but by now it seems beyond dispute that his sociological and ethnological observations are in any case based in part on his personal experiences with Gypsies.[231] Above all his Aunt Maria, for a season the mistress of a 'bastard Gypsy', was said to have initiated him into the world of the dancing, singing and soothsaying Gypsies. She had exposed him to Gypsy tales from the time he was a child, enabling him to mine them as a rich lode of local colour for his account of Preciosa, 'the idealized embodiment of his dream-aunt María, the romantic victim of a cruel destiny'.[232] According to Gypsy expert Starkie, not only was Cervantes the first in Spain to describe many familiar Gypsy customs and characteristics, he is also said to have accurately sketched their relations with other Spaniards in those days.[233] Cervantes demonstrated that Gypsies had exercised a strong influence on the songs and poetry of Andalucía and that the nobility and clergy as well were under the spell of Gypsy culture – their dancing, songs and customs. Furthermore he commended the chastity of Gypsy women – a topic about which Borrow would also boast two centuries later. He has Preciosa sing the praises of virginity as the pearl in the life of a woman.

We rediscover many of the Gypsy motifs from *La Gitanilla* in Borrow's two books on Spain (and her Gypsies). The ghost of Don Quijote, moreover, hovers near, recognizable to every reader of *The Bible in Spain*. The rambling knight and his servant bear a strong resemblance to the man who, centuries after them, similarly in the company of extraordinary sidekicks (usually guide, cook and interpreter) journeyed through a land fraught with perils, defying both the forces of nature and the distrust of the inhabitants of remote villages. In the struggle which the colporteur Borrow had to wage with the Spanish ecclesiastical authorities, just like his fictional ancestor, after dark, along with his servant, he regularly knocked on the door of yet another Spanish inn, crossing the path of bizarre characters without any irresolution in his calling. He had so much in common with the archetypical knight Don Quijote in his battle against delusions which he conjured up himself, that John Hasfeld, the friend with whom Borrow had enjoyed port, vodka, *Tijl Uilenspiegel* and other literature in St Petersburg, wrote after reading him: 'Did it never strike you how much you resemble the good hidalgo *Don Quijote de la Mancha*? To my notion, you might readily pass for his son.'[234]

Master and servant are also, to be sure, a well-known combination in the picaresque novel, although in this genre the servant is usually the protagonist. In Cervantes' novellas, such as *Lazarillo de Tormes*,[235] it is possible to point out themes that belong to the standard elements of the picaresque novel or rogue's tale. Yet Geremek has pointed out that although the exemplary novellas are replete with a rich assortment of personages from the lowest levels of Spanish (urban) society, with each of them Cervantes wanted to make some moral point, whereas what the picaresque genre depicts is rather the social disintegration of individuals. The form adopted was autobiographical most of the time, populated as a rule with charlatans, parasitical ne'er-do-wells, ruined gentlemen of leisure, bandits, beggars and vagabonds, in short people who in times of social crisis had to rely on their wits to keep from going under.[236] Their exotic, unfamiliar ambience, their secret language, the life of the parasitical, marauding knight, all combined to generate a treasure trove of stories about the unequalled exploits of people in resistance against a society that treated them as social outcasts.

In Borrow's *The Bible in Spain*, in particular, we come across many such figures from the nether regions of society who spin colourful tales about their attempts to maintain their social standing. By bestowing attention on their ups and downs and portraying the aristocracy and clergy with a good deal of cynicism, Borrow places himself in a Spanish literary tradition where fact and fiction are inextricably intertwined. His book nevertheless revolved primarily around George Borrow. We see a figure loom up who overcomes hosts of dangers without ever succumbing to be anybody's victim; who kindles the flame of Protestantism in a Catholic country and in punishment is tossed into prison among genuine criminals, but whose light, like Christ's, shines forth undiminished; who keeps confusing people with his great gift for languages; who need back down from no physical confrontation, owing to his lanky, athletic prowess; who for long nights in succession rides through the woods, at times nearly crumpling from exhaustion, but who always reaches those who need him in the nick of time; who excels in patriotism in a land of semi-barbarians. Examined closely, Borrow thus functions as the adventuresome hero of the picaresque novel that was his life.

THE RECEPTION OF BORROW

Having reached the end of this chapter, I return to my point of departure: Borrow's reputation as the first 'Romany Rye'. Not only gypsiologists after him, but also contemporary reviewers spread his fame widely.[237] With the publication of *The Zincali*, the author's talents instantly received wide exposure, although there was considerable negative criticism about sections of the book. There has always been agreement about the vivacity of Borrow's style, his lively narrative skill and his ability to bring Gypsy characters vividly to life. When, during the 1850s, doubts were heard concerning the verisimilitude of his fiction, practically no reviewer omitted to mention that the novels nevertheless included a wealth of enchanting scenes, that the Gypsies in them were described with great gusto and that Borrow's literary vitality never deserted him for a moment. Similarly, there was just as little difference of opinion about his familiarity with the way of life of the people about whom he wrote with such flare.[238] Some reviewers found that his identification went so far that he deserved the honorary title of 'Prince of the Vagabonds'.[239]

Typical of the reception of Borrow is the explanation offered for the success of his work. It would be remarked that everyone knew what Gypsies were because, owing to the beauty of their appearance and their mysterious way of life, for centuries they already comprised a popular theme in literature.[240] What Borrow's work – written in his romantic missionary period – added was that he had shown how Gypsies, physically and morally, were the same all over the world and could be recognized by their penetrating glance and an unmistakable wickedness. By portraying their lives from the inside, however, and presenting them in a series of exciting anecdotes, Borrow had at the same time seen to it that his readers became intrigued and came to feel a certain sympathy for the Gitanos. He had revealed a previously unknown, magical realm and had done so in such a convincing fashion that no one doubted his profound expertise.

His literary descriptive powers won him much praise, as did his command of Romani, which enabled him – in imitation of others, although few reviewers mentioned this – to tear back the veil from Gypsy history and disclose the mystery of their origins. Not everyone was equally impressed by his linguistic stunts,[241] but in the ranks of those who were his admirers, people emphasized the authenticity of the prayers, poems and songs that he interpolated and the inestimable value of his vocabulary lists.[242] Only one reviewer found his attempts – in the footsteps of Grellmann and Marsden – to use linguistic evidence to establish India as the Gypsies' original homeland to be anything but convincing.[243] He pointed out that since Sanskrit was the mother of most European languages, comparisons would always bring similarities to light.

Of all Borrow's books, *The Zincali* and *The Bible in Spain* prompted the most aspersions about the truthfulness of their contents. A few reviewers emphasized explicitly that Borrow had recorded the remains of a culture in decay as a veritable historian,[244] although they found it a pity that he had not compared the Gitanos with English Gypsies.[245] He was also said to have been carried away by Romantic literary motifs so that his work became an amalgam of fact and fiction, a mix compromising the credibility of its argument. With the appearance of his two-part semi-autobiographical writings, this objection was sounded again, much more pointedly than before. The author was told that he had handed in a portfolio of disconnected sketches, had allowed himself to be dragged along by his prejudices, and had pushed his narcissism to its outermost limits.[246] Yet the *communis opinio* in the biographical literature about the belittling of these works by the critics rests on the lack of an overall view. The reviewers for a number of leading periodicals may have vented their disappointment in no uncertain terms because they 'had expected a second Marco Polo, but had gotten a 19th-century Defoe';[247] most critics had delighted in how Borrow, historian and poet rolled into one, had played, lyrically, with *Wahrheit und Dichtung*.[248] The only part of his work which charmed nobody was the appendix to the *Romany Rye* in which he shamelessly thundered against Catholicism and all kinds of other targets which were, in his eyes, evidence of decadence.

The scholarly foundation of *The Zincali* was challenged by only a few; more attacked, principally, Borrow's disconnected mode of presentation and lack of a unified vision. These points were elaborated at greatest length in a French review by Philarète Chasles,[249] who, while he found it one of the most curious books to appear in England in recent years, objected to Borrow's having no underlying philosophic idea. The author's analytic ability was inadequately developed and he was said to have forfeited the credulity of his readers through his naive and simplistic portrayal of things. It was a murkily written account which failed to consider the most interesting questions. Passages taken from life were adulterated by inclusion of fictional fragments.[250] Only the persevering reader would be repaid, Chasles felt, with a wealth of new insights and findings – which he illustrated, as dozens of his English colleagues had done, with a large number of telling citations. He was above all struck by Borrow's complete and detailed portrait of the Gitanos, with whom he was said to have identified entirely. Chasles classified him as an indefatigable missionary of scholarship who had written an exceptional, valuable and, above all, picturesque book.[251] He contended, however, that Borrow was not sufficiently intellectual to do anything more with his raw material than merely present it, so he had shed little light on the history of the 'Gypsy race' and had not come up with an explanation for the immutability of their ethics and customs down through the ages. According to Chasles, the Hindu institution of the caste system was the key to the puzzle. Through this legacy they, like the Jews, would always keep to themselves, inaccessible to change.[252] Supposed parallels with Jews as a separate people in the diaspora were also drawn in various English reviews.[253] In his lengthy review of *The Zincali*, the hispanist Richard Ford wrote:

... both wanderers and outcasts on the face of the earth – both branded Cain-like – both inspiring dislike and distrust, which they repay on those who despise them with tenfold interest – both 'peeled nations', living alone amongst all others, never amalgamating, but hermetically sealed up and palisadoed with deep-rooted prejudices, which neither time nor space, persecution nor increasing civilization, have been able to break down.[254]

NOTES

1 Yates (1953, p. 11). 'Romani Rai' means, literally, 'Gypsy lord' and 'Romani Rawnie' means 'Gypsy lady'. The terms are used for a man or woman who, especially interested in Gypsies, makes friends with them.

2 The initial series of the *Journal of the Gypsy Lore Society* appeared from 1888 to 1892 in Edinburgh; the second from 1907 to 1916; the third from 1922 to 1973; the fourth from 1974 to 1978; in 1991, a fifth began in the United States.

3 In 1984 a bibliography of the published works and manuscripts of George Borrow appeared, compiled by Collie and Fraser; an annex (No. 2) devoted to the editions printed by Murray also specifies the size of printings. Only for *The Zincali* did I read the first edition, for it was more extensive than later ones, a number of which I looked into too. For Borrow's other works, I was content with later editions (see references).

4 This opinion is also expressed in Mayall's standard work on the nineteenth-century history of Gypsies in England (1988, p. 72). In his analysis of image-formation among the English, he refers to Borrow's far-reaching influence as a novelist and 'gypsiologist', and calls him the leading figure of his day in this area, subsequently to concentrate in his analysis on the members of the Gypsy Lore Society.

5 The history of this influential society, which in 1994 still comprised a reflection of the themes dominating Gypsy studies, i.e. ethnology and linguistics, has not yet been written. In Mayall's study (1988, pp. 71–93) he is critical about their findings, whereas Fraser (1990, pp. 1–14) saluted their learning and enthusiasm. Voerst van Lynden, in the course of her research, analysed the work of two of the founders of the society and reported on her findings in her master's thesis 'Gentlemen of the Roads', completed in 1993. She subscribes to Mayall's most important assumptions.

6 So wrote MacRitchie and Groome in the founding circular of the GLS, May 1888, which is part of the *C. G. Leland Collection* in the British Library, London, Add. Mss. 37.174/131. Borrowed from Voerst van Lynden (1993, pp. 4, 68).

7 See, for example, Boas (1929, pp. 51–67, especially 66–7) on Borrow's unique position in the English Romantic literary movement.

8 In 1899 Knapp's two part biography of Borrow, for a long time the most authoritative, was published. The reigning opinion among 'Borrowians' is that Knapp has turned out to be an unreliable guide to Borrow's life. One does acknowledge the value of the biography as a reference work, however, owing to the unique collection of letters and other documents which it contains, only a part of which can be found in the *Hispanic Society* archives in New York. Archer Milton Huntington, the founder of this museum with its extensive archives, idolized Spain as well as Borrow, and considered Knapp as his mentor. This explains why he purchased Knapp's legacy from his widow. For a critical introduction to the existing biographies of Borrow, see Collie and Fraser (1984, pp. 1–9). Whoever wishes to understand how manuscripts (fragments) from Borrow's legacy have come to rest

in so many scattered locations throughout the world, read Fraser (1990, pp. 182–9).

9 In this context it is worth mentioning Fraser's recent (1982, 1984) editions of the letters George Borrow wrote to a Danish friend in St Petersburg. In 1981 Fraser already published a volume with letters that Borrow wrote from eastern Europe.

10 For this reconstruction I adhere to the main lines of the latest biography of Borrow by Collie (1982), without going very deeply into the controversies occasioned by some of Collie's interpretations.

11 On grounds of the symptoms which Borrow himself describes, Collie (1982, p. 8) is led to think of epileptic episodes, but Allderidge (1990, pp. 44–53, here p. 52), basing her diagnosis on talks with psychiatrists, is much more cautious, inclining to go along with Borrow himself and to speak of severe melancholy.

12 Letter of 20 January 1824 to Roger Kerrison who trained further in London to become a lawyer and in whose house in London Borrow would lodge for some time. From Collie (1982, p. 31 ff.).

13 To form some idea of the desperation of Borrow's situation in those days, it is sufficient to read his letters reproduced in Knapp (1899, Vol. II, pp. 249–52). See, too, the *Hispanic Society*, *George Borrow Collection*, in particular the Knapp folder, 1824a.

14 Published in six parts in 1825. Derived from Collie (1982, pp. 32, 253).

15 About Borrow's slave labour as an editor, see Howsam (1993, pp. 1–9).

16 Citation from Collie (1982, p. 42).

17 See Shorter (1913, pp. 147–50) for a description of Borrow's efforts to procure letters of recommendation that would enable him to enlist, successively, with the Greeks, French, Belgians and British. According to Shorter in the back of Borrow's mind there was constantly the design of his being stationed in the Orient, not so much driven by wanderlust but because he had all sorts of translation projects in his head.

18 See, for example, Fraser (1988, pp. 2–13). Ridler's unpublished 1983 doctoral dissertation 'George Borrow as a Linguist: Images and Contexts' is relevant here as well.

19 In 1991 Howsam's general history of the BFBS appeared. In an article in 1988 she had already described Borrow's relation with the Bible Society.

20 Thus Howsam (1988, p. 48). The board consisted of 63 members. None was an editor or linguist. They were in the first place people of a practical bent, for example merchants, bankers and shopkeepers; a quarter of them did regularly work out their ideas in written form, however.

21 Cf. *Targum. Or Metrical Translations from Thirty Languages and Dialects* (1835) and *The Talisman. From the Russian of Alexander Pushkin. With Other Pieces* (1835).

22 See Fraser (1992, pp. 25–47).

23 Letter dated 24 February 1836 from Madrid. Printed in Knapp (1899, Vol. II, pp. 271–2). At the bottom he had written: '(Burn this!)'

24 Collie (1982, p. 113).

25 See, for example, Collie (1982, pp. 144, 157). On p. 246 he even writes: 'She was steadily affectionate, and the possibility remains that Borrow would have married her had her mother not been determined to marry him.'

26 Knapp had people search to no avail for these letters in the Bible Society's archives. Yet fate willed that they were located shortly after the appearance of his biography. T.H. Darlow, Literary Superintendent of the BFBS, took on the task of editing the entire packet of letters, providing notes. In 1911 they appeared in book form. Collie and Fraser (1984, p. 39) estimate that Borrow based roughly one fifth of his book on the letters.

27 The crucial turmoil which the writing and publication of this book occasioned in Borrow's life is described extensively by Collie (1982, pp. 184–228) in the chapter: '*Lavengro*: the "book which is no humbug".'

28 Collie (1982, p. 220). This biographer, it should be said, has an inclination to model his hero after the image which he apparently has of Borrow in his head as a kind of socialist/anarchist partisan fighting for minorities such as Jews, Gypsies and Quakers and opposed to all the forces of conformity in society. He doesn't gloss over the bourgeois side of the writer whom he greatly esteems but it does not weigh heavily in the scales when he interprets Borrow as an (almost consciously) eccentric Victorian.

29 Collie (1982, p. 230).

30 This last original work of Borrow's stemmed from two vacation trips which he, in part accompanied by his wife and step-daughter, had made between July and November 1854 and August and September 1857. The first edition of *Wild Wales: Its People, Language and Scenery* came out in December of 1862. In the twentieth century it would come to be regarded as one of the classics of Welsh travel literature. See Collie and Fraser (1984, pp. 73–4).

31 See Collie and Fraser (1984, pp. 79–81).

32 Thus Webster (1888–89, pp. 150–3). See also Jenkins (1912, p. 12, note 2), who adds that he was unable to find confirmation of this story anywhere.

33 See Vesey-FitzGerald's biography of Borrow from 1953.

34 This was indeed not true for his mother, for according to this line of reasoning it was she who was of Gypsy origin or had taken a Gypsy lover. Shorter had already exposed this story as a fable (1913, pp. 12–13); nor was Fréchet in his biography of Borrow (1956, pp. 5–7) particularly impressed by the arguments FitzGerald brought forward. There has never been any corroborating evidence whatsoever.

35 See Fraser (1972, pp. 60–81) who characterized FitzGerald's suppositions as vague, refutable and impossible of proof.

36 See the issue of the *Morning Herald* for 12 May 1838, a copy of which can be found in the *Hispanic Society* (Knapp folder 1838a). Fraser (1992, pp. 25–47) writes that the rough version of the piece in question in Borrow's own handwriting is also there, but I was unable to locate it.

37 Ridler may bestow credulity on Borrow's meetings with Gypsies in his youth, yet even she cannot subdue her doubts when she speaks of his inclination to generalize and to exaggerate as soon as Gypsies are his subject. She advises caution in efforts to reconstruct Borrow's actual contacts with Gypsies (1982, pp. 49, 55, 395–6).

38 From the pen of Pastor Jessopp (1900, p. 8). Seven years before this author had also written two articles about Borrow (see the list of references).

39 See Thompson (1909–10, pp. 162–74).

40 See Shorter's (1913, pp. 41–5) interpretation of their contact.

41 See Knapp (Vol. II, 1899, p. 268).

42 See the Berg Collection, sign. 64 B 4845: *Biographical sketch of George Borrow. Holograph, unsigned and undated.* Here there is a reference to a list with 1,127 words, transcribed from the mouths of English Gypsies – without, however, the list itself being attached. In this sense the evidence is a bit shaky.

43 See Darlow (1911, pp. 92–5) and *The Zincali* (1841, pp. 7–11).

44 Ibidem, p. 94.

45 Ibidem, pp. 166–71; *The Zincali* (1841, pp. 219–38), written with somewhat more restraint and with a number of added dialogues about personal encounters, and finally, *The Bible in Spain* (1842, pp. 105–21), with many allusions to the scenes in the first book. A short description of both first meetings can be read in 'The Gipsies in Russia and in Spain', *The Athenaeum* (20 August 1836) pp. 587–8.

46 Darlow (1911, p. 169).

47 Ibidem, p. 188, with Borrow's report on the Gypsy quarter of Triana, in the vicinity of Seville (5 December 1836) and Darlow (1911, pp. 430–2) on the sale of Gypsy Bibles in San Lucar, in Borrow's report from Tanger (4 September 1839).

48 See Napier (1842, pp. 73–95). There is, moreover, the indirect testimony of the

49 Marquis of Santa Coloma who had told Webster (1888, pp. 150–3) about his meetings with Borrow in Spain and about Borrow's contacts in Seville with a Gypsy leader who also went along with him on his trip to Madrid.

49 See Collie (1982, pp. 192–6) and Knapp (Vol. II, 1899, pp. 41–3) who is surprised that Borrow seems to have made no notes pertaining to the expedition.

50 Historical passages from the section on Hungarian Gypsies in the first edition of *The Zincali* (pp. 11–16) were in subsequent editions (1901, p. 12) replaced by a prayer in the language of Gypsies from Hungary and Transylvania. Borrow had heard the prayer often in these countries, he wrote. He also added a page and a half of text about Wallachia and Moldavia which, however, did not include any personal observations (1901, pp. 12–13).

51 Published by Winstedt (1950, pp. 46–54, 104–15 and 1951, pp. 50–61). He refers here to a manuscript of Borrow's entitled *Vocabulary of The Gypsy Language as spoken in Hungary and Transylvania, Compiled during an intercourse of some months with the Gypsies of those parts in the year 1844 By George Borrow*. This manuscript, which I have not seen, is in the British Museum in London.

52 See Letter 5 from Fraser's 1981 collection.

53 See Shorter (1913, p. 311), who has in mind here a piece by Elizabeth Harvey in *The Eastern Daily Press* of 1 October 1892.

54 Egmont Hake (1881, p. 209).

55 His biographer, Knapp (1886, pp. 121–3), wrote that when he had called on Gypsies in the famous neighbourhoods of Seville and Granada, they had all known who he meant when he spoke of the Englishman.

56 *Hispanic Society*, New York, George Borrow Collection, folder Knapp 1889.

57 See, for example, the newspaper article 'An old Romany' in *Eastern Daily Press* (19 August 1896), in which the journalist lets three Gypsies air their memories from the era when they could still wander about England in comparative freedom. One on this occasion said that he also recalled camping on Oulton in his youth. George Borrow visited them regularly there in the camp: 'He was something of a gipsy himself, and could talk the gipsy language like a Romany.'

58 Letter no. 12 in the volume G. Borrow *Letters to his mother Ann Borrow and Other Correspondents* (1913). A copy of this private edition is in the Berg Collection of the New York Public Library.

59 Borrow's journal covering his trips in Wales is in the Hispanic Society in New York. This citation is from Fraser (1980, pp. 163–73, here 169).

60 See, also, Fraser (1968, pp. 38–47).

61 Borrow *Wild Wales* (1906, p. 557).

62 Fraser (1968, p. 46). The passage from Crabb that I allude to occurs in the 1832 edition, p. 168.

63 Thus Fraser (1994, p. 44, note 25), referring to the draft of a letter from Borrow to Clarendon in the Harry Ransom Research Centre, University of Texas in Austin.

64 From Ridler (1983, p. 390, note 54).

65 See Boswell (1955, pp. 129–33). In 1970 he also wrote a book about his own life *The Book of Boswell. Autobiography of a Gypsy*, in which his grandfather indeed appears anew, but not his relation with Borrow.

66 Boswell (1955, p. 130).

67 Ibidem, p. 131.

68 Such as Smart and Crofton, Groome and Morwood, who all made use of Wester Boswell as an informant in their work on English Gypsies.

69 Boswell (1955, p. 132).

70 This information comes from, among others, Fraser (1994, pp. 29–44).

71 Ibidem, p. 35, referring to Samuel Widdrington *Spain and the Spaniards in 1843*. Part II (1844) pp. 304–6.

72 See Knapp (1899, Part II, pp. 272–3, 276–7) for translations of the letters from

Bailly to Borrow dated 13 and 27 February 1839, from which it can be concluded that Manuel, for a fee, transcribed from memory the Gypsy poetry composed by one Luis Lobo and that Bailly had begun a search on Borrow's behalf for the manuscript of a Gypsy vocabulary that he had hopes of procuring through a friend.

73 On 28 July 1839 Borrow wrote to another Spaniard: 'Since I have been in Andalusia this last time, I have made efforts to collect all that those who call themselves *Maestros del Caló* had noted down' (Knapp, Part II, p. 283).

74 In *The Zincali* (1841, Part II: 59 ff.) Borrow wrote that the manuscript of the collected Gypsy poetry of Luis Lobo had fallen into Manuel's hands in his youth. He had learned it by heart and could later recite it on command. According to Fraser (1994, p. 35), the plethora of people who supplied imitation Gypsy poetry makes it difficult to distinguish specimens of original Gypsy verse in the collections that Borrow published.

75 In a footnote to his article in the *JGLS* Webster (1888–89, p. 153) had referred to this project.

76 In the Borrow-collection from the Knapp legacy in the archives of the *Hispanic Society* there is a list of sources, some Spanish, some Latin, for *The Zincali*. (The list is in a handwriting that I don't recognize.) At the top it is written, in Spanish, that the writers mentioned had treated the evil customs of this useless and destructive rabble, namely the *gitanos* and *Cingaros*. In the left hand margin abbreviated titles appear, many with a note about which chapters had to do with Gypsies. Strangely, Knapp made no use of this extraordinary information in his biography when describing Borrow's sources.

77 This highly incomplete description of titles included in Knapp's biography (Part I, pp. 350–1), he simply lifted, comparison shows, from references to literature in *The Zincali*.

78 The manuscripts in question are Juan Quinones *Discurso contra los Gitanos* (Madrid, 1631) pp. 24 ff.; Torreblanca's *De Magia* (1678); and a series of laws from Ferdinand and Isabella from 1499 until Carl III in 1783 that appear almost letter for letter in *The Zincali*, Chapter 11, p. 151 ff.

79 This was verified on the spot by the Dutch hispanist Piet van der Loo who also wrote the complete titles of the works in question down for me.

80 Thus Fraser (1994, p. 30), with reference to a letter from south Derbyshire to Borrow about Mr. Yuda, who did the copying.

81 From Fraser (1994, pp. 31–3) who refers to a note from Borrow to Usoz to be found in his copy of *The Zincali* in the National Library in Madrid. Usoz had also drawn up a list of words in Caló, as we know from his annotations in the back of his edition of the *Gypsy Luke* in Madrid, according to Fraser recently published by Margarita Torrione as *Diccionario caló-castellano de don Luis Usoz y Río* (Perpignan, 1987) (not checked by me – W.W.). Only, Fraser relates, in Usoz's case there were 1,268 entries, and in Borrow's 2,130. That may be true, yet comparison of the Caló words which Usoz lists beginning with *a* (copies of which are in my possession) with the vocabulary that Borrow published reveals strikingly many similarities.

82 Fraser (1994, p. 37).

83 *The Zincali* (Part I, pp. 63–73). This analysis was carried out by Hitchcock (1994, pp. 45–52).

84 The reference is to the *Didascalia multiplex* (1615) of this prebendary who was highly revered among academics and church authorities and whose treatment of Gypsies in the last chapter of his book contained a concise account of their origins.

85 According to Hitchcock (1994, p. 47), Krantzius (1580) took his material verbatim from Münster (1550), in which he is mistaken. In reality in his *Cosmographie* (1550) Münster had instead strongly diverged from Krantzius' *Saxonia* (1520). Moreover, he, in his turn, had drawn heavily on earlier chronicles, as described in my introduction concerning 'protogypsiology'.

86 Ibidem, p. 49, with reference to Sancho de Moncada (1619) and Juan de Quinones (1631).
87 Ibidem, p. 48, with reference to the *Memorial histórico apologético la ciudad de Logroño* by Fernando de Alvia y Castro (1633).
88 Bright's *Travels* (1818) pp. 109, 188, 519–43, supplement LXV ff. According to Groome in the *Lavengro*-edition of 1901 (p. xxiii) and also Fréchet (1956, p. 196) this was one of Borrow's direct sources.
89 A letter from 1874 from Groome to Leland, cited in Pennell's biography (1906, p. 141). According to Fréchet (1956, p. 196) the original of this letter resides in the British Museum (additional MS 37.173).
90 Bright (1818, p. ix).
91 Ibidem, pp. 109–10.
92 Ibidem, pp. 188–9.
93 Ibidem, p. 530.
94 Ibidem, p. 530 ff.
95 Ibidem, p. lxix.
96 Ibidem, pp. lxxii–iii.
97 Ibidem, p. lxxviii ff.
98 *The Zincali* (1901, pp. 2–3).
99 Ibidem, p. 54.
100 Ibidem, pp. 48–9.
101 Ibidem, p. 354.
102 Ibidem, p. 50.
103 Idem.
104 *The Bible in Spain* (1904, p. 105 ff.).
105 *Romano Lavo-Lil* (1905, p. 210).
106 *The Zincali* (1901, p. 15).
107 Ibidem, p. 200.
108 *The Romany Rye* (1903, p. 263).
109 *The Zincali* (1901, pp. 203–5).
110 *Romano Lavo-Lil* (1905, pp. 179–80).
111 *The Zincali* (1901, p. 110 ff.).
112 Ibidem, pp. 112–3, 255–65 and *Romano Lavo-Lil* (1905, pp. 197–203).
113 Ibidem, pp. 101–2.
114 Ibidem, pp. 261–2.
115 *Lavengro* (1904, pp. 381–97).
116 *The Bible in Spain* (1904, pp. 115–24).
117 *The Romany Rye* (1903, p. 77).
118 *The Zincali* (1901, p. 34).
119 Ibidem, pp. 266–8.
120 *The Romany Rye* (1903, p. 67).
121 *The Zincali* (1901, p. 269–71).
122 *Romano Lavo-Lil* (1905, p. 241–8).
123 Ibidem, p. 248.
124 *The Zincali* (1901, p. ix).
125 Ibidem, p. 299 ff.
126 *The Zincali* (Part II, 1841, p. 5). According to Niemandt (1992, p. 291) the choice of words and themes in the *coplas* reveals that they were not produced by Gypsies.
127 *The Zincali* (Part II, 1841, p. 161).
128 *The Bible in Spain* (1904, pp. 687–8).
129 *Romano Lavo-Lil* (1905, pp. 215–6).
130 Ibidem, p. 260.
131 *The Zincali* (1901, pp. 27–9).
132 Ibidem, p. 14.

133   *The Zincali* (1901, p. 213).
134   *Romano Lavo-Lil* (1905, p. 182).
135   *The Romany Rye* (1903, p. 80).
136   Ibidem, p. 56.
137   *Romano Lavo-Lil* (1905, pp. 176–223).
138   *The Romany Rye* (1903, p. 67).
139   Ibidem, p. 68.
140   *Romano Lavo-Lil* (1905, p. 9).
141   From Ridler (1983, Annex TA–8).
142   See Cunningham (1897, pp. 254–71) for a sketch of the influence of political refugees from continental Europe on the English social climate during the early decades of the nineteenth century.
143   Ridler (1983, p. 175).
144   Ridler draws the parallel (1983, p. 176). See, too, Lady Arthur Grosvenor (1909, pp. 161–79).
145   See Knapp (Vol. II, 1899, pp. 4, 7). For the passage on Whiter in *Lavengro*, see pp. 155–6 in the 1904 edition.
146   Ridler (1983, pp. 176–8) writes that it is not known whether they ever met each other in person but she is convinced of Whiter's great influence on Borrow.
147   Cited by Lady Arthur Grosvenor (1909, p. 162).
148   Ibidem, pp. 164–5.
149   Ridler (1983, pp. 176–7) with a reference to H. Aarsleff's *The Study of Language in England 1760–1860* (1967) pp. 78–9 where the author writes: 'But one wonders how it ever found its way into print.'
150   Cited by Grosvenor (1909, p. 163) from the *Dictionary of National Biography* (1975, pp. 121–2).
151   Thus Ridler (1983, p. 178) with reference to a review in *Critical Review*, Vol. 32, pp. 361–71.
152   Ibidem, pp. 178–206.
153   Ibidem, p. 228, with reference to J.C. Adelung's *Mithridates oder allgemeine Sprachenkunde* (2 Parts) (1806 and 1809). Adelung expounded on the idea of 'language as descent'. His work was extremely influential. In *The Zincali* Borrow names him as one of his sources.
154   Ibidem, pp. 234–6. She points out here the parallels between Herder's *Stimmen der Völker in Liedern* (2nd edition 1807) and Borrow's *Targum* and *Songs of Europe*.
155   Ibidem, p. 249 which refers to Richard Head's *The English Rogue* (1665), to Daniel Defoe – whom Borrow greatly admired – and to Samuel Pegge's *Anecdotes* (1814).
156   Ibidem, pp. 249–50, under reference to R. Robins *A Short History of Linguistics* (1969, p. 181).
157   Discovered by Ridler (1983, pp. 308–9). Borrow is said to have turned down invitations to join a number of other societies.
158   Borrow expresses his belief in Lavater's moral physiognomy, for example, in *Lavengro* (1904, p. 140).
159   This letter of Goddard Johnson, dated 16 January 1843, is in the Norfolk Record Office (Ms 11342, Vol. I). As far as I know, the manuscript *A History of the Gypsies* never appeared in print.
160   See, for example, Cann (1990, pp. 55–63).
161   See Darlow (1911, pp. 1–2).
162   Ibidem, p. 8 for the complete text of this letter from Norwich, dated 10 February 1833.
163   Jenkins (1912, p. 98) wrote, on the basis of Borrow's letter to Cunningham late in December 1832, reproduced in Knapp (II, p. 268), that Borrow was asked to draw up a vocabulary of the language of Mr. Petulengro (n.b., a fictional character) on his return to Norwich.

164   Holmes provides a good introduction to Samuel Roberts (1976, pp. 233–46). There is also the *Autobiography and select remains of the late Samuel Roberts* (1849) in which the author portrays the frustrating years of his youth as a difficult pathway that had to be followed to reach God; a trivial article in the *JGLS* by his grandson *(Roberts 1911–12, pp. 161–6); a family chronicle low on information, Some Memorials of the Family of Roberts, of Queen's Tower, Sheffield, as exemplified by kindred, affinity, and marriage* (1924); and a number of concise passages in Odom (1926, pp. 99–101).

165   See Roberts (1816, pp. 97–124 and 1830). An extensive edition of the latter work appeared subsequently under the title *The Gypsies* (here the 5th edition from 1842).

166   Roberts (1830, pp. v–xii).

167   Ibidem, p. viii.

168   Ibidem, p. x.

169   Ibidem, p. xii.

170   Roberts (1842, p. 293).

171   Ibidem, pp. xxiii–xxiv.

172   On 27 March 1843 Borrow did write to his publisher Murray to send a copy of the *Bible in Spain* to Mr. [Samuel] Roberts, Park Grange, Sheffield. See Knapp (Vol. II, 1899, p. 310). He also incorporated a note in the second edition of *The Zincali* (1843, pp. 351–2) with a friendly reference to the letter that he had received from Roberts and with the declaration that he had indeed read his book. In later printings this addition dropped out.

173   See Borrow's article in *The Athenaeum* (20 August 1836) p. 587.

174   Cann, the archivist of the Bible Society, wrote to me on 26 August 1993 stating that memoranda from the years 1831 through 1836 are missing from the collection. There is only a single letter from James Crabb dated 28 December 1836 in the archive in which he requests a number of Bibles to pass out among Gypsies. Further correspondence with members of the Southampton Committee has not been handed down. The archivists of the University of Southampton and the Southampton City Record Office wrote to me on, respectively, 22 and 13 October 1993 that they, too, had nothing in their collections about this society, or about Borrow or Crabb. Finally the Royal Commission on Historical Manuscripts in London let me know in writing on 9 November 1993 that their indices contained no references to archival material about the society.

175   See the entry on him in the *Dictionary of National Biography* (1891, pp. 132–3) and Fairley (1907).

176   From the biographical lemma, which was written by the famous Gypsy folklorist Groome. The rumour of a marriage, spread by the Gypsy expert Simson (1865, p. 380), is rejected by Groome as unproven. Fairley (1907, p. 2) wrote that George Offer, the editor of Bunyan's works, had told him that Hoyland had been enchanted by a young Gypsy lass.

177   Hoyland (1816).

178   In this vein Groome wrote, in his entry on Hoyland, that Hoyland's book was still of value, although to this he added that it was primarily based on Raper's translation of Grellmann.

179   Thus Hoyland wrote (1816, p. 169) that much of the data he collected was confirmed by Riley Smith, for years the head of the Gypsies in Northamptonshire; his answers were written down by two of his neighbours, both salesmen.

180   Ibidem, p. 155.

181   Ibidem, p. 179.

182   See Mayall (1988, p. 147) and Cottaar et al. (1992, pp. 42–66).

183   Hoyland (1816, p. 186).

184   Ibidem, p. 233.

185   Ibidem, pp. 76–80.

186 Ibidem, p. 222. See Fraser (1992, pp. 112–22) for the historical background of these regulations.

187 Here I am reluctant to leave unmentioned a number of publications about the 'Gypsy colony' in Kirk Yetholm, none of which appreciably enriches the data assembled by Hoyland, except for adding a few personal anecdotes. They form a series that no doubt could be expanded with many titles, and which is of such interest because the pattern of authors who copy each other can be so clearly discerned: Howitt (1833, pp. 219–50 on Gypsies), Woodcock (1865), Lucas (1882), Stuart (1883) and Brockie (1884).

188 See Hoyland (1816, pp. 229–58), under the reference to the *Christian Observer*, Vol. II, p. 91; Vol. VII, pp. 496–7, 712; Vol. VIII, p. 286; Vol. IX, pp. 82–3, 278–80, 554–5.

189 See Mayall (1988, pp. 97–129) for an analysis of attempts to evangelize and reform Gypsies in England during the first half of the nineteenth century when dealing with social problems was still mostly a matter of private initiative.

190 The committee published various reports (cf. list of references). The principal points of the first reports can be found in Crabb's book.

191 The book, moreover, prompted similar initiatives in other parts of the country, in Kirk Yetholm among other places, where the Quakers had entrusted the local cleric, John Baird, with investigating possibilities for converting the approximately 1,000 Scotch Gypsies; he wrote up his findings in a pamphlet that appeared in 1839. In fact Baird based his work wholly on Grellmann and Hoyland, with Crabb as an illuminating example. Through improvement and instruction, he felt that the Gypsies must be brought to the point where they would see the wrongness of their itinerant life and leave it behind them. See Mayall (1988, pp. 111–29) for other such initiatives in London, and in Chettle and Farnham (in Dorset).

192 See under Crabb in the *Dictionary of National Biography* (1887, p. 427). His involvement with Gypsies is also treated at length in Rudall (1864, pp. 132–60).

193 Crabb (1832, p. 27).

194 Ibidem, pp. 27–8.

195 Ibidem, pp. 33–5.

196 Ibidem, p. 38 ff.

197 Ibidem, p. 48.

198 Ibidem, p. 49.

199 Idem.

200 Samuel Roberts (1816, p. 111) had also identified this mechanism in his first publication and, to put the matter in proper perspective, he had pointed out how few convictions followed accusations.

201 Crabb (1832, p. 50).

202 Ibidem, p. 51.

203 Ibidem, p. 75.

204 In this context Crabb (1832, pp. 92–112) wrote at length about the positive experiences of William Blankenburg in the German Gypsy colony Friedrichslohra during the 1830s and about similar conversion campaigns in Bristol.

205 Ibidem, p. 138–9.

206 According to his biographer Rudall (1864, pp. 143–4).

207 Shorthouse (1905, p. 67).

208 See Ridler (1983, p. 367). In this context she refers to Collie who, in his biography, even accuses Borrow of being hypocritical where religion was concerned. Cann (1990, p. 62), on the other hand, would have us see Borrow as a man who throughout his entire life was involved with religion. According to her, he knew the Bible thoroughly and was no stranger to personal spiritual experience or agnostic doubt.

209 See, too, Robertson's article in *George Borrow Proceedings* (1992, p. 17) who discusses Borrow's plans to spread the gospel of Jesus in schools in Portugal 'for the mental improvements of the Portuguese'.

210 Borrow *Bible in Spain* (1904, p. 531).

211 Ridler (1983, p. 399) believes that Borrow truly felt himself to be the Christ figure that he presented himself as being. In this context she cites a passage from a letter to his Danish friend Hasfeld written on 20 November 1838 in which he talks of 'the humble desire of carrying my Maker's Gospel to the end of the old world'.

212 The aggressive missionary activities of Borrow and J.N. Graydon, another field representative of the Bible Society at the time, stirred up such resistance that all activities of the society in Spain were forbidden by the Royal Decree of 10 May 1838. Borrow, however, would not let up, so the church began a fierce campaign to have him put out of the country. The government behaved with more ambivalence because they did not wish to insult England, then amiably disposed towards it, by ungraciously hounding her subjects. See Giménez (1990, pp. 19–31, especially pp. 20–4) for an analysis of 40 articles about Borrow which appeared in the Spanish political and religious press.

213 That Borrow also had an evangelical intention with *The Zincali* is something which I conclude from a letter to Mary Clarke dated 10 January 1839 in which he wrote: 'Pray let Hen [his step-daughter – W.W.] continue to collect as much money as possible towards affording spiritual instruction to Spanish Gypsies. I am shortly about to publish, on my own account, a work which will prove of no slight spiritual benefit to these unhappy people' (*Berg Collection*, Sign. 310947 B).

214 *The Zincali* (1901, p. 281).

215 See, for example, 'The Scholar Gypsy', in: *The Nation* (12 July 1913) pp. 560–1. Cf. further the section which comes later in this chapter about the reception of Borrow's work.

216 *Lavengro* (1851, 1904 edition, p. 362).

217 See Geremek (1992, translated from Polish). His literary–historical analysis with its sociological foundation leads him to the conclusion that in this literature about the poor and rootless, in which Gypsies are prominent, we may speak of a cosmography of the 'anti-society'.

218 Only a few, predominantly descriptive studies in this area are available. The sole comparative study, from 1954 and mentioned already, was published in its entirety a short while ago: Hans-Dieter Niemandt (1992). Another dissertation, only available on microfilm, restricts itself to Germany: Berger (1972). For discussion of the same literature, see also the self-published thesis of Koeman (1993), his Chapter 5 in particular, 'Die Rezeption der Zigeuner-Episode' (pp. 301–64). The somewhat older dissertation by Boas is only mildly interesting in its analysis (1929; a copy is in the library of the University of Amsterdam). This, in part, takes notice of Borrow's two novels. Boas praises the author's Gypsy characters as true to life.

219 This is the assertion of Berger (1972, p. 71) and Koeman (1993, p. 359).

220 In the first edition of *The Zincali* (Part 1, 1841, pp. 83–4) Borrow emphatically praises Pushkin's heroine in *Zigáni* for being a lifelike portrait of a Gypsy.

221 Bloshteyn (1992, pp. 24–9) analyses the influence of Pushkin and Russian Gypsy literature on Borrow's work. She was the first to make recent publications in Russian on this subject accessible to a wider audience.

222 It appeared for the first time in Vol. 16 of the collected works (the Norwich edition). According to Collie and Fraser there is a manuscript version of this translation in a draft dating from the end of 1850 in the British Library. Interestingly, Prosper Merimée, one of Borrow's literary descendants, also translated *Zigáni*, publishing it together with his *Carmen* in 1846 (from P. Henry 1972, p. xxiii).

223 See Bloshteyn (1992, p. 29, note 7) who, in this context, refers to three recent publications about Russian Gypsy choruses: Efim Druts and A. Gessler 'Tsyganskie

khory Rossii', in: *Druzhba Narodov* 10 (1986, pp. 210–30); E. Druts and A. Gessler 'Tsyganskii mif', in: *Druzhba Naroda* 2 (1989, pp. 190–8); I.U. Dombrovski 'Tsygany shumnoiu tolpoi' in: *Vorprosy Literatury* 12 (1983, pp. 187–202). See, too, Fraser (1992, p. 205).

224 *The Zincali* (Vol. I, 1841, p. 8).

225 Ibidem, pp. 9–11.

226 Bloshteyn (1992, p. 27).

227 See P. Henry's Pushkin edition of 1962.

228 *Romano Lavo-Lil* (1874, 1905 edition, p. 241).

229 In the first edition of *The Zincali* (Part I, 1841, pp. 80–6), Borrow had also included several passages from this novella which were omitted in later printings.

230 See Niemandt (1992, pp. 79, 94–5), but especially Wurzbach's article (1901, pp. 391–419).

231 See Niemandt (1992, pp. 71–2) under a reference to various Spanish studies from the nineteen forties. The Gypsy expert Starkie (1960, pp. 131–51) wrote that Cervantes owed most of what he knew to hearsay.

232 Starkie (1960, p. 144).

233 Ibidem, pp. 145–51.

234 From Knapp (Part I, 1899, p. 175).

235 To which Borrow referred emphatically in *The Bible of Spain* (1904, p. 682).

236 See Geremek, who refers to countless works of literature. He interprets the *picaro* as a figure who represents resistance to society, and the picaresque novel as a manifestation of a period of social crisis.

237 The body of reviews which I have compiled consists of 80 pieces. The largest number of them are a combination of many citations intended to generate interest in the writer on the strength of these high points. An extensive critical judgment was a rarity. See Annex 4 for an overview.

238 *British and Foreign Review* (1842, p. 367). In addition see *The Quarterly Review* (1843), *The Monthly Review* (1841, p. 108) and the *Revue des Deux Mondes* (1843, pp. 145–6) in which P. Chasles wrote that Borrow was the friend and chronicler of the race which had escaped from India: 'C'est par l'intimité de ses relations avec tous les bandits et parias de la société espagnole que Mr. Borrow est parvenu à faire un livre tout à fait nouveau' (p. 159) ('It is through the intimacy of his relations with all the bandits and pariahs of Spanish society that Mr. Borrow has come to produce a book unlike any other').

239 *American Whig Review* (1851) and *Southern Literary Messenger* (1857).

240 See, for example, *The North American Review* (1842, p. 75). In a pair of Russian reviews of *The Zincali* (from 1841 and 1842), but especially in the discussion of *The Bible in Spain* (from 1857), emphasis falls on the romantic image of the captivating Borrow. For an analysis of these reviews, see Bloshteyn (1993, pp. 10–17).

241 His reviewer in the *Magazin für die Literatur des Auslandes* (1841, p. 266) was unimpressed. After the appearance of such works as *The Bible in Spain* and *Lavengro*, some began to be annoyed by Borrow's use of fragments of Gypsy language, which they found confusing. Thus the critic for *Blackwood's Edinburgh Magazine* (1851, p. 337) carped: 'We are sick of the Petulengros and their jargon, and Mr. Borrow ought now to be aware that he has thoroughly exhausted that quarry.'

242 Above all in German circles. See L. Diefenbach in *Allgemeine Literatur-Zeitung* (1842, p. 540) and the *Göttingische gelehrte Anzeigen* (1844, p. 998).

243 *Dublin University Magazine* (1843, pp. 251–3).

244 E.g. *The New Monthly Magazine and Humorist* (1841, p. 282), the *Miscellen aus der neuesten ausländischen Literatur* (1842, p. 392) and the *Allgemeinen Literatur-Zeitung* (1842, p. 537). Cf. also the reviewer for the *Revue des Deux Mondes* (1857, pp. 109–43), who found that Borrow had reproduced reality in a naturalistic fashion.

245 *Blackwood's Edinburgh Magazine* (1841, p. 354).
246 See, for example, *The Athenaeum* (1851), *The Literary Gazette* (1851), *Spectator* (1851) and *Fraser's Magazine* (1851).
247 *Tait's Edinburgh Magazine* (1851, p. 271).
248 Of the 26 reviews of *Lavengro* I have been able to trace, 18 were unequivocally positive. Tilford jr. had already found as much, earlier (July 1944, pp. 442–56 and January 1949, pp. 79–96). According to Tilford the biographer Knapp was responsible for introducing into the world the erroneous idea that critics had not done justice to Borrow's two-part semi-autobiography.
249 In *Revue des Deux Mondes* (Brussels 1841, pp. 203–15).
250 Ibidem, p. 203.
251 Ibidem, p. 206.
252 Ibidem, p. 207. According to Emile Montégut in his review of *The Romany Rye* in *Revue des Deux Mondes* (1857, pp. 109–43, here p. 131) the immutability of the Gypsy community was the consequence of the fidelity of Gypsy women to Gypsy moral values and customs, a point Borrow himself also made.
253 See *The Westminster Review* (1841, p. 268) and *New Monthly Magazine and Humorist* (1841, p. 281).
254 *British and Foreign Review* (1842, p. 370).

4

The heirs of George Borrow

INTRODUCTION

The criticism that was formulated in 1874 upon publication of *Romano Lavo-Lil* came primarily from the gypsiologists who were Borrow's heirs; they pointed out their predecessor's indebtedness to other linguists and maintained that the lists of words that he published gave an inadequate idea of Romani as it existed.[1] As for the Gypsy songs and sayings that Borrow included, he was said to have made part of them up or to have filtered them through his own idiom of expression. Yet criticism of his philological abilities had already been heard in the circles of linguists who were busy with Gypsy languages. In the second part of his standard work from 1845, August Pott had written that Borrow's vocabulary lists should be carefully verified – although he himself had lacked the time and the will to carry out such a check, in part because he believed the jargon of the Gitanos contained little of interest, given its slight etymological value.[2] Later prominent figures from the Gypsy Lore Society would say still more trenchant things about Borrow's philological qualities; it is possible, however, that professional jealousy sharpened their tongues.[3] Nor was the biographer Knapp able to muster much respect for Borrow's translations in Caló. He was of the opinion that there was no scholarly basis whatsoever to Borrow's Spanish Gypsy vocabulary, rather it was '… a kind of philologico-literary *gazpacho* (…) badly put together, and the poetic and prose specimens badly copied and accented.'[4] Matters were said to be no better with Borrow's Hungarian Gypsy word lists and the linguistic material that was incorporated in *Romano Lavo-Lil*. The reason to attach importance to Knapp's judgment on this point is that he appears to have mastered the Gypsy languages of England, Spain and Turkey, lecturing on them at an institute for comparative philology in the United States.[5] Appreciation of Borrow as an expert in Romani dialects was subject to rather violent fluctuations in the following decades.[6] Only his publication of the Gospels according to Luke in Romani garnered some praise, particularly in nineteenth-century Spain, even though by modern standards it can no longer be considered authoritative because of the way forms from different Gypsy dialects slipped into the translation.[7] According to Knapp not only did the *Gypsy Luke* exercise great influence in Spain, but he maintains that no small number of Spanish scholars also copied entire sections of Borrow's *The Zincali* without acknowledging their source, adding a new chapter to the tradition of plagiarism.[8]

There can thus be no doubt that many Gypsy experts owed a lot to Borrow's stimulating work. I have already alluded to his role as the inspirer of the literary Romantic school which would explore to the full the themes of the freedom-loving Gypsy and the mysterious Gypsy woman, and certainly not in England alone.[9] Prosper Merimée can be singled out as a direct heir of Borrow's writings on Spanish Gypsies, the creator of the fiery beauty Carmen, a temptress who acquired world renown through George Bizet's 1875 opera.[10] Moreover, Borrow's influence, both thematic and in terms of his spirit, is demonstrable in the publications of the authors who made the Gypsy Lore Society famous. In Mayall's standard work on the Gypsy-travellers in nineteenth-century England, the contribution of the first generation of gypsylorists to the evolution of the image of the Gypsy has already been extensively described.[11] Accordingly I will pay only limited attention to the founders of this society. Much less is known about the contribution in this area of Austro-Hungarian folklorists. This is why I am going to spend more time considering their findings, which will also enable me to make a transition to Gypsy scholarship on the continent where, in Germany in the 1930s, gypsiology would become coloured by a eugenic approach embodying the culmination of nineteenth-century thinking about Gypsies as we have come to recognize it.

THE GYPSY LORE SOCIETY

We may justly call the folklorists, linguists, ethnologists and (amateur) historians who by now have populated the columns of the *Journal of the Gypsy Lore Society* for some 100 years Borrow's principal heirs. The society has yielded a succession of writers whose importance for the development of Gypsy studies cannot be mistaken. They were, however, interested primarily in 'true Gypsies' who were assumed in social, moral and racial respects to be far superior to other travellers and in print had grown into aristocrats of the road.[12] Wholly in keeping with Borrow's spirit, this category of GLS publicists was intent on preserving the remains of Gypsy culture, searching to achieve this end as romantically inspired 'archaeologists' for the last traces of a people they saw as vanishing:

Gypsies are the Arabs of pastoral England, the Bedouins of our commons and wastelands. In these days of material progress and much false refinement, they present the singular spectacle of a race in our midst who regard with philosophical indifference the much prized comforts of material civilization, and object to forego their simple life in close contact with Nature, in order to engage in the struggle after wealth and personal aggrandizement.[13]

The idea of founding such a society was suggested in 1874 in a letter from the American writer and folklorist Charles Godfrey Leland to the orientalist E.H. Palmer from Cambridge. Palmer was at once enthusiastic and replied that he was convinced that, besides linguists, there were a large number of intellectuals from other disciplines 'who are Bohemians in heart and taste'.[14] They would surely be interested in a society of 'Romany Ryes' and appreciate having a journal of their own. Both agreed that, in any event, George Borrow had to be asked to join. The fire of their initial excitement flickered out, however, as suddenly as it had flared up. Only in 1887 would the idea again be put into words, this time in the folkloristic periodical *Notes and Queries* by the mathematician W.J. Ibbetson who collected lists of Gypsy words in his free time. The Scottish amateur-historian David MacRitchie worked the plan further out for him. Thanks to these intermediaries, Leland and other authorities in Gypsy studies came to see eye to eye. Within a year both the society and its journal were accomplished facts, but the founders had not yet agreed altogether about how the society should be set up, or the kinds of participants that they were aiming for. Their discussion revolved around a subject that would become one of the society's most important preoccupations: the Gypsy language. Leland strove the most openly for an exclusive club and initially only wished to admit members with a command of Romani: 'I should prefer a small and poor society, but a real one even with Gypsies in it, to an amateur theatrical company.'[15] MacRitchie and also Francis Hindes Groome, another leading figure in the society, took a more practical position. By themselves interested linguists would produce insufficient funds to cover their own publications, a realization that led them to advocate expansion to include scholars in such fields as history, ethnology and folklore. The next step was to solicit subscriptions from all American and European writers about Gypsies. Thanks to this strategy, the first issue of the *Journal of the Gypsy Lore Society* could appear in July 1888, a little more than six years after Borrow died. The first series of the quarterly would run until 1892, acquiring a great deal of international esteem, even if primarily among the ranks of Gypsy researchers themselves.

It is notable that the founders never officially sought affiliation with the English Folk Lore Society which was established ten years before them.[16] It could be that Charles Leland and Francis Hindes Groome, two leaders from the very first hour, found that Gypsy Lore embraced more than folklore alone. It is also possible that the English Folk Lore Society, in its turn, was not very interested in the products of a marginal population group and, moreover, felt little affinity for the linguistic and historical subjects that dominated the first volumes of the Gypsy journal so strongly. Nor, however, did the GLS ever try to link up with other academic disciplines. For a long time it remained in isolation and its influence on scholarly history, archaeology and ethnology was minimal. The journal depended heavily on the enthusiasm of a small group of fans with no academic training.[17] In point of fact GLS-experts, like the groups they studied, have always functioned on the academic periphery, a position that they have continued to occupy down to the present day. They had (and have) a mouthpiece all their own and rarely published anything outside it. This was a form of splendid isolation that has not proven beneficial for the development of the field.

This holds extremely true for Leland and Groome in particular, two figures who were decisive in determining the image of the GLS during the first decade of its existence. The key concepts for their work include: devotion, hobbyism, affinity with Gypsies, an ability to organize, intelligence, literary talent and editorial skill. In these founders we recognize the characteristic methods and themes of generations of gypsylorists. Considering their exemplary function in the history of Gypsy studies, I will present a brief sketch of their lives and work.

Charles Godfrey Leland (1824–1903) was the son of a rich merchant from Philadelphia, with leanings towards the supernatural which he himself explained as the result of an incident in his youth when a Dutch children's maid cast a spell on him. Already as a child he distinguished himself by writing poems and stories, but his passion for literature and for adventure were only awakened fully during a journey through Europe which he made to round off his studies. He travelled through France and Italy, stopped off in Heidelberg where he fell in with liberal German students, and stayed a while in Paris where he appears to have taken part in the Revolution of 1848. Once back in the United States he elected to lead a journalist's and writer's life, becoming actively involved in the Civil War. As a contributor to countless newspapers he acquired fame with his humorous poems, written in a mixture of English and German, about the adventures of the picaresque vagabond Hans Breitman.[18] After his father's death in the 1870s he left for England where he was a welcome guest in artistic and literary circles and came into contact for the first time with Gypsies.[19] Years earlier, however, he had already read Borrow's books, writing an article on them in 1844 in which he was rather explicit about his view of Borrow's romantic way of looking at Gypsies:

> One of the most remarkable men of the present century is George Borrow, author of the *Zincali* and *The Bible in Spain* (…). Many of his younger days were spent amongst prowling bands of gipsies, gratifying his 'strangely fascinating desire' to understand this most singular race of beings. He resorted to their encampments (…) he mingled with them, but was not one of them, this tall, erect, manly boy, with his thoughtful frow, was even then storing away, in a memory as vast, profound and retentive of its treasures as the sea, the jargon of the Romany.[20]

In England he would set out by himself with a small notebook and stop in at Gypsy camps, a paternalistic stranger dressed in tweeds who delighted in surprising his 'victims' with a comment in their language, a basic facility that he had acquired from the linguistic work of August Pott and others. Here we see the 'collector' at work in full glory. Without fundamental linguistic training he went into the field, determined simply to compile for future generations as many anecdotes, scraps of conversation, borrowed words and fables as possible. With money and small presents he, just like his great example Borrow, came far. Even he, in the long run, began to doubt the effectiveness of this approach. He read aloud to his primary informants from a Hindi dictionary and for each word that they recognized he promised them a shilling. That got him so many words that he became suspicious. Gypsiologists after him were several times more critical of this anything but scientific method.[21] Nevertheless, after the publication of *The English Gipsies and their Language* (1873) and *The Gypsies* (1882), people both in England and abroad regarded him as Borrow's obvious successor, which accounts for why he was invited to become chairman of the GLS.[22] In the ensuing years he turned into a travelling ambassador for the society. Thus, at the invitation of the well-known Hungarian gypsiologist Anton Hermann in 1889, he was in Budapest for the founding of a national folklorist society. A short while before, in Paris, he had argued at a folklorist congress that Gypsies were the most important dispersers of folklore in Europe.[23] For him folk traditions were a kind of religion, the original form of which was still to be found among 'racially pure Gypsies'.

In the course of the 1880s Leland's philological and folklorist interest began to develop ever more intensely in the direction of the magical-spiritual aspects of the Gypsy community; he became intrigued by the mystic side of these people whom he saw as the last representatives of an antique way of life. The result was his *Gypsy Sorcery and Fortune Telling* (1891) which is all about magic ceremonies, spells and incantations, amulets and love potions. In it, however, his orientation was primarily towards publications on east-European Gypsies and he was highly selective about the subjects he included.[24] In imitation of Borrow he none the less wrote that everything he knew came from personal observation, which didn't keep him from inserting long extracts in his books from the work of known European Gypsy experts.[25] Moreover, his material turned out not always to be equally reliable, for he adapted the Gypsy tales and songs which he collected as he thought best, at times restoring them in the original Romani-spirit, as he himself put it. By virtue of his affinity with Gypsies and his poetic talent he considered himself entitled to undertake such reconstructions. When necessary, indeed, he even thought up stories himself, variations of anecdotes that he had heard in 'rough form'.[26] As a result of his work methods, Leland's writings never earned much respect in folkloristic circles. That was not true for his reputation among fellow gypsiologists, who lauded his feeling for the romance of Gypsy life and the evocative, poetic powers he revealed in his descriptions of Gypsy ways and the affection with which he brought his friends to life.[27] It was therefore not suprising that Gypsies greeted him like a brother and placed their trust in him, despite their supposed natural aversion to *gorgios*. Leland was happy to boast of his rapport with them and according to him his tent companions were livelier, politer and more grateful than the 'lower strata of other European or American races'.[28] They were even said to approximate most closely the idealized 'noble savage' of Enlightenment philosophers: '... freer than any wild beast from care for food, free from imaginary cares, no religion, no tie to a spiritual world, no fear of a future.'[29] At the same time he found that they had known how to retain the natural distinction of the Easterner, despite so many centuries of persecution and discrimination against them. Their tactfulness had often struck him. In his time, thanks to their mixing with Anglo-Saxon blood, they were braver than ever before, which on occasion cost them dearly. The 'true Gypsies' were said to still be the freest by nature, less inclined to practise deceit, more frequently to be found in honourable vocations, and more fluent in Romani. This was a romantic-mysterious image which afforded even less room than Borrow had for the actual social and economic circumstances of the groups in England known as Gypsies or travellers.

This practically mystical preoccupation with racially pure Romani, an elite category that was said to distinguish itself morally, socially and culturally from other groups of travellers, was also not foreign to Francis Hindes Groome (1851–1902). It explains as well his resistance to policy aimed at their assimilation (or emancipation) which contained the lurking danger that the Gypsies' unique culture would crumble away still further. The son of an archdeacon from Suffolk, Groome, despite his gifts, left university after two years of loafing about and opted for a life of alternating adventure and hack writing. The story goes that already at an early age he had lessons in Romani from an amateur Gypsy scholar in Ipswich. An encounter at the age of 20 with Borrow may also have increased his 'scholarly' interest in Gypsies, considering the deep impression that the writer made on him.[30] Groome, however, also spoke from experience. According to his own report, at the age of 20 he fell in love with a 17-year-old Gypsy girl, Britannia Hughes, with whom he ran away and travelled for a year through England. With tent and caravan, they lived from his winnings at the horse races. Some years later he described this youthful adventure in a letter:

> You know how beautiful some Romani *raklis* are. This one was by far the prettiest I have ever seen. She was living in Oxford with a sister, who was married to a *gorgio*, & so I saw her repeatedly, & in time she became to me as my wife, though never lawfully *romedi* in a *kongeri*, & so she remained till the day of her death, 10 months ago.[31]

For a long time the young Groome led a rather directionless life, without steady work or financial support from his father. He wound up, among other ports of call, in Göttingen where presumably he studied with the orientalist Theodor Benfey, the founder of comparative research on fairy tales. Next he criss-crossed Germany, Hungary and Romania to visit Gypsies there and transcribe their vocabularies, but he also corresponded with such Gypsy studies luminaries as the French archivist Bataillard and the Austrian linguist Von Miklosich with whom he primarily talked about the Romanes of English Gypsies. He kept comparing words that he had copied down himself directly from their lips with published sources. He also digressed about aspects of his own life history – for instance about the two thousand English Gypsies with whom he was allegedly acquainted already at the age of 21 and the vast vocabulary that he had accumulated over the years, without, however, being willing to publish anything about it because he was loathe to abuse the trust of his Gypsy friends. Until Miklosich's death in 1891 the two men continued to write each other sporadically.

Groome's relations with Gypsies increased in intensity when once again he fell in love with a young beauty, Esmeralda Lock. As a 17 year old she was married off to a Gypsy scholar 40 years her senior, Hubert Smith, with whom Groome also corresponded. When Groome, who had been Smith's house guest, left, Esmeralda followed him, upon which the deceived husband demanded an enormous sum in compensation. The desperate youth felt himself obliged to flee the country with his darling. Only after a great deal of moving about did he dare to go underground in Edinburgh, where he tried to make ends meet as an editor. The case fizzled out once it emerged that Smith had abused his wife and in 1876 the young gypsiologist and his Gypsy love married. Yet this union, too, would not last long. Later Groome said that a Gypsy woman's natural instincts could not be suppressed and that to survive Esmeralda needed the free life among the members of her family. At home she only got on Groome's nerves. This led to divorce, although until the end of Groome's life the pair continued to exchange letters.[32] This bond, and his many contacts with Gypsies, gained him a reputation in Gypsy studies circles where he soon became acknowledged as an authority. Consequently, in 1878 he was offered a prestigious commission to write on Gypsies for the new edition of the *Encyclopaedia Britannica*. Later, as assistant editor-in-chief, he would enter the services of the Chambers brothers, who also brought out an encyclopedia. It is of interest that Groome, as he himself once wrote, had learned a great deal about Gypsies from one of Esmeralda's uncles, the Welsh harpist John Roberts. Roberts spoke Welsh, English and Romanes and could even write the latter, although, according to Groome, he was *not a full-blooded Gypsy* (my italics – W.W.).[33]

For a long time, Groome's ties with English Gypsy families held him back, he claimed, from writing about their language, customs and private life. He knew that they would feel insulted if he exposed their language to the public at large and he forbade those with whom he corresponded on the subject to reproduce the information he sent them in print. The only exception he permitted himself was writing entries for encyclopedias. Until 1880, when giving in – he was then still not yet 30 – he wrote *In Gypsy Tents* about his experiences with Gypsies in east England. Critics found that he achieved a photographic image of the Gypsy community in his book and that his characters breathed the same degree of reality as Zola's.[34] His interest in Gypsy folklore, a field in which he considered himself an amateur, only began late, fixated, as he himself said he always was, with the collection of words.

Groome's oeuvre would remain modest and he was always of two minds about granting the world access to things he learned about in personal settings. Apart from the general articles in encyclopedias that I have mentioned, which were subtly shaded sketches, he acquired his reputation principally for his *Gypsy Folk Tales* (1899), his *magnum opus*. He himself tells us that despite his earlier resolve not to write about Gypsies, he felt compelled to pick up his pen by his indignation over the way in which the socially-motivated philanthropist George Smith from Coalville approached the Gypsy 'question'. He had little sympathy for the preoccupations of scholars and regarded all Gypsies, showmen, travellers and vagrants as a single category of starvelings who lived in pitiful circumstances. This prompted his plea for a government policy to promote assimilation, which would lead to the vanishing of this 'blot on society'.[35] Groome staunchly opposed any such determined offensive to civilize the needy which overlooked the diversity of itinerants. He only agreed with Smith that a survey among Gypsies should be held to determine to what extent problems of criminality and illiteracy existed. Nor did he oppose the registration of caravans and tents, although he did not wish this to be connected to the (forcible) improvement of the Gypsies social conditions. After registration, he believed, they should – just as in Germany – receive an identity card and, upon showing this card, they should then be allowed to set up their camp on traditional pitches. When carrying out registration, he proposed employing people who were conversant with Romani, for he regarded language as the most significant indicator for differentiating authentic Gypsies from unauthentic ones. He was prepared to concede that by now there was no such thing as racial purity, given the frequency of unions between Gypsies and other itinerants. Indeed, this had emerged clearly from his own investigation of the family trees of a number of Gypsy families.

With Groome, genealogical research into the extent of the Gypsies' racial purity made its entry into Gypsy studies. This was an important turning point, despite the contradictory results,[36] the consequences of which would emerge in full a half century later. Groome, for that matter, had difficulty reconciling his own conclusions on racial mixing with his thoughts and observations of the hierarchy within the Gypsy community. He let the Gypsies in his work regularly disparage half-castes, running them down as Irish Crinks and using other currently popular insulting names for people of the road. Yet above all Groome continued his commitment to protecting the way of life and culture of true, racially pure Gypsies who, in his view of things, came from India, spoke Romani and whose character and appearance were such as they had come to be known in the literature ever since Grellmann.

In advocating that the Gypsies retain their own identity, Groome especially emphasized the value of their store of narratives. With his international study of fairy tales, he plunged into the debate then raging in folklorist circles about the origin and dissemination of folk tales. According to the brothers Grimm, fairy tales were remnants of old Aryan myths, a supposition to which Theodor Benfey and the French-man Thomas Cosquin added that India was the cradle from which the fairy tales spread throughout the world as part of both oral and literary traditions. Opposed to these supporters of diffusionism were such evolutionary folklorists as Andrew Lang and Alfred Nutt who maintained that myths had originated in prehistoric times among the primitive ancestors of contemporary man. Traces of these myths were said to be detectable among the primitive peoples of the nineteenth century. Groome's allegiance was with the diffusionists: he claimed that Gypsies, whose language was said to be indicative of their Indian origins, had once, heading westwards, spread Indian fairy tales in the countries through which they passed. Along the way they had picked up new stories, added elements of their own and then, as it were, had sown these in the next country they reached. He thus saw the Gypsies as the disseminators, the hawkers of folklore. As born story tellers they were said to have entertained the nobility at court in bygone days and then later to have brought diversion to peasants in the countryside with their music, dancing and tales. His colporteur theory never really caught on among folklorists because at the close of the nineteenth century the idea of a communal pool of fairy tales rose to prominence. In diffusionist circles, however, people were appreciative of the extraordinary material that he had collected in his most important book, culled from many international collections.[37]

AUSTRO-HUNGARIAN FOLKLORE

In the wake of the Gypsy Lore Society, in the immemorial ethnic crucible of the Donau monarchy at the end of the nineteenth century, a strong interest arose in the cultural traces of the Hungarian and Transylvanian Gypsies. Ethnologists like Heinrich von Wlislocki and Anton Hermann moved among them and were the first to publish the results of their fieldwork. Hermann also took the initiative, in 1903, in founding the short-lived *Gesellschaft für Zigeunerforschung* which put out the *Mitteilungen zur Zigeunerkunde*, an ethnological periodical that can be regarded as the continental equivalent, on a much more modest plane, of the *JGLS*.[38]

A Hungarian Gypsy Census

The Hungarian situation is so interesting primarily because we can compare the assertions of recognized nineteenth-century gypsiologists from the region with the published findings of a demographic survey of Gypsies carried out in 1893 at the orders of the Hungarian Ministry of the Interior.[39] The Ministry wished to sharpen its policy with respect to itinerant Gypsies for reasons similar to those that had already been formulated a century earlier, to wit that itinerant elements should not be part of Hungarian social life and were out of place in a civilized state. They interfered with intellectual and material progress, encumbered state administration, and constituted a danger for public order and morality. In the interests of public safety the government intended, therefore, to put an end to the way of life of its itinerant subjects. A goal which contains an echo of Grellmann's work: 'Der Zweck aber wäre, zu bewirken, dass die Zigeuner menschenwürdige, civilisirte, glückliche Mitglieder der Gesellschaft, nützliche Bürger des Staates, treue Söhne der Nation und des Vaterlandes werden.' ('The aim, however, was to see to it that Gypsies became decent, civilized, happy members of society, useful citizens of the state, faithful sons of the nation and the fatherland.')[40]

The results of the population count of all Gypsies in Hungary and Transylvania contradicted the prior assumptions of the officials involved and of the research co-ordinator, Anton Hermann. Only 3 per cent of the 274,940 Gypsies enumerated turned out to be itinerants (i.e. 8,938 *Wanderzigeuner*); some 7.5 per cent were semi-sedentary; the over-whelming majority had already been sedentary for a longer while. In selecting Gypsies to interview, the local authorities who conducted the census with questionnaires could not rely on objective criteria such as language, way of life, external characteristics or self-definition. In determining who was eligible to be counted, a simple criterion was used: was a person known as a Gypsy? At the local level popular anthropo-logical-racial notions and tradition were followed for determining who belonged to the Gypsy people, rather than any formal indicator. Reality, however, proved more varied than expected. For example, only 30 per cent of all those surveyed reported Romani as their mother tongue; 20 per cent were more or less familiar with it; and more than half claimed Hungarian or Romanian as their first language.[41] The vocations of those included in the census also displayed much less deviation from the norm than anticipated. The total number of employed Gypsies in the survey population was 134,454. From the 154 different vocational activities that they reported, a differentiated picture of their social status emerges. Thus the 17,000 who said they were musicians (12 per cent) were not merely settled, but to judge by the evaluation in the census, they were respectable and earned a good living. The same was true for the (copper) smiths, collectively about 36 per cent of the group. There were also brick makers (9 per cent), Gypsies who worked in agriculture (2 per cent) – including landowners and tenants – traders/peddlers (3 per cent) and artisans/shopkeepers (36 per cent).[42] Yet the survey of their vocational activities summarized here did not lead to a sensitive perception of how they functioned economically. The idea prevailed that many of their reported lines of work simply provided camouflage for illegal transactions, that they made too little use of their abilities and consumed more than they produced. In this regard the census spoke of *'ein beträchtliches nationalökonomisches Deficit'*.[43]

The findings of this survey also offer a number of indications that Gypsies in central Europe had advanced a long way towards integration,[44] but the published results never led to any change in the generally negative image of this population category as socially immiscible. That is not so strange if we realize that the census was meant to provide a basis for preparing government measures to curtail the Gypsies' existence. That certain facets of the diverse ways Gypsies led their lives deviated from the standard idea of the 'average citizen' – they had no steady work, did not always live in well-maintained housing, and were predominantly illiterate – appeared to provide sufficient incentive for subjecting them to separate policy. Moreover, ethnographers of a folklorist inclination concentrated exclusively on the part of the Gypsy population that was itinerant and lived in tents, further reinforcing the existing image. The same was true for Anton Hermann, who had analyzed the census data, thus placing his expertise directly in the service of the government. By taking such a position he brought about a shift in Gypsy studies, from a scholarly-folklorist interest to the performance of a policy supportive role. Although little more may be known about Hermann's functioning as a policy adviser, on the grounds of what we do know we can consider him as a transitional figure between George Borrow and Robert Ritter. Almost half a century later, in Germany, it would be Ritter who combined his intellectual interest in Gypsies still more directly with activities at the policy level.

HEINRICH VON WLISLOCKI

The best-known east European representative of this tendency in Gypsy studies was Heinrich von Wlislocki (1856–1907). Until recently he has been regarded as an authority in the areas of story-telling, social organization, and the religious imagery of Gypsies.[45] The growth of legends about him after his death was inspired primarily by the thought that Von Wlislocki's intimate knowledge of the world of the Gypsies had been accumulated while he travelled about with them for an indeterminate period of between three to 12 years. Moreover, until the 1930s, people were convinced it was marriage to a Gypsy that enabled him to get to know the world about which he wrote from the inside. In 1986, Ruch was the first to point out that such an interpretation is untenable and that Von Wlislocki had only a limited familiarity with central European Gypsies. Ruch was able to make important factual corrections in accepted opinion about the gypsiologist's life and work after he came across a correspondence consisting of 178 letters and cards in the legacy of Arnold Hermann.[46] This evidence, which spans the period from 1880 to 1896, supports the conclusion that Von Wlislocki only spent a few months among the Gypsies in the summer of 1883, followed by some weeks in the winter of 1886. Furthermore, in the 1880s the recently graduated student found himself obliged by a lack of funds to write as many small pieces for magazines as possible, many of them consisting of translations of Gypsy fairy tales. His industry resulted in a list of some 80 publications on Gypsies. He and Hermann also at times published under each other's names, if it was convenient.

Von Wlislocki, son of a tax collector in Kronstadt (Transylvania), studied German, philosophy, and Sanskrit at the University of Klausenburg. Under the influence of the theory of one of his teachers about the Indian origins of the greater part of the themes and motifs in European folk narratives, Von Wlislocki arrived at the hypothesis that Gypsies, as migratory carriers of culture, had brought these stories from India to the Balkans. In his work, right to the very end he continued to accept the premise that Indian origins were at the root of Gypsy texts, trading, and religious imagery. His study of German was a second important influence; in Klausenburg the rather free translation of folk tales was common practice; one hardly felt bound by the language of the original. Through the lack of comparative textual editions it is no longer possible to ascertain the accuracy of Von Wlislocki's free interpretations of oral transmissions. This is no trivial matter when we consider that Von Wlislocki has been accused of having copied original texts from other (non-Gypsy) collections. We also know from his letters that he screened and abridged the material collected, anticipating possible objections on the censor's part or deciding himself that certain texts offended prevailing norms of decency.[47] At the very least the consequence of this practice is that the reader is offered a body of texts adapted to contemporary taste, as well as reconstructions of the fabric of ideas common to a small group of itinerant tent-dwelling Gypsies in Hungary-Transylvania – without the author's rendering further account.

From the personal letters an image emerges of a lonesome man, constantly undermined by illnesses, a problem drinker living in poverty because for years he was unsuccessful at finding a teaching position.[48] He struggled to support himself by building bird cages – sold by a Gypsy woman![49] In 1880, a year after finishing his studies, he published his first volume, containing 40 Gypsy songs, under the romantic title *Haideblüten*, a title remarkably similar to an anthology published seven years previously by Martin Möckesch. The title aside, Ruch unjustly suggests that Von Wlislocki was imitating this song collection.[50] From his own work we can see that he turned to the subject after being alerted to it by his teacher Meltzl, who himself, several years before, had published a number of Gypsy folk songs.[51] There was no ethnographic interest driving the enterprise. Von Wlislocki's motive was rather to preserve the 'archaeological' remains of a vanishing culture. In the process among other materials he made use of a body of folk songs collected by his grandfather Andreas Roth during the period 1818–25 while he travelled aimlessly through Transylvania and Saxony.

It appears from the letters that, in the course of 1887, a controversy arose between Von Wlislocki and Hermann over remarks about style and a rebuke for plagiarism (*Raubwirtschaft*), on the occasion of the appearance of Wlislocki's *Volkskunde*.[52] At various times in his life he had also published anthologies in which the collections were recognizable or a reissue of previously published contributions. Whoever reads the fragments of the letters Ruch cites, in which the nervous fits and grave illnesses from which Von Wlislocki suffered are described, can only be amazed that he still managed to find time to devote himself to his work. Not until 1890 did he manage to land a post in Zombor at a small gymnasium where, among other subjects, he taught French. In this way he secured a little peace. Later he lived and worked in Wildbad Jegenye in Transylvania, and, from 1894 onwards, in Budapest.[53] The 1890s were the most productive years of his life, although, as just mentioned, practically all of his publications at this time contained condensations of earlier work; Von Wlislocki never performed (new) fieldwork after the 1880s. None the less, he gained social status through his work. He joined the *Ungarische Ethnologische Gesellschaft* and contributed many articles to Hermann's periodical. His stability, however, did not endure and, in 1899, Von Wlislocki succumbed to insanity.[54]

In his analysis of Von Wlislocki's work methods, Ruch first invokes Hermann's criticism, which amounted to chiding his friend for working too hastily, permitting his texts to be printed without very much scholarly reflection. To which Von Wlislocki himself answered as follows:

> Was die Art meines Arbeitens anbelangt, so wäre es gut, wenn jeder so arbeiten würde, ich bin kein 'Gelehrter', auch kein Genie u. arbeite das auf, was u. wie ich es finde (…) Ich kann nicht eine Arbeit tagelang liegenlassen. (As far as the nature of my work goes, it would be a good thing if everybody worked like that, I am no 'scholar', nor a genius, and plainly use what I find and how I find it (…) I cannot put aside a piece of work for days.)[55]

In a manner analogous to the way in which others dealt with such themes as superstition among Romanians or animals in folk tales, he selected from his collections of Gypsy texts, those which fitted together best. The texts acquired their specific meaning through the context of this comparative ethnology. As the years passed, Hermann's criticism of his friend's linguistic competence became more acerbic. His commentary on the errors in the Gypsy grammar of Archduke Joseph Karl von Habsburg (patron of the *Gesellschaft für Zigeunerforschung*), a book on which not only he but Von Wlislocki, too, had worked, were shrugged off by the latter. Others, eventually made public their reservations about Von Wlislocki's qualities as a linguist.[56]

In addition to choosing for his anthologies the best and most beautiful texts from his collections of Gypsy poetry, when he had different versions of a tale at his disposal he picked the one which best lived up to his literary-aesthetic norms and was consistent with his theory of the Gypsies' Indian origins. In form, content and ideology, he aspired with his anthologies to create a romantic, idealized image. Thus many fairy tales start off with 'once upon a time', the texts are literarily embellished, and in the figures who appear one can detect the stereotypical picture of nomads who set out from India, complete with deviant customs. In his search for relics from Indian or Indo-German prehistory, he selected his mythical motifs from different cultural regions (France, Germany, Poland, Turkey) without acknowledging his sources.[57] This was a method that left him even more dependent than Grellmann a century earlier on his powers of imagination and his gift for pointing out analogies. In this context Von Wlislocki bragged that as a 'brother' of the Gypsies and an initiate of their mysteries he had managed to penetrate to the heart of their customs. They were said to have considered him a clan member – the usual self-legitimizing claim prevalent among Gypsy experts since Borrow: '... nach meiner – übrigens schwer erwirkten – Aufnahme konnte ich aber unter den Mitgliedern "meines" Stammes unbesorgt wandeln; doch nicht im Kreise der andern Stämme, deren "Genosse" ich nicht bin.' ('... after my acceptance – not easily achieved – I could move freely among the members of "my" tribe; but not in the circles of other tribes, whose "comrade" I am not.')[58]

Elsewhere, however, he commented that, as a 'naturalized' Gypsy, he was recognized everywhere as a member of this ethnic group. The reader doesn't learn anything more about the nature of his relations with these Gypsy groups and must rest content with the assertion that in their most unadulterated form they were to be found only in the region of the Donau. Ruch places such passages against the background of the conservative culture pessimism that dominated the work of Von Wlislocki and many of his contemporaries. One of its characteristics was the glorification of traditional folk culture and an anxiety in the face of modernism[59] which manifested itself as a virulent rejection of social-democratic ideas and the demands of the burgeoning workers' movement. For folklorists such as Von Wlislocki the threat lay precisely in an improvement of the material and social circumstances of those who belonged to this folk culture, for this would lead inevitably to the corruption of the object of their study: the 'authenticity' of the people in question. He regarded them as the representatives of a natural, uncultivated way of life, people among whom the submerged cultural heritage of human civilization could still be experienced. That further clarifies why Von Wlislocki only studied the small group of intinerant tent-dweller Gypsies whom he considered representative of the true Gypsy life. In such a perspective the (half-)sedentary Gypsies in cities were merely social-democrats who 'von dem Kosmopolitismus das Schlimme, aber weniger das Gute angeeignet haben' ('who have adopted the bad rather than the good of cosmopolitanism').[60] Tent Gypsies, he believed, also wanted nothing to do with those who had settled, seeing them, it was said, as traitors to the ancient culture that they originally carried with them from the Indian *Heimat*. He argued that, because of their criminal behaviour, they were expelled from the original group of nomadic Gypsies and that, having intermarried with the bottom echelons of the sedentary population, they had lost every feeling of solidarity. Von Wlislocki allowed himself to be swept along by such culture pessimistic and romantic notions about people who still lived in the era of mythological prehistory and who, despite their moral shortcomings, were alleged to still have retained something of the purity which modern life, in his opinion, so sorely lacked.

With this vision Von Wlislocki made a name for himself in Gypsy folklore – one which he has kept right up to today, even though already during his lifetime his work prompted many questions.[61] That it nevertheless earned him an enduring reputation within Gypsy studies can perhaps only be understood by pointing out the more or less accepted practice in comparative mythology in those days of exercising a free hand while compiling collections of fairy tales and stories.[62] All the same, what did the criticism amount to? First of all in his *Vom wandernden Zigeunervolk* Von Wlislocki had copied many passages from Richard Pischel and Johann Schwicker, giving a twist to their findings whenever that worked out better for his argument.[63] He was also said in his translations to have often sacrificed the meaning of original texts to meter and rhyme. Ruch bluntly writes that he was seldom able to keep in check his 'Neigung zur lyrischen Verniedlichung und geschwätzigen Geste' ('taste for lyrical innocence and eloquent gestures').[64] Furthermore reasonable doubts have arisen about the many Gypsy analogies that Von Wlislocki tracked down in the course of the years. Not only did some ask themselves whether the themes and motifs were so gypsy-specific,[65] but the collective's fantasy was also subjected to discussion.[66] During his life and in the following decades Von Wlislocki was harshly criticized. In 1943 Tancred Borenius published three fragments from his correspondence with the Finnish gypsiologist Arthur Thesleff who, in 1898, had undertaken a journey through Hungary and Transylvania and was said to have shown the texts of Von Wlislocki's publications to his informants. This test led him to make the following judgment:

> [I have satisfied myself as to the complete atheism of the Gypsies.] Wlislocki is wholly irresponsible in my view. Almost everything he says is his own imagination, scientific sensationalism. He turned Gypsy and died amid fumes of alcohol. I simply ignore all his works. I have met his Gypsy friends who, on being told of his accounts about the various deities, the visions of ghosts, etc. burst out laughing, delighted that they had been able to fool him so completely.[67]

Later criticism was aimed not only at the ingenuity with which Von Wlislocki had given a 'Gypsy tint' to his folklorist assertions but also at an entire generation of folk tale collectors who did not know how to free themselves from their national expectations and mythological pre-suppositions. The spirited attacks that appeared in the 1960s, which specifically took exception to Von Wlislocki's study of the language of Transylvanian Gypsies, dismissing what he wrote as philologically neither authentic nor accurate, can be seen as latter day extensions of such criticism.[68] Thus it appears that most of the linguistic material that he presented did not come from Transylvania but from Slovakia and had already been published in Hungarian by György Ihnátko in 1877. He, for that matter, in his turn, was said to have taken a great deal – without acknowledgement – from a linguistic publication by Anton Puchmayer, based on the speech of Bohemian Gypsies, which had appeared in Prague in 1821. Ihnátko had adapted his material in such a way that his derivations were indistinguishable from the Slovakian Gypsy words. Von Wlislocki went a step further by modifying the phonetic spelling of his derivations to fit the rules of Sanskrit. This induced critics to recoil: 'Wlislocki's Beschreibung der Zigeunersprache ist und war für die Sprachwissenschaft völlig wertlos.' ('For linguistics, Wlislocki's description of the Gypsy language was and remains totally worthless.')[69] After an analysis of 15 of the fairy tales that he published, one again reaches the conclusion that mystification was being practised, and thus that a body of fictitious Gypsy narratives were being presented as real, and were put into Romani (or some variant of Romani) by Von Wlislocki himself. Serious reservations are accordingly called for about the reliability of his publications as genuine sources of nineteenth-century popular Gypsy culture.

ANTON HERMANN

The scholarly career of Anton Hermann (1851–1926) is worthy of mention. The major collection of Hungarian Gypsy folk poetry that he and Von Wlislocki planned may never have materialized,[70] but from his many folkloristic activities it appears that he always served as spokesman for Austro-Hungarian Gypsy studies. In 1889 he established the *Ungarische Gesellschaft für Volkskunde*, two years after founding the periodical *Ethnologische Mitteilungen aus Ungarn* which continued to appear under his editorship until 1911, producing several special numbers entirely devoted to Gypsy studies.[71] From the very beginning it was Hermann's intention to provide his journal with a continental counterweight to the *Journal of the Gypsy Lore Society*, whose initial appearance in 1888 he, as representative of the 'klassische Land des Zigeunertums',[72] had experienced as an insult. His periodical, however, secured few substantial contributions, certainly in comparison with its English rival, which was an outlet for researchers from many countries. Ruch interprets the enterprise as nothing more than a publicity offensive by Hermann, motivated in part by his need to guarantee the financial support of patrons interested in Gypsy studies, especially Archduke Joseph von Habsburg.[73] His later proposal for a *Gesellschaft für internationale Zigeuner- und Vagantenkunde*, which incorporated a number of principles that Ruch found meaningfully expressed (for example, that research should be action-oriented and aimed at improving the Gypsies' social circumstances) also never advanced beyond the conceptual phase. Every few years Hermann tried to breathe new life into his plans but his undertakings were doomed to remain weak reflections of the firm position occupied by the English sister-organization, GLS – certainly after the GLS journal started a new series in 1907. From this time onwards, to be sure, Hermann began in his publications to refer rather explicitly to the corrupting influences of Gypsy culture (songs, music) and narrowed his field of vision to the Hungarian nation.

FRIEDRICH SALOMO KRAUSS

In the work of folklorists we encounter a number of standard arguments with which they justify their involvement with groups who occupy such a marginal position in social consciousness, as we can conclude from a small collection of Gypsy songs published by Moritz Rosenfeld in 1882.[74] The most well known of these is that they occupy themselves with the cultural-historical products of Gypsy groups to 'save-what-can-be-saved'. They search for characteristic evidence of a vagabond people whom they believe will not outlive modernity and are menaced with extinction. In short, acting with due haste, they record the relics of a vanishing natural folk. The paradox here is that they attribute hardly any uplifting or educational value to these culture products. The songs are said to be superficial, with no content to speak of, and the researcher, beforehand, apologizes for publishing them, pleading their uniqueness as his justification.

The contradictoriness of this common attitude, which combines the social rejection of a (presumed) people with interest in its cultural products, appears all the more striking when compared to the work of one of the rare researchers who had an eye for both the social-cultural circumstances and the cultural-historical products of the Gypsies. Such a figure was Friedrich Salomo Krauss (1859–1938),[75] who not only analysed the state of methodology in folklore at the turn of the century, but also earned his spurs as an empiricist. His study of sources revealed to him that most fairy tales, songs and religious imagery that folklorists had accumulated were the common property of all the peoples on earth. Indeed, through the consistent application of the principles of comparative ethnology, Krauss believed he could demonstrate that, for example, as far as themes and motifs were concerned, Von Wlislocki's collections of the folk poetry of Transylvanian and Hungarian Gypsies were virtually identical to those of non-Gypsies from Slavic-, German- and Romanian-speaking areas. Later Krauss went a step further by postulating, in the introduction to his own collection of Gypsy humour, that there had always been a lively interchange between Gypsies and the peoples surrounding them.[76] Certainly since the fourteenth century, the white Gypsies (the so-called assimilated Gypsies), according to Krauss, had lived together with the Serbs and Croatians and were so integrated that ethnographic research into specific cultural components did violence to reality. Krauss demonstrated his awareness of contact between population groups. He was constantly discerning parallels in customs, imagery, narratives and forms of social interaction where others accentuated existing differences, real or imaginary. In addition – and this was something unique for his day and for a long time thereafter – he expressed himself in notably positive terms about his Serbian Gypsies, to whom he hoped to have done justice in his publication.

ENGELBERT WITTICH

The criticism mentioned here levelled at Von Wlislocki by his contemporaries and by later gypsiologists did not really tarnish his reputation, nor prevent others from making use of his work freely.[77] This can be illustrated by the work of Engelbert Wittich (1878–1937), a controversial amateur publicist, a number of collections of whose writings have recently been issued by Joachim S. Hohmann.[78] The appearance of Hohmann's first anthology in particular sparked vigorous protests from the *Verband deutscher Sinti und Roma* because Wittich was said to have betrayed Gypsies and Jews to the police during the Nazi era. This did not keep Hohmann from bringing out the same work again later with modifications, arguing that Wittich himself as *Landfahrer* had suffered under the Nazi regime and that he harboured no doubts about the value of his writings. That Wittich enjoyed some credit was primarily the result of his being taken to be a Gypsy. Hohmann maintained in 1982 that Wittich was of Gypsy descent,[79] and as early as 1909, R.A. Scott Macfie, the former secretary of the *Journal of the Gypsy Lore Society*, appealed to the members of his society to support the impecunious Wittich. Finally they had among them a 'full-blooded Gypsy', one who was even prepared to brave the accusations of his comrades that he gave away their secrets. Doubts about his origins were dispelled by expert witnesses:

> Engelbert Wittich aus [sic!] Pforzheim is so exceptional a man that, were it not for the careful inquiries of Geheimrat Prof. E. Kuhn and Mr. B. Gilliat-Smith, and the personal investigations of Prof. Karl Brunner, one might have suspected that he was no true Gypsy. He is, however, a full-blooded Romanischel.[80]

The mere idea that it was a member of this ethnic group who was writing about his own culture increased the authenticity of his work in the eyes of these authors. The same held true for Krauss, who considered Wittich to be an inspired observer, even though in 1927, in a foreword to the latter's book, the former wrote that the author owed his information primarily to his Gypsy wife.[81] Siegmund Wolf, in his standard work from 1960, proved far more critical, at least about the linguistic material Wittich presents, for which Wolf argues he had Joseph Denner, his wife's former husband, to thank. He was also said to have too easily tossed together German and south-European material without any justification: 'Wittich, der sich gern für einen Vollzigeuner ausgab, hat nachweislich manchen gutgläubigen Zigeunerforscher und Romani-philologen erfolgreich getäuscht.' ('Wittich, who liked to pose as a full-fledged Gypsy, succesfully deceived many a gullible gypsiologist and Romani-philologist.')[82]

This remark of Wolf's induced Ruch to investigate whether Wittich had possibly borrowed his published material from other sources. In the process he chanced upon a significantly large number of parallels with the work of the criminologist Liebich from 1863, and an even stronger indebtedness to Von Wlislocki's publications on amulets and (superstitious) religious imagery.[83] He also suspected Wittich of having used the sketches that Von Wlislocki had made of Gypsy amulets and statuettes as models for commissioning the manufacture of the objects themselves, then reproducing these in his publications accompanied by practically the same descriptions. According to Ruch, empiricism figured only in Wittich's 1927 collection on south German Gypsies, *Blicke in das Leben der Zigeuner* where the author drew exclusively from his own experience. He went on to add that a certain distrust of Wittich, who served as spokesman for Gypsy scholars involved in policy decisions during the Nazi era, is called for. Thus Eva Justin – whose own relevance to this study will emerge in the following chapter – in her 1944 dissertation on Gypsy children states explicitly that she had received personal information from Wittich concerning a married Gypsy couple.[84]

With this colleague of the youth psychiatrist and eugenist Robert Ritter we have arrived at the Nazi era when scholars and political leaders approached 'the Gypsy problem' like mindedly. This period also marked the culmination of the power of academics and policy makers to make definitions and impose labels. The consequences for Gypsies were enormous, and, especially during time of war, fatal, but the repercussions in the post-war period should also not be underestimated. In order to make the connection comprehensible, I will first turn to the discussion which went on in Germany during the 1950s and 1960s about reparations for Nazi victims.

NOTES

1 See Groome (1874, pp. 666–7), who wrote that Borrow had helped himself generously to material in Bright's *Travels in Hungary*, and see the Orientalist Palmer (1874), who rejected Borrow's book as an anachronism which contained nothing the author hadn't already published 40 years earlier. In 1905 the tide had turned to the extent that a reviewer in *The Academy* wrote that Borrow's feeling for Gypsy life and humour was unique and that he might justly be called the greatest 'Romany Rye' of them all: 'There is but one Romany race, and Borrow is its prophet' (p. 751).

2 Pott (1845, Foreword). The gypsiologist Predari also dismissed Borrow's vocabulary as of little value and wrote in his *Origine e Vicende dei Zingari* (1841, pp. 260–1) that Borrow as a rule had only allowed corrupt Castillian words and the Arabic terms which Gitanos in Spain used to pass for Gypsy language. From Ridler (1983, p. 64).

3 Thus Ridler (1983, pp. 72–3) who carefully attempts to defend Borrow's name as a 'Romani' scholar.

4 Knapp, Part 1 (1899, pp. 350–2).

5 Thus Ridler (1983, p. 78, note 46) who derived this information from a letter Knapp

sent from Madrid in March 1870 to the editorial superintendent of the *British and Foreign Bible Society*.

6   See Ridler (1983, pp. 80–92), who examines Borrow's controversial reputation as a linguist at length.

7   Ibidem, p. 118, under the reference to a short article by Carlos Clavería, 'Gitano-Andaluz Devel-Undevel', in *Romance Philology*, 11, 1 (August 1948) pp. 45–6.

8   See Knapp (1886, pp. 121–3). According to Ridler (1983, p. 117, note 166) the tradition of silent reproduction began with Francisco de Sales Mayo's *El Gitanismo, Historia, Costumbres y Dialecto de los Gitanos* (Madrid: Victoriano Suarez, 1870) and was continued by Tineo Rebolledo *Gitanos y Castellanos* (Barcelona: Casa Editorial Maussi, 1909); F.M. Pabanó *Historia y Costumbres de los Gitanos* (Barcelona, 1915) and B. Dávilla and B. Pérez *Apuntes del Dialecto 'Caló' o Gitano Puro* (Madrid, 1943). The last three authors referred to neither Borrow nor Mayo.

9   See, for example, Niemandt (1992, pp. 146–7) on the great influence of Borrow's works in French-speaking territory.

10   In this context I would like to refer to Northup (1915) and to Fraser (1951, pp. 2–16) who came to virtually the same conclusions 36 years later without, strangely enough, citing Northup's publication.

11   See Mayall (1988, pp. 71–93) on the existing definitions and stereotypes of Gypsies that also circulated among members of the *Gypsy Lore Society*.

12   Ibidem, p. 73 ff., who offers an illuminating résumé of the most important pre-occupations of the *Gypsy Lore Society* and the consequences of their definitions. See, too, Acton (1974) for a critical sociological analysis of historical shifts in the concept of the 'true Gypsy' in England.

13   Smart and Crofton (1875, pp. xvi–xvii). In this section I will depend heavily on the findings of Voerst van Lynden who, under my supervision, wrote a master's thesis on the GLS. For purposes of orientation I also read Leland's *The Gypsies* (1882; here the 1924 Boston/New York edition with an introduction by his biographer Elizabeth Robins Pennell) and Francis Hindes Groome *In Gypsy Tents* (1880; here the reprint from 1973 with a foreword by A.J. Clinch). In addition, at the University of Pennsylvania I consulted the typescript of Varesano's unpublished doctoral dissertation on Leland (1979).

14   Pennell (1906, p. 163).

15   Ibidem, pp. 198–9.

16   The illustrious history of this society is recounted in Dorson (1968).

17   David MacRitchie, one of the founders, claimed that, during the first recruitment drive for members, only one British professor had enrolled and in the following years there would be no change in the situation. For a long time the total membership remained limited, with no more than some 100 persons and institutions. Above all foreign Gypsy studies experts kept the society going, such figures as Von Miklosich, Kopernicki, Von Sowa, Von Wlislocki and Hermann. See Voerst van Lynden (1993, pp. 10–12) on the membership of the GLS.

18   See Varesano (1979, pp. 19–66) for the literary fad which Leland ushered in with his creation of this Rabelaisian figure.

19   Ibidem, p. 82, based on Leland's memoires from 1893.

20   Ibidem, pp. 127, 139 under the reference to Leland's article, 'George Borrow and the Gipsies', *The Nassau Monthly*, 3, 3 (January 1844) p. 79.

21   Groome, for example, and Sampson. See Voerst van Lynden (1993, pp. 56–7).

22   Voerst van Lynden (1993, p. 53).

23   Varesano (1979, p. 134); here she cites Pennell (1906, p. 206).

24   Voerst van Lynden (1993, p. 61) who here relies on E.B. Trigg *Gypsy Demons and Divinities* (1973, p. 24).

25   For example, Von Wlislocki, Friedrich, Krauss and Gerard; see Voerst van Lynden (1993, p. 58).

26 Varesano (1979, pp. 89–92, 131–2).
27 Voerst van Lynden (1993, pp. 59–62).
28 Ibidem, p. 63, under the reference to Leland's *The English Gipsies* (1873, p. ix).
29 Ibidem, p. 63, under the reference to Leland (1873, p. 24).
30 Ibidem, p. 20, under the reference to a number of Groome's reminiscences published in *The Bookman* in 1893.
31 In an undated letter from the 21-year-old Groome to the well-known Austrian (Gypsy) linguist, Franz von Miklosich. From a pack of 20 letters from Groome in the Austrian National Library, *Handschriftenabteilung*, Autograph 134/110 (1–20) in Vienna, which contains the entire correspondence with Miklosich. With thanks to the slavist Prof. Stanislaus Hafner from Graz who drew this collection to my attention.
32 Dora Yates (1953, p. 105).
33 Voerst van Lynden (1993, p. 25) under a reference to Groome's *Gypsy Folk Tales* (1899, p. vii).
34 Ibidem, p. 25.
35 Mayall (1988, pp. 130–49) discusses the work and campaigns of the demagogic George Smith from Coalville at length.
36 Mayall (1988, pp. 83–5) has shown convincingly that nineteenth-century Gypsy experts, with their probing into family trees, family names and language, did not succeed in arriving at a conclusive definition for the category of 'true Gypsies'.
37 See Voerst van Lynden (1993, pp. 36–8) who in her reconstruction of Groome's diffusionist theory depends upon Dorson (1968, pp. 270–3, 306–7).
38 The main line of the findings presented here comes from Ruch (1986, pp. 191–315). I checked all his assertions about the secondary literature that he consulted, but not his statements based on analysis of archival sources and difficult to trace publications.
39 See *Ergebnisse* (1895, pp. 1–98). Ruch, however, relied on the brief and also imprecise summary in the periodical *Globus* 70 (1896, pp. 321–2).
40 *Ergebnisse* (1895, p. 4).
41 Ibidem, p. 57.
42 Ibidem, pp. 73–98, about vocations.
43 Ibidem, p. 73.
44 This can also be deduced from the following figures: in 7,962 of Hungary's 12,693 municipalities, Gypsies turned out to be living there, in 7,220 permanently, in 2,874 mixed with the rest of the population (40 per cent) and in 596 (8 per cent) partly mixed, partly segregated. In Transylvania, the place for Gypsies, the largest number of municipalities were located which had an integrated population. See *Ergebnisse* (1895, pp. 27–8).
45 See Ruch (1986, pp. 198–296).
46 At present in the library of Attila University in Széged, Hungary. See Ruch (1986, pp. 207, 346).
47 Ruch (1986, p. 266) deduces this, among other conclusions, from the following undated passage: 'I am not sending any Gypsy fairy tales – although I have almost 100 of them of a highly obscene nature and poor textual quality – so that the *K. Gesellschaft* edition will not be delayed.'
48 This picture is confirmed in an article by one of the founders of the *Gypsy Lore Society* written after a visit to Von Wlislocki in Zombor. See MacRitchie (1913, pp. 46–55).
49 According to Ruch (p. 222), who here draws on a letter from Von Wlislocki to Hermann dated 5 October 1885, this female vendor was his only contact in these years with the Gypsy world.
50 It is solely on the basis of the title *Haideblümchen* that Ruch (p. 217) suggests Von Wlislocki was imitating Möckesch. He could not check further because, according

to him, the volume couldn't be found. I consulted the copy in the Romany Collection of Leeds University and noticed no similarities. In the forewords to both anthologies the authors make it clear that the songs collected are those sung by Gypsies in Transylvania.

51 *Jile Romane. Volkslieder der transilvanisch-ungarischen Zigeuner. Originaltexte mit gegenüber stehenden Übersetzungen von H. Meltzl* (1878).

52 Ruch (pp. 227–8) refers here to letters from Von Wlislocki dated 29 March, 28 April and 30 May 1887.

53 The correspondence up to 1890 in Hermann's legacy is written in German; the 20 letters and cards from the period 1890 to 1896 were in Hungarian. Ruch did not get around to translating them, which accounts for the meager information he offers about the last period preceding Von Wlislocki's madness (p. 233). I myself have never set eyes on the letters.

54 Ruch (p. 234) has this information from the obituary by Hans Helmolt in *Das literarische Echo*, 21 (1907) pp. 1632–5, which also revealed that Von Wlislocki had married a certain Fanny who, on 8 March 1907, had her brother-in-law, Alfred von Wlislocki, write a letter to Hermann claiming her inheritance from her husband. Ruch couldn't find out what ultimately happened with that material and observes that we still know little about the last period of Von Wlislocki's life. To this he adds that the German researcher, Kirsten Martins-Heuss, once, resolved to write a biography of Von Wlislocki. Her widower, Herbert Heuss, told me in a conversation, however, that she died without acting. Ruch (p. 347) also writes that from a letter he has inferred that Von Wlislocki's whole life long he had kept a kind of diary. All reasons to launch further study of his legacy.

55 Ruch (p. 231) cites here from a letter dated 17 October 1890.

56 E.g. Meyer (1893, pp. 107–17). This criticism, however, was restricted to a comment on the lack of a linguistically responsible method in Von Wlislocki's work, without wishing to question its cultural-historical value.

57 Ruch (p. 243), in this context, alludes among other criticism to the objections of Von Wlislocki's contemporaries A. Hermann and F. Krauss who condemned as unscientific his construction of an analogy system of myths, which was, according to them, a faulty approach practised by many folklorists at that time.

58 Von Wlislocki (1890, p. 78).

59 See Ruch (pp. 245–9).

60 Von Wlislocki (1890, p. 166).

61 See Ruch (pp. 259–315).

62 See Schenda (1983, pp. 24–8) who invokes a large number of telling examples of this method of working which was common in the second half of the nineteenth century.

63 See Willems and Lucassen (1990, p. 34).

64 See Ruch (pp. 265–7). Here he also cites the similar criticism of W. Golther in *Archiv für Anthropologie*, 20 (1891/92) p. 249. This is remarkable, for, according to MacRitchie (1913, p. 51), Von Wlislocki himself read Golter's review as praise.

65 The questioners included Francis H. Groome in *Chamber's Encyclopaedia*, V (1892) p. 489. Already prior to Von Wlislocki Groome to be sure had pointed out in the *Encyclopaedia Britannica*, X (1879) p. 615, that Gypsies had fulfilled an intermediary's function between Asia and Europe as story tellers. Yet within Europe, too, according to him, they had spread folkloristic themes and motifs.

66 See, for example, the review by his friend Anton Hermann in *Ethnologische Mitteilungen aus Ungarn*, 2 (1890/92) p. 181. MacRitchie (1913, p. 54) also wrote: 'It is not unlikely that a lively imagination may have led him to indulge in a considerable amount of embroidery.'

67 Borenius (1943, pp. 1–9, here p. 8). Borenius, however, did not go more deeply into Thesleff's criticism of Von Wlislocki. He introduced the citation with the comment

that his friend had great admiration for George Borrow.

68 Ruch (pp. 279–84) here deals extensively with the criticism of Jiri Lipa *Über die Fragwürdigkeit des Zigeunerforschers Heinrich von Wlislocki* (typescript, translation from the Czechoslovakian magazine *Slovo a Slovesnost*, 29 (Prague, 1968)); and with the remarks of Karel Horalek 'Beitrag zur Textologie orientalischer Märchen' in *Asian and African Studies*, II (1966) pp. 24–37. I have verified neither of these titles.

69 See Ruch (p. 281) who here quotes Lipa (1968, p. 7).

70 See Ruch (1986, pp. 284–303) about Anton Hermann's activities. In the library of Attila University in Széged (Hungary) there is an extensive legacy from him, administered in the mid-1980s by Dr Istvan Monok. There are also many 'Gypsy poems' in it that were never published, written in Hungarian, albeit without the original transcribed texts. Hermann actively worked on the 1893 census which registered the social conditions of Gypsies in Hungary, and the collected data, in all more than 4,000 pages, is also housed with his legacy.

71 These special numbers appeared very irregularly and with different titles, such as *Organ für allgemeine Zigeunerkunde* (1893–97) and *Mitteilungen zur Zigeunerkunde* (1903–4, 1911). All issues can be found in the Romany-Collection in Leeds.

72 Hermann (1890–92, p. 193).

73 See Ruch (1986, pp. 296–303). The archduke himself (1833–1905) also published a Gypsy grammar that received a mixed reception among his contemporaries. Through it, he acquired some fame, certainly within the Gypsy Lore Society. Following in the footsteps of his ancestors Maria Theresa and Joseph II, he even ventured to try to reform a colony of 36 Gypsy families on his own land in Alcsúth. The project is said to have lasted no longer than a year.

74 For Moritz Rosenfeld's 'Lieder der Zigeuner', *Ungarische Revue* (Leipzig, 1882) pp. 823–32, see Ruch (1986, pp. 303–5).

75 Ibidem, pp. 306–15. From the way he handles Krauss's work, Ruch reveals his own ideological preferences very emphatically. He prefers scholars who aspire through their work to improve the Gypsies' lot.

76 See Krauss (1907). In this anthology, for the rest, I found not a single (critical) reference to Von Wlislocki.

77 In addition to Ruch's dissertation itself, see the critical comments of Hohmann (1980) and Fraser (1989, pp. 3, 8).

78 See Hohmann (1984), Hohmann (1986), Wittich's *Beiträge zur Zigeunerkunde* (edited, introduced and published by Hohmann, 1990).

79 See Hohmann (1982, p. 29) and Wittich's Foreword (1910, p. 268).

80 Cited in Ruch (1986, pp. 320–1) under a reference to *JGLS*, 3 (1909–10) p. 1.

81 In a foreword by Wittich (1927, p. 11).

82 See Wolf (1987, p. 40).

83 See Ruch (1986, pp. 323–33) where he treats a large number of passages which Wittich took, often word for word, from Richard Liebich's *Die Zigeuner in ihrem Wesen und in ihrer Sprache* (1863) and Heinrich von Wlislocki's *Volksglaube und religiöser Brauch der Zigeuner* (1891). The similarities are indeed significant. Moreover, I found the image on one of Von Wlislocki's amulets in more or less identical form in Crabb (1832, p. 44) who spoke of a Gypsy soothsayer who had rendered the emblem of her calling in metal, 'a half-moon, seven stars, and the rising sun'.

84 See Ruch (1986, p. 335) for the reference to Justin (1944, p. 31). Let me mention here that this, the only reference in Justin's work to Wittich, occurs as a casual remark in a citation.

5

Robert Ritter (1901–51):
eugenist and criminological biologist

INTRODUCTION

Whoever sifts through German jurisprudence from the 1950s and 1960s concerning reparations for suffering incurred under the National Socialist regime encounters a reluctance, if not a downright unwilling-ness, on the part of the judiciary to recognize Gypsies as victims of the government's policy of racial persecution.[1] Until as late as 1963 the Federal Court adhered to the guideline that Gypsies had only been persecuted on racial grounds after the implementation of the Himmler decree on 1 March 1943, from which moment the deportation of Gypsies and 'those like Gypsies' to Auschwitz followed. In the preceding years all policy measures were said to have constituted part of attempts to combat asocial befdcccccccchaviour and to prevent crime; and after the outbreak of the Second World War in 1939, policy had been motivated by military and security considerations (fear, for example, of espionage activities).[2] It is true that, for many years, the courts in Germany's several states did not have access to all kinds of policy documents that came into being during Nazi predominance, so it was difficult for them to arrive at a judgement regarding the legal validity of the claims that Gypsies were making. The idea that, as undesirables and criminals, they presumably had deserved confinement in labour and concentration camps, con-formed so closely with the prevailing (prejudiced) social view of Gypsies, that we need not search far for an explanation of the judges' hesitation to confer compensation. Only in the case of the Jews had the courts found that there had been persecution from the very beginning on racial grounds – in other words, the Nazis had attributed their supposed deviant and anti-social behaviour, their criminality and other such taints directly to racial descent.[3]

The turnabout in judicial opinion that manifested itself in the early 1960s was partly a consequence of the fact that relevant documentation became available. Here the real eye-opener was a scholarly publication by the historian Hans Buchheim in which he showed that from the time of the evacuation of 2,800 Gypsies to occupied Poland in May 1940, at the instigation of Heinrich Himmler (head of the SS and German police) one has to speak in terms of a policy of racial persecution.[4] In the wake of these new insights, there followed in 1961 the first judicial opinion in which it was acknowledged that Gypsies and others considered their equivalent[5] had, along with the Jews, been defined as belonging to an inferior race since the Nuremberg race laws of 1935.[6] The Himmler-decree of 8 December 1938 ordered that Gypsies and 'those with Gypsy blood' had to be registered nationally and undergo biological examination to determine their race. From that moment on they were exposed to racial persecution.[7] These registration and examination procedures were condemned by the Federal Court in 1962 as measures of National Socialist oppression. Subsequently, those who had been compelled to submit to those measures were eligible for reparations.[8] In practice, however, it proved to be no easy matter for Gypsies to demonstrate that they had in fact been persecuted as a consequence of these ordinances.[9]

The tardy implementation of the *Wiedergutmachung* for Gypsies was in part a result of the lack of written evidence that would have enabled Gypsies to show that they had been evacuated, sterilized or deported because of their assumed membership of a 'foreign race'. This was especially true for the racial diagnoses that were written out by research organizations to provide government bodies, and the police in particular, with a conclusive answer to whether or not the (forcibly) examined individuals belonged to an undesirable population category. In addition to the police centre in Munich which had concentrated on Gypsy affairs since 1899, after 1933 the *Reichsstelle für Sippenforschung*, also a division of the Ministry of the Interior, occupied itself with Gypsies, whom they classified as non-Aryan. Yet in actuality it did not turn out to be easy to agree upon precisely who met the requirements to be labelled a 'Gypsy'. As a bold move to resolve the growing struggle between the research bureau and police organs, a separate *Erbwissenschaftliche Forschungsstelle* was set up within the *Reichsgesundheitsamt* (Ministry of Public Health) in 1936. This was placed under the leadership of the Tübingen youth psychiatrist Robert Ritter who, from then on, with his racial and criminal-biological studies of the non-sedentary, would impose his ideas on how these groups were to be defined at the policy level, beginning with Gypsies and those 'of mixed Gypsy blood'. Indeed, in 1962, when the Federal Court spoke of coercive measures,[10] it meant the research activities of this very institute, which would later be called the *Rassenhygienische und bevölkerungsbiologische Forschungsstelle*.

According to the judge, Ritter agreed to such an extent with Nazi racial doctrine that he believed in the superiority of the Aryan race and allotted Gypsies to the category of non-Aryans. He felt racial-hygienic measures were called for to prevent the Gypsies from mixing with

Germans. The registration, which he completed between 1937 and 1940, with files on all persons who were known to be Gypsies, part Gypsy, or 'Gypsy-like', together with the scientific conclusions that Ritter attached to his research, were of fundamental importance to the policy of persecution enacted against these groups.

Thus the intertwining of science and policy in German Gypsy studies during the 1930s and 1940s reached a culmination that prompts a number of questions. First of all, was it at all possible during the Nazi era to carry out independent scholarship and was Ritter's career exemplary for these years or an exception to the rule? Was he a Nazi fanatic who saw his chance to prove scientifically that the German people must be purged of a 'hostile race', or was he not? Did he simply put into words the prevailing ideas of his time and his branch of research? If this last formulation should prove accurate, how can it be explained that a social scientist could identify to such an extent with the goals of an inhumane political system? When we look through texts about the fate of the Gypsies under the Nazis, we notice that Ritter's ideas are seldom examined in detail and there is little understanding of what made him tick.[11] There appears to be unanimity that Ritter was not merely one of those responsible for the genocide practised against Gypsies, but that he was also directly involved.[12] Was that indeed true, or, if we look deeply into the matter, was Ritter no more than a follower whose deeds had far-reaching consequences?

In what follows I will try to formulate an answer to these questions, relying in part on a number of biographical sources about Ritter that I recently discovered and which have enabled me to learn about the youth psychiatrist's background.[13] These consist of a series of personal letters from the period between 1908 and 1947 and an autobiographical manuscript from the summer of 1945. Here Ritter not only sketched a self-portrait, he also analysed different phases of his scientific and personal development. Furthermore he went into expansive detail about the nature of the research he conducted and his position with respect to the regime. I am well aware that the manuscript was written after the fall of Hitler and that certain passages should therefore be interpreted as self-justifications. Wherever possible I have checked Ritter's words against official (archival) sources.

THE AMBIVALENT LIFE HISTORY OF ROBERT RITTER

Advocate for his own youth

On 14 May 1901 in Aken, Martha Ritter-Gütschow brought Robert Ritter into the world. Her husband, a naval officer, died when his son was 15 years old.[14] Later Ritter described his father as an authoritarian man whom he had always looked up to and whose aura he found daunting: a man of rigid principles who made a profound impression on a boy who, as he himself wrote, had inherited extreme sensitivity from his mother. The lack of self-confidence which accrued from his relationship with his father was something that Ritter himself says he tried to compensate for through a limitless eagerness to learn. His father's dominance, however, meant that he proved to be a late-bloomer. Between the ages of 14 and 17 he suffered, above all, from fits of severe depression for which his parents showed little understanding.[15] Others also failed to show any recognition of the symptoms of an adolescent crisis, a crisis which, Ritter explains looking back, clarifies his later interest in the problems connected with bringing up children. This professional concern of his which was thus said to have been spawned by feelings of abandonment and frustration, was further strengthened by events during the First World War. When, at last, as a 16-year-old he ended up seeing an understanding, psychoanalytically-trained neurologist, the foundation was laid for a life-long fascination.

In his autobiography Ritter describes how, at an early age, he already discerned that reason, upbringing and experience did not determine the course of peoples' lives, but rather laws of character and disposition did. Reasoning further along these lines he regarded goodness as something that was not a personal achievement and he rejected any connection between wickedness and guilt because fate determined the course of one's life. As a cadet in the Prussian military academy in Lichterfelde, where he was judged to be too much a civilian by nature to pursue a military career in the footsteps of his father, Ritter experienced the truth of his ideas at first hand.[16] Nevertheless, in 1919 he reported for duty as a voluntary border guard in the east of Germany. His apprenticeship would be brief, for after two months he came down with a paratyphus infection that landed him in the military hospital in Königsberg. In the years during the aftermath of the First World War and the collapse of the German empire, Ritter felt an enthusiasm for the folk ideals of the German national *Jugendbund*,[17] a youth movement in which conservative and liberal strains of thought coexisted. The war had been lost and a part of Germany's youth wanted to join forces to build a new future for Germany in Europe.[18] They formed an alliance in their common fight against democracy as a form of government. They were against the Weimar Republic and for a *Wahlaristokratie*, rule by the elite, but they were for nationalistic purity as well and against 'alles Undeutsche und Fremde, gegen alle Unnatur, gegen "Schmutz und Schund in Wort und Bild"' ('everything un-German and alien, against everything unnatural, against smut and trash in word and picture').[19] At the time Ritter would very much have liked to have made a name for himself in politics, but relations after the war were such, in his mind, that he instead chose to concentrate on more social goals for the time being.

In the meantime he complied with the emphatic wishes of his mother and grandmother and, in the spring of 1920, began work as an apprentice in a branch of the German Bank in Koblenz. He made better use of his free time by performing services for a certain clergyman Gräber who had started up a Christian, charitable help organization and was committed to allaying the distress of youth. This man inspired Ritter to pursue social work. All other employment palled beside his idealistic leisure-time activities, so that in April 1921 the bank dismissed him.[20] Since his mother no longer wished to support him, he decided to prepare himself for a state examination and subsequently to study.[21]

The versatile student

Ritter's years as a student were characterized by his breadth of interest in medicine, the social sciences and the humanities. He moved about a great deal, from university to university, and his compulsion to combine scholarship with practical experience led him to devote most of his free time to work in clinics, psychiatric centres and reformatories. His ambition was so multifaceted that at an early stage he wanted to be a doctor, a psychologist and an educationist, as well as a social and spiritual counsellor. His physical and mental condition were so unstable, however, that hypertension or a serious infection would inevitably put him out of action from time to time. From Ritter's letters to his grandmother, and later to his wife, a picture emerges of a young man who invariably looks on the dark side of things, is troubled by periods of depression and is incapacitated regularly by nervous excitation. During his initial semesters at university he attended classes in philosophy and medicine in Bonn and Tübingen where he showed particular interest in practical psychology and child psychology. He also audited lectures on theology and philosophy, and during his vacations acquired practical experience working in the nursing home Stetten in Remstal where he had mentally deficient and epileptic boys as patients. After six weeks there he fell gravely ill and appears once again to have contracted paratyphus. Ever after he was to suffer from a chronic stomach and intestinal disorder.

He studied in Marburg in the ensuing semesters, with youth psychology among his subjects, and he came into contact with instructors in the Theology Faculty and with Norwegian students. During the summer of 1922 he improved his skills as pedagogue in Ilsenburg, a country house for problem children in the Harz. He took the work extraordinarily seriously. When he received a considerable sum as a bonus for his extra effort from the father of one of his charges, he decided to take a trip to visit German Borstals. Next he headed for the Swiss city of Bern. At this time, too, he twice went to a spa in the mountains to receive treatment for asthma. He would continue to be plagued by asthma and hay fever so that every June, until far into the 1940s, he invariably sought relief in the mountains. In his own terminology this was without doubt a question of an inherited susceptibility to allergies.[22] For his studies, after Bern, he also travelled to Copenhagen (in Denmark) and Oslo (in Norway) where he became enamoured of a Norwegian student. He broke off with her, however, because in her youth she had suffered, just as he had, from moods of gloom. They considered themselves and each other as poor marriage partners in terms of hereditary science. This stand on principle indeed weighed heavily on them.[23] The inflexible way in which Ritter later acted as a marriage counsellor was possibly rooted in his own Norwegian attachment.

In May 1924 Ritter returned to Marburg to sit for examinations for his bachelor's degree, then to move on to Munich where the interface between medical studies and pedagogy especially seized his interest. For the first time in Munich his life consisted of more than only studying and he built up an extensive circle of friends who put him in touch with professors, publishers and artists. At the time religious, metaphysical and parapsychological subjects held everyone's interest so that even Ritter, later so caustic in his opposition to all kinds of sorcery and superstition, came into superficial contact with them: 'ausserdem selbst schon zum Beispeil hypnotische und telepathische Experimente gemacht hatte' ('besides which, for example, he himself had already carried out experiments in hypnosis and telepathy').[24] Furthermore he established relations with local psychotherapists and took part in *Erziehungsberatungsstunden* (pedagogic consulting hours) during which parents could seek advice about the best way to bring up their children. During vacations, among other jobs, he worked on the psychopathology ward of the teaching hospital where degenerate girls, as they were called in those years, were housed. At the same time while fulfilling the practical requirements of his study he came into contact with youths who were 'misfits'. In 1927 he acquired his degree in philosophy *cum laude* for his thesis on *Sexualpädagogik* written under Alfons Fischer.[25]

Munich was also the city where Ritter came to know his future wife, who was born as Hildegard Cesar in Cologne in 1901. Although it was art history that interested her, on his advice, she first dedicated herself to nursing, with her eye on presently becoming a doctor's wife. Shortly thereafter, Ritter travelled on to Heidelberg, in continuation of his studies, to work under the youth psychiatrist August Homburger, with whom he also wanted to take his state examination in medicine. Among his acquaintances there he counted Marianne Weber, the widow of the sociologist Max Weber who died young; she maintained a salon frequented by many of the prominent personalities of the day. The winter after Ritter was awarded his degree, he enrolled in Berlin to deepen his knowledge of youth psychiatry. There he crossed paths with the leading figures of the democratic woman's movement; as a consequence of his dealings with them he grew estranged politically from the 'freikonservativen Einstellung' that had been characteristic of his adolescent years. He married on 10 January 1928 while in Heidelberg. Two years later, under Homburger, a man whom they both admired, his wife would earn her doctorate for her thesis entitled *Die seelische Entwicklung schwer erziehbare Kinder* (Mental Development of Problem Children).[26] Ritter took yet another university seminar, one on criminal law pertaining to youth, and he also attended lectures on 'social hygiene' – developments that were not without importance considering Ritter's later development.

Ritter made his first acquaintance with the NSDAP at the end of the 1920s. Together with an eccentric whom he'd called 'uncle' since his youth, he went to a party meeting where Hitler gave a talk. Ritter wrote that he was appalled by the fanaticism with which Hitler spoke of the future and by his biting criticism and total belief in his own infallibility. It fed his concern about the growing popularity of the NSDAP in 1929. Yet, according to Ritter, many Germans continued to be confident that the 'ship of state' would pass into the hands of trustworthy people before it was too late. In an emergency the army could always intercede to maintain order. People then saw Hitler still primarily as the drummer he himself claimed to be. Idealistic and politically engaged young people in Heidelberg, Ritter among them, united in the meantime in the *Arbeitsgemeinschaft für jung deutsche Politik*, a kind of middle-of-the-road political party of conservatives, democrats and the socially and religiously inspired. This initiative caught on in other regions and cities of Germany and a national party with a broad base appeared to be in the making. In the elections of the summer of 1930, however, only the *Sozial-demokratische Partei* (SPD) made real gains. As a result those with other convictions became isolated. Ritter's political activism had in the interim cooled down in any event, above all because he had shifted his field of study abroad.

In 1930 in Heidelberg Ritter earned his degree as a doctor of medicine, once again cum laude, with his study, later published as an article, on the *Vererbung der allergischen Diathese*. The text analyzed the case histories of a family circle consisting of 101 people.[27] Next he went, with his wife, to work in the youth sanatorium of Gmelin in Wyk on the Frisian Island of Fohr. There, from November 1930 to March 1931, they had a grant from the E.R. Schmid Foundation in Paris for an internship. They attended lectures by Heuyer in the *Clinique de neuro-psychiatrie infantile*. Drawing on their network of contacts in Heidelberg, they came to meet various French ministers and bank directors, but also writers such as Viennot and the later fascist Pierre Drieu La Rochelle[28] with whom they exchanged ideas about a unification of Europe worth struggling for and shared his anxieties that developments in Germany would impede realizing such solidarity. From Paris Ritter and his wife moved on to Zürich where they successfully applied for positions at the psychiatric institution Burghölzli.[29] Not long before, at a congress, Ritter had been deeply impressed by a talk given by the director on eugenics and the tasks of social-medical science. In Zürich, as head of the division, he was in charge of giving advice about youthful delinquents, while his wife was employed as an orthopedagogue. They also took advantage of the opportunity to participate in a psychotherapeutic seminar given by Carl Gustav Jung.

Eugenics and Nazism

During the time he studied and worked in Switzerland a shift took place in Ritter's thinking that would not only prove decisive for his later positions both in matters of science and policy, but would also help clarify his attitude towards young people. Prior to Zürich he had seen himself first and foremost as an advocate who took the side of youth, but through his work in the clinic the idea won ground that sometimes it was more urgent to protect the community against young people who had gone astray. His advocacy, as he himself dubbed it, was torn between alternatives from then on. The general guideline to which he subsequently clung was to decide, for each case, which side was on the receiving end of injustice and therefore was in need of protection. In other words he no longer wanted to be carried away by his sympathy for juveniles and he considered it his task to provide help preventively. He came to the realization that psychotherapy was no panacea for all ills; some youths might reap benefits from in-depth treatment but not those with an inherent disposition that was incurable. This understanding led him to the conviction that, for patients who were in some way abnormal or incurably sick, only eugenic intervention could do any good.[30] In April 1932, when Ritter returned to Germany, he therefore regretted that he ascertained there were as yet no possibilities on hand, just as in Switzerland and the United States,[31] to prevent certain people from reproducing themselves, a measure which in his opinion was justifiable from a socio-medical point of view. At a congress on eugenics in the service of national well-being organized in Bonn during the summer of that year by the German Society for Psychic Hygiene, Ritter observed that the idea of voluntary sterilization of persons with hereditary defects indeed had supporters in Germany but that there were political reservations about the racial hygiene legislation that had been drafted.[32] To deepen his understanding of the subject, Ritter attended a seminar for three months at the Social Hygienic Academy in Berlin during the summer semester of 1932.[33]

At this time Ritter was once again intensively engaged in the stormy political developments going on in Germany, participating actively in politics and debating with the supporters of national socialism. Thus in newspaper articles he openly opposed what he considered to be the party's nihilistic ideology:

> Leitet die National-sozialistische Partei die Jugend heute nicht irre, leitet Sie ihr bestes Wollen, ihren gesunden Instinkt, ihre lebendige Begeisterung nicht auf falsche Bahnen, wenn Sie unduldsam nationalen Geist und soziales Empfinden nur bei sich sieht, wenn Sie gleichzeitig andersdenkende deutsche Volksgenossen als Verräter hinstellt, wenn Sie gegen fremde Meinung rohe Gewalt setzt, Unfrieden und Zweitracht schürt? ('Is the National Socialistic Party not leading today's youth down the wrong path, is it not misdirecting their best will, their healthy instincts, their lively enthusiasm, when they lay exclusive claim to an uncompromising national spirit and social feelings while at the same time depicting fellow Germans who think differently as traitors, when they unleash rough violence against differing opinions, and sow discord and division?')

In this piece in the *Kölnische Zeitung* of 11 January 1931 Ritter wrote that while it was true that he could identify with the concepts 'national' and 'social', he rejected the NSDAP's ideology. In the same newspaper on 25 January 1931 Ritter became the butt of a response to his article by a young NSDAP supporter, a law student, who accused him of an excessively passive method: 'Aber, Herr Dr. Ritter, es geht nicht an, Duldsamkeit zu predigen und zu gleicher Zeit die Altersgenossen im nationalsozialistischen Lager verständnislos zu kritisieren.' ('But, Dr. Ritter, it won't do, to preach tolerance and at the same time to criticize meaninglessly contemporaries in the National Socialistic camp.') In Berlin he attended sessions of the *Reichstag* which evoked from him the remark that, in this period of crisis, popular representation had lost touch with all seriousness and sense of responsibility. Like many of his German contemporaries, he was convinced that the authority of the state had to pass into the hands of a strong politician who would send the representatives home.[34] President Von Hindenburg was already an old man besieged on all sides, according to Ritter, by many with ambition who hoped to exercise influence over him.

In August 1932, Ritter relocated to Tübingen where he had applied to Director Robert Gaupp for a post as head of the children's division of the University Psychiatric Clinic.[35] He also set up a polyclinic advice service for matters connected with child-raising, an *Erziehungsberatung*, soon consulted in large numbers by people from the surrounding area: parents, social workers, teachers from Special Elementary Schools and civil servants who worked with youth. This success, however, was over-shadowed by the Nazis' seizure of power as a result of which, Ritter wrote in 1945, the atmosphere of the clinic changed instantly, in part because of the *Gesetz zur Wiederherstellung des Berufsbeamtentums* (Law to Re-establish the Professional Civil Service) which went into effect on 7 April 1933 making it possible to discharge state employees who were Jewish or politically undesirable.[36] The regulation meant that several Jewish colleagues left the clinic without fanfare. It was no longer possible to enter into public debate over political affairs – indeed, the presence of the new doctors who came as replacements and who, it went without saying, were closer in outlook to the NSDAP would have been enough to act as a deterrent to free discussion. Fear of informers arose, especially after the *Reichstag* fire when countless people were rounded up and shunted into concentration camps. Everyone soon knew about the methods of torture that the Nazis were using there. From then on anyone who was not a party member had to be careful. Moral pressure to join the party also increased; to fail to do so meant risking one's job and income. As the years passed many actually succumbed. This did not hold true for Ritter who consistently refused to become a party member. Indeed for years he lived with the fear that the letter which he had written while still a student in Switzerland to Von Hindenburg expressing his criticism as a psychiatrist of Hitler's authority-undermining behaviour[37] would one day end up costing him his position, if not his life.[38] For a long time he could justify his reservations about joining the NSDAP by pointing out the need to protect the independence of his research. Illustrative of the ambivalent attitude of those days is Ritter's description of the way in which, after initial confusion about the Nazis coming to power, the notion gained ground that things could still work out well with this party, for idealists who were known to be trustworthy were also accepting membership. In 1945 he wrote that it was only in the second half of the 1930s when he perceived that every turn for the better would prove illusory. According to him, the Nazis had no clear party programme and he considered their hatred of Jews as the single unifying element of what they stood for. It is certainly more than likely that Ritter himself, as without doubt most Germans at that time, was afflicted with anti-semitic resentment.[39]

There was only one area in which he greeted the party's aspirations with approval and even worked hard himself to see them realised: eugenics. In 1934 the Nazis had laid a legal basis for eugenics with their *Gesetz zur Verhütung erbkranken Nachwuchses* (Law to Prevent the Birth of Offspring with Hereditary Illnesses) which provided for the possibility of proposing people with a hereditary illness for sterilization, on grounds of 'health considerations'.[40] In the context of the post-war discussion of what the concept of 'eugenics' entailed, the following statement of Ritter's is pregnant with meaning: 'Man brauchte fürderhin zwar das international anerkannte Wort Eugenik nicht mehr, sondern sprach nur noch von Rassenhygiene, was jedoch dasselbe bedeutet.' ('From now on one did not use the internationally recognized word *eugenics* anymore, but instead spoke only of racial hygiene, which, however, meant the same thing.')[41]

Wholly in keeping with the spirit of these principles, in the spring of 1934, alongside his *Erziehungsberatung*, Ritter set up a *Rassenhygienische Eheberatungsstelle* where couples who intended to get married could secure advice about the risks (including the legal risks) that they would face where genetic inheritance was concerned.[42] In January of 1936 he became a member of the *Erbgesundheitsgericht* for the region of Tübingen.[43] These activities led to Ritter being regularly asked to give talks and organize courses on racial hygiene issues.[44] He also began to build an archive in Tübingen with files about the hereditary health of people who consulted him, the *Erbgesundheitsarchiv* which, in the following years, continued to expand. While attending congresses abroad Ritter did not dare speak about internal relations in Germany, fearful that the *Gestapo* would take him into custody as an enemy of the state. Scholarly recognition was coupled with a degree of self-censure, certainly where political matters were concerned. Actually, life in its entirety in Germany until 1945 was governed by a taboo on the subject of National Socialism. Afterwards Ritter himself described the falsity characteristic of the period as follows:

> Zu den überwachten Spielregeln des öffentlichen Lebens gehörte aber der sogenannte 'deutsche Gruss', der Gebrauch der Vokabel 'Führer' und das Flaggen einer Hakenkreuzflagge je nach Befehl. Beachtete man diese angeordneten Verhaltensweisen und zahlte man die vorgeschriebenen Beiträge an Arbeitsfront und die Nationalsozialistische Volkswohlfahrt und hielt man im übrigen seinen Mund, so konnte man sich der Hoffnung hingeben, ungestört seiner Arbeit nachgehen zu können. ('To the rules of

public compliance, however, belonged the so-called "German salute", the use of the utterance *"Führer"* and display of a flag with the swastika when ordered. If one adhered to this decreed behaviour, paid the prescribed contribution to the *Arbeitsfront* and the National Socialistic *Volkswohlfahrt* (organisation for social work) and furthermore kept one's mouth shut, one could nurse hopes of being allowed to carry on one's work and not be disturbed.'[45]

Survival strategy or opportunism?

What kept Ritter going, he tells us, were his attempts, first as a child psychiatrist and marriage counsellor, later as *Kriminalpsychologe* and *Kriminalbiologe* (criminological biologist), to exercise some influence on the policy that was being carried out. In Tübingen he did not have much success because very soon so-called hereditarily inferior youth monopolized attention there and healthy young people faded from the picture. Only the feeble-minded, epileptics or other such organically sick juveniles were still admitted. The idea prevailed that healthy young people with problems would be put back on the right track by the *Hitler-jugend*. From the very beginning of his career Ritter had been especially interested in the puberty crisis, attempting to find out how youths who were treated during adolescence by a neurologist made out in later life. As a result of the announcement of the 'sterilization law' in 1934, however, many people began to withdraw from his research. They were no longer willing to talk about any possible nervous disorder or mental disease during their youth because of the possible consequences. At the same time, Ritter was also confronted in his practice with children from 'notorious' Tübingen poorhouse families with, to put it in his terms, many loafers, alcoholics, vagabonds, thieves and thugs among their number. Very pragmatically he began to shift his attention and to concentrate on the family relationships and the descent of these children. Ritter processed the results of that study in a dissertation completed in 1937.

In the summer of 1935, while working on this dissertation, he met Alfred Ploetz, one of the champions of eugenic thinking in Germany, who appeared extremely interested in Ritter's research findings and invited him to speak in Berlin at an international congress on population studies.[46] In his presentation Ritter recommended preventing not only the mentally deficient from bearing progeny, but also social misfits whose grandparents and parents had been known to behave in the same manner. Opposition to the further generation of 'gemeinwidrig lebenden Menschen' was something that Ritter considered to be a necessary racial-hygienic measure. He urged that certain things should be fixed in law.

This talk led to great interest in Ritter's work among his fellow professionals and also to an invitation to the Ministry of the Interior, where officials demonstrated their readiness to support Ritter's project. In a talk with Director General Arthur Gütt,[47] head of the Public Health Department, Gütt told him of his plans to found a government institute of hereditary sciences within the Ministry of Public Health. Known scholars such as the hereditary pathologist Otmar von Verschuer and the bacteriologist Ernst Rodenwaldt had been approached to direct this institute but they had other commitments, which brought him to inquire whether Ritter, whom various people had recommended to him, might like to take on the post. Ritter had his doubts. Instead of the leadership of a large institute that would be occupied with what for him was a new area of science, he would prefer financial support for his research among the riff-raff of Tübingen. In his autobiography he listed the considerations that influenced his decision at the time, writing that the most important advantage of Berlin was that he would move closer to the centre where decisions were taken so that perhaps he might acquire a voice in the much-discussed *Bewahrungsgesetz* (probation system). This law was to see to it that renegade, hostile and criminal youths would no longer walk around free. At the start of 1936 Ritter's greatest quandary was whether he would know how to navigate safely between super-critical, party-affiliated nit-pickers and the, by his estimate, more pragmatic policy-making officials employed by the ministries. After extensive discussion with Hans Reiter, the President of the Ministry of Public Health who had Ritter's interests at heart, Ritter finally accepted Gütt's offer.[48]

The core of his project came to consist of a mobile team (*fliegende Arbeitsgruppe*) with a modest number of co-workers and supplementary funds from the state committee for public health.[49] As compensation for the time he had to spend as advisor to all sorts of bodies, Ritter received a bonus of 250 to 300 RM a month. Furthermore Gütt promised to be his advocate for a professorship at the university in Berlin. All in all, seductive conditions for the ambitious Ritter who headed in October 1936 for the Ministry of Public Health in Berlin, trailing in his wake the physician Odenwald, a former comrade from his student years whom he had appointed to his staff, and Eva Justin, with whom he had already worked in Tübingen for some years.[50] He arrived carrying plans in his pocket for three research projects: one concerning the population of wine growers in Tübingen (to be carried out by the anthropologist Adolf Würth), a second about a community of traders of Jewish origin near Buchau on Feder Lake, and the third targeting a settlement of social undesirables in the hamlet of Schlossberg in Württemberg (to be carried out by his childhood friend Manfred Betz).[51] First, however, he had to add the finishing touches to his book on the vagrants of Württemberg.[52]

Upon Ritter's arrival in Berlin, it turned out that both Arthur Gütt (of the Ministry of the Interior) and Hans Reiter (of Public Health) had overplayed their hands. Ritter landed in a bureaucratic labyrinth of departments that were pitted against each other. The creation of a permanent position for Ritter met for a long time with insuperable objections. He felt himself to be a pawn in a power struggle. At this point the fact that he was not a party member made itself felt. In this context he referred to a phenomenon which in post-war literature came to be known as the polycratic politics of the Nazi power élite. What this amounted to was that in any given professional area different bodies were conjured into life at the same time so that, if necessary, under the tense situation characterizing relations between the party and the state, they could be played off against each other.[53] Thus within the Ministry of Public Health at practically the same time as Ritter's *Rassenhygienische Forschungsstelle*, an *Erbwissenschaftliches Institut* and a *Kriminalbiologische Forschungsstelle* were established. Owing to the fact that all three occupied the same work terrain in practice, Reiter often used the term *Bevolkerungskundliche Forschungsstelle* in dealings with the world at large. To make things still more complicated yet, the ministry lumped all of Ritter's activities together under what it called the *Sozial- biologisches Forschungsinstitut*.

The principal task that Ritter was assigned by the Ministry of the Interior was to devote himself to the study of non-sedentary population groups, with special emphasis on Gypsies. Having reached this point he asked himself in his autobiography whether as a child psychiatrist he hadn't drifted too far away from his original field. In retrospect he managed to identify a line of continuity leading from his work as a youth and marriage counsellor, through his involvement with questions connected to heredity and social misfits, and on to research involving Gypsies. In his reasoning Gypsies never grew out of childhood, so it wasn't all that illogical for a child psychiatrist to occupy himself intensively with them. According to him civil servants had all sorts of romantic images of Gypsies in those years: as child thieves, cannibals, spies and bandit chieftains. His challenge would consist of testing the scientific possibilities for ridding society of these parasites, as he called them, and at the same time to search for living conditions for Gypsies which suited their nature. This was a line of reasoning that enabled him to see himself as the advocate for both parties.

Later I will speak about the continuation of Ritter's career. Here it is apposite to inquire into the nature of the connection that existed between his individual development, including his research and policy ideas, and prevailing intellectual currents in and beyond Germany in the 1930s and 1940s. In the process, we deal with the history of eugenics, the roles played by medical and psychiatric professional groups and by anthropologists within the field of eugenics, and the arguments that dominated the debate about population policy.

SCIENCE AND GOVERNMENT POLICY IN THE 1930s

A biological inheritance: social-Darwinism and eugenics

The literature on the intellectual roots of German eugenics and its connection with the racial population policy of the Nazis has grown so extensively in recent years that it is more than I can do here to provide a resume of the most important developments.[54] I will restrict myself to indicating a number of aspects that collectively clarify the background of Ritter's personal and scientific development and which make it possible to place his Gypsy research in a broader context. To this end we should realize in the first place that in the Germany of the 1930s a number of traditional and contemporary academic schools of thought converged. Thus a revitalization occurred of Herder's eighteenth-century ideas about the *Volksgeist*, emanating from historical chronicles, old myths and literary sources, and forming an important stimulant to the nationalism in a number of European countries in the nineteenth century which reached its culmination in the so tardily forged German nation under the Nazis. In addition the notion of an *Aryan race* that was rooted initially in anatomy and in comparative linguistics came to prevail[55] but gradually became transformed into the more anthropological concept of *cultural race*, the ultimate incarnation of which, as bearers of the most civilized culture, were presumed to be the Aryans. To the historical-mythical concept *Volk* (a people or a nation) and the anatomical-anthropological and cultural concept *race*, in the course of the nineteenth century, was added the social-Darwinian idea of *man as a social-biological being*, as the carrier of characteristics that could be genetically transmitted. All these notions fused in the Nazi movement which drew from this arsenal at will.

This is also a source of the post-war confusion concerning whether Nazi policy had been based on heredity or race.[56] In any event, a utopian theory with a biological foundation was central, one which on the one hand wanted to create a new, optimally socially serviceable man, and which on the other hand, engaged in battle against every (supposed) illness or form of otherness and in the process adopted race as a battle standard (*Kampfbegriff*). From the literature it is difficult now to determine which motives were decisive in the development of this theory: political, racial, economic, demographic or considerations of a medical or psychic nature. However, scientists from all these disciplines made a contribution to the legitimization of the ideal state to which they aspired.

A popular slogan in the 1930s was that National Socialist politics put biology into practice, to which I hasten to say that many of the ideas implemented between 1933 and 1945 were certainly not exclusively German.[57] They conformed to an international trend, oriented to achieving efficiency and control over human progress. Their historical origin lay in social-Darwinism which applied the biological principles of evolution and selection to social processes. For Darwin, a process of natural selection whereby the best-adapted survived and reproduced lay behind the variation in forms among living creatures, including man. While Darwin formulated this theory of evolution as a dynamic principle of development he had not fully worked out idea about its end result. The (social-)biologists who followed him thought that they also recognized the principle of evolution at work in society around them. They conceived of a people, of the state, in fact of a culture as a whole as a living organism to which the individual is subordinate. They elevated the principles of Darwin to moral norms which meant in practice that they believed that, in the course of evolution, the strong, the healthy (those who work!) and the attractive had to carry on.

This position expressed positive expectations of human advancement, only practice appeared not to accord with theory. Indeed statisticians had calculated that those who reproduced the most vigorously were not the successful but people who were less highly socially esteemed. Interpreted in social-Darwinian terms, they curbed the forward progress of civilization. This discovery of the principle of biological counter-selection led to pessimistic conclusions and sparked the wish to correct, through social interventions, the process of natural selection that had been disturbed. The reasoning behind this stance was that the Industrial Revolution, modernization and technology, along with incremental medical and social care, had enfeebled the natural laws that Darwin had revealed. These developments were said to have contributed to a situation where the weak, the handicapped, the social-economically less productive, the carriers of hereditary illnesses and the racially 'impure' had more possibilities of survival than ever before. This was the origin of the ever more loudly resounding call to protect one's own race and prevent the incursion of hereditarily tainted blood.[58] Whereas during the Enlightenment emphasis had fallen on the changing of people through the improvement of their circumstances, a tendency that had grown stronger and continued to figure in the Christian-middle class civilizing policy of the nineteenth century and among Marxists, the social-Darwinists believed that humanity required specifically biological improvement. Not culture, but nature was all decisive to their way of thinking. Humanity needed to take its destiny into its own hands.

For those determining the criteria for intervening in social selection, the question of which biological or racial motives merited priority intruded itself. Hindsight reveals that the influence on policy of (physical-)anthropology, which had managed to win respect in the nineteenth century with skull measurements and other methods of comparative anatomy, remained limited. True, peoples were differentiated on grounds of genes, prevalence of blood groups and suchlike, but ultimately the results that this yielded were not especially usable. None the less, strong ideas about racial characteristics came into currency in this branch of anthropology, inspired by cultural value judgments. The influence of this race ideology – for that in fact is what it was – may certainly not be underestimated.[59] It was, however, the eugenics movement above all, with its roots embedded in the principles of genetics, which would trace, along scientific lines, the factors by means of which people believed the human race could be made better.

The founder of this movement was Francis Galton (1822–1911), a nephew of Charles Darwin. He based his ideas on genealogical research and arrived at the conviction that gifts and talents were congenital and required extra social exertion to be able to flower fully. With his proposals to encourage marriages between members of the so-called upper echelons and to oppose those of 'inferior persons', Galton was the first to direct attention to the possibility of regulating reproduction. He felt that eugenics should become a national science with the help of which a breakthrough could be achieved in the, as he described it, passive and mechanistic process of evolution. He almost presented his doctrine as a religion which had to be embraced in order to improve the inherited attributes of the race and to raise humanity to a higher level of perfection. By *race* he understood *a group with the same inherited characteristics* which propagate themselves down through successive generations. He regarded the dissemination of understanding of genetic biology among the population as a practical task for scholarship, together with the assembling of as much material as possible regarding the circumstances under which large, prolific and gifted families best flourished. He was the first to champion the inclusion of eugenic regulations in the national health system.

Early in the twentieth century these ideas found a zealous proponent in Germany in Wilhelm Schallmayer (1857–1919)[60] although medical science comprised the point of departure for his thinking. In his solidarity with Galton's proposals he described preventive medicine as a highly promising strategy for containing, if not reversing, tendencies towards, to express it in his terminology, the degeneration of human civilization. He built further on the theme of selective reproduction, as a consequence of which hereditary traits in human societies would but slowly change. Upper classes often regulated their fertility, according to him, through the use of contraceptives. Thus they produced the fewest offspring which meant that the regenerative stock of the race itself was being weakened, since the lowest levels were the very ones to bring so many children into the world.[61] He interpreted this one-sided limitation of births as evidence of a degeneration that could only be halted by means of an active biological state policy consisting of prohibitions against certain marriages and the propagation of some kinds of people. In the absence of such policy, the further degeneration of the 'white civilized nation' was inevitable, and this entailed that it would lose the physical and mental properties to which it owed its position at the top of the cultural ladder. Thus Schallmayer linked inheritance theory, which accentuated the ominous deterioration of hereditary qualities, with the concept of 'degeneration' which came originally from psychiatry but which in practice had expanded into a collective term denoting such phenomena as criminality, alcoholism, begging, homosexuality, irregular employment, unwed parentage and other forms of what was described at the time as inadequate functioning, either medically or socially.[62]

In his proposals concerning the prevention of the degeneration of the German people, Schallmayer did not ally himself with racial-anthropological typologies and theories about the superior Aryan or Nordic race. He was anchored first of all in a medical-psychiatric tradition, an observation not without importance here since Robert Ritter must be similarly placed. They interpreted the concept of 'race' along Galton's lines, as a social category of people with the same hereditary characteristics; the tools and techniques of physical anthropology were for them altogether irrelevant. As doctors and psychiatrists, they described the defects of society in biological terms and conceived of their proposals for betterment as social hygiene, thus basing their ideas on fundamentally different classifications from anthropologists, however far the groups which they had in mind may in practice have overlapped and despite the difficulty, for scientists and policy makers as well, of distinguishing between them.[63]

Alfred Ploetz (1860–1940), the Nestor of German racial hygiene – as Robert Ritter called him in the foreword to his dissertation – also stood in a medical-eugenics tradition.[64] He presented himself as an opponent of the socialists' ideology of equality, because he believed that natural selection had been disturbed through the protection of the weak. As a physician he distanced himself from the idea that the health of the individual was of the utmost priority and became inspired by the views of racial hygiene as a method to ameliorate the condition of mankind as a whole. That Ploetz also managed to make racial hygiene *salonfähig* in sociologists' circles came about because he conceived of society as an aspect of the phenomenon of 'race' and emphasized that every individual and each group was subject to the laws of racial biology. Unlike Schallmayer he also spoke enthusiastically about the value of the Germanic race and stressed that the German most closely approximated his (romantic-mythical) ideal of the Aryan race. Initially, when talking of Aryans, he had primarily meant people of European origin whose preferential treatment, racial-hygienically, would assure the higher development of humanity, but during the Nazi regime he converted openly to a partiality for the Nordic race.

A figure who linked the racial *hygienists* and the racial *ideologists* of the *Völkische Bewegung* in Germany (with their myths about the Nordic race as the hero of history, creator of Aryan languages and cultures, and explorer of the world) was the physician Fritz Lenz (1887–1976).[65] To be sure the thought that the Nordic race was superior wasn't by any means restricted to Germany but was widespread in the 1930s.[66] In Lenz's way of looking at things, genetic diseases could only be eliminated through the negative selection of families who were 'contaminated' with them. That those who allowed themselves to be led by such notions were none other than medical doctors themselves is to be explained by the dominant thought in eugenic circles that much human suffering was the result of hereditary illnesses whose proliferation should be brought to a stop.[67] Already, in 1931, Lenz had made it apparent that he regarded as highly commendable the attitude of the NSDAP, at the time the second largest party, towards the doctrine of racial hygiene; to elucidate his standpoint he cited passages from Hitler's *Mein Kampf* since, according to him, Hitler had understood the essence of the movement so well and had, in the style of a prophet, formulated its premises for a political mass movement. He had far less affinity with the one-sided emphasis on Jews as the polar opposites of the Aryans and he also appears to have rejected the violent use of power by Hitler and his henchmen. He showed himself to be a supporter of positive eugenics, that is to say of measures to promote large numbers of children accruing from 'good' marriages and counselling in all essential areas of life. The actual breeding of a better kind of people, analogous to the breeding of animals, appealed to him less, as did coercive sterilization or the carrying out of euthanasia, which belonged to the political programme of negative eugenics.[68] In the literature we read that not only did he fail to take into account the fanaticism of the Nazis, but in the end, he joined the party for opportunistic reasons and profoundly influenced many of the NSDAP leaders with his writings.[69]

From the combination of racial hygiene and social-Darwinism the Nazis derived their ideological motivation to tackle all groups that were undesirable in their eyes, employing the argument that in the 'struggle for survival' there could be no compromise. They thus exploited science to impose a new ethic and to realize a new social-technocratic strategy. The Nazi idea of the construction of a new man and a new state matched well with the points of departure of eugenics as inspired by social-Darwinism. A specific value was attributed to the hereditary qualities of people (*Erbgut*), defined in terms of good and evil, and with social qualifications as guiding standard. Thus it was thought possible to measure the degree of degeneration; the results were then put to use to carry out a racial population policy. Here we should not lose sight of the fact that in the first decades of this century the eugenics movement was international and the measures that derived from its principal concepts, such as the sterilization of the hereditarily contaminated, were acted upon in various countries. In 28 American states, even before 1930, 15,000 people had already been sterilized, most of them against their will, a total which was to rise to 30,000 by 1939. Thus, with the exception of putting people to death, the principle of negative eugenics in Germany was far from novel or unique. In 1924, moreover, the United States had taken the lead by instituting restrictive immigration laws, as well as laws in southern states against racially mixed marriages. These sprang from eugenic theories about degeneration, based on medical-genealogical, empiric studies of inherited diseases within families.[70] Since sterilization laws were also supported in the United States, after the war the allied authorities could not classify sterilizations as war crimes; only those who could prove that they had not been sterilized because of a 'genetic defect' were eligible for reparations.[71]

The joint effort of disciplines certainly does not constitute the only explanation for the political efficacy of heredity policy in the Nazi period. A shift in the orientation of values also played a part, such as thoughts about the economic value of people which began to gain currency from the beginning of the twentieth century. As early as 1911, in Germany, an essay prize was announced on the theme of what people who were inferior cost the state. Lack of statistical material meant that no adequate account was submitted at the time. At the end of the 1920s, however, during the economic crisis, the theme increased in timeliness, for even the health services did not escape from budgetary cuts. Radical racial hygiene proposals were then well received as a result of the general feeling that the hereditarily contaminated cost the community too much. Marriage counselling bureaus were also in the spirit of the times. At first they were a private initiative but in 1926 the government stepped in to lead the way. At the same time the discussion about the sterilization of individuals who were regarded as inferior, and of groups, steadily gained in prominence; to keep inferior individuals from propagating themselves further was certainly far less expensive than confining them for years in an institutional home.

Scientific notions about racial hygiene and political goals derived from them were incorporated into Nazi ideology in radicalized, strongly utilitarian form. Not only could the *Völkische* ideas of the Nazis be scientifically legitimized in this manner but researchers also saw their chance to promote the interests of their own field and to exercise influence on policy. Thus Eugen Fischer and Fritz Lenz were govern- ment advisers on population and race policy and worked out plans for the sterilization of so-called children of mixed-blood. In addition, after the race laws became operative, they wrote countless race diagnoses for the *Reichssippenamt*, relying heavily in the process on hereditary biological interpretations of their subjects' physiognomical traits.[72] In this respect they demonstrated far more of a physical-anthropological orientation than Robert Ritter's subsequent work with Gypsies would. They did not have much influence, however, on the way in which, in the end, those in power applied their ideas. From 1933 on all institutes involved with racial hygiene were placed under state surveillance or housed, as Ritter's institute was, under the *Reichsausschuss für Volks- gesundheitsdienst*.[73] Thus the racial hygienists provided the framework but were themselves scarcely involved in the practical implementation of their proposals where political or economic motives were far more likely to prove decisive.

Hereditary health prognoses and registration systems

We have seen how Nazi political doctrine had roots in a number of scientific disciplines, but what has failed to emerge clearly so far is how science set to work to trace such an array of undesirable elements and in what way academics supported the state in the realization of policy which put into practice what had already been advocated during the preceding years. For we must not forget that some eugenists had already, in the 1920s, more-or-less written off some 20 per cent to 30 per cent of the population on a basis of their hereditary health prognoses and had drawn up data banks that contained genetic information about diverse groups.[74] Various professional associations felt a need to compile personal dossiers with hereditary-biographical resumes of individuals, families and groups. Doctors and psychiatrists who were searching for connections between inherited defects did so; social and criminological biologists who were interested in the 'socially inferior' and in criminals as the carriers of genetic defects did so; and researchers studying race did so in the course of mapping entire family trees (*sibben*) in order to be able to determine the degree of German descent. All this was carried out with the intention of making the German people healthier, a heredity policy from which academics (physicians, anthropologists and others), judicial organizations, government organs and political parties alike benefited.

The first wave of registration rules after the Nazis assumed power was aimed against Jewish and politically undesirable civil servants who, on the basis of a law introduced on 7 April 1933, could be removed from office. After arrests, systematic investigations and registration rapidly followed in order to deprive *artfremd* (not real Germans) colleagues of their jobs. Such internal purges even took place among physicians until, in 1938, non-Aryans were forbidden to enter the medical profession. A fifth of the total number of physicians appear to have been victims of this ban. In addition all genealogical societies under government authority were joined together in 1935 in a *Reichsstelle für Sippenforschung*[75] which, drawing on disparate sources, began to create files for German residents in order to establish if someone was an Aryan, or *deutschblütig*, as it was put, and to collect diagnostic data about the hereditary health of the person in question. Similarly, since the late 1920s eugenically-inspired researchers gravitating around Eugen Fischer in Berlin and the psychiatrist Ernst Rüdin in Munich[76] had been busy amassing and processing statistical material about the congenital defects of Germans, scouring the archives of countless institutions such as reformatories, psychiatric hospitals, Special Elementary Schools, clinics for alcoholics, homes for the deaf and dumb and the blind, and sanatoria for the tubercular.[77] The same held true for the *Kriminalbiologische Gesellschaft* founded in 1928, which regarded the criminality of the lower classes as a genetically determined predisposition and accordingly activated a network of criminal-biological assembly points where data about delinquents could be registered and complemented by medical-psychiatric diagnoses. With the help of such files they hoped to achieve the improvement of criminal punishment.[78] Detection of the 'inferiors' who accounted for the dreaded (social-) biological counter-selection had thus an early start but would expand under the Nazis into a genuine hunt. Eugenists who became involved as advisers to the four committees of the Ministry of the Interior in the formulation of population and race policy seized the opportunity to have their scientific notions codified in laws and regulations. It is in this context of ministerial concern with health we must also place Robert Ritter's work as researcher and consultant.

The institutionalization of the hereditary biology baseline studies which had been under way since the 1920s, was realized under the Nazis when they opened 650 public health bureaus throughout the country. These, in keeping with guidelines laid down in legislation unifying the health system (3 July 1934), served as *Beratungsstellen für Erb- und Rassenpflege*, but also, and especially, as central organs for collecting and registering data about the genetic antecedents of families on the grounds of which, for example, involuntary sterilization could be imposed on people. The interests of the state and community enjoyed priority in this public health policy; hereafter, it was society rather than the individual that collectively had a right to health. In defining the concept of *health* a social-economic perspective prevailed, that is to say that only someone able to look after his own livelihood was considered to be healthy, whereby the government emphatically dissociated itself from the sick and the poor, and discontinued social welfare measures. Wherever possible the public health bureaus saw to it that only 'sound offspring' were brought into the world, in part by means of extensive marriage counselling. In Frankfurt am Main – where the bureau is of special interest to us because Ritter himself worked there as a physician for some years after the war – this resulted in a growth in the number of personal files contained in the heredity archives from 60,000 to 330,000 during the period 1933 to 1943. This total meant that there were files for two-thirds of the inhabitants of the city.[79] In collecting information the bureau made use of the services of countless institutions, including the registries of births, marriages and deaths, churches (for genealogical data from baptism registers), schools (for children's achievement levels) and child welfare boards. Advice bureaus had unlimited access to all such material included in the personal files. Thus if the director of a nursing home or penitentiary wanted to propose sterilization, or the Social Welfare Department wished to know if someone might wrongly be the recipient of state assistance, or if a government body required a person's racial diagnosis, the bureau offered its information freely.[80]

An application for sterilization had to be submitted to one of the 1,700 *Erbgesundheitsgerichte* which were subdivisions of the cantonal courts and which included a jurist, a medical health inspector and a physician with experience in the field of eugenics. They passed judgement on the proposals of doctors who, believing that they had identified a congenital illness in a patient, reported this to the local health inspector. Once the *Erbgesundheitsgericht* had given its approval, sterilization could follow. It appears that 90 per cent of the proposed sterilizations were endorsed as valid and, of those who appealed to one of the 181 *Erbgesundheitsobergerichte* against the decision, a scant 3 per cent won their plea.[81] Those who balked at being sterilized usually wound up in a concentration camp. Approximately 400,000 people were sterilized during the

Nazi regime under the provisions of an heredity protection law, with a peak of 50,000 a year during their first four years in power.[82] After the outbreak of war the annual cohort of sterilizations decreased because attention had in the interim shifted from the category of the 'congenitally ill' to those who failed to measure up to norms of social achievement.[83]

In the stepped-up post-1936 pursuit of the registration of riff-raff, the mentally and/or physically less valid and ethnic minorities, the Ministry of Public Health, especially the division to which Ritter's institute belonged, fulfilled an important function.[84] With his detailed registration of Gypsies and 'Gypsies with mixed blood' he demonstrated the methods that were necessary to exercise control over diverse categories of *Gemeinschaftsfremden*. In the early 1940s, however, the Nazis enlarged the scope of their racial population policy to such an extent that all deviant categories were eligible for 'social annihilation' including not only the congenitally ill in institutions, but detainees who were registered as biologically predisposed to criminality by prison doctors, national minorities such as Jews and Gypsies, and also in part the *deutschstämmige Gemeinschaftsfremden* (a label for innumerable kinds of individuals considered to be undesirable).[85] So abrupt was the acceleration of Nazi elimination policy that scientists involved found themselves too deeply entangled to extricate themselves, too distant from the centre of power to be able to influence political choices, should they have wished to do so.

RITTER'S PUBLICATIONS: A CLOSE READING

A culture pessimistic world view

The previous pages have offered a conspectus of the world of ideas inhabited by scientists and policy-makers in Nazi Germany and of the concept of man and society that comprised its foundation. We saw how science and policy at the time became more closely intertwined than ever, as exemplified by the career of Robert Ritter, who, through his research, exercised great influence on the way in which government institutions defined individuals and groups as ethnically or socially different – separate persons, peoples, races – with all the consequences which such distinctions entailed. A closer reading of Ritter's work is indicated here to obtain some idea of the background that underpinned policy enacted towards Gypsies, but also to determine what Ritter owed to previous Gypsy scholars and what new accents he himself was responsible for introducing.

In many of his publications Ritter sketched an image of Gypsies and related groups that can be interpreted as presenting a kind of negative image of what he considered to be a desirable society. He only waxed more or less explicit about his ideal view of the world in one of his youthful works from 1928. At the same time in this preliminary effort towards a pedagogy of sexuality he already broached a number of themes that would recur later in his writing. Thus he regarded the sexual crisis that he felt he perceived all around him as one aspect of the general social crisis in which Germany languished in the 1920s. According to him this crisis found its expression in economic materialism, feminism, and the moral decay of German youth. He identified the transition Germany was undergoing from an agrarian to an industrial state as the cause behind the shift in morality. This had led to a flight from the countryside to urban areas where, wholly alienated from nature, people had to carry out factory drudgery. Moreover, they were exposed to the sensations and stimulations of the big city, such as prostitution. In this connection Ritter wrote about the 'degenerating influence' of major centres of population. In his opinion post-war relations in Germany, characterized by broken families and in their wake alcoholism, unemployment, housing shortages and increasing tension between generations, also left a demoralizing mark on society.

All these elements were part of the culturally pessimistic image of dissatisfied modern man that thrived during that era.[86] A romantic longing for the unsullied past was part of the unhappiness expressed as well, pining for the natural harmony of body and spirit that had been lost. Germane to this vision was unrelenting anxiety about undermining forces at work in that epoch – forces that, in a medical metaphor, were imagined as germs that weakened the body of the German state: '... unser Volkskörper in hohem Masse durch Geschlechtskrankheiten, durch nervöse und psychosexuelle Störungen geschwächt ist' ('... our *Volkskörper* will be weakened to a high degree by venereal diseases and nervous and psychosexual disorders').[87] In this initial publication Ritter found words and phrases for a number of key ideas that would recur again in his later work: influences harmful to the people, degeneration, pathological, disruptive for the community, and asocial. In line with such concerns was his interest in unfavourable inherited traits, such as feeble-mindedness, all kinds of anti-social behaviour (alcoholism, prostitution, sporadic work) and criminality. His view of Gypsies whom he described, depending upon the context of the research he was conducting at the time, as vagrants, *Gemeinschaftsfremden*, incorrigible criminals or degenerates with mixed blood, should also be placed against this background. At the same time Ritter had an image of the true Gypsy, a practically mythic being, endowed with traits we can recognize from the ethnographic portrait perpetuated by Grellmann and from Borrow's romantic imaginary figures.[88] In practice, however, during the course of his research he hardly ever managed to track down any specimens of such authentic Gypsies (as he called them). In any event it appeared to be no simple matter to locate any groups of Gypsies who manifested the distinguishing characteristics then attributed to them, such as communal vagabondage, a language of their own, authentic mores and customs, recognizable physiognomy, group-specific vocations, unusual names and racial purity. The trail led him rather to various German groups and individuals who also fulfilled a number of these criteria, just as there were people who were known as Gypsies but who, for example, led sedentary lives, who in appearance were indistinguishable from other Germans, who, in short, hardly matched the image of the Gypsy handed down from the past.

The methodological problems with which Ritter had to contend in his efforts to arrive at a conclusive definition of the concept 'Gypsy' derived to some extent from the multidisciplinary character of his research. Thus as a medical person and youth psychiatrist his initial focus was on the diagnosis of someone's personality – on how this person functioned, socially and psychologically. In addition, however, he plumbed dossiers and archives, drawing up family trees to establish an individual's genealogical history, which meant that he had to rely on definitions made by people other than himself, especially those recorded by police authorities down through the centuries. Furthermore he had anthropological research carried out which, it should be said, never led to uniform findings or to a complete categorization of the physical traits specific to one people. This explains why the results are not included in Ritter's publications. What mattered to him first of all was to demonstrate that Gypsies were the carriers of unfavourable hereditary characteristics. In the context of one study this induced him to use a medical-psychiatric definition of Gypsies, in the context of another a biological or eugenic definition, in yet another a sociological, historical, ethnological, or even criminological one.

The reader should keep it firmly in mind therefore that the terminological variation I make use of in the sections that follow reflects the diverse ways in which Ritter himself defined the groups which he was describing. Going by a reading of his texts it sometimes seems as if there existed a clear-cut difference in Germany between *Gypsies* (a people of foreign origins with a vagrant way of life), *Jenischen* (indigenous people with an itinerant way of life) and *sedentary misfits*. In some publications, however, Ritter also used the term *Jenischen* to denote a mixed population of Gypsies and Germans, sedentary or not, but definitely, of in his eyes, inferior social calibre.[89] On one occasion he used the term

Deutsche Landfahrer, without, incidentally, discussing their characteristics, and on another *Jenische Landfahrer*, similarly without
explanation. In the first instance he specifically had in mind indigenous
German caravan dwellers, in the second, Gypsies and 'Gypsies with
mixed blood'. In one place the children born from relations between
Gypsies and *Jenischen* are called 'Gypsies with mixed blood', in another
'*Jenischen* with mixed blood'. The label *Jenische Menschenschlag*,
moreover, serves as a collective designation for everything which Ritter
considered to be shiftless, anti-social, criminal, pathological, of Gypsy
descent (no matter from how far back) and undesirable. To complicate
things still more, in his ethnic characterization of Gypsies he drew a
distinction between 'domestic groups' and those from Burgenland (from
the region of the Austro-Hungarian border). All these distinctions, I
repeat, ultimately existed only on paper; in practice his work obliged
him to resort to a far simpler classification, although it remains unclear
what criteria proved decisive in the process.

In order to impose a semblance of order on Ritter's confusing
application of scientific labels to those whom he studied, I will begin by
describing the prototype that served Ritter as a standard for appraising
the degree of authenticity of Gypsies in Germany and Austria during
the 1930s. I will subsequently delve into his actual work methods,
indicating step by step the group distinctions to which his approach led
and how he arrived at the conclusion that almost the only Gypsies who
survived were degenerate and who, through their intermarriage with
the dregs of the German nation, had to be regarded as the root of the
current evil. What lurked under the epithet of 'asocial' and why such
persons should be especially branded as criminals also deserves
clarification. Finally I will dwell on Ritter's ideas with regard to racial
hygiene as a preventive method and on the measures that he proposed
in order to curtail the festering – as it was portrayed at the time – of all
these forms of unworthy human life.

The Gypsy: a mythic prototype

In the tradition of Grellmann, Gypsies constituted for Ritter the
prototype of those who lived a non-sedentary life. The function of that
prototype in his work was twofold. He could attribute what he saw as
the unalterable desire of Gypsies for an untrammelled existence to the
original core of their ancestry and he could show that for them as well,
as for sedentary Germans, the mingling of their blood had generated
undesirable admixtures. His ideas on this score underwent a significant
development in the course of time. In his earliest work he sketched the
traditional stereotype of the 'true Gypsy', complete with the inevitable

mesocephalic skull and a special propensity to eat hedgehogs.[90] To the extent that his empirical knowledge concerning diverse groups of Gypsies in Germany and Austria increased, this image began to assume an almost mythic character. At a given moment he had already asked himself whether the Gypsy population that had left India some 1,000 years back had indeed comprised a single ethnic group.[91] He didn't dispute that they had belonged to the caste of pariahs but the contemporary variation that his studies brought to light might very well, he believed, derive from their originating from a number of nomadic tribes. The influence had also made itself felt of the peoples among whom they had resided: 'Denn man kann neben deutlich indiden Zügen viel orientalische, vorderasiatische, mediterrane, dinarische, ostische und andere Einschläge bei ihnen beobachten.' ('For among them one can observe, in addition to clearly Indian traits, many oriental, near-Asian, Mediterranean, Dinaric, and Ostic features.')[92]

Later he elaborated on the aspect of their presumed primitivity which, along with restlessness, he considered to be an essential characteristic of non-sedentary man, taking his readers with him back to prehistory.[93] There the Gypsies' forefathers roamed around as hunters and gatherers in subtropics which bestowed on them all they needed. They were driven by natural needs, not by spiritual needs, and for thousands of years their lives had gone on unchanged. Ritter pictured them as exotic children of nature, with immutable primitive instincts, entirely dependent on nature and destiny, with an intense emotional life and at the mercy of impressions that they did not comprehend. This, he added, further explains their belief in supernatural powers. Fantasy and reality were so intertwined for them that they could very well identify with what they imagined. With this line of reasoning Ritter explained their strong gifts of persuasion and their credibility as soothsayers, and he also supposed that it helped him better understand their criminal behaviour. The world around them would, he fancied, seem unreal, with the consequence that they would not feel bound to abide by its laws. Even the tribal struggles among themselves, which according to Ritter were so typical of Gypsies, failed to surprise him. This was certainly the behaviour that was inherent in 'savages' and 'natural man' whose temper soon boiled over so that, like children, they misbehaved.

In Ritter's image of the Gypsy as mythic prototype we see a confusing cluster of representations merge. In the first place there is the notion of Gypsies as a collective designation for tribes who emigrated from India and who were said to have broken away from the caste of untouchables. Ritter differed from Grellmann in that, reasoning on the basis of the variations he came into contact with in Germany, he regarded them as socially unitary, but ethnically not. In addition, more in keeping with the folkloristic romantic tradition of Borrow, he sketched Gypsies as an exotic, primitive people who ever since prehistoric times had wandered about, lacking the capacity to adapt to changing social circumstances. Ritter denied that these two historical interpretations were difficult to reconcile. Moreover, he rejected the reconstruction of the prototypical form of the true Gypsy as a pure primitive in so far as he maintained, without supporting argumentation, that in his day only Gypsies with mixed blood survived. In this context he referred to the *Jenischen* whom, like the Gypsies, he made into a relic of a prehistorical population, but in their case one that was ethnically related to other Germans – thus, socially considered, a backward segment of the German people whose most important characteristic was their itinerant way of life. The reasons why they had become steadily more marginal, feeble-minded and criminal down through the ages had to do, according to Ritter, with the infusion of sedentary 'German blood'.

Mixed-bloods as the root of evil

I now wish to consider the diverse categories of wandering lineages that Ritter distinguished in his writings throughout the years.[94] He cited two categories a number of times, without, however, further comment: honourable (commercial) travellers and traders, and individual vagabonds who were compelled by social-economic circumstances to desert hearth and home. Besides these he distinguished two categories which, he found, had much in common: Gypsies and *Jenischen* (*Land-fahrer*). In the impressionistic portrait that he sketched of them, a number of corresponding traits can be pointed out. Both groups were said to be restless, continually under way, roving in families (with their belongings in a cart or caravan) and using hawking as a protective mantle for begging. Furthermore Ritter emphasized their cunning in intercourse with settled people, characterized, it was said, by the use of a traditional system of secret signs and a strange language with which the government was not familiar. Ritter also distinguished a number of differences between Gypsies and *Jenischen*. With Gypsies it was said to be possible at first glance to see that they were a foreign race and their clothing, according to him, was distinctively bold in colour; their women wore long, spreading skirts and abundant jewellery. The language they spoke was Romanischel which was part of the Indo-Germanic family, whereas *Jenischen* resorted to an artificial language, Rotwelsch, if they wanted to guard secrets in the presence of outsiders. In practice, Ritter went on to say, even these ethnological characteristics were not a great help owing to the emergence of a category of mongrels – the offspring of mixed marriages between Gypsies and *Jenischen*. It was Ritter's conviction that extensive research into their descent was needed to establish to which group they belonged.

Thus, in Ritter's view, a person's hereditarily determined nature decided the question of his authenticity as a Gypsy. When he spoke of racially pure or true Gypsies, he did not base his views on anthropo-metric or medical data such as blood tests. Findings from physical-anthropological or medical-biological research are indeed conspicuously absent from his publications.[95] He paid just as little heed to cultural characteristics, although this did not keep him from referring regularly to how Gypsies lived in a traditionally tribal fashion, honouring tribal laws. With these remarks he was alluding to the strict taboos that Gypsies observed – although it remained unclear what these specifically prohibited – to the supposed chastity of their women and to their rigorous endogamy. In this ethnographic portrait, segregation and in-breeding accounted for why Gypsies had remained so racially pure. Ritter believed that their resistance to sedentary society expressed a strong consciousness of race and feelings of solidarity among them-selves. The only problem was, what truths emerged from the family trees that he traced? The kind of Gypsies whom he portrayed as anchored in tradition simply didn't exist in the Germany of the 1930s. Even those whom had been judged to be the most racially pure invariably turned out, on closer inspection, to have some German blood coursing through their veins.[96]

These findings show us how, as Ritter's research progressed, he formed a more differentiated picture of the various Gypsy populations in Germany and Austria. Nevertheless this failed to lead to a more subtle appreciation of their existence and mode of life. Any sociological, or anthropological perceptions were in the end subordinated to the science of hereditary biology, with its racial foundation and its essential mission of detecting genetic threats to the German people. Moreover, the criminological component in Ritter's work increased in importance, which is hardly surprising considering his ever-closer ties with judicial and police institutes. Thanks to co-operation with the *Zigeuner Polizei-zentrale* (Central Office) in Munich, the *Bayerische Landesverband für Wanderdienst* and the *Reichszentrale zur Bekämpfung des Zigeunerunwesens*, which, like one of Ritter's own institutes, fell under the *Reichskriminal-polizeiamt*, it proved possible to keep on expanding his archive on Gypsy families. The last official count in one of his own publications reported that 30,000 persons were included as of February 1941: 19,000 in the former German state and 11,000 in Austria and Sudetenland. He estimated the total at large at about 35,000.[97]

In the interest of order he imposed the following, rather crude ethnic categories on the records he had compiled at that time. The German

Sinte comprised the largest group (some 13,000 strong), with a 'talented musical tribe' as a sub-group among whom asociability was unknown.[98] Next he differentiated a group of 1,800 *Rom* or *Lovari*; Hungarian Gypsies who were said to have come to Germany around 1860 to 1870 and who differed from the *Sinte* both genealogically and anthropologically as well as linguistically. For the most part they were reasonably prosperous horse traders or textile merchants who frequently drove about in richly adorned caravans. They did not beg, and tried to respect the law. For them the old Gypsy mores no longer mattered. According to Ritter they went to great lengths not to look like Gypsies. It was his idea that, together with many other racial characteristics, they shared the business mentality of the Jews.[99] The *Kelderari* made up a separate sub-group within these *Rom*; they were tinkers who were alleged to have been living in Germany since 1864. Ritter had little to say about them. He also distinguished a group of 500 *Lalleri* who struggled to survive in Bohemia and Moravia, begging, telling fortunes, and committing petty theft, and 2,700 Germans who lived in caravans – about their characteristics he was brief, mentioning them but once as such in his work. He placed some 8,000 Burgenland Gypsies in Austria (which Germany had annexed). These, according to Ritter, constituted a population of bastards and mongrels with all the usual negative traits. Yet he also mentioned a settlement where they were regarded more favourably. He maintained that these exceptions also looked better: not such pitch black hair and less swarthy skin. Socially they were said to have been much better adapted and could only with difficulty be recognized as Gypsies any more. A similar tone dominates Ritter's discussion of the *Litautikke* or *Masurtikke Sinte*, a Gypsy group of unspecified size in East Prussia. He hypothesized that they had mixed more intensively with sedentary Germans because they did not live in caravans but rented living quarters and were frequently wage labourers or farmhands. Some even owned a little land, which they also farmed themselves. Their children attended school regularly and their misdeeds were confined to pilfering things to eat from the woods and fields. They were said to be fluent in the Gypsy language but they usually spoke East Prussian. The old *Sinte* laws and precepts didn't matter to them very much any longer. On the heels of this notably positive depiction of a Gypsy group, followed the 200 former bear-leaders who in Gypsy fashion roamed widely and were known as Turkish Gypsies of west Balkan origin. In 1941 Ritter had not yet completed his collection of information about their descent.

It may be possible to extract from Ritter's publications a varied picture of ethnic (sub-)groups among the Gypsies, yet he himself, while engaged in research, overlooked such differentiations entirely. As mentioned earlier, he concentrated on genealogical research, and that brought to light that 90 per cent of the people who fell into the categories listed above had mixed blood. It was Ritter's conviction, unsupported by the printing of any statistical evidence, that most reports of Gypsy crime involved the *Jenische Menschenschlag* who moved about like Gypsies. As early as 1934 Ritter had formed an idea of what Gypsy mixed-bloods – his preferred name for the category – were like. Throughout the coming years it would not undergo any change worth mentioning. All the positive characteristics of the 'true Gypsy' seemed to be missing from this product of a crossing of races, while all the traits worthy of condemnation could be found in them. These people, he maintained, were, even in the eyes of 'true Gypsies', the roots of the evil: 'Das Halbblut ist auch einen Hund, was den Reinrassigen zum Unreinen stempeln würde.' ('The half-breed is also a dog, which the racially pure would brand as unclean.')[100]

Official criteria for distinguishing the categories of 'Gypsies', 'half-castes' and the 'Gypsy-like' were only established quite late in Ritter's work. In practice, for purposes of classification, the police authorities had for a long time latched onto external appearance, way of life, and language and names, in combination with occupations. From the time of Heinrich Himmler's decree of 16 December 1938 they, and the *Reichszentrale zur Bekämpfung des Zigeunerunwesens*, saw themselves obliged to use as their point of departure the racial diagnoses which Ritter's institutes had drafted on grounds of genealogical data and the social evaluation of a person's individual family history. Both the police authorities and the Gypsies in question – if at any rate the term in this connection is still fitting – were, according to Ritter, informed of the results of the diagnosis and could contest it by handing over genealogical documents with contradictory information. These racial diagnoses, known in German as *gutachtliche Äusserungen*, served as the basis for the selection of Gypsies and 'Gypsy-like' individuals for Auschwitz,[101] but they have never been analysed because after the war they became dispersed throughout Germany and to a large extent apparently became lost.[102] Remarkably, in February 1941, Ritter wrote that he had completed 10,000 of them,[103] whereas it appears from the copies of racial diagnoses that I collected that on 8 July 1941 number 2,322 was written; the person in question was classified as ZM (+), that is to say a Gypsy with mixed blood of predominantly Gypsy descent.[104] Under Ritter, racial diagnoses continued to be written out until January 1945, at which time number 24,411 was completed.[105] In this instance diagnosis took into account a number of categories, although Ritter's publications leave us in the dark about what criteria were decisive. In any event the formal rubrication was as follows:[106]

- A Gypsy is someone who has three pure Gypsies among his grandparents;
- A Gypsy half-caste (+) (first grade) is anyone with fewer than three pure Gypsies among his grandparents;
- A Gypsy half-caste (–) (second grade) is anyone who has at least two Gypsy half-castes among his grandparents;
- Non-Gypsy: all other cases.

Stricter criteria were thus applied for Gypsies than for Jews, since those who were not part of the Jewish religious community and had four half-Jewish grandparents were not regarded to be Jews or Jewish half-castes. The underlying thought was that 'Jewish half-castes' of the first or second grade had been, from a social-biological perspective, absorbed within the German population. On the other hand, with Gypsies, as Ritter put it, the influence on others of intermarriage was intensely poisonous. Throughout the process of mixing with all sorts of persons from German society who were considered to be inferior, the Gypsy character, according to him, was preserved. That is why he still assigned Gypsies, whether first or second grade, to the category of 'Gypsy half-castes'.

The genealogical tables of the science of genetics

It can be deduced from the preceding analysis of Ritter's publications that he was above all a proponent of the science of genetics. He was determined to find out the extent to which certain illnesses and character traits, alienation from society and even criminality were congenital and to ascertain their prevalence among the groups which he studied. He did this by means of medical-psychiatric diagnoses, but his genealogical research ultimately proved decisive. Using his most authoritative study of drifting families, completed in 1937, I will show how we should understand Ritter's work method within his practice as a physician. Towards this end I will first reconstruct how his method developed down through the years, thereafter pointing out some inconsistencies in his approach.

Ritter dedicated his 1937 study to Alfred Ploetz, the Nestor of racial hygiene, introducing it as an initial sketch of comprehensive research targeting vagabonds, thugs and deceivers. It all started in his medical-psychiatric practice in Tübingen where, in the early 1930s, among the steady stream of youths who came to consult him, he believed he had discovered, after lengthy observation, a new variety of mental deficiency. To denote his discovery he introduced the term *getarnte Schwachsinn* (hidden feeblemindedness).[107] The picture that he presented of these young people reflected his own mixed feelings of esteem and repulsion. Thus he talked about adolescents who at the same time emanated a remarkable rascality and awkwardness. Restless and alert, they took in their surroundings but, at the same time, their bodies communicated a striking degree of aggression and self-confidence. Closer observation, outside his office as well, taught Ritter that they were constantly moving about, and combed through the garbage for things they could salvage and sell. They trapped sala-manders, frogs and toads and sold them to all kinds of institutions. They knew a great deal about herbs, mushrooms, roots and crops. They were always up to something, but displayed, according to him, a preference for pulling off swindles. What was said to distinguish them from others most of all was their roving, their being left to their own devices at an early age, their tendency to beg in some veiled fashion and to feign innocence if they were caught at their mischief. The children gave no cause for complaint at school until they reached the age of eight; after-wards their mental growth stagnated. They distrusted outsiders and, with their expressive faces and gifts of speech, they knew how to conceal their lack of knowledge and to invent plausible excuses for just about everything. They acted in a self-important manner, but were said to lack ambition. Ritter concluded that the fact that they were not capable of steady and organized work, also came from their supposedly not having any self-insight or knowledge. Everything for them revolved around their own profit and longings: an unadulterated egocentric approach to life. They had a good grasp of things that were immediately relevant to them, but had difficulty with abstract thinking. Their ability to concentrate was also said to be limited in its development. They lived from day to day, heedless and carefree.

After formulating this group diagnosis, Ritter's attention shifted to the youths' background, to the origin of their – in his eyes – hidden mental deficiency.[108] In the process he came across a group of families who for 60 years had been a nuisance to the government of a city not further identified by name. Their dependence on social welfare had been especially burdensome. Most lived in railway cars or sheds on the edge of the city or in poorhouses. They avoided work, hung about without any goals in life, demonstrated a lack of hygiene and discipline, and were rapacious. The women squabbled and shrieked, the men were slaves of drink and carried out a forbidden trade in dog meat, killing the animals and butchering them, it was alleged, in their homes. From documents in government institutions it was clear to Ritter that these peoples' grandparents had lived in the same way. By following the genealogies of these families back in time he arrived at lineages of wine growers and craftsmen who had always intermarried among themselves. From the moment, late in the eighteenth century, when 'foreign blood' (from non-sedentary partners) first commingled with the old stock – which Ritter believed he could trace by means of family names – things were said to have gone wrong. The descendants of these – to his way of thinking – mixed marriages had relations with others who were 'socially inferior' and the resultant social-biological degeneration would lead, after a number of generations, to the concealed mental deficiency from which the youths whom he received in his practice suffered. With this line of reasoning Ritter believed he had laid bare the hereditary destiny of certain family lineages.

Here, then, was a combination of social disapprobation for an erratic way of life and medical psychiatric notions concerning biological deviation. The idea was that whenever offspring considered to be socially or medically inferior – that is to say persons who enjoyed a low social esteem because they followed an ambulant vocation, did not work regularly or, for example, were feeble-minded – managed to fuse with a 'healthy family' of people who lived sedentary lives with a fixed occupation, the inferiority spread itself rapidly. This occurred socially, in the form of anti-social behaviour, and also biologically, in the form of mental weakness. 'Hidden mental deficiency' manifested itself most seriously among people whose ancestry included the feeble-minded as well as tramps or vagrants. Ritter regarded living without a fixed abode as, by definition, an hereditary deviation, or a social defect. It took four generations, according to him, before the consequences of a mix with inferior blood could be neutralized by mating with 'healthy blood'.[109]

Whereas genealogists as a rule occupy themselves with drawing up the family tree of a single individual, Ritter combined trees from all the members of an entire family into one massive genealogical table, for he was convinced that foreign influences could have infiltrated via distant branches of the *Erbstrom*. By bringing together the genealogical tables of socially related family groups he believed he could arrive at a social-biological portrait of a specific human type (*Menschenschlag*). During this process of tracking heredity back through time for families who numbered many with 'hidden mental deficiency' among their descendants (as evidenced by youthful cases who consulted Ritter in his psychiatric practice), Ritter found himself led to the eighteenth-century world of vagabond and street-trader colonies. Having arrived at this point his research took a decisive turn, for in the government archives he chanced upon *Gaunerlisten*, police records of the tracing of all kinds of suspects. In addition to names these documents contained much personal data.[110] He then decided to select a number of family names known to him (as founders of a lineage), to choose a certain region, namely the north-western part of the Württemberg Black Forest

District, and to follow these families from the eighteenth century down to the twentieth century, using all the social-historical documents that he had at his disposal. He used, for example, a hundred folio volumes with official records of judicial hearings from 1760 to 1820 at which accused persons gave testimony, compiled in part by someone we encountered in the introduction to this study, detective Jacob Schäffer, who joined the service in 1780 in Sulz.[111] Ritter also extracted information from court indictments, penal registers, investigation ledgers and documents of the *Kriminalpolizei* of the kingdom of Württemberg which offered a unique insight into the criminality of large groups of people during the span of half a century. Finally he had researchers comb through the minutes of city council meetings, case histories of illnesses, doctors' reports, child welfare board documents, the registers of poor-houses and nursing homes, and other such institutions.[112] All these sources combined were to yield conclusive information about the path of development of individuals and families, with sedentariness serving as an important indicator for assessing the extent of an individual's social adaptation.

With this method, Ritter, if we may believe what he has written on the subject, managed to draw up more than 20,000 *Erbtafel*, a kind of genealogical chart with data about the hereditary traits of the people mentioned in it. In his book, however, he only discusses one charac-teristic example at any length.[113] This one case also continued to constitute the core of his theory for years after the appearance of his book. He called the family under scrutiny Romsch to protect their privacy, even though three years previously during a lecture he had explicitly identified them as the Pfaus family.[114] In later publications he would refer time and again to this one 'vagrants' lineage' living in the vendors' colony of Schlossberg near Flochberg because they so pointedly illustrated what Ritter wished to argue – the widely branching hereditary transmission of unfavourable biological traits.

Ritter deals primarily with the descendants of the youngest son of one of the families of the principal stock who married a woman from a notorious family of miscreants. In his historical reconstruction Ritter called attention to a number of changes that occurred circa 1870.[115] Many municipalities, according to him, no longer knew what to do with these people and were said to have put entire families onto ships for America. We can only speculate about the historical accuracy of this inter-pretation. Of those who remained behind the largest part were said to have married people like themselves, such as tramps, beggars and semi-sedentary traders. Thus, in Ritter's terminology, a comparatively pure hereditary strain of criminal blood came into being which determined the disposition of the people from these dynasties and created a definite human type (*Menschenschlag*).[116] Some of them later left for the big cities where they were not recognized and these had mixed with the population. Yet others were said to have managed to find impoverished winter quarters in border areas. Around the turn of the century, they had been able, so Ritter maintained, to carry on with their age-old tricks of fraud and begging in only a small number of places, driving here and there, for example, in a wagon.[117] By about 1930 their descendants belonged to the very poorest in the vagrant colonies and in the slums of the major cities. Some 90 per cent of the 240 Romsch who, in this period, were known to the *Kriminalpolizei* of Württemberg were said to belong to the offspring of this branch.

Ritter rounded off his study with an impressionistic sketch of the contemporary Romsch in broad strokes. These people were, according to him, the parents of the hidden feebleminded juveniles who visited his practice. These people were on relief, unlicensed street-traders, beggars and the down and out. Among the women, vice was said to be common and the children frequently ended up in reform schools. The families had no shortage of children, many of whom, Ritter claimed, were mentally defective. It was his conviction that the people who belonged to this biologically determined lineage simply lacked the capacity to adapt socially. He diagnosed them as unstable and beyond any hope of improvement, emphasizing that they lived like parasites at the expense of the settled community. In his terminology they were asocial or antisocial psychopaths, or socially defective types.[118]

It doesn't strike me as useful to explore the methodological shortcomings of Ritter's study in detail, especially since he himself hardly tried to justify the way in which he carried out his analysis. Nevertheless I would like to take a look at certain aspects of his method briefly in order to provide some insight into the shaky foundations of his work and the questionable ethics of his scientific approach. First of all, it is necessary to comment on the way in which he constructed a representative lineage, for in practice this is what his study amounted to. Before he introduced this family in his book, he went on at length about the marked improvement in social position both of the sons of one male ancestor and of one particular son of a second founding father. He cited three reasons for their rise in society: one hereditary-biological, one social, and one individual. It was above all a tie with a sedentary woman which he considered to be advantageous for them in the long run, for according to Ritter she passed on a disposition towards a settled existence to her children which eroded in time their hereditarily determined compulsion to wander aimlessly. Ritter similarly considered a change of milieu as a means to achieve a higher social position. In this context he explained that sedentary people continue to look on the children of vagabonds as socially suspect, with all the concomitant stigmatization of such views. This was why the children often kept moving from one place to another, before having a chance to earn some respect anywhere. This line of reasoning, I feel, reveals a certain understanding of the processes of social interaction that might have led Ritter to a more differentiated vision of the possibilities for social-economic improvement open to people in a disadvantaged situation, but not for a moment did Ritter allow this perception to disturb the main line of his argument, his preoccupation with heredity. For him everything revolved around social conformity. Children who managed to acquire superior social opportunities, had inherited that ability from their sedentary mother. Position, class and race are, for those who share such thinking, inextricably bound up with each other.

Another methodological flaw in Ritter's work methods is that, while interpreting the history of itinerant groups in Germany, he relies entirely on the contents of sources from government archives, even though he certainly discerned the limits of the policy enacted.[119] He was sure that the persecutory measures and the initiatives towards socialization, settlement and emancipation would fail because they were based on erroneous suppositions. Governments forgot that they were dealing with a biologically determined sort of person, one who was essentially immutable and who, by virtue of his high fertility, compensated for losses incurred through persecution with natural increments. It is worthwhile to contemplate this development which he sketches at some greater length, for here Ritter presented his vision of the social history of people with ambulant occupations, including Gypsies and those who were gypsy-like. Except in *Ein Menschenschlag* he was writing about knaves, tramps and vagrants. Similarly, we can deduce from other publications that the portrait he presents of these low-life types bore a stark resemblance to how he saw the (Gypsy) mixed-blood population. According to him these people had always optimally exploited the geographical features of Schwabia which were so favourable for the kind of life which they led. Hilly surroundings, deserted valleys, thick forests, remote villages, inns and mills standing in isolation.[120] Yet Germany was also split into countless small enclaves each with its own counts, dukes, knights and other lords so that, if persecuted in one place, people quickly fled to a neighbouring area. Owing to the weak co-ordination of government policy this situation could drag on and on. Using lists of wanted persons, the head of police in Sulz, Jacob Schäffer, managed, at the end of the eighteenth century and beginning of the nineteenth century, to register a population of some 3,000 criminal types in Schwabia and to carry out their repression more effectively. As a consequence of the growing number of sentences of death or life imprisonment, many vagrants had fled away, or turned semi-sedentary. They never wholly settled down because, according to Ritter, the large landowners did not make meadows or farmland available to the vagabond-colonists on their terrain so that they were compelled by a lack of work opportunities to return once again to their roaming ways. Once more Ritter, to my mind, expressed here a social-economic perception which could have led to greater nuance in his vision of the history of these groups.

The label of asociability

To Ritter's way of looking at things, asociability was one of the most disadvantageous inherited characteristics of rovers. Only in the early 1940s would he declare the label to be applicable to a far larger category of people.[121] Then, in fact, it became a collective designation for everyone, excluding the sick and invalided, who cost the community time, money and energy. Closer reading of his publications also discloses that, in a certain sense, he was constantly concerned with the same – in practice poorly-demarcated – categories of people, whether writing about Gypsies, *Jenischen*, half-castes or marginal riff-raff. Only he was constantly shifting his perspective. The point of departure of his research on asociability in the 1930s (which, indeed, was not confined to Germany) was that many people hardly had any economic value for the community. The spotlight was accordingly turned on families and communities of paupers, recipients of welfare, and the neglected. The concept of asociability in the first decades of the twentieth century became increasingly an expression of a kind of moral criterion. People who were earlier referred to as dishonourable or who were known as notorious good-for-nothings in these years became tagged as asocial. Since this was a word from a foreign language, it was replaced under the Nazis by such terms as *gemeinschaftsfremd* and *gemeinschafts-unfähig*.[122] In this context Ritter cited a ministerial decree from 18 July 1940 with guidelines for evaluating hereditary health. Here *gemeinschafts-fremd* pertained to all persons with an inclination towards one form or another of condemnable behaviour (including psychopaths, addicts and trouble-makers) and whose nature precluded any possibility of amelioration. Ritter attributed five social attitudes to these people which, one by one, he found fault with: they were weak, troublesome, destructive, recalcitrant and hostile.[123] He fails to mention how he applied these in the execution of his research. Under the label 'alienated' (*Gemeinschaftsentfremdeten*) he grouped those whose asocial behaviour was induced solely by environmental factors, for example people neglected by their parents.

The definition of 'asocial' was thus rather inclusive. All persons without education or training about whose usefulness the government was in doubt and whose way of life was seen as a nuisance or counter-productive for the community could be labelled as socially defective. It was then necessary to determine whether this was a matter of a hereditary lack of social skills, an individually determined abnormal disposition, or if extreme circumstances had generated the socially disruptive (*gemeinschaftszerstörende*) behaviour. Genealogical family tables were relied on to furnish conclusive evidence. Having reached this juncture, Ritter posited that the *Jenische Menschenschlag* constituted the nucleus of the asocial population.[124] Other studies to which he referred in this context, which together were said to contain an inventory of the asocial population, came, Ritter maintained, to the same conclusion.[125] By descent the asocial were said to be immune to influence and incorrigible and to cost the community a great deal of money. They lived restless lives and, in keeping with life's rule that 'like seeks like', were prone to become involved with Gypsies. Another generally accepted finding was that all these groups of asocials were distinguished by a comparatively high fertility.[126] In essence, according to Ritter, they were representatives of a primitive, degenerate sort of people. Some researchers spoke of them, he said, as unformed, unripe or undeveloped. What was actually true, according to his notions, was that, by nature, they were not capable of social adaptation. Owing to a congenital inability to work or act communally they existed as parasites, as *gemeinschädigende* members of the body politic.[127] A description in which it is easy to recognize Ritter's portrait of the *Jenische Menschenschlag* and his prototypical Gypsy.

The mark of criminality

One of the most important categories under the label *Gemeinschafts-fremden* was that of hereditarily tainted criminals, so-called born wrong-doers.[128] They, too, according to Ritter, seldom came from a sedentary milieu. They usually belonged to the ranks of the mentally less-developed and were economically and socially weaker members of society, which was also how he looked upon casual labourers. These people, in his view, had no steadfastness, and shifted about restively. The need to do research aimed specifically at this category, especially in wartime, was, according to Ritter, twofold. Society should be protected from dangerous characters and *Gemeinschaftsfremden*, and those fit to work and socially adjusted (*Gemeinschaftsfähigen*) should be employed in places where their productivity was badly needed.[129] He did not assume, indeed, that the criminal type could be identified at a glance. He was of the opinion that contemporary research had rendered obsolete Lombroso's criminological-anthropological notions about atavism, the reversion of people to an (ancestral) state of primitiveness. He did not believe that someone's natural bent could be read from external features – proof yet again that he had little confidence in physical anthropology. Only by analysing genealogically the hereditary circle of the criminal under scrutiny was it possible, Ritter found, to achieve results.[130]

In the last publication from his pen, an article from 1944 about the nature of juveniles who broke the law, Ritter went into depth about his methods as a researcher into heredity. What is at once striking is the eclectic way in which he links features (characteristics, traits) from different areas of life, in this respect remaining true to the spirit of his earliest writings. Thus during his medical training in Heidelberg he had begun with a study of hereditarily determined susceptibility to allergies and its relation to nervous disorders.[131] Later he became fascinated by red hair as a physical phenomenon and pointed out a correlation among racial hybridization, crime and the frequency of this hair colour.[132] This finding proved useful to understanding why so many men at the core of the Romsch lineage, the family which according to Ritter was a typical product of the crossing of inferior Germans and Gypsies, whether of mixed blood or not, had red hair and beards.[133] In 1944 he coined a phrase which, suitable for printing above his work as a credo, gave explicit expression to his anxious view of the world: 'Niemand von uns weiss, ob er nicht Träger einer sich ungünstig auswirkenden Anlage ist.' ('None of us knows whether he might not be the carrier of a predisposition with unfavorable consequences.')[134]

For accused criminals, Ritter enumerates a whole series of their traits, such as: emotional impoverishment, lack of willpower, an inclination to defraud, pathological lying, aggression, sloth (a sin against middle-class morality) and a volatile temperament. In his multidisciplinary approach the deviations piled up. There is one salient aspect that I am unwilling to skip without mention. Ritter wrote that when a woman is weak, vain, or unwise this need not mean that she will commit any punishable offence. Should a boy inherit these qualities from his mother, on the other hand, it is extremely likely that he will go astray. Should the hereditary taint not be discovered in the immediate family circle of the youth in question, then further research along the branches of his family tree, moving back in time, is requisite until the person is located who passed on the damaging trait. Ritter cites a complex of social defects – as defined by the middle class – as a guideline for the researcher: illegitimate children, divorces or shattered relations, a constant changing of vocation, lack of cohesion in a family, the disappearance of family members, suicide among relatives, family members reduced to poverty by gambling, suspect sources of income such as prostitution or pimping, an uncle shipped off to America because of a youthful folly, a relation who is continually initiating court cases, a sectarian fanatic.[135] Although Ritter had remarked elsewhere that it was not yet known how complex character traits were inherited, in the genealogy of families he thought he could locate enough evidence to go on to stamp people with the mark of criminality.[136]

THE RECEPTION OF RITTER AND HIS RELATIONS WITH CONTEMPORARIES

Reviews of Ein Menschenschlag

We can get some idea of the scientific value that contemporaries attributed to Ritter's research from reviews in professional journals and popular periodicals. In so doing, however, we should keep in mind that few writers at the time would have dared to comment critically on the politically sensitive subject that Ritter broached. There was nothing like an open scientific forum. It is thus a possibility that the reviews primarily reflect official ideas about research during the 1930s and early 1940s.[137] In any event, medical-psychiatric, criminological, specialized racial and racial-hygienic, ethnological and genealogical, anthropological, psychological as well as more general periodicals devoted some paragraphs to *Ein Menschenschlag* (1937) or at least noted its appearance.

Reviewers were unanimous that the book was extraordinarily readable, accessible, and vividly written, easy to understand for the layman and a valuable acquisition for professional colleagues. Some read the family portraits that were included as if they were mini-crime novels. The author was praised for his painstaking attention to detail and his indefatigable animus for research, for his cultural-historical and hereditary-biological insights, as well as for the way in which he extended previous genealogical research on particular deviant families to a much larger population in an innovative way.[138] The work was said to merit recommendation to pedagogues, teachers, psychiatrists, doctors, sociologists, neurologists, (criminal) judges, detectives, administrators, geneticists, racial hygienists, and – not to be forgotten – young people growing up who could learn the responsibility from it that rested on them in contracting marriage. From notices in medical-psychiatric publications it is easy to see that Ritter's hereditary biological findings met with great appreciation. Nor did reviewers omit to mention the importance of his specific attention to Gypsies, vagrants, the asocial, beggars, prostitutes and the mentally deficient. They spoke as well of what they qualified as the original way in which, via his psychiatric practice for juveniles and his use of social-historical sources, he had hit upon a biological human type – never previously described in this way – which, through the mechanics of heredity, passed on to following generations its genetic group's identity. His discovery that below the surface of apparent integration into German society and a 'hidden feeblemindedness', there lurked a biologically coherent cluster of hereditary defects, won him recognition on all sides. He also scored in demonstrating a blood tie between descendants of criminals and Gypsies (from the beginning of the fifteenth century), as well as demonstrating that this was not a case of individuals whose social fall came about because of poverty or losing their way, but rather of hereditarily contaminated cheats and asocial psychopaths who constituted a state within the state. From the perspective of public health, reviewers attached importance to Ritter's point that asociability was not an isolated form of degeneration but was connected to other inherited genetic impairments such as feeble-mindedness and wanderlust. Here was said to lurk a double threat since fertile people were involved who were extremely ill-suited as marriage partners for hereditarily healthy Germans. It was necessary to take practical steps to prevent this social-biological branding iron from leaving its imprint on society.

It is also worth mentioning that a number of reviewers called attention to the fact that the human type Ritter described bore no special stamp of race and thus could not be told apart from other Germans through prominent, deviant external characteristics.[139] That is probably also the reason why an article by a specialist on race called for anthropological research to test Ritter's findings.[140] The comments of another reviewer with a similar scientific background were consistent with this obser-vation to the extent that he voiced his regrets that Ritter had not performed any physical-anthropological research. The reviewer felt that this was a pity since it was indeed information about racial traits that could add considerably to Ritter's hereditary pathological insights into 'elements of alien blood within the territory of German sovereignty'.[141]

The single answer which Ritter still owed to science, wrote two reviewers, was how to explain the yearning to wander psychiatrically.[142] A reviewer in a criminological publication put a similar doubt into words; he began by emphasizing the utility of the study for combatting crime and for criminological biology, then went on to call Ritter's acceptance of a congenital compulsion to roam questionable from a psychological point of view.[143] There was no difference of opinion concerning the consequences of Ritter's research results for racial policy. One reviewer pointed out that, in the interests of inclusiveness, it was important when applying radical racial hygienic measures to leave an ample margin when drawing the line demarcating asocial or criminal mental defectives, or the less-gifted.[144] A second reviewer took the position that should this kind of person truly constitute a hereditary biological entity, its representatives should fall under the dictates of the sterilization law.[145] A third found that thanks to Ritter it was possible to distinguish clearly between racially pure Gypsies, of whom there were said still to exist several thousand (at that moment – in 1943! – labouring, according to the reviewer, in separate camps) and the incorrigible *Jenischen*, sprung from German soil, for whom he considered separate eradication measures were required.[146] In genealogists' circles Ritter's study was also received with immense enthusiasm. People praised it as a text book for genealogists, an exemplary scholarly work that would nurture racially responsible behaviour. It was considered ideal material for instruction of children older than 16 and as a pedagogic handbook for teachers, 'weil in ihnen alles Wesentliche in voller und erschütternder Lebenswirklichkeit da ist' ('since true to life it contains everything essential in complete and moving terms').[147]

Contemporary researchers studying Gypsies

In September 1937 an article appeared by Carl-Heinz Rodenberg, a psychiatrist and head of the *Erb-und Rassenpflege* division of the national committee for Public Health Services, in which, in an almost pro-grammatic fashion, he explained that Germany, having come to recognize the racial biological danger presented by Jews, had taken adequate protective measures against them, so that now it was time to focus policy-making and scientific attention on the nomadic Gypsies, as he called them. Indeed they, too, said to be a racially exclusive and *artfremde* group, were consequently a biological threat to the German people.[148] In his discussion he devoted attention to the most important findings of Gypsy research in recent years; in addition to Ritter's work, he commented on Otto Finger (1937), Robert Krämer (1937), Martin Block (1936), Norbert Vogel (1937), Dr Günther (1937–38) and Joachim Rómer (1937).[149] Although, for the most part, Rodenberg invoked articles based on partial research, these nevertheless reinforced his conviction that laws and regulations were needed to muster racial-hygienic resistance to Gypsies and other asocials as well. The projects launched by Ritter's institute shortly thereafter, under the aegis of the Ministry of Public Health, meshed smoothly with this proposal to intensify Gypsy research.

It has been suggested that interest in Germany in the (racial) scientific study of Gypsies increased sharply in these years, landing Ritter in a competitive situation[150] but I have found no decisive evidence to confirm such a claim. In contrast to his broad, racial hygienic research, elsewhere in Germany only isolated initiatives were undertaken, usually without any follow-up and without anything being published. Nor have I turned up the least corroboration for the idea that radicalization of measures against Gypsies was in part a consequence of growing competition in wartime between Ritter's institute and the *Amt Ahnenerbe* of the SS.[151] I did, however, find two indications which help put things in perspective. These concerned first of all the train of events centered around the anthropologist Wolfgang Abel who was employed by that bureau. He indeed appears to have studied Gypsies, in Scotland among other places, but he never published an integral work on them. In his attempts in 1942 to create an independent institute for anthropology and racial biology, he met with no encouragement at the ministerial level.[152] He can therefore scarcely be called a serious rival. I unearthed another reference to the activities of the *Amt Ahnenerbe* in this field of study in a letter dated 14 January 1943 in which the Criminal Investigation Department in Vienna was asked to allow Johann Knobloch to carry out research into the language and morals of Gypsies in concentration camp Lackenbach in Burgenland, a project for which both Himmler and Arthur Nebe had given their permission.[153] From Knobloch's publications we learn that, in the spring of 1943, he transcribed a number of texts from the mouths of Gypsies confined in that camp.[154] He was thus also hardly a competitor for a figure like Ritter with his broad racial hygiene approach. The same holds true for the activities of the SS's *Rasse- und Siedlungs-Hauptamt* which was said to have appropriated Gypsy research in occupied Austria for itself as early as 1938.[155] Much more likely is that the bureau, which we know bore co-responsibility in 1942 for the evacuation of politically undesirable persons – such as all coloureds, half-castes, Gypsies, (half-)Jews, asocials and the mentally ill – to occupied territories in the West, with *rassische Wertung* as the prevailing criterion for selection, made use of the racial diagnoses completed by, among others, Ritter's institutes.[156] The racial hygienic proposals generated by Ritter's research and the political consequences that Himmler and his consorts attached to them, namely internment in a concentration camp, were not so different in principle, however, that speculation about competition between institutions becomes necessary.

Most authors to whom Rodenberg refers asked themselves the same questions as Ritter himself did. They let themselves be led, moreover, by the same population policy fears (large number of children, increased asociability, criminal mixed bloods) and their proposals did not essentially differ from the solutions Ritter had formulated.[157] Nevertheless I want to pause to consider two aspects of their work, for I believe these are representative of how someone's scientific viewpoint apparently unavoidably intertwines with his social attitude towards his research subjects – in this instance Gypsies.

In my analysis of Ritter's main work I have already alluded several times to the fact that someone interested in the history of Gypsies in nineteenth-century Germany could read between the lines that many of them were to a certain extent integrated in Germany's economic and social life. The same holds true for Mayor Günther's publication about the Gypsy colonies on the edge of the municipality of Berleburg in the south of Westfalen. In his historic sketch, based on local sources, a remarkably positive image prevails of the well-disposed reception accorded to Gypsies by the local nobility and officials of the church, with mention being made of high positions held in the army, honours conferred for significant services rendered, and the performance of such responsible occupations as nightwatchmen; all contributory reasons for their receiving permission in the eighteenth century to settle in the vicinity.[158] Their descendants in the nineteenth century were registered, according to Günther, as day labourers and wanderers and in the 1930s many of them still appeared to have vocations that kept them on the move. Of the 65 vendor permits issued in 1935, 51 went to residents of the Gypsy colony. In this context Günther reports that the district union of those who worked at an organized ambulant vocation had also accepted Gypsies from Berleburg in their midst, for me clear proof of their far-reaching integration but for the mayor simply provocation causing him to exclaim that this was a tragicomic coincidence. Still he was willing to concede that: 'Es soll nicht verkannt werden, dass einige durchaus arbeitsam und stetig ihrem Erwerb nachgehen, wie sich nach der Anzahl der von ihnen geklebten Invalidenquittungskarten feststellen lässt.' ('It should not be denied that some of them lead an industrious life and make a steady living, which we can establish from the number of stamps in their books for disablement benefits.')[159] What especially worried him was the rapidity with which they reproduced according to statistics. They were, he continued, for a long time no longer the pure Gypsies of the past, but were rather the degenerate offshoots of once proud dynasties. Above all, since the First World War they appeared with some regularity to have been guilty of criminal and other asocial behaviour. Günther overlooked any possible connection with altered economic and political circumstances, blaming their ongoing intermarriage with marginal figures for the social-biological degeneration that he believed he could detect and which, it was said, was so costly to the government in terms of money and energy.

The ethnological-anthropological image of the true, racially pure Gypsy that runs like a red line through the history of Gypsy studies may also be observed popping up again and again in discussions during the Nazi era. A rough division seems justified. On the one side there are researchers who, like Ritter, were rather taken with eugenics; among them the notion of the true Gypsy had assumed practically the character of a myth that served to reveal existing Gypsies as degenerate specimens who no longer observed the authentic laws of the tribe, were no longer fluent in their own language, and married with non-Gypsies.[160] Opposed to them were those with an anthropological training who clung for a much longer time to the idea that there were still indeed racially pure Gypsies,[161] dividing them into ethnological categories which they then attempted to characterize physically. That this racial ideological or theoretical approach matched poorly with heterogeneous reality – wherein itinerants of diverse origin had carried on marrying each other down through the centuries, as Ritter's research along genealogical lines also demonstrated – can be strikingly illustrated by work of the Austrian SS officer, Karl Moravek published in 1939. Indeed, in that very year, Moravek worked for Ritter although very briefly.[162] Like Gerhard Stein, he placed himself in the anthropometric tradition of Gypsy researchers such as L. Glück (1897), A. Weisbach (1889) and V. Lebzelter (1923).[163]

Moravek's publication contained a report of his findings about a sample of 113 so-called Burgenland Gypsies from the border area between Austria and Hungary, but it was basically part of an extensive, comparative anthropometric study of 460 Gypsies and 2,000 indigenous natives which, however, never found its way into print. This is to be regretted because, in his foreword, Moravek disclosed that the sedentary Burgenland Gypsies were not a racial entity and, anthropologically speaking, they constituted a mixed population. Nevertheless he still rejected the designation 'mixed-blood population' because he believed that, from an ethnic-sociological viewpoint, a distinct group was concerned. Since he had worked in the region as a surveyor for years, he asserted that his experience enabled him to recognize their typical Gypsy characteristics.[164] This experience brought him to the conclusion that his subjective impressions were more reliable than the indicators used for group classifications – hardly to be measured objectively – which were needed to distinguish sub-categories of Gypsies. Relying on literature and his research data, augmented by what experience had taught him, he was of the opinion that a division into four principal groups was justifiable: the *ziganid* (clearly identifiable members of the Gypsy people); the *fremdrassigen* (to the extent that they were not readily recognizable as Gypsies); those who bore *the stamp of south-eastern Europe* (a kind of mixed category); and those who were indistinguishable from indigenous locals.[165] Their economic and living conditions varied considerably, the musically talented 'true Gypsies' often earning their money at the roadside and those who were the most European in appearance usually being better off.[166] Those of mixed blood were, for the most part, loafers and ne'er-do-wells, which was why the native population wanted nothing to do with them, although Moravek had heard from different informants that, in the past, when smaller numbers were involved, relations with them were said to have been better.

What makes Moravek's study so especially interesting is the tension that we find in it between the crude ethnological concepts that the author presents and the concrete anthropometric findings that he handles. Thus, at a certain point, referring to the authors mentioned above, he writes that there was a fundamental consistency to research findings among Gypsies in Hungary, Serbia and Burgenland. Then immediately afterwards, when he indicates that there were diverse observations about the skin colour of those studied, he offers the absence of clear-cut criteria as an explanation for such variety.[167] He encountered similar discrepancies with respect to the hair colour, alluding to such complicated factors as baldness, closely-shaved heads and colour changes from the summer sun. True Gypsies were said to have the blackest hair, but in practice he came across primarily black-brown gradations. The small number of Gypsies with dark irises also clashed with his standard image, which he interpreted as revealing a high level of intermarriage with Europeans. The body size of the members of Gypsy groups, both on the whole and within separate categories, also seemed to vary considerably. The only interim conclusion that he dared to draw was that skin colour among 'Gypsies with mixed blood' was a much better gauge for judging the extent of exogamy than either the colour of hair or eyes.[168]

The fragmentation of his research population was extremely evident to Moravek when he was unable to discover significant connections between the characteristics that he distinguished. Fieldwork indicated that there were no anthropometrically demonstrable racial relationships among his diverse sub-categories.[169] These findings, however, did not induce him to speak of any shortcomings in the methods of physical anthropology or in any way to call into question the pretensions of that discipline. To his way of thinking, the half-castes were the ones who were clouding the picture with their physically impure traits which triggered his concluding remark that from a racial hygiene perspective it was advisable to oppose further mixing of the races. He hoped that the laws that were then being drafted governing the Gypsies would assure the prevention of new relations between them and indigenous peoples.[170]

GYPSY POLICY BEFORE AND DURING THE
NAZI REGIME

Continuity and escalation

Proposals to introduce a Gypsy law did not materialize out of thin air but dovetailed with the social exclusion of people with a Gypsy-like way of life that had already been set in motion years before. The Nazis, however, carried this policy to the utmost extremes.[171] The question that interests me in this context is the role that Ritter played in these developments. What was the nature of the relationship between the research activities of his institutes, the policy regulations that he proposed, and their implementation during the Nazi regime? In attempting to arrive at an answer we run into an interconnectedness among all sorts of institutes that can hardly be disentangled. That is also the reason why, during preliminary court investigations after the war, Ritter and his colleagues were never nominated for further judicial probing and why, even in 1989, the public prosecutor could dismiss as unproven the charge that Ritter's research institutes had co-operated in the planning of genocide.[172] To be sure, justicial bodies had not enough documentation at their disposal at first to make an accurate estimate of the situation, yet a reluctance also existed to acknowledge the contributions made by countless vocational groups to the Nazis' racial policy. In the 1970s and 1980s, charges became nullified by the statute of limitations; the accused were psychologically or physically no longer able to appear in court, and even the discussion of the importance of racial diagnoses for determining who was sent to concentration camps had reached a dead end.

During a preliminary investigation launched against Ritter's former associates Sophie Ehrhardt and Adolf Würth in the early 1980s, the public prosecutor in Stuttgart even displayed unabashed scepticism about the very existence of racial diagnoses, the criteria on the basis of which they were said to be drafted, and their use by the Gestapo.[173] He had asked advice from Hans W. Jürgens, who was known as an expert on the subject of Nazi population policy and performed research himself on marginal social elements during the Nazi regime, and who controlled the legacy of Hans Weinert, director of the Anthropological Institute in Kiel from 1935 to 1955.[174] On 7 April 1982 Jürgens wrote that anthropological diagnoses were still always used to characterize genetically isolated population groups. For Gypsies in wartime, however, that would not have been true, since they were seen as asocials. In his view documents from the *Kriminalpolizei* rather than diagnoses along racial lines had dictated their selective admission to concentration camps.

An observation to which he added: 'Letzteres wäre nach der Ideologie der Nationalsozialisten auch ein Widersinn gewesen, da es sich bei den Zigeunern immerhin um "Arier" handelt.' ('The latter would also have been an absurdity according to the ideology of the National Socialists, because of the fact that Gypsies, after all, are "Aryans".')[175]

One can ask in all conscience how it is possible that a public prosecutor in the 1980s could still mistake such a misinterpretation of the foundations of the Nazis' racial policy towards Gypsies and why he ignored jurisprudence concerning the *Wiedergutmachung* in which it is stated explicitly that copies of the racial diagnoses which Ritter wrote out for the *Reichskriminalpolizeiamt* were used to implement regulations against Gypsies? Here, to my way of thinking, we can see the impact of the image of Ritter as an anthropologically-oriented expert on race, an image that has still not disappeared from the literature, despite the fact that after the war various of his former colleagues confirmed that for him it was descent which had above all weighed decisively in his categorization of people.[176]

Let me return, however, to the discriminatory regulations and laws affecting Gypsies that had already been enacted decades before the Nazis came to power. In this context it is necessary to point out that criminological biologists such as Ritter were part of a long-standing tradition of criminologists. In Chapter 2 of this study, concerning the German historian Grellmann, I described how his approach had a great influence on later authors who dealt with the issue of Gypsies in one justiciary capacity or another, such as Avé-Lallemant (1858), Liebich (1863), Gross (1894), Dillmann (1905) and Aichele (1912).[177] Their interest, too, at first primarily concerned the Gypsy language, which amounted to the compilation of word lists or the notation of new words from the lips of arrested Gypsies, attached to which there were usually observations about Gypsy history and group characteristics. The belief was current that police work was made considerably easier once the police authorities had mastered the Gypsy language and acquired some insight into their group character. Tracing people, determining someone's identity, verifying alibis, comparison of interpretations, and getting to the bottom of the Gypsies' cultural background (their essential being) would then give rise to far fewer difficulties.

Around the turn of the century, attention seems to have shifted to identification and registration – activities from which criminologists expected wonders in combatting the 'zigeuner *Unwesen*' or Gypsy peril as the policy towards these groups had come to be known.[178] The Bavarian Central Bureau for Gypsies, set up in 1899, fulfilled a pivotal function in this approach. The centre operated as a division of the police directorate in Munich under the leadership of Alfred Dillmann, whose handbook on Gypsies, which appeared in 1905, would come to serve as a guide for judicial organs. In his foreword he characterized Gypsies as a morally inferior and criminally inclined population group, although according to him they were no longer a separate people in Germany but consisted almost exclusively of mixed-bloods and, in some small part, of people of local origin: 'Die rassechte Zigeuner gehört bei uns zu den Seltenheiten.' ('With us the racially pure Gypsy is a rarity.')[179] This is why he defined the category of persons who should be registered as broadly as possible, encompassing all who had itinerant vocations with no fixed place of abode. In his manner of sketching this social category we recognize the standard eighteenth-century portrait of Gypsies: they roam about while, with petty trade as camouflage, they beg, poach, endanger public safety as tramps, spread infections, steal, cheat people and exploit the superstitiousness of country people.[180] The greatest problem for the police in those years – and the same actually always held true – was to identify suspect persons conclusively as 'Gypsy' or 'Gypsy-like'.[181] The intentions of the Justice Department appear to have been at cross-purposes with villagers who simply offered Gypsies a roof over their head, gave them food, or let them do chores. Dillmann also complained that local police authorities issued licenses to vendors much too readily or were satisfied to drive Gypsies beyond the boundaries of their municipality instead of checking on their behaviour and, in the event of ascertaining any infractions, taking direct action.[182] Actually he was looking for ways to make each region gypsy-free without indicating what central policy measures were necessary to achieve an adequate solution. Implicitly he conveyed his conviction that roving as a way of life should vanish.

To reach this goal he built up, just as all his pro-eugenics contemporaries did, a central register of persons from wandering families who were known to the police, making use of data from the courts and municipal authorities in Germany and in Luxembourg, the Netherlands, Austria, Switzerland and Hungary. This registration and identification system would be progressively refined in the coming years, until finally, during the Nazi regime, it operated in all major places in Germany.[183]

In the criminological literature from the turn of the century we recognize other themes that will come to dominate the foreground in the 1930s. Here I am alluding especially to the idea that Gypsies were not a cultural race and were *artfremd* to the Germans.[184] In his Württemberg-oriented study, the same area where Ritter's research also primarily took place, Aichele had depicted them not only as a group that had never advanced beyond the childhood phase of civilization, but also as a kind of mythical primitive, the remnants of an original core of cultureless gatherers, living on what nature had to offer, at the mercy of an irresistible urge to wander and compelled by penury to live as social parasites at the expense of a host population.[185] All the inconsistencies which mark the profile of Gypsies in the 1930s and 1940s crop up in Aichele's portrait of them: rovers about whom racial science can not yet say anything definitive, who, ethnographically-speaking, are Aryans but, physically and anthropologically speaking consist for the most part of mixed-bloods.[186] The criminological biologists were the ones who would attribute the deviant behaviour of this population category to genetic factors. In the spirit of racial hygiene, they compiled elaborate personal files in order to map case histories of criminal or asocial families, subsequently making proposals to sterilize, isolate or confine indicated persons in a concentration camp, invoking, as they did so, the law for preventing crime.[187]

How could these criminological ideas ultimately lead to such far-reaching policy measures? To understand how, we should realize that some 150 ordinances were passed against Gypsies in Germany between 1900 and 1933, the largest share of them in Bavaria. Yet, as a result of this political criminalization, the number of complaints about the *Zigeunerunwesen* only kept increasing. A sort of self-fulfilling prophecy was set in motion, which was not helped by the inadequacy of the police apparatus. Hence in 1926 in Bavaria, special, separate laws were enacted against Gypsies, *Landfahrer* (a generic term for all 'gypsy-like beings') and 'the work shy', a triad in which we recognize the clustering of race, way of life and social esteem which also would characterize later Nazi Gypsy policy. The law spoke explicitly of the *reinrassische Zigeuner* and brought an itinerant way of life into disrepute by lumping together all people who tried to earn a living without settling down as workshy.[188] Even then the government thus drew a connection between a shifting existence and asociability, and presented the 'Gypsy race' as the personification of this way of life. Once the Bavarian law was put into effect, anyone older than 16 who had no steady wage labour could, without any kind of trial, be put into a workhouse or house of correction for two years. From then on one needed to apply to the police for a permit in order to travel around with a caravan or cart. The police, if they could have had their way, would have put an end to such movement entirely, for they saw in it a threat to the public order, property and health – but legislators were not prepared to go that far. In 1927 the Prussian lawmaker did decide that fingerprints and photos of all Gypsies had to be taken for a special card, the *Zigeunerausweis*. The necessity of coming up with a practical definition of what precisely a 'Gypsy' was began to make itself felt with increasing urgency.

When the Nazis rose to power in 1933, at first they seemed to show little interest in 'the Gypsy problem'. The calm, however, would turn out to be deceptive. It would take us too far afield to review all the laws between 1933 and 1945 by which step by step Gypsies were sidelined.[189] Citation of the most important ones, enacted by the Ministries of the Interior and Justice, will suffice here. The sterilization law introduced in 1933 and designed to prevent people with an 'hereditary defect' from reproducing, offered the option of defining a Gypsy as asocial in order subsequently to nominate him for sterilization. The Nuremberg race laws of 1935 had more far-reaching repercussions for anti-Gypsy policy: they determined who was eligible for citizenship. People with foreign blood in their veins were excluded. Yet Gypsies, in contrast to Jews, still were not mentioned in either the *Reichsbürgergesetz* or in the *Gesetz zum Schutze des deutschen Blutes und der deutschen Ehre*. In a 1936 commentary on these laws, however, explicit mention was made of the fact that Jews and Gypsies were the only races in Europe with *artfremdes Blut*.[190] As a consequence of this, they were no longer considered *Reichsbürger* (from 1943 onwards they even lost German citizenship). To enter into marriage with someone of German blood was thus no longer permitted, on penalty of sterilization or compulsory confinement in a work or concentration camp. Moreover, from 1936 onwards the Ministry of the Interior was preparing a separate law for Gypsies and the Ministry of Justice a law specifically for asocials (*Gemeinschaftsfremdengesetz*).[191] Up to the end of the war, however, the actual adoption of these laws was constantly being postponed until some time in the distant future. This was probably, first and foremost, a consequence of opposition from Hitler, who wanted to have his racial policies executed without ministerial interference or restrictive legal measures.[192]

Persecution and annihilation

The persecution of Gypsies cannot be ascribed simply to official legislation. Given that Hitler wished to realize his objectives outside the state's bureaucracy, preferably with secret directives, in this way pre-empting opposition as far as possible, many decrees and ordinances were issued especially by SS-bureaus such as the *Reichssicherheitshauptamt* and the *Reichskriminalpolizeiamt*.[193] In this context we must understand that the Nazis, as far as police and judicial action were concerned, constituted a state within the state.[194] In the course of the 1930s, in keeping with his polycratic policy, Hitler even succeeded in breaking the state's power monopoly by having regulations carried out in the name of the party without there being any legal basis for them. The most powerful body was the SS to which, in 1933, Hitler had assigned responsibility for guarding the concentration camps. The strongest weapon of this organization was the *Schutzhaft*-policy which empowered the police to detain persons in protective custody who, in their eyes, endangered state security. By virtue of this authority, political opponents of diverse kinds, including criminals and the work-shy, could be removed, consigned to a concentration camp without trial or judicial review. For a long time the Ministry of Justice, which was virtually put out of action in this way, and the Ministry of the Interior protested against such arbitrary intercession on the party's part – but in vain.

From 1936 onwards, Himmler's Gestapo operated almost independently as a political police force with extensive executive powers. If this force found that the Ministry of Justice was not satisfactorily pursuing the racial political goals of the party, then it was empowered to intercede autonomously, citing its mandate to protect state security. There was thus nothing barring it from eliminating or liquidating all kinds of undesirable groups and individuals. Thus in the years 1938–40 Hitler's own chancellery, for example, perpetrated wild euthanasia actions against the mentally handicapped and others deemed to be congenitally ill.[195] The powers of the Gestapo as a special police force even increased at the outset of the war when Hitler authorized it to execute criminals without a preliminary trial. At the end of 1941 special ordinances followed against persons branded as *Volksschädlinge*, after which penal executions could take place, especially in occupied areas, without any form of legal proceedings. As for the situation in Germany and Austria, here opportunistic use was made of the findings of registration and identification studies carried out at ministerial level. By silencing ministerial organs and by refusing the Ministry of Justice jurisdiction over what went on in the concentration camps, the SS succeeded in carrying out many illegal measures in wartime without reprisal.[196] Moreover, in the fall of 1942, the new Minister of Justice, Otto Thierack, who in contrast to his predecessor was a fanatic devotee of the tenets of the racial politics of Hitler and his consorts, voluntarily ceded prosecution of Poles, Russians, Jews and Gypsies to Himmler, so that as of 1 January 1943 the police could eliminate all 'fremdvölkische und rassisch minderwertige Menschen' on German soil, or deport them to a concentration camp where the policy of *Vernichtung durch Arbeit* would accomplish their purposes.[197]

What now were the consequences of SS involvement for policy towards Gypsy-like groups? To answer this, to start with, we need to go back to 14 December 1933 when the (unpublished) decree about preventing crime was enacted, which amounted to making anybody who in the eyes of the authorities behaved asocially, or who was a threat to the general welfare, open to arrest by the *Kriminalpolizei*. In practice it turned out that officials had their eye here primarily on domestic and foreign Gypsies (described as a subgroup of the *Landfahrer*), asocials, the unemployed, criminals, traders with no fixed abode, beggars and Jews.[198] The Himmler Decree of 8 December 1938 went a step further, being intended explicitly to staunch the 'Gypsy plague', imposing still further restrictions on those for whom roaming was a way of life. To this end extensive identification and registration were required, and this took place on a basis of race by distinguishing officially among three groups: Gypsies, Gypsies with mixed blood, and 'persons who stray about in a Gypsy-like fashion'. One result of this decree was that many Gypsies lost their jobs.[199] Shortly after the outbreak of the war, on 17 October 1939, Heydrich, the head of the *Reichssicherheitshauptamt*, issued a decree that forbade Gypsies (and those of mixed blood) from leaving their houses. In the following years many additional measures made it more difficult for Gypsies to marry, diminished their chances of finding work,[200] enhanced the possibilities of their (involuntary) sterilization, cut back on the welfare facilities available to them, eroded their legal rights, and facilitated their deportation.

Since 1935 local administrators and welfare organizations had exerted pressure on the police to confine Gypsies in separately con-structed camps, the so-called *SS-Sonderlager*, guarded by the SS, gendarmes or city police in uniform. These camps quickly became reservoirs of forced labour, genealogical registration and compulsory sterilization. During the 1930s they developed from local internment camps into camps where people were amassed for deportation to concentration camps.[201] Before 1939 a number of deportations of Gypsies to concentration camps also already took place – to Buchen-wald, Dachau and Sachsenhausen among other places – the authorities invoking the decree over crime prevention. Once war began, the deportations accelerated, although Heydrich's plan to deport 30,000 Gypsies, in the wake of Jews and Poles, to occupied Poland was never wholly realized but stalled after the evacuation, mentioned above, of 2,800 German Gypsies in May 1940.[202] The decree Himmler issued on 13 October 1942 concerning 'racially pure' *Sinti*-Gypsies was wholly in keeping with the spirit of Ritter's almost mythical ideas about 'genuine Gypsy descendants'.[203] In the future he wanted to permit them, together with 'good mixed-bloods' nominated by Gypsy headmen, a certain freedom of movement by allowing them to roam about in a designated area where they could live observing their own mores and customs. His plans for these 'true Gypsies', however, proved a casualty of Hitler's annihilation directives. The lists which the Gypsy headmen handed in, moreover, had to be checked against Ritter's genealogical data base, with strict norms obtaining. The most drastic regulation was proclaimed on 29 January 1943 by the *Reichszentrale zur Bekämpfung des Zigeunerunwesens*, the so-called Himmler decree which condemned Gypsies to be deported to Auschwitz-Birkenau. Authentic *Sinti-* and *Lalleri-*Gypsies were exempted, as were Gypsies of mixed blood singled out as being of a good sort by the Gypsy headmen who were approached, Gypsies who were legally married to Germans, lived socially adapted lives in the eyes of the local *Kriminalpolizei* (five years' steady work and a fixed abode), were still in military service or could prove they had foreign citizenship. All of them, 12 years and older, had to undergo sterilization – which also actually appears to have taken place.[204] To what extent these 'Gypsy exceptions' finally wound up in Auschwitz remains a point of discussion. It certainly appears that Hitler himself, just as Bormann, Thierack and Goebbels, ordained *Vernichtung durch Arbeit* for all Gypsy-like persons, regardless of how little or how much mixed blood they had.[205]

In the course of 1943 and 1944 many Gypsy-transports from the occupied territories followed. A little over one year later, on 2 August 1944, the Gypsy family camp in Auschwitz-Birkenau was abolished. By this time 13,614 Gypsies had died from malnourishment, diseases, medical experiments and exposure to harsh conditions; 6,432 were gassed, 32 shot down during an attempted escape. Of the 23,000 German and Austrian Gypsies deported to Auschwitz, only 3,000 survived.[206] After the Himmler decree of early 1943, as far as we know, no further official decrees or ordinances pertaining to Gypsies were issued by the *Reichssicherheitshauptamt* or the *Reichskriminalpolizeiamt*.

That was the situation in Germany and Austria, but how did things stand elsewhere in Europe? Various documents from the early 1940s make it clear that, especially in eastern-occupied areas, summary executions of Slavs, communists, partisans, asocials, Jews and Gypsies took place on a large scale without any form of trial or possibility of resistance. In the ideology of the SS these were all categories of *Untermenschen* so that hundreds of thousands of them were shot down in cold blood without any individual distinction among them.[207] The refined registration- and identification-activities which in Germany, Austria and the Western occupied territories served to implement a differentiated racial policy, were unheard of in the East. Appearance, way of life, name, but above all how someone was known in the area (as a Gypsy, Jew or communist, for example) proved decisive in selecting people for deportation or liquidation. The exact number of Gypsies who perished during the Nazi regime still remains unknown. In a recent collection of overview articles the cumulative total of Gypsies who died in concentration camps is estimated at 220,000, but we can only speculate about the mass murder of Gypsy populations in the Ukraine, the Crimea, Croatia, Serbia and other regions.[208]

The role of Ritter's research institutes

To be able to appreciate the role which Ritter and his research institutes fulfilled in this persecutory spiral, we need to recall that he worked for not only the Ministries of Public Health and the Interior but also for the *Reichskriminalpolizeiamt* of the SS – which also formally fell under the Interior. The pre-eminent position that Ritter began to enjoy during the 1930s as far as research on Gypsies was concerned was, without doubt, connected to the aspects of his work that seemed to support government policy. He hoped that the government would use the results of his studies, executed in close co-operation with the *Landeskriminal-polizei*, to take racial hygienic measures with respect to the Gypsies.[209] Consequently it is relevant to examine the course of his career during the Nazi regime more closely. Distributing his research among a number of institutes and, moreover, financed during the war because of the importance which those in power attached to his studies, Ritter managed to cast the net of his research projects over the whole of Germany and part of the occupied territories.[210] Through close col-laboration with regional police authorities, he was able to build up a widely branching registration system from which he drew data for his genealogical and in part also his anthropological studies. This proceeded step by step and began with exploration of relations with Gypsies in south-western Germany since the beginning of the eighteenth century.

After his appointment by the Ministry of the Interior in 1936, Ritter had formed small work groups which carried out independent research in various regions, including Schwaben, Baden and the Pfalz. Genealogy had the highest priority, but the ethnology and psychology of Gypsies were also studied, as well as the extent of their social adaptation and records of their criminal misdeeds. It did not take long before the *Kriminalpolizei* displayed an interest in the research, as expressed by Arthur Nebe and his stand-in, Paul Werner. Nebe would function as a central figure in Ritter's career, especially because after he was assigned the task of setting up a *Reichskriminalpolizeiamt* in Berlin he immediately wanted to take over Ritter's institute. Matters didn't come to such a pass; rather, an agreement was reached that Ritter would serve as adviser to the RKPA in exchange for which the rural *Kriminalpolizeistellen* lent him their support in collecting local information for his studies.

For their study of Gypsies and indigenous wanderers, Ritter and his associates visited their subjects in the field. To facilitate communication, they mastered the rudiments of the German Gypsy dialect, although on occasion an elder from the group also went along with them as an interpreter. In order to immerse himself more deeply in the life, mores and customs of Gypsies, Ritter – at least if we go by what he writes in his autobiography – undertook various journeys for his work, to Hungary and Romania, among other places, where he visited Budapest and Bucharest. He wrote that he even laid eyes on Turkish Gypsies in the Dobrudscha, and had observed Gypsies in Ploesti, Kronstadt, Hermannstadt and Klausenburg, as well as in Copenhagen, Zürich, Vienna, Karinthie and Burgenland.[211] It strikes me, however, that this account of his scouting is rather apocryphal, for neither in archives nor in his official publications do we detect a trace of all these peregrinations. What would have preoccupied him in Germany was the extent to which young Gypsies could be raised in keeping with sedentary norms and how well they could fit in socially. Just as Grellmann had done a century and a half earlier, he asked himself if it made sense to take children from itinerant parents and force them to go to school. His colleague Eva Justin would devote her dissertation, which appeared in 1943, to that topic. Finally she arrived at the conclusion that all Gypsies and Gypsy half-castes of the first degree brought up as Germans – whether socially adapted or asocial and criminal – should, as a matter of principle, be sterilized. Socially adjusted mixed bloods of the second degree could become *eingedeutscht* if their mainly German heritage was irreproachable, whereas asocials and mixed bloods of the second degree, saddled with questionable German blood, should also be rendered incapable of reproduction.[212]

Given that Ritter's mandate was nothing less than to study all non-sedentary groups in Germany, he was quick to strive for the expansion of his scientific team, but he did not succeed in attracting physicians other than Odenwald. Anthropologists did offer their services, which led to a shifting of attention to a terrain in which he was not intensely interested. Anthropometry and photography also yielded results that were scarcely able to be incorporated within the more social-biological and historical-sociological perspectives with which he preferred to work. The scientific projects to which Ritter's institutes devoted themselves served – in letter, if not spirit – the interests of the state, but he always remained dissatisfied with how this connection worked out. Above all his problematic relationship with the *Reichskriminalpolizeiamt*, so keen to follow his advice about individual cases but irresponsive to his attempts to influence general policy, troubled him. He retrospectively interpreted all kinds of haphazard actions as the inevitable outcome of the lack of a general policy fixed in law, which in the summer of 1945 prompted the dubious conclusion: 'Das Zigeunerproblem wurde vom nationalsozialistischen Regime nicht gelöst.' ('The Gypsy problem was not solved by the National Socialistic Regime.')[213] In addition to research on Gypsies and asocials, at the end of the 1930s Ritter threw himself again, even more intensively than during the preceding years, into youth psychology,[214] criminal psychology and genetic characterology.

In line with his contention that the mingling of Gypsies and asocial Germans had negative consequences for both parties, Ritter proposed sheltering men and women in separate camps. In this context he spoke of reservations for asocials.[215] It was also possible for them to be quartered together, but only after sterilization. Request for an operation, according to him, had to come from the individual concerned; in this way the problem of the asocials would resolve itself in the long run. This is how he depicted things in his 1945 autobiography. In his publications, however, Ritter's premise was invariably that sterilization be imposed. Nowhere in his work have I come across the idea that those who had to submit to sterilization could exercise any influence on the selection process. From a letter he sent in 1944 to the German Research Fund (DFG) we can conclude that his proposals for sterilization were indeed acted upon: 'Ein grösserer Teil der begutachteten asozialen Zigeunermischlinge wurde sterilisiert, während Mitglieder geordnet lebender Mischlingssippen mit vorwiegend deutschem Blutsanteil auf sozialen Gebiet eine Behandlung wie Deutschblütige erfahren.' ('The majority of racially diagnosed antisocial Gypsy mixed bloods are sterilized, whereas members of clans of mixed bloods with pre-dominantly German blood who lead orderly lives are treated socially the same as persons with pure German blood.')[216]

In 1941 Arthur Nebe considered the time ripe for the *Reichskriminal-polizeiamt* to have its own scientific criminological biological institute;[217] his first choice for director was Ritter, who, when approached, if we are to take him at his word, was not enthusiastic about the idea. He came around when he was assured that his post in the Ministry of Public Health would not be endangered, he would retain his scientific freedom, and he could carry on with his university work. In addition he was exempted from membership in the SS. According to Ritter, Nebe was playing for high stakes by nominating him, for this was counter to Himmler's wish that Nebe choose between two SS protégés. The *Sicherheitsdienst* had, moreover, solicited advice from a number of renown scholars who also had spoken very favourably of Ritter. The sole concession he had to make to the party was to tolerate an SD officer at his side. Among his initial duties, he counted the building up of a card file to include all asocial and criminal families in Germany and the accumulation of documents that would enable him to provide scientific advice to police investigators about individuals who should be registered according to the law that was pending for *Gemeinschaftsfremden*.

Through his closer co-operation with the police, Ritter even hoped to acquire some influence over the obscure relationships in the concentration camps. Tales were legion about the capriciousness of what took place there. Which brings me to the point of how much Ritter knew about the horrific fate of Gypsies transported to Auschwitz. He was not unaware of the existence of concentration camps, nor was he ignorant that Gypsies and other 'asocials' were brought there. Thus Eva Justin, in connection with a request from a German woman for a divorce on racial hygienic grounds from her *Jenische* husband (the term denoting an indigenous person with an itinerant occupation), something which in principle was not permitted under law since the marriage was a union of Germans with each other, wrote about the kind of people called *Jenischen*: 'Heute sind diese Menschen unter dem starken Druck des Staates entweder in den Arbeitsprozess eingegliedert *oder als unverbesserliche Asoziale in die Konzentrationslager überwiesen*' ('Today, owing to strong pressure from the state, these people have either once more been incorporated within the labour process *or been sent away to concentration camps as incorrigible antisocials*') [my italics – W.W.].[218] In 1939, moreover, Ritter and his staff had conducted research among Gypsies in Sachsenhausen and Jews in Dachau: 'Wir haben hier 400 Zigeuner im Konzentrationslager Sachsenhausen untersucht mit Blutabnahme. Dr. Odenwald, der auch 8 Tage hier arbeitete, untersucht jetzt schon seit 3 Wochen mit frl. dr. Ehrhardt in Dachau Juden.' ('We have done blood tests on 400 Gypsies in concentration camp Sachsenhausen near here. Dr Odenwald, who also worked here for eight days, has been conducting research with Dr. Ehrhardt among the Jews in Dachau for three weeks now.')[219]

Auschwitz-Birkenau was exceptional, however, since it functioned as both a work camp and annihilation camp.[220] The question is whether Ritter knew (or wanted to know) that Gypsies who were sent there were almost certainly going to be exterminated. Around 1942 many in Germany were to a certain extent aware of the *Endlösung* ('final solution') that was under way but chose, whether consciously or otherwise, not to ponder the details.[221] The Nazis never issued written extermination orders; the crimes transpired clandestinely. The consignment of asocials and criminals to work camps continued throughout the duration of wartime to depend on arbitrary policy initiatives. This in no way affected Ritter's lack of belief in the standard training techniques and punishments prescribed for these groups since, according to him, these were undeveloped, primitive beings whose hereditarily determined *Un-Art* was immutable. The solution that he had thought up for these tens of thousands of *Gemeinschaftsschwachen* was in principle practically as rigorous as that of the Nazis. He wanted them excluded from society, set apart in a kind of alternative community: a fenced-in area far from the civilized world, under strict surveillance. His ideas assumed – once again, looking back – almost romantic-idealistic forms:

> Die Gemeinschaftsschwachen könnten je nach Geschick und Talent einem sie befriedigenden Beruf nachgehen, sie könnten ihren eigenen kleinen Haushalt führen, sie könnten in ihrer Freizeit Bücher lesen, Lichtspiele besehen und sich an Musik erfreuen oder auch Sport treiben. ('The socially weak could, in keeping with their gifts and talents, practise a satisfying vocation; they could run their own little household, read books at their leisure, go to the cinema, enjoy music or engage in sports.')

The residents of these miniature societies also were supposed to submit to two conditions: the limitation of their freedom of movement and the sterilization of all sexually mature males to protect the hereditary health of the German people from new contagion in the future. Good behaviour could lead at a later stage to a recommendation for release. In the summer of 1945 Ritter's opinion was still consistently unambiguous: 'Meines Erachtens sollte man jeden Menschen, den wir aus erbgesund-heitlichen Gründen *niemandem* [Ritter's italics – W.W.] zur Ehe empfehlen können, grundsätzlich auch von jeder ausserehelichen Fortpflanzung ausschliessen.' ('In my opinion we should exclude from bearing children, even indeed out of wedlock, every human being whom on eugenic grounds we cannot recommend to anyone as a marriage partner.')[222] Any other solution was, for him, inconsistent and would lead to the suffering of many people. To be sure, Ritter's ideas about preventing crime fell, as he himself tells us, on deaf ears, for they conflicted with strategies that the Nazis had devised. In this respect he referred to tensions between the *Reichskriminalpolizeiamt* and the Ministry of Justice's correctional division concerning the increasing lust for power of the *Sicherheitspolizei*. It all revolved around two questions: who had to answer to whom, and what means to exercise power were available? The Ministry of Justice, Ritter maintained, was still intent on incorporating his institute within its walls, but he chose to limit co-operation with them to the provision of advice.

One of Ritter's most important contacts in the Nazi party was Arthur Nebe, the head of the *Kriminalpolizei* in Germany, a man who, we know from the literature, for years played a double role in the SS. Because of his strategic position for the opposition movement against Hitler (culminating in 1944 in the Stauffenberg putsch), he found himself obliged, despite ever-increasing conflict with his conscience, to remain at his post until the bitter end.[223] Ritter and he shared an affinity for the study of the deviant and apparently respected each other's ambitions. Moreover, they drew steadily closer in their doubts about the path that the *Führer* and his consorts chose to pursue. They simply lived in widely different worlds, and this made it difficult for them to be candid with each other. On many occasions, over the years, Nebe had tried to convince Ritter that he would strengthen his position considerably if he were to accept membership of the NSDAP, join the *Sicherheitsdienst*, or at least leave the church. As it was he still belonged to the category of people who may have won respect for their scientific work but who hadn't been able to shed their aura of not being altogether politically correct. If we go by what Ritter himself has written on the subject, Nebe was eager to form a union with him. Towards this end he had the idea of establishing a criminological academy in Berlin, with a technical, a biological, and a medical institute, and someone with the title of professor at the head of each. Ritter's ambitions, however, leaned more in the direction of an independent institute at the national level in which all criminological biological divisions from the world of public health, justice and the police would join forces. Without doubt he would have imagined himself directing such an institute. In talks with Ritter through-out the war years, Nebe regularly dropped hints that his own influence on developments in Germany was declining. The system had become so complex that, when one government body refused to carry out a certain assignment there was always a second presenting itself to attend to the dirty work. Such conversations fortified Ritter in his conviction that it made little sense for him officially to join the ranks of the police.

In the light of Ritter's ideas on hidden feeblemindedness it is ironic, to say the least, that in his autobiography he so often pointed out the ambiguous position in which he and many with him found themselves during the years of the Nazi regime. During the war he often experienced self-doubts and asked himself whether a latent melancholy may not have been the underlying cause of his criticism of the system and his lack of belief in those brandishing power. He found that he had no natural talent for dissembling all the time and going through life crouched behind a kind of mask. The tension between his self-censuring behaviour in the external world and his inner emotional world runs like a red line through his narrative. In those days people said: 'Wer schweigt, lebt länger.' ('The silent lives longer.')[224] Ritter took this warning very much to heart. A remarkable ambiguity characterizes a point he raised during a talk with Nebe in December 1943 when they were returning from an inaugural party for a criminological-medical institute in Vienna. Nebe steered the conversation to what the consequences would be for Germany should Hitler suddenly die. Ritter's response was that his demise would, he thought, plunge the country into chaos because in that case the question of whether the *Führer* was a genius or mentally unbalanced could no longer be answered and dissension on this point would split the population into two camps, with a possible civil war in the offing.[225] The following year, on 20 July 1944, it turned out that an attempt was actually made on Hitler's life. In the subsequent wave of arrests, many people Ritter knew were taken into custody but what troubled him most was that, shortly after the attack was made public, Nebe went underground. For Ritter there was no doubt that Nebe, having joined forces with those who opposed Hitler, had made himself scarce. Later this proved an accurate assessment, for Nebe was hanged for his participation in the abortive assault on Hitler on 3 March 1945.[226] Considering the fact that Nebe, but not only Nebe, knew exactly how Ritter felt about Hitler and the Nazis, Ritter feared that his own fate, too, was likely to be sealed in the foreseeable future.[227] Yet, despite the Gestapo's policy of terror, which lasted for months, Ritter emerged unscathed.

Identification and arbitrariness

For a better grasp of Ritter's share in Gypsy policy during the Nazi regime it is necessary to analyse the relationship between his institutes and the headquarters for the national data bank on Gypsies and for co-ordination of all police activities, the *Reichszentrale zur Bekämpfung des Zigeunerunwesens* which Himmler placed under the RKPA in Berlin in October 1938.[228] Shortly after this installation, the decree was promulgated to fight the 'Gypsy plague'. In the ensuing specifications about the application of the decree, at the beginning of 1939, the law which was supposed to entail a well-reasoned prohibition of mixed marriages, guidelines for sterilization and also rules governing the life of the 'Gypsy race' in the new Germany was invoked. A first requisite was the extensive, systematic genealogical registration of Gypsies by the local police and public health authorities, together with a photo-bearing identity card to be issued to all Gypsies, each sub-category coded with a different colour. The *Reichszentrale* was entrusted with this task.[229] Ritter's institution in the Ministry of Public Health was required to write out differential racial diagnoses based on this data and on available genealogical documentation:

> Es gibt sehr viel einzurichten, da wir durch den neuesten Reichseinheitlichen Zigeunererlass des Reichsführers SS mit der verantwortllichen Entscheidung über die Rassenzugehörigkeit der ca. 40.000 Zigeuner und Zigeunermischlinge beauftragt sind. Bis zum 1. April [1939] müssen wir mindestens 3000 Gutachten

liefern. ('We have a lot to take care of, for by the latest, general Gypsy decree of the *Reichsführer SS*, we have been given responsibility for deciding on the racial background of about 40,000 Gypsies and Gypsy mixedbloods. By 1 April 1939 we have to deliver at least 3,000 racial diagnoses.')[230]

These racial diagnoses were also used in selecting Gypsies for evacuation to occupied Austria in 1940 where, at a certain moment, Ritter's colleague Adolf Würth appears to have been summoned with his card system to the transit camp Hohenasperg (Ludwigsburg) for the purpose of deciding if the Gypsies there whom the *Kriminalpolizei* had rounded up on a basis of their own criteria might, from a racial biological perspective, be qualified as 'Gypsy'. It turned out that various of the internees were diagnosed by Ritter's institute as 'non-Gypsy'.[231] This sequence of events alerts us to the tension that apparently existed between the criteria which Ritter and his co-workers applied and the felt needs of communities, in the wake of the party's racial politics, to say good riddance to their 'Gypsy-like persons'. We should also pause to realize that Ritter's criteria were certainly not absolutely clear-cut. Rather there was room for subjective interpretation and, in practice, one relied above all on genealogical data.

To illustrate what this could lead to, I cite the discussion that arose in relation to the case of Liselotte W. in Karlsruhe.[232] Her father, Wilhelm Krems W., born in 1890, was decorated for valour as a soldier in the First World War. He married a German woman and lived a totally integrated existence. One of his sons met his death in France in 1940 and his four remaining offspring did respectable work; his sons even belonged to the *Hitlerjugend*. At a certain moment in the public health services in Karlsruhe, doubts arose about his origins and the authorities wrote to Ritter's institute at the Ministry of Public Health; after studying the matter the institute concluded that William W. had to be considered a Gypsy and his children, accordingly, were half-castes. Further study would be needed to determine if this family, with its adapted way of life, fell under the terms of police ordinances. On 8 August 1941 Eva Justin wrote that perhaps Wilhelm W.'s descent marked him as a Gypsy ('only one grandmother was not real'), but he had impressed her as a mixed-blood, so that she was eager to examine his children. According to her they did not fall under the police ordinances, but she did find that they should be prevented from having any more descendants. On 17 October 1942 the children, who until then had known nothing of their father's Gypsy roots, petitioned the RKPA by letter to regard the entire family as being Germans. The Karlsruhe police supported this request in an accompanying letter because the children had never left their birthplace, held down steady jobs, did not consort with Gypsies, were, in short, wholly assimilated in society: 'Es müsste als besondere Härte angesehen werden, wenn man sie aus den Berufen infolge ihrer rassischen Abstammung herausreissen wollte.' ('It would be regarded as extremely harsh if they were to be removed from their jobs because of their racial descent.')

On 21 January this same police bureau reported to the *Reichszentrale* of the RKPA that the Gypsy mixed-blood Luise Liselotte W., in the fifth month of pregnancy, had voluntarily asked for sterilization on the condition that she be allowed to marry the German Richard Meissinger, who echoed her request. Meissinger was a soldier, private first class, although he had deserted a short while before which made him liable to execution. The *Reichszentrale*-functionary Hans Maly reacted on 27 January 1943 that Liselotte, despite her pregnancy, should be taken into protective custody and he asked for the papers necessary to effect her arrest. In the house of detention, however, the prison doctor wrote that she was not in any condition to work or be admitted to a camp, since she was within a few months of delivering a child. The arrest papers and the doctor's diagnosis, however, induced Maly, on 20 February 1943, to order that Liselotte be deported with the first following collective transport to the concentration camp at Auschwitz. She was 21 years old. Two written pleas from her father in the ensuing months to gain his daughter's release were rejected. On 16 March, in the fullness of her pregnancy, Liselotte was put on the train to Auschwitz, where on 7 May 1943 she died in the camp hospital from diarrhoea. As for the rest of the family, Maly decided that the father and his children could keep their lives but had to be sterilized. After Liselotte's death the family was not harassed further.[233]

The procedural aspects of this case are eminently important for my argument. What took place exactly? The health services in Karlsruhe approached Ritter and were told, after some research, that their suspect's Gypsy descent had been proven. As a consequence, the sterilization of all family mixed bloods was proposed without further police interference. Thereafter, on its own, the *Reichszentrale* of the RKPA decided otherwise and deportation to Auschwitz even followed. This does not lead me to conclude, as Hohmann does,[234] that the Central Bureau was under Ritter's intractable influence but much rather – in line with earlier comments – that where the solution of the 'Gypsy question' was concerned the two institutes were striving after partially different goals. The Gypsy Bureau within the *Reichskriminalpolizeiamt* was a police identification, registration and tracing institute that worked as a support service for the *Reichssicherheitshauptamt* and also for Himmler's Gestapo. Individual Gypsies, as supposed asocials had, for years, already been victims of the powers of these political police. Responsibility for deportation to concentration and annihilation camps lay with the Gestapo. The exceptional groups that Himmler had included in his 1943 decree were, however, selected for deportation by the Gestapo on the basis of lists of names acquired by the RKPA which were based on racial diagnoses made by Ritter's institutes and their interpretation by the local *Kriminalpolizeistellen*, who had to bring the designated Gypsies in. Indirect proof of this hypothesis is that Robert Hecker, employed by the Ministry of Justice during the war, declared as part of his testimony dated 17 March 1947, that prior to the sensational accord reached between Himmler and Thierack in the autumn of 1942, as well as Poles and Jews, certain categories of Gypsies whom Justice held in custody were delivered to the Gestapo, and many ended up in SS concentration camps. This train of events is confirmed by an eyewitness account by Dr Hans Mayr, who also worked for Justice.[235]

The answer to the question of how Ritter construed these developments remains uncertain. From the testimony of former associates during preliminary investigations after the war we know that, from 1943 onwards,[236] if not earlier, he realized that taking Gypsies and 'gypsy-like' persons into custody in a concentration camp was not wholly in accord with his own ideas about necessary isolation and sterilization because of the many who died there. In 1960 Anna Tobler, whom Ritter employed from 1937 to the end of the war in a non-scientific capacity, claimed that she was aware that in the Gypsy camps in Auschwitz and Bialystok 'grauenhafte Zustände' ('gruesome situations') prevailed, with inmates dying in droves from malnourishment and pitiful hygienic conditions. At Ritter's instigation, she appears to have familiarized herself with the situation in Bialystok and then to have briefed her director. In the records can be read: 'Aus späterer Sicht gesehen könne man aus der Tätigkeit für das RKPA *eine gewisse moralische Schuld der Mitarbeiter* der kriminalbiologischen Forschungsstelle des RGA für die Vernichtung von Zigeunermischlingen ableiten, glaubt Frau Tobler.' ('Mrs. Tobler believes that, from a later perspective, one could see that owing to their activities for the RKPA *employees of the criminal biological research centre of the Reich Health Office (RGA) bore a certain moral guilt* [my italics – W.W.] for the destruction of Gypsy mixedbloods.')[237]

We can deduce from fragmentary sources that, during the War, Ritter continued to cling to the idea that separate laws for Gypsies, as well as for outsiders (in other words, asocials) still belonged to the realms of possibility, the execution of which would be entrusted principally to the Ministries of the Interior and Justice. He might even have regarded internment in the Gypsy camp at Auschwitz as a temporary measure. A public prosecutor also concluded, during a pre-trial investigation in the 1960s, after perusal of 15,000 Gypsy dossiers, that the three actions during which Gypsies were gassed in Auschwitz-Birkenau were exceptional and distinct from the systematic gassing perpetrated against the Jews. The three gassing actions involved 1,700 Polish Gypsies who were suspected to have typhus at the end of March 1943; 1,035 Polish and Austrian Gypsies on 25 May 1943 at the instigation of camp physician Josef Mengele, also on grounds of typhoid infection; and some 4,000 Gypsies (among whom those deported from the Netherlands) on 1 August 1944 under the responsibility of camp commander Rudolf Hoess himself. The prosecutor went on to say:

> Da man in Auschwitz angesichts des immer wieder angekündigten Zigeuner-Gesetzes die Anwesenheit der Zigeuner offenkundig nur als eine Zwischenstation dieser Internierten-Gruppe angesehen hatte, infolge der Kriegslage aber nicht mehr mit ihrer Abholung (zum Abtransport nach Osten) rechnete, dürfte sich die örtliche Lagerleitung entschlossen haben, den Zigeunerblock für die Neuankommenden zu räumen. ('In the light of the repeatedly announced Law for Gypsies the presence of this group of inmates in Auschwitz evidently was considered as a transitional stage, but because of developments on the front, the local camp command, no longer counting on their removal (transport to eastern regions), probably decided to clear out the Gypsy-block for newcomers.')[238]

Ritter, an ambitious and diligent man, did not wish to see his scrupulously careful scientific work serve only as a prop for administrative organizations, aiding them to execute their racial policies, which steadily escalated during the war years and to which the vast number of Gypsy victims in the eastern occupied territories bore irrefutable witness. Perhaps his contact with Nebe also blinded him to what went on behind the scenes at the SS. And from his stubborn insistence on official legislation, I conclude that he completely underestimated the destructive delusions of Hitler and his supporters, failing to comprehend the enormity of what actually transpired in Auschwitz-Birkenau.[239] Indeed it is also conceivable that this is something that he refused to know.

THE AFTERMATH

Ritter's last years in Frankfurt am Main

After the war, in the six years that remained to Ritter, he did not dissociate himself from his eugenic and racial hygienic principles. Indications exist, however, that he felt weighed down by guilt owing to the fruits these ideas bore. He put his troubled feelings into words in a letter to his wife in May 1947 in which first of all he expressed his concern about what he viewed as the excessive anti-fascistic sentiment that suddenly gripped Germany after the war. These feelings led him to fear that his work would never again be judged on its merits, whereas he always believed he had done his best for the most freedom-loving of all peoples, the true Gypsies. For years he had urged the passage of separate laws for the purpose of allowing Gypsies to lead their own lives on a secure reservation. The accompanying restriction on reproduction was in his eyes a humane, social-medical solution to forestall the generation of new misfits and criminals. His was, he felt, a standpoint that had nothing to do with racial ideology. Yet he hinted that he couldn't wash his hands altogether of guilt:

> Sollte es mir versagt sein, weiterhin meiner Berufung zu leben, dann möge man mit mir mein Ende als ein Opfer ansehen, das gerne gebracht wird in dem Bewusstsein, dass jeder von uns zu seinem geringen Teil die unermessliche Schuld mit abzugelten hat, die unsere Volksgenossen in ihrer Verblendung – aber nicht nur sie allein – auf sich geladen haben. ('Should I be denied the further practice of my profession, one might consider my end as a sacrifice, readily made in the awareness that each of us in some small part must attone for the immeasurable guilt incurred by our fellow-citizens – but not by them alone.')[240]

As for Ritter's professional activities, after the close of the war he devoted himself first and foremost to renewing his abortive academic career. His credentials for lecturing on criminological biology, earned from his university in Berlin,[241] were transferred, once he was obliged to leave that city late in 1943, to the Faculty of Law and Economics in Tübingen. At the outset of 1946 he had broadened the scope of his classes to embrace the theme 'Gegenwartsfragen der sozialärztlichen und kriminalpädagogischen Jugendfürsorge' ('Contemporary problems of youth care in a social-medical and criminological-pedagogical perspective') and appears to have been put forward for a chair in criminology (*Verbrecherkunde*).[242] The rector of the university supported his nomination but the faculty withdrew it rather abruptly in August of the same year. What led them to do so was probably a letter from the inspector of police who had heard that Ritter had been one of the intellectual pillars of Nazi ideology in the field of juvenile law. He insisted on an investigation of Ritter's record, and this prompted the faculty to forget its intention to award Ritter a chair, despite the favourable tenor of the references they had collected which praised the nominee highly for his scientific and ideological integrity.[243] During the process of political cleansing in the region of Reutlingen that fell inside the French military zone in south-west Germany, the conclusion was also reached that there were no objections to Ritter holding a position in the service of the state.[244]

In September 1945 Ritter had already sent an open solicitation letter to the directorate of Justice in Württemberg in which he spelled out three fields in which he could serve the state. He had a preference for teaching and research at a university. In addition he felt his expertise, insights and practical experience would prove useful in a judicial criminological-biological institute, the likes of which, he was firmly convinced, would certainly be feasible in Württemberg. In that context he referred to the abundance of sources on the region, placing special emphasis on the extensive research material in his possession which could constitute the basis for a separate service. This could occupy itself with giving advice of all sorts: about (juvenile) delinquents and difficult children in reformatories, prisoners and correctional institutions, about pedagogic and marriage problems at health bureaus. Detectives and police, moreover, could avail themselves of the institute's services. To his mind, forecasting the course of society should have the highest priority, hence the importance of advice about the character of diverse groups. He proposed talking about it as a social-medical institute, for he was acutely conscious that people would not readily co-operate with criminological-biological research. As a third possibility he alluded to his original metier, social work with young people and orthopedagogy, envisioning a position for himself as head of a psychiatric institute or other kind of residential home for youths, ideally in combination with a professorship in social-medical youth affairs.[245]

In this last field he also actually managed to land a job – with the municipal health service in Frankfurt am Main where, as of 1 December 1947, he assumed duties as a child physician, rising some months later to the position of head doctor (*Obermedizinalrat*). A salient detail is that two years later, effective retroactively from 1 April 1936, Ritter was considered to be a civil servant, something that his refusal to join the NSDAP had made impossible during the Nazi regime.[246] From correspondence with Ritter and between the concerned aldermen in Frankfurt we can deduce that negotiations were under way for a post as head of the *Fürsorgestelle für Gemüts- und Nervenkranke* and the youth psychiatry division.[247] He would be appointed to an independent post as chief physician and research leader of the Department of Psychopathology and Neurology – of children and adults. One had also led him to believe he would assume leadership of the Hermannsheim government reformatory that had been forced to shut down in 1933 after the dismissal of its director (the Jewish child and youth psychiatrist Walter Fürstenheim).[248] Ritter had demanded, as a condition for his acceptance of the position, that he must be able to work independently, and he wanted to make the care and psychiatry of youth, together with combatting youthful criminality, his highest priorities. He went along with a plan to expand the post at a somewhat later stage to include agreed criminological research tasks. For the time being he assumed leadership of the medical bureau for youth care and succeeded in creating a psychologist's post there for his loyal friend of many years, Eva Justin.[249]

Ritter did not derive much satisfaction from his new function and the city of Frankfurt will also have regretted hiring this so-highly qualified associate. The aftermath of the war took its toll, morally, physically and psychologically. Thus, beginning in 1949, various legal inquiries into Ritter's past were launched which brought him into serious discredit as a doctor although he was never brought to trial. First of all he was accused of dishonesty for omitting to mention in the de-Nazification forms that he had been required to complete in that he had held the rank of *SS-Obersturmbannführer*. Later it would turn out that there had been a number of misunderstandings.[250] A second legal inquiry was the consequence of accusations voiced by some Gypsies concerning Ritter's involvement in crimes committed against them during the Third Reich. Public prosecutor Schulze, however, had second thoughts about bringing charges, for the accusations could not be proven. None the less he considered the case, for what the Gypsies concerned had to say was serious. It is no longer possible to reconstruct the exact chain of events relating to these preliminary investigations – yet a third was initiated on 12 August 1950 – for the legal documents have been destroyed.[251] Hohmann, in his book on Robert Ritter (1991), nevertheless probes this case extensively, partially on the evidence of documents from the attorney general of the district court in Frankfurt.[252] Forty years on, he rejects the grounds of the public prosecutor's defence, namely that he chose not to prosecute since direct guilt had not been established. Hohmann also jeers at the authorities because they failed to construe the testimony of the Gypsies involved as serious evidence. It is unfortunate that the author refers in his argument to documents whose existence is improbable. He makes Ritter, for example, a member of the SS, something that he never was: 'Nach einem dem Verfasser vorliegenden Dokument trat Ritter am 26. Juli 1934 – noch während seiner Tübingen Zeit – in die NSDAP und im Jahre 1936 in die SS ein.' ('According to a document in the possession of the author Ritter became a member of the NSDAP on 26 July 1934 – still during his Tübingen days – and a member of the SS in 1936.')[253] This is not to say that the manner in which

Ritter, and his lawyer, Hermann Stolting II, expressed themselves in writing about the Gypsy witnesses against him didn't display a flagrant lack of compassion for the suffering inflicted upon them, partially through his doing, during the Nazi regime.[254] The fragmentary passages that have come down to us do little to sustain the image of a man who, in hard times, would have sprung into the breach for true Gypsies. He referred emphatically to their untrustworthiness and their talents of invention, thereby playing on social prejudices that, since Grellmann, had been part of how Gypsies were portrayed as a group and which, during the war, were clearly a trump card that the Gestapo did not hesitate to play.

That the developments did not leave him untroubled, however, and that guilt had perhaps penetrated deeper than Ritter himself could admit, are conclusions I draw from descriptions of his ill health during the post-war years while he worked for the municipality of Frankfurt. From a report by the physician in the Caritas Sanatorium in Bad-Neuheim, written on 14 August 1948, we learn that Ritter spent some time there under treatment. He is portrayed as a busy but hypersensitive man, quick to become agitated, prone to bottling up his emotions and, for months floundering in a crisis with high blood pressure and heart complaints as a consequence. The Personnel Division of the municipality was advised to give Ritter more scope for his talents in his work but the large number of days that Ritter was absent from his job because of sickness progressively diminished his chances of being appointed as a youth psychiatrist to a research position. When the municipality, after the third legal inquiry in August 1950, looked into the matter of the de-Nazification procedure which its continuously ill civil servant had undergone, they were told that, on grounds of the *Gesetz über den Abschluss der politischen Befreiung* (Law for the Ending of Political Liberation) in Hessen, he would presumably be classified as '*Mitläufer*' ('hanger on') a categorization that did not constitute a reason to discharge him.[255] The de-Nazification courts classified people according to five categories: *Hauptschuldige*, *Belastete*, *Minderbelastete*, *Mitläufer*, and *Entlastete*. Most of those investigated appear to have emerged as *Mitläufer* which, as a rule, entailed no punitive consequences for them.[256]

Before deciding whether he could be kept in his responsible position, the personnel division first wanted a thorough diagnosis of the condition of his health. Upon admission to a teaching hospital for observation, Ritter turned out to be totally unfit for work: his brain and optic nerves were damaged and he could no longer stand up to the mental stress. The examining physician prescribed a stay in the sanatorium Hohe Mark, advising the city to speak to his wife for the continuation of his employment did not seem very likely. Between mid-1948 and the beginning of 1951 Ritter spent no fewer than 428 days sick at home or in a sanatorium, with diverse complaints, such as high blood pressure, infections, hay fever and heart trouble.[257] He would never recover and died on 15 April 1951 at 23h30.[258]

A splintered heritage: police, science and policy

The story did not end with Ritter's death, however. The scientific heritage that he left behind continued to exercise enormous influence in Germany on post-war attitudes towards Gypsies on the part of police authorities, academics and policy makers. To start with, let me linger over the question of what happened to his research material. At the end of July 1943 Ritter proposed to President Reiter of the Ministry of Public Health that his institute be relocated to a building outside Berlin. Goebbels had rallied all Berliners with the cry: 'Leben und Gut aus der Grossstadt zu retten!' ('Save lives and goods from the town.') Ritter wanted to transport all his accumulated youth doctor, criminological biological and population materials to Württemberg. Here he had found a number of rooms in the psychiatric nursing home Mariaberg where, with Eva Justin and his employee Bremer, he would carry on with his work. Two other associates found refuge in the psychiatric institution Winnenthal, while the materials of the Criminological Biological Research Institute of the *Reichskriminalpolizeiamt* were housed in Fischerhäusle, a small summer vacation hotel near Herrnskretschen in Sudetenland. The *Reichszentrale zur Bekämpfung des Zigeunerunwesens*, which controlled the archive with personal data on Gypsy families, ended up in a *Führerschule der Sicherheitspolizei* in Drögen near Fürstenberg.[259] A number of colleagues remained in Bavaria where, apparently together with the former Gypsy centre of the Munich detective force,[260] they carried on with the registration of *Jenische Landfahrersippen* (as they were suddenly called).

Ritter's reception in Mariaberg was less hospitable than he had hoped and, to his mind, was typical of how German war refugees were treated in their own country. He found the institution a place that was out of touch with the world, one where the staff lived in hermetic isolation from the war. At the same time it was so bustling that his and his two female associates' concentration seems to have suffered severely. Within next to no time an internal power struggle arose, for Ritter regularly had critical comments to make about how things were being run.[261] The management, however, was unable to show any appreciation for his unsolicited advice. As the result of bombardments at the end of 1943 the Ministry of Public Health and the *Reichskriminalpolizeiamt* were gutted by fire, news which reached Ritter together with notice of his promotion to director within the Ministry.[262] At that time he and his colleagues at Mariaberg and Winnenthal were fully engaged in criminological-genealogical research on asocial families living in south-west Germany and, in Herrnskretschen, on, primarily, criminal and occupational groups.

Falling bombs set Ritter's residence on the Züricherstrasse in Berlin ablaze on 24 March 1944. His library, which contained many special volumes and into which over the years he had pumped considerable funds, went up in smoke.[263] After moving all that could be salvaged to safety, he left for the *Jugendschutzlager* Moringen. There, in the meantime, the police had taken over responsibility for deciding the fate of the young internees, wholly, according to Ritter, on the basis of advice from a handwriting analyst. In the summer of that year he acquired further teaching credentials enabling him to lecture on the nature of youthful offenders as a member of the Law and Economics Faculty of the University of Tübingen.[264] Yet for him, as for most Germans, the last year of the war meant above all living in dread of bombardment and in hope of a rapid end to the dictatorship. In the autumn of 1944 a telegraph informed Ritter that, owing to the all-out war effort, both of his institutes were summarily closed down and most of his staff were drafted to work in the weapons industry. All that remained for him to do was to try to assure the safety of his scientific material. The Ministry of Public Health endorsed these instructions and allowed the K Division – the Criminological Biological Research Institute – to cease all work at once. In 1942 the party leadership had ordained that the only departments that could be maintained were those engaged in research serving Germany's defence, which is also why this institute passed the war years as a criminological biological centre and separate work groups functioned as research annexes. In 1936 the ministerial public health services had set up all kinds of institutes of its own, an equivalent in Berlin of the famous *Kaiser Wilhelm Institut für Genealogie und Demographie* in Munich. Now these, too, had to cede a considerable percentage of their personnel to the war industry, which, in practice, amounted to shedding everyone except civil servants who belonged to the original management. Ritter did his best to arrange for his associates to find positions with, among others, the *Kriminalpolizei* and the Criminological Biological Research Institute of the *Reichskriminalpolizeiamt* in Herrns-kretschen, where, as mentioned earlier, his massive Gypsy archive had in the interim also been housed. His own small workgroup in Mariaberg was not disrupted. In the course of the ensuing months he tried to convey as much research material as possible to the nursing home, packing it in suitcases to store it where bombs could do no damage.

In January 1945 he made a trip to Moringen to give advice on whether or not to induct the youths who were still there into the army. For two months he moved into the old inn *Zum Ratskeller* to be able to carry out his work with no disturbance. Later he claimed in self-exoneration that it was thanks to his efforts that this youthcamp never became a concentration camp and escaped falling within the sphere of the Gestapo's influence. Considering his earlier complaints about the influence on the camp of this very corps, his assertion does not have a very likely ring. We know from the literature, moreover, that such an interpretation is contestable, not to say false.[265] In any event, it seems improbable that Ritter co-operated directly with the secret state police. In their political affairs they tolerated no external influence or counsel, which also accounts for why his work terrain remained confined to his own division of the *Reichskriminalpolizei*.

So much for what happened to Ritter's empirical material during the last years of the war. Why is it important to know what happened to it afterwards? At the beginning of my narrative about Ritter I pointed out that the stagnation of the *Wiedergutmachung* was partially a consequence of the lack of documents that Gypsies could use to substantiate their claims for reparations.[266] Also during the post-war preliminary investigations conducted against Ritter, his associates, and institutes involved in the persecution of the Gypsies, public prosecutors sorely lacked written evidence.[267] For decades, uncertainty prevailed about the nature of the empirical material Ritter and his team used to arrive at their research findings and since only an occasional copy of one of his racial diagnosis came to light, insight into the background of the Nazis' racial persecution policy towards Gypsies remained limited. Owing to the efforts of advocacy organizations, however, the suffering inflicted on them during the Third Reich has, in the interim, been officially acknowledged, although the government agencies involved do not always take into consideration the factor 'asociability' when weighing individual claims for the period prior to 1938. In these cases Gypsy specialists are also called as expert witnesses who refer to Ritter's ideas about racially pure and impure Gypsies. The latter are said to have landed in concentration camps primarily on account of their asociability and criminality, and died there in large numbers from contagious diseases as a consequence of their unhygienic way of life.[268]

The most important evidence about the registration and deportation of Gypsies that could have brought about a change in peoples' way of thinking was kept in the archive of the *Reichszentrale zur Bekämpfung des Zigeunerunwesens* of the RKPA, housed, as we saw, in Drögen near Fürstenberg since the end of 1943 but, at the end of the war, destroyed by the *Sicherheitspolizei*.[269] This does not hold true for the diverse collections of empirical material that Ritter's institutes accumulated during a decade and a half. It is likely that scarcely anything of their contents has been lost. From his correspondence, we know that in June 1947 Ritter was busy visiting all the places where such material had been stored, with the intention of subsequently depositing it in some central location, although there are indications that it was still in Mariaberg awaiting transportation a year later.[270] For it was Eva Justin who wrote to her employer on 14 June 1948: 'In dem früheren Wohnsitz von Herrn Obermedizinalrat Dr. Ritter befinden sich noch Akten, Bücher und Photogeräte unseres früheren Institutes, die wir für die hiesige Arbeit der Jugendsichtungsstelle dringend benötigen.' ('In the previous domicile of *Herrn Obermedizinalrat Dr. Ritter* there still remain documents, books and photo equipment from our former institute. We are in urgent need of these for our research work here with younger people.') She asked for leave in order to fetch that material from the neurological institute in Mariaberg.[271]

For details of the route that the material later travelled, I rely principally on what the historian Mathias Winter has written about it.[272] Winter maintains that, on 21 May 1949, Eva Justin handed over the genealogical material (films and card files) and copies of 24,000 racial diagnoses to Rudolph Uschold, the official in charge of Gypsy questions within the *Zentralamt für Kriminalidentifizierung und Polizeistatistik* in Munich.[273] National Socialist laws may have been abrogated then by the occupying American forces, but in 1949 Bavaria continued the prewar tradition by setting up a new *Landfahrerzentrale*, with a separate Gypsy police, so that the criminalization of itinerant groups would not disappear during the 1950s and 1960s.[274] In a publication from 1951, Uschold urged separate legislation aimed at so-called 'asocial travellers' (*asoziale Landfahrer*) – which two years later was actually realized – referring to Ritter's research material which was then with his office. To judge from this author's terminology, we can deduce that after the war the criminological biological tradition was carried on without a hitch by the judicial authorities:

> Die Sichtung der Jenischen, der Zigeuner und der Zigeuner-mischlinge hat aufschlussreiche Ergebnisse über die verschiedenartige Herkunft und Kriminalität der genannten Gruppen gezeigt. Die kriminalwissenschaftlichen Erkenntnisse dieser Arbeiten werden auch in Zukunft der erkennungsdienstlichen und kriminalpolizei-lichen Arbeit dienlich sein. ('The research on Jenischen, Gypsies and Gypsy mixedbloods has yielded informative results concerning the different origins and criminality of the groups mentioned. The criminological knowledge produced by this work will in the future

also be helpful to the identification services and to the criminal investigation department.')[275]

In publications from 1957, written by another police official in the same service, we read that, for strategic reasons, a rather loose definition of the concept of *Landfahrer* was used: '... wer aus eingewurzelten Hang zum Umherziehen bzw. aus Abneigung gegen eine Sesshaftmachung (...) im lande umherzieht.' (one who has a deep-seated urge to wander and who, driven by an aversion to sedentary life (...) roams about the country.')[276] To be sure, the police primarily had in mind people of 'Gypsy-like origins', but given the fact that the Constitution forbade application of the principle of descent as part of any policy directed at a group, the labelling was modified.[277] For the record the author added to his explanation that the people concerned were the descendants of primitive nomads from India where, in the ninth century, they had belonged to the pariah caste – an image from Grellmann that has not yet disappeared from criminological literature. The anti-Gypsy policy of the pre-Nazi period seems to have been perpetuated, using the identification and registration material that Ritter's auxiliary institutes had collected during that regime.

Another part of Ritter's legacy, after his death, was made available to the Landauer physician Hermann Arnold, one of the most prolific of post-war authorities on Gypsies (and other non-sedentary groups) in Germany. For a long time Arnold, because he was regarded at ministerial level as a prominent expert, knew how to impress his standpoint on policy discussions about Gypsy affairs. Among his activities in the service of the Ministry of the Interior, he carried out research. The *Landfahrerzentrale* placed material at his disposal. In the 1970s Arnold would become, explicitly, Ritter's self-appointed advocate, even though the two men never knew each other personally.[278] What they shared was a belief in genealogical research as the method of choice for tracing the roots of 'asocial behaviour' in a family context. In a letter to an unnamed correspondent which Arnold wrote in 1965 concerning the man's genealogical study of non-sedentary groups, he wrote:

Ihre Genealogien sind vorbildlich breit angelegt und wunderbar exakt gezeichnet. Es ist sehr schade, dass Sie nicht seinerzeit mit der Ritter'schen Arbeitsgruppe des Reichsgesundheitsamtes in Verbindung getreten sind, denn Ihre Kenntnisse und Fähigkeiten hätten dort sicherlich Anerkennung gefunden. ('Your genealogical trees are exemplary in their breadth and drawn with wonderful exactness. It is really too bad that at the time you did not get in touch with Ritter's team at the Reich Health Office, for they certainly would have recognised your knowledge and capabilities.')[279]

As a physician Arnold followed in his predecessor's footsteps, providing medical-criminological advice to all kinds of official bodies, including police stations, courts (in their evaluation of *Wiedergutmachung*-applications, for example) and homes for youths. He was also, like Ritter, a proponent of eugenic regulations to solve the 'problem of asocials' which was said above all to plague large cities – an observation which also has a pre-war familiarity to it! In a comparative textual analysis, Winter shows convincingly that Arnold's major works on 'Gypsies', '*Jenischen*' and 'social outcasts' (from 1958, 1964, 1965 and 1983) are not only heavily indebted to Ritter's work, including his unpublished lectures and other material from his legacy, but that he also closely followed Ritter in his use of language and his ideology. Arnold employed literally the same concepts, phrases and passages of text, often without references. Arnold stated regularly that Ritter's genealogies, so valuable in his opinion, contain important objective information about the extent to which Gypsies mixed with other groups. Anthropometric material, he suggests on a number of occasions, may indeed also have been preserved, but it still needed to be processed.[280]

In an exchange of letters in which Arnold was involved at the end of the 1950s and in the early 1960s with the jurist Hans-Joachim Döring, who in 1964 published a controversial book about Gypsies under the Nazis, he wrote that he shared his opinion that it would be useful to introduce a system of *apartheid* for Gypsies, to which he added that at the present moment, however, such a measure would not stand a chance of succeeding. Döring pressed him to urge Eva Justin, against whom a preliminary investigation was then in progress, to continue with her Gypsy research.[281] Winter maintains that, in September 1958, Justin had presented Arnold with the genealogical material from Ritter's institutes on microfilm, together with his scholarly library. With these to refer to, he could appear as an expert witness on her behalf at the investigation in which she was one of the accused, reassuring the public prosecutor that the family trees did not serve as a basis for the selection of Gypsies for deportation to concentration camps.[282] Because no racial diagnoses were produced – the missing link between the family trees and the deportation lists of the *Reichskriminalpolizeiamt* – it was not possible to marshal conclusive evidence of guilt. From Winter's reconstruction, I deduced that these key papers were, until 1964, with the *Landfahrerzentrale* which wanted at the time to destroy them since they were incriminating material. Through his ministerial contacts Arnold managed to prevent this from happening, whereupon the documents were deposited as scientific resource material with the health bureau in Landau, where Arnold worked at the time.[283] As the years passed, like his predecessor, he managed to acquire a pre-eminent position with respect to research and policy advice concerning Gypsies and other 'socially isolated' groups in West Germany, with Ritter's empirical legacy as the basis of his authority, supplemented with material which he himself collected in the course of the post-war decades.

In addition to the Gypsy registration, the racial diagnoses, and the family trees, Arnold also had access for years to some of Ritter's unprocessed anthropological gypsy-related data, although he did not publish anything separate based on it. He did, however, keep in touch with those professionally interested in such material, such as Hans W. Jürgens, whom we have already encountered as an expert witness, because of his own social-biological study of asocials. In his doctoral dissertation of 1961, Jürgens championed the forcible imposition of sterilization on a larger scale, something which, he believed, would be regarded as perfectly normal in the culture of the future state. In 1962 Arnold, Jürgens and Otmar Freiherr von Verschuer, all three members of the German Academy of Population Sciences, were asked by the Ministry of the Interior to apply their minds to the problem of promoting the integration of Gypsies and the asocial into society. This initiative led to the setting up of a documentation bureau with material on non-sedentary families, led by Arnold until 1979. It was his intention to bring together as much material as possible about asocials, laying a basis for legislation which would be developed by future policy makers.[284] Apparently he was bent on completing Ritter's interrupted work. In the 1950s Arnold shared with Jürgens, the later director of the Central Institute for Population Studies in Germany, a strong interest in Gypsies from a racial sciences point of view. The terminology which the like-minded pair used seemed directly derivative from Ritter's eugenics vocabulary:

Aus Ihrem Brief vom 11.11 ersehe ich, dass mit mir einmal wieder der Anthropologe durchgegangen ist, der nicht nach Personalien fragt und nur nach dem Rassentyp sieht. (...) Wenn Sie gelegentlich mal Zeit haben, würde ich mich freuen, wenn Sie Ihr Restlager an Zigeuner- und Zigeunermischlingsbildern in einen Karton packen und mir für kurze Zeit überlassen könnten. Vielleicht finden sich noch weitere schöne Typen für Anthropologen. ('From your letter of 11.11, I gather that once more it is the anthropologist in me who does not investigate personal particulars, but only studies racial type, who finds acceptance. (...) If you could find a chance to pack the rest of the pictorial material you have on Gypsies and Gypsy mixedbloods in a carton and let me have it for a short time,

I would be extremely pleased. Maybe there are still further beautiful (proto)types for anthropologists among these remains.')[285]

The bulk of Ritter's anthropometric material was located, however, in the Anthropological Institute of the University of Tübingen where his former co-worker, Sophie Ehrhardt, was employed. After the war, under her leadership, a number of publications appeared about the racial-specific dactyloscopic characteristics of Mid-German Gypsies, based on data that the racial hygiene institute had collected.[286] She herself succeeded, doubtless by referring to this empirical treasure house at her finger tips, in landing a major research project to be carried out for the DFG (German Association for Research), entitled *Populations-genetische Untersuchungen an Zigeunern*. She worked between 1966 and 1970 on this project together with the American (statistically-trained) anthropologist, Norman Creel. When Horst Ritter (no relation!) assumed direction of the Anthropological Institute in Tübingen in 1969 and forbade work with data from the Nazi era, Ehrhardt gave Creel the basic material to take with him when he found work in 1969 in Mainz. In 1972 he was said to be returning to New York. Their joint book that was to be published two years later never materialized.[287]

The direct social importance of Ritter's legacy for the support of Gypsies' claims for damages was only recognized in 1979 when the *Verband Deutscher Sinti*, in part owing to a reference in one of Arnold's publications during the previous year, began to insist that the government make it possible for the public to have access to Ritter's material by having it transferred to the State Archives in Koblenz. At that time Ehrhardt must have realized the explosive nature of the material she had passed on with Creel to Mainz, for on 19 June 1980 she had it sent to the University Library in Tübingen and asked the State Archives to keep the material on hand, available to her for her project, until the year 2000. She was then 77 and considering the history of her project there is no doubt that not much progress would have been accomplished with such arrangements.[288] Gypsy interest groups had, in the meantime, become so alert that they simply forced transfer of the material to the State Archives by occupying the University Library in Tübingen on 1 September 1981. That very night 16 metres of bookshelf headed for Koblenz with documents from Ritter's Racial Hygiene and Crimino-logical Biological Research Institute.[289] Of the racial diagnoses, however, there was not a trace. Nine years later the Federal Court in Saarbrücken ruled that Arnold had indeed received this Nazi material in 1964 – which was still of importance for legitimizing Gypsy reparations demands – from the *Landfahrerzentrale*. Expiration of the statute of limitations, however, protected him from prosecution, apparently bringing to an end, temporarily, the story of this lost legacy.[290]

NOTES

1 This jurisprudence can be found in the publication *Rechtsprechung zum Wiedergutmachungsrecht* (RzW) in which the motivations involved in Gypsy cases are described. See volumes from 1953 to 1974.

2 See Calvelli-Adorno (1961, pp. 529–37).

3 See, for example, *RzW*, 10, 3 (1959, p. 121).

4 See Buchheim (1956, pp. 51–60). On 7 November 1960 the court in Kiel was the first to pronounce that the evacuation was a racially motivated persecutory measure. The Federal Court confirmed the Kiel opinion on 18 December 1963. See *RzW*, 12, 2 (1961, pp. 59–60); 15, 5 (1964, pp. 209–11).

5 The policy relied on a principle of categorization according to which persons who lived 'in a gypsy-like way' also were designated as belonging to the same race. See Calvelli-Adorno (1961, p. 536).

6 These included the *Reichsbürgergesetz* and *Blutschutzgesetz* which denied citizenship and the possibility of marriage with a German to '*artfremdes Blut*' (of alien blood).

7 On 2 May 1961, the court in Frankfurt am Main was the first to point out that in the Stuckart-Globke commentary on the Nuremberg race laws, in addition to Jews, Gypsies in Europe were considered to have 'artfremdes Blut'. Racial discrimination against Gypsies would thus already have begun in 1935. See *RzW*, 12, 12 (1961, pp. 544–6). The decree of 1 June 1938 issued to all police stations by the *Reichskriminalpolizeiamt*, who was one of Himmler's subordinates, specified that in the summer of that year, with the prescribed registration and examination in mind, among those who qualified for preventive imprisonment were 'Gypsies and people wandering around in a gypsy-like way, if they have not shown their intention of working on a regular basis or have committed a penal act'. From Calvelli-Adorno (1961, pp. 536–7).

8 See *RzW*, 13, 9 (1962, pp. 396–8) for commentary on the court's pronouncement.

9 For a discussion of the complicated administrative aspects of indemnity claims on these grounds, see Stanicki (1968, pp. 529–35).

10 *RzW*, 13, 9 (1962, pp. 396–8).

11 Not until the 1980s in Germany, and even later elsewhere, would any serious scholarly attention be paid to Gypsies as Holocaust victims. It speaks volumes that Kenrick's and Puxon's pioneering English publication of 1972 only appeared in 1981 in a German translation.

12 Thus Müller-Hill wrote (Dutch version 1986, p. 107): 'I absolutely do not shrink from calling the murderers murderers, even if the German courts have spoken of the statute of limitations and manslaughter (...) as in the case of Dr. Ritter, the academic organizer of the genocide against the Gypsies.' We find most of the authors in the collection *Das Reichsgesundheitsamt 1933–45 – eine Ausstellung* (1989) hold a similar opinion. See, also, Hohmann (1991). In this study, more than half of which consists of integrally reproduced documents, the author consistently omits citation of the sources that provide him with his information. Since the accuracy of most of his statements can not be verified, his publication falls short of acceptable standards for an historical study.

13 The typed manuscript contains 158 pages. There are 32 personal letters covering three periods: 1908–25, 1932, 1945–47. A distant relative of Ritter came into possession of these documents several years ago and was prepared, when I managed to trace him, to make copies of them available to me. Out of consideration for the relative's privacy, I can not divulge any name. Anyone interested, however, can request copies of the documents from me. It is my intention to persuade the person in question to deposit the originals with a public archive in due time.

14 Max Ritter died on 30 March 1917 at the age of 57. From a letter, a copy of which

is in my possession, from Robert Ritter to his mother dated 8 May 1917.

15 Between 1918 and 1921 Ritter wrote various letters to his grandmother, with whom he had a close bond, about his mother's acute nervousness and their emotional differences of opinion, as well as about her distant behaviour during the years of his adolescence.

16 Although at the time he entertained visions of a twofold career as naval officer and diplomat. Information from a letter Ritter sent to his grandmother on 14 February 1918.

17 For further information about this cosmopolitan movement oriented towards social reforms, see Weindling (1989, pp. 67–73).

18 That Ritter also still nourished such political idealism many years later emerges from an article entitled 'Europaische Jugend. Die politische Jugendbewegung in Deutschland' which he wrote for the *Neue Zürcher Zeitung* of 22 December 1929.

19 Ritter (1945, p. 4).

20 From a letter Ritter wrote to his grandmother on 6 April 1921.

21 From Ritter's letters to his grandmother dated 14 and 20 April 1921. On 4 August of the same year he took his lyceum school-leaving examination successfully in Betzdorf Kirchen.

22 We can conclude from a letter which Ritter sent his grandmother on 1 May 1921 that his mother suffered from asthma, too.

23 Ritter (1945, p. 8).

24 Ibidem, p. 10.

25 On 12 July 1926 Prof. A. Fischer filed a petition for awarding the doctorate but there was a delay because treatment for asthma prevented Ritter from taking one of his oral exams on time. He finally received his degree on 8 July 1927. For the extensive correspondence concerning Ritter rapidly making up the missing examination – necessary because Ritter had already enrolled in the University of Berlin – see the University Archives of Munich, sign. O-N prom. SS 1927.

26 She received her degree in March 1930. I have the title of her thesis from a curriculum vitae written by Ritter on 20 December 1931 in Zürich which can be found in the University Archives of Tübingen, Ritter's personal file (sign. 308/3201).

27 He passed his examination on 1 May 1930. For further details about his study time in Heidelberg, see the University Archives there, sign. H-III-862/56.

28 In the 1920s and 1930s Drieu La Rochelle (1893–1945), known as an anti-Semite, abrogated the role of the conscience of his generation with his literary work, diligently searching for new ideals for Europeans, whose civilization, as far as he was concerned, had sunk to its nadir. He agitated against the spirit of the times, above all against parliamentary democracy, which he branded as a paralysing force. He was on the look-out for a powerful, authoritarian ideal and recognized what he sought in fascism. Accordingly, he became active in the fascist party in France in 1940. A 'spiritual collaborator' throughout the war, he committed suicide shortly before liberation.

29 In response to my request, on 8 May 1992 Prof. Jules Angst of the *Psychiatrische Universitätsklinik Zürich, Forschungsdirektion* informed me that he could locate no file for the Ritters, neither husband, nor wife. From the annual report 1931–32 it is nevertheless clear that they had worked there as assistants at the time.

30 Ritter (1945, p. 21).

31 See below the more extensive treatment of this point in the section entitled 'A biological inheritance: social-Darwinism and eugenics'.

32 See Noakes (1984, pp. 83–4).

33 A duplicate of the diploma that he received for successfully completing the seminar is in the City Archives of Frankfurt, the personal file for Robert Ritter, sign. 18.576 (p. 7).

34 Ritter also gave journalistic expression to this train of thought in his article, 'Der neue politische Mensch', which appeared in the *Kölnische Zeitung* on 15 September 1930.

35 For the correspondence about this position between Ritter and the psychiatrist

Gaupp (from 26 October 1931 until 31 May 1932) see the University Archives of Tübingen, Ritter's personal file, sign. 308/3201. Gaupp, in his much talked about Berlin publication *Die Unfruchtbarmachung geistig und sittlich Kranker und Minderwertiger*, had proposed sterilization as a racial hygiene measure as early as 1925. Taken from Weingart et al. (1988, p. 293, note 101).

36 See Roth (1984, p. 63, note 129).

37 Ritter (1945, p. 21). The letter concerned, ostensibly from 1931 or 1932, has proven impossible to trace. Ritter wrote that Von Hindenburg had sent him a formal thank you note in reply. Adolf Würth, who worked with Ritter, told a similar version of this story in an interview with Benno Müller-Hill (English version 1988, pp. 147–8), adding that, according to him, Ritter was always afraid that after 1933 the letter would still surface somewhere. On 29 April 1946 Irmgard Engeling, a physiotherapist and another former colleague, also wrote about how Ritter feared he would land in a concentration camp because of what he had put in his letter. See the State Archives of Frankfurt, Robert Ritter's personal file, sign. 18.576.

38 In his article of 11 January 1931 in the *Kölnische Zeitung*, moreover, he had openly criticized the practices of Hitler and his consorts.

39 At any rate there is a passage which says a lot in a letter which the young Ritter sent to his grandmother (1 March 1920) when he had just found a room with a family named Stern: 'An antisemitic inclination I should not show too overtly (s. Stern). But I think the grandfather has already been baptized, although I could be mistaken.'

40 This law was passed on 14 July 1933 and became operative on 1 January 1934.

41 Ritter (1945, p. 27).

42 The *Rassenhygienische Eheberatungsstelle* in Tübingen was established on 15 March 1934 with the assistance of the *Deutsche Gesellschaft für Rassenhygiene*. In the *Tübinger Chronik* of 14 March 1934 Ritter expounded his thoughts about this marital advice bureau, which he did as well in the pamphlet *Sind Sie erbgesund?* Both documents are located in the City Archives of Tübingen, sign. no. A 150/4859.

43 See the University Archives of Tübingen, sign. no. 308/3201, a letter from Gaupp to (his successor) Hoffmann, dated 10 March 1936. Later in this chapter I go more deeply into the phenomenon of *Erbgesundheitsgericht* in the section entitled, 'Hereditary health prognoses and registration systems'.

44 On 4 February 1935, for example, at the home of Prof. Dr H. Dold, chairman of the Tübingen branch of the *Deutsche Gesellschaft für Rassenhygiene*, on the subject 'Erbkundlichen Untersuchungen über Zigeunermischlinge'. See the City Archives of Tübingen, sign. no. A 150/4857.

45 Ritter (1945, p. 30).

46 Ritter's talk appeared later as 'Erbbiologische Untersuchungen innerhalb eines Züchtungskreises von Zigeunermischlingen und asozialen Psychopaten' in: H. Harmsen and F. Lohse (Eds.) *Bevölkerungsfragen, Berichte des Internationalen Kongresses für Bevölkerungswissenschaft 1935 in Berlin*, Part 7, pp. 713–18.

47 Arthur Gütt (1891 to 1949) was one of the drafters of the *Gesetz zur Verhütung erbkranken Nachwuchses* (1934) and of the *Blutschutz- und Ehegesundheitsgesetz* (1936).

48 His decision was prompted in part by a drastic labour dispute in Tübingen which had left rather deep scars behind. Now he had an opportunity to start again elsewhere with a clean slate. For the extensive correspondence concerning the drawn-out conflict between Ritter and a colleague who was supported by Director Gaupp, see the University Archives of Tübingen, Ritter's personal file, sign. 117/565. Ultimately a higher authority would rule in Ritter's favour and discharge his opponent, but working relations had been damaged severely. From the flurry of letters, Ritter emerges as an ambitious schemer, but also as a hypersensitive neurotic. It should be noted, too, however, that his enemy was ready to stoop to

just about anything to bring Ritter into discredit. See the University Archives of Tübingen, sign. 308/3201 for the correspondence between 9 March and 8 August 1936 about Ritter taking on his new position.

49   Exactly how the financing of Ritter's projects worked cannot be deduced satisfactorily from the documentation I was able to compile. For years, along with the Ministries of the Interior and Public Health, the *Deutsche Forschungs Gemeinschaft* (DFG) also provided funding. For Ritter's correspondence with the DFG, see the State Archives in Koblenz, sign. R73/14005. From perusal of Robert Ritter's file in the *Berlin Document Centre* it is possible to calculate that between 2 July 1935 and April 1944 a total amount of RM 226,286 in research funds was transferred to Ritter for various projects.

50   Eva Justin was born in Bautzen on 23 August 1909 and joined the staff of the University Hospital in Tübingen on 10 October 1934. See the University Archives of Tübingen, sign. 308/1804. A rather detailed sketch of Eva Justin appears in Hohmann (1991, pp. 238–71).

51   Concerning the progress of this project, an extensive exchange of letters between the Tübingen research group and the institute in Berlin has been preserved which covers the period from 26 April 1938 to 27 September 1939. See the State Archives in Koblenz, UAT 164 and sign. R 165/ 000237, 238, 239, 241. No report or publication concerning this project, however, was ever produced. True, Ritter's choice of his friend, the sociologist Manfred Betz, had not proved to be brilliant. Upon completion of his studies, the man had gone to work as the head of the export division of the firm Saba-Radio. In March 1935 he had a nervous breakdown which would render him inactive for years. Only in August of 1937 was he allowed to leave the sanatorium Bethel near Bielefeld. While employed on Ritter's project he was also prostrated by nerves several times.

52   For which Ritter earned his Ph.D. in Tübingen on 7 July 1936. The formal exchange of scholarly ideas with his examiners, which formed a part of this occasion, concentrated on the subject of the *'Zigeunerbastarde'*. More information about the awarding of Ritter's degree, including the high praise paid to Ritter's dissertation by Heinrich Hoffmann (Robert Gaupp's successor to the chair of psychiatry in Tübingen) can be retrieved from the University Archives of Tübingen, sign. 125/59.

53   For Nazi polycratic policy, see, among others, Ganssmüller (1987, p. 178) and, in relation to Gypsies, Zimmermann (1989, pp. 42, 126). The struggle for power at the judicial and police level waged among the Ministry of Justice, the SS and the *Kanzlei des Führers* is recounted in detail in Gruchmann (1988, pp. 1115–46).

54   Two interesting, if detailed studies in this area are Weingart et al. (1988) and Weindling (1989). My remarks are also based on Noakes (1984, pp. 75–94), Ganssmüller (1987), Proctor (1988), Pross and Aly (1989), Bäumer (1990), Becker (1990, pp. 500–620).

55   A trend initiated with Blumenbach's skull measurements, and, as far as linguistics is concerned, with the nineteenth-century distinction between Aryan and Semitic languages.

56   So Ganssmüller maintains (1987, pp. 3–4).

57   Derived from Proctor (1988, pp. 22–8) according to whom, until 1938, Germany even shared an institute for racial biology, located in Moscow, with the Soviet Union.

58   For these developments, see, among others, Ganssmüller (1987, pp. 10–11) and Becker (1990, p. 599). Further, see George J. Stein (1987, pp. 251–73) for an analysis of the biological-political foundation of Nazism, using Hitler's *Mein Kampf*.

59   Cf. Becker (1990, pp. 514–7).

60   See Weingart et al. (1988, pp. 38–50).

61   Proctor (1988, p. 20) has pointed out the inconsistencies in such reasoning, citing, for example, Minister Frick of the Ministry of the Interior who, in 1933, warned

against the 'racial-suicide' of the German people as evidenced in the plunging birth rate, only to go on and plead in the same breath for more German *Lebensraum*. Concern about population growth, according to Proctor, had more to do with political interests than with any real anxiety based on demographic facts. In other words, war against other peoples and the occupation of foreign territories had to be defended.

62 See Pross and Aly (1989, p. 122 ff.) about the medical-psychiatric influence on genetic studies.
63 This accounts for why Proctor (1988, pp. 24–30) rejects the recent twofold division imposed by German historians who set the movement that propagated the supremacy of the Nordic race off against the movement of racial hygienists who thought in medical terms rather than in terms of anthropology. In academic terms this division did indeed exist, but in practice, both where research and policy-making were concerned, the two were inextricable.
64 For the ideas and influence of Alfred Ploetz, see especially Weindling (1989, pp. 64–89 and passim).
65 See Bäumer (1990, pp. 83–5) about Fritz Lenz.
66 Proctor (1988, p. 58) has pointed out that the book written by Erwin Bauer, Eugen Fischer and Fritz Lenz, *Grundriss der menschlichen Erblichkeitslehre und Rassenhygiene* (1921) was recognized in many countries as the standard work on human eugenics and was even regarded in English-speaking areas as a masterpiece.
67 Ibidem, pp. 48–9.
68 The *Rassenpolitische Amt der NSDAP* dictated how this 'new man' should look. Thus in 1935 Himmler set up the bureau *Lebensborn* within the SS and tried to put into practice so-called positive breeding measures between the women who were admitted there and SS recruits: 'The goal we are striving for is families of German and Nordic origins with a clean bill of hereditary health.' From Ganssmüller (1987, p. 5).
69 Among others, see Bäumer (1990, pp. 83–5).
70 See Proctor (1988, pp. 99–101).
71 Ibidem, p. 117.
72 See Pross and Aly (1989, pp. 132–3).
73 See Bäumer (1990, p. 88).
74 Derived from Karl Heinz Roth, '"Erbbiologische Bestandsaufnahme" – ein Aspekt "ausmerzender" Erfassung von der Entfesselung des Zweiten Weltkrieges', in Roth (1984, pp. 57–100, here p. 71).
75 This organization was the consequence of the earlier bundling of (race hygienic) genealogical organizations by Achim Gercke, an active NSDAP supporter, who in February 1933 launched the *Reichsverein für Sippenforschung* in the Prussian Ministry of the Interior. This body, including its leadership, was incorporated in 1935 within the *Reichsstelle für Sippenforschung*. Derived from Roth (1984, pp. 63–4). See also Weindling (1989, pp. 525–8).
76 For an analysis of the work of Ernst Rüdin, active in the *Deutsche Forschungsanstalt für Psychiatrie* in Munich, see Roth (1984, p. 58).
77 Roth to be sure concluded (1984, pp. 68–9) on grounds of his analysis of the publications of the most important eugenists among the Nazis that hereditary biology in its entirety was based on probabilities and the arguments of recognized authorities.
78 Ibidem, pp. 59, 64.
79 From Bauer et al. (1992, here p. 94). With its 420,000 personal index cards and 330,000 health files, the biological heredity data bank of the city of Frankfurt am Main was one of the most extensive in Germany.
80 See Bauer et al. (1992, pp. 93–101).
81 This information about how sterilization decisions proceeded in practice is from Proctor (1988, pp. 102–7).

82 From Bock (1986, pp. 230–46). See also Proctor (1988, pp. 107–9).
83 See Roth (1984, p. 93) and Proctor (1988, pp. 110–15). The latter points out that after the outbreak of war more draconian methods gained the upper hand, such as euthanasia programmes and the annihilation of people in concentration camps. He attributes this radicalization of policy in part to an internal power struggle between the Ministries of the Interior and Justice, and the party's SS-organs.
84 Roth (1984, p. 94).
85 Ibidem, p. 95.
86 In this connection the great intellectual influence in Germany of a man such as Oswald Spengler comes to mind. For discussion of this influence, see Boterman's dissertation (1992). Spengler's ambivalent attitude towards National Socialism, displaying recognizable similarities to Ritter's, is described in Chapter 9 (pp. 289–351). Becker (1990, p. 506) has attributed the strong culture pessimism of Germany to the idea of a 'verspätete Nation': powerful neighbours, being caught in the middle, the loss of the First World War and the humiliating Treaty of Versailles.
87 Ritter (1928, p. 7).
88 Ritter's references to literature indicate that he was familiar with the contents of both Grellmann and Borrow.
89 Where necessary, I will indicate in which sense of the term Ritter was using Jenischen; yet let me remark for the record that he was far from consistent. According to Kluge Rotwelsch I (1901, p. 176) the word Jenisch has the same origin as Jauner or Gauner, to wit jana (meaning to cheat or deceive).
90 Above all Ritter (1934, pp. 25–34).
91 Ritter (1936, pp. 6–10).
92 Ibidem, p. 6.
93 See, especially, Ritter (1940, pp. 197–210).
94 See Ritter (1938, pp. 71–88), Ritter (1939, pp. 2–20) and Ritter (1941, pp. 477–89).
95 This is not to say that no anthropological research was conducted in his institute. Ritter, for example, submitted a requisition in 1937 to the Deutsche Forschungs Gemeinschaft (German Research Fund) for sets of anthropological instruments (Augenfarbentafeln, Haarfarbentafeln, measuring tapes, equipment for determining blood types) and he referred several times to race-biological and anthropological research among itinerants. See Ritter's letters of 15, 21 and 22 December 1937 to the DFG in the State Archives in Koblenz, sign. R 73/14005. The only publication deriving from research at one of Ritter's institutes which contained any anthropology was Ehrhardt (1942, pp. 52–7).
96 Ritter (1938a, p. 77).
97 Ritter (1941, p. 483).
98 Ritter (1939, p. 10).
99 Ritter (1941, p. 484). See also Ritter (1939, p. 11) where he discusses this group at greater length.
100 Ritter (1934, p. 32).
101 Thus, for example, the State Archives in Magdeburg (sign. Rep. C 29) still contain 600 personal files from the principal police station there that burned down in the war. On many cards is the notation: 'KZ Auschwitz eingewiesen (admitted to concentration camp Auschwitz).'
102 See the section entitled 'A splintered heritage: police, science and policy' at the end of this chapter.
103 Ritter (1941, p. 486).
104 See Greifswald Landesarchiv, pers. akt. 15721/242, Gutachtliche Äusserung no. 2322, 8 July 1941. In the Landeshauptarchiv Sachsen-Anhalt in Magdenburg (C 29 Anhang II no. 84/1, 54R) GA no. 3,369 from 25 July 1941 was turned up, signed by Dr Ritter with the annotation: 'Zur Zeit (at present) im Konz. Lager (concentration camp) Buchenwald.'

105 In the *Brandenburgisches Landeshauptarchiv* in Potsdam (Rep. 30 Berlin G Polizeipräsidium tit. 198 A 3, Gypsy no. 133). The file, however, does not contain a copy of the racial diagnosis indicated, although the correspondence in it refers to *Gutachtliche Äusserung* no. 24,411 from 2 January 1945, completed by the *Rassenhygienische Forschungsstelle des RGHA*. In this Gypsy half-caste's file it is recorded that he/she deserves to be considered a non-Gypsy. The GA with the highest number that Ritter mentions in any of his publications is diagnosis 23,822, dated March 1944. Information from a letter which he wrote on 6 March 1944 to the DFG. See State Archives in Koblenz, sign. R 73/14005. Up to now, the date which holds for the last day on which a racial diagnosis was written is 15 November 1944 (Gilsenbach 1988, p. 125). It is extremely regrettable that copies of these documents, so significant from both scholarly and documentary points of view, have never systematically been collected. In large part they were in the possession of rural *Kriminalpolizeistellen* and later found their way into various state archives. I myself collected a series of copies of these racial diagnoses, partly during actual visits to archives and partly by means of specific requests for such documents addressed to other archives. In answer to my requests, I was usually forwarded a number of representative examples edited in such a way as to make identification of any individuals impossible. Their total is too modest to permit my attempting any meaningful generalizations.

106 From Ritter (1941, pp. 482–3).

107 Ritter (1937, pp. 13–19).

108 Ibidem, pp. 20–2.

109 Ibidem, p. 26.

110 In the introduction to my chapter on the Göttingen historian H.M.G. Grellmann, I also referred to the importance of these lists of wanted persons (*Gaunerlisten*) for labelling people as Gypsy and gypsy-like.

111 See Lucassen (1997, '*Zigeuner*', Chapter 3, 'Wo sind die Zigeuner?') for a full sketch of Schäffer whom Lucassen considers to be the first criminal lawyer.

112 Ritter (1937, pp. 31–49).

113 Ibidem, p. 51. In a note he promises his readers that he will presently publish a series of instructive *Erbtafel*, something that he never did. In retrospect it is no longer possible to reconstruct how many of these genealogical tables Ritter and his assistants worked out in detail and how they went about the task. A part of this material has ended up in the State Archives in Koblenz where, until now, it has remained unanalyzed.

114 Unpublished lecture, untitled, on vagrants and Gypsies delivered at the Congress for psychiatrists in Giessen (1934). Copies in the State Archives in Koblenz, sign. R 073/014005.

115 With the unification of Germany in 1870, all ordinances that concerned only Gypsies became defunct and the *Freizügigkeitsgesetz des Norddeutschen Bundes* came into effect. Everyone could subsequently live wherever he wished. Separate regulations were enacted, however, to keep out strangers considered to be Gypsies and to prevent them from being given patents or identity papers, measures which in practice meant sharper control of all 'Gypsyish types'. See Cottaar et al. (1992, pp. 51–5).

116 Ritter (1937, pp. 60–1).

117 Ibidem, pp. 102–5.

118 Ibidem, p. 109.

119 For a more subtle reconstruction of the interactions between Gypsies and diverse governments in nineteenth-century Württemberg, see Fricke (1991).

120 In Fricke (1991, p. 29 ff.) we read that in the second half of the eighteenth century vagrants, vendors, beggars and felons eagerly sought out south-west Germany. As the result of wars, failed harvests, discriminatory judicial regulations and social-

economic developments, eighteenth century Schwabia at times had a cumulative vagrant population which amounted to 20 per cent of its total population; Gypsies would have accounted for merely a modest proportion of these.

121   See Ritter (1940b) and Ritter (1941, pp. 137–55).
122   Ritter (1941b, p. 139).
123   Ritter (1940b, p. 12).
124   Ritter (1941b, p. 142).
125   Ibidem, p. 143.
126   Ibidem, p. 148.
127   Ritter (1941b, p. 153).
128   See Ritter (1941, pp. 38–41), Ritter (1942a, pp. 535–9), Ritter (1942, pp. 117–19) and Ritter (1944, pp. 33–60).
129   Ritter (1942a, p. 117).
130   See Ritter (1942, pp. 536–7) and Ritter (1941a, pp. 38–9).
131   See Ritter (1936, pp. 289–303).
132   See Ritter (1935, pp. 385–90).
133   Ritter (1934, p. 11).
134   Ritter (1944, p. 37).
135   Ibidem, pp. 37-8.
136   Thus in a letter dated 2 February 1938 he wrote to the DFG that, in his hereditary biological and anthropological research, he was primarily concerned with the relationship between race and crime and between race and illness. Studies in these directions were still, he felt, in their infancy. See the State Archives in Koblenz, sign. R 73/14005.
137   See Annex 6 (at the end of this study) for a list of 41 reviews that Ritter's book received, rarely longer than half a page, and for a justification of the work method that I followed.
138   He garnered kudos from diverse reviewers for examining an entire hereditary stream in contrast to classical genealogical studies that concentrated on a single family tree.
139   From the medical-psychiatric world such commentary came from a review in the *Deutsche Zeitschrift für die gesamte gerichtliche Medizin* (1937, p. 124) written by Ritter's colleague Von Neureiter and a piece by the psychiatrist Villinger in the *Zeitschrift für menschliche Vererbungs- und Konstitutionslehre* (1942, pp. 626–7).
140   In the *Archiv für Rassen- und Gesellschaftsbiologie* (1937, p. 270), by Friedrich Stumpfl, Director of the *Erb- und Rassenbiologisches Institut* in Innsbruck between 1939 and 1945.
141   In *Anthropologische Anzeiger* (1937, p. 133), a piece by the Austrian Albert Harrasser, an associate of Ernst Rüdin in Munich. Eugen Fischer wrote in *Zeitschrift für Morphologie und Anthropologie* (1940, p. 174) that the way Ritter depicted it, the closed *Blutkreise* of vagrant families bore considerable resemblance to a race(!).
142   In the previously cited article by Villinger in *Der Nervenarzt* (1938, pp. 222–3).
143   In the *Archiv für Rechts- und Sozialphilosophie* (1937/38, pp. 530–2), by Alfred Vierkandt whose work straddled the frontier between sociology and psychology.
144   F. Steiner in *Der Erbarzt* (1937, p. 127).
145   F. Köhrle in *Zeitschrift für Psychologie* (1937, pp. 367–8).
146   Hans Hartmann in *Illustrierte Zeitung* (1943, p. 34).
147   In, among others, *Hessische Blätter für Volkskunde* (1937, pp. 148–50) and *Blätter für Württembergische Familienkunde* (1937, p. 77).
148   Rodenberg (20 September 1937, pp. 437–46).
149   Otto Finger was an assistant physician at the *Institut für Erb- und Rassenpflege* run by H.W. Kranz in Giessen and on the staff of the *Rassenpolitische Amt der NSDAP*; Robert Krämer, employed by the *Hygienische Institut der Westfälischen Wilhelms-Universität* under the leadership of K.W. Jötten in Munich (and not, as

Zimmermann (1989, p. 26) wrote, working for Lothar Loeffler in Königsbergen) based his article (1937, pp. 33–55) primarily on a piece by the Mayor of Berleburg, Dr Günther (1937, pp. 262–8); the ethnologist Martin Block, feet planted squarely in the tradition of Wlislocki and the Gypsy Lore Society, produced a study in 1936 about 'racially pure Gypsies' in south-eastern Europe; Norbert Vogel of the university polyclinic in Munich carried out criminological biological research in the tradition of Dugdale et al. on a family of vagrants (1937, pp. 85–91, 110–21, 147–56); and, finally, Joachim Rómer of the *Rassenpolitische Amt der NSDAP* wrote several articles (1937, pp. 281–8, 321–8 and 1934, pp. 112–13), concluding that Gypsies had to be detached completely from the German people.

150 See Zimmermann (1989, pp. 26–7). Also relevant, however, were remarks which he made during a *Podiumsgespräch* several years ago (unpublished, no date) implying that at the same time that Ritter was busy others were conducting studies of Gypsies in Giessen, Munich, Berlin and Königsbergen.

151 Ibidem.

152 From Weindling (1989, p. 555).

153 From document NO 1725 from the State Archives in Nuremberg.

154 See his contributions on the subject in *Zigeunerkundliche Forschungen* I, which he edited together with Inge Sudbrack (1977). For Knobloch, see further Hohmann (1991, pp. 320–3).

155 See Zimmermann (1989, p. 35).

156 This interpretation was suggested to me by document NO 1499 from the State Archives in Nuremberg which concerns news dated 28 September 1942 about this evacuation conducted by the *Rasse- und Siedlungshauptamtes-SS*.

157 The proposal to resort to sterilization on a large scale also flowed from the pens of Kranz (1937, pp. 21–7) and Küppers (1938, pp. 183–93) who depicted the *fremdkörperische* danger in strident colours.

158 Günther (1937, pp. 262–3).

159 Ibidem, p. 266.

160 Someone like Küppers (1938, pp. 192–3), who made various journeys through the Balkans and there visited countless Gypsy groups, even spoke of the 'racial decay of gypsydom'.

161 An example of someone with this approach during the Nazi regime is Gerhard Stein (1941, pp. 74–114) who reported in an article on his research among 227 Gypsies (124 *Rom* and 123 *Rumungri* or *Sinte*) and – *nota bene* in 1941! – concluded on grounds of psychological and ethnological impressions – familiar with the latter through the literature – that most Gypsies living in Germany were racially pure. This he deduced from their character – so entirely their own – even though his physical anthropological research had only brought to light a limited number of racial characteristics, such as a husky voice (p. 106).

162 Moravek (1939). For biographical information about Moravek, see Hohmann (1991, pp. 271–5).

163 Both Stein and Moravek refer to the anthropometric research of: L. Glück 'Beitrag zur physischen Anthropologie der Zigeuner in Bosnien und der Herzegovina', *Wissenschaftliche Mittheilungen aus Bosnien und der Herzegovina* (Part 5, Vienna, 1897, pp. 403–33) – which concerned 66 Serbian Gypsies; A. Weisbach 'Die Zigeuner', *Mittheilungen der anthropologischen Gesellschaft in Wien* (Part 9, 1889, pp. 107–17); and finally V. Lebzelter 'Anthropologische Untersuchungen an serbischen Zigeunern', *Mittheilungen den Anthropologischen Geschichte* (Part LII, Vienna, 1923) which dealt with 41 imprisoned Serbian Gypsies.

164 Moravek (1939, p. 11).

165 Ibidem, pp. 12–13.

166 Ibidem, pp. 2–3.

167 Ibidem, p. 16.

168   Ibidem, p. 29.
169   Ibidem, p. 73 ff.
170   Ibidem, p. 90.
171   For a critical discussion of historical writing about Gypsy policy during the Weimar Republic and under the Nazis, see Lucassen (1995, pp. 82–100). Apart from the ground-breaking work of Kenrick and Puxon from 1972, the publications of Michael Zimmermann from 1989 and 1992, the collection of articles, *Feinderklärung und Prävention* (1988), the representative regional study by Karola Fings and Frank Sparing (1992), and the summarizing review by Sybil Milton (1992, pp. 1–18) all offer cogent introductions to the subject.
172   See file StA Hamburg 2200 Js 2/84, p. 802 (*Zentrale Stelle der Landesjustizverwaltung Ludwigsburg*) about the pre-trial investigation of Ruth Kellermann, a staff member of Ritter's research bureau in the Ministry of Public Health.
173   See File 415 AR 314/81 (*Zentralstelle Ludwigsburg*) which concerns case StA Stuttgart 19 Js 928/81 during which the prosecutor (p. 442) reached the conclusion that the systematic use of racial diagnoses in the selection of Gypsies for the camps was not proven.
174   From Weindling (1989, p. 514). Hohmann (1991, p. 445) lists in his bibliography Hans W. Jürgens' *Asozialität als biologisches und sozialbiologisches Problem* (1961). In 1935 Hans Weinert wrote *Rassen der Menschheit* that is rife with racial myths. From Köbben (1971, pp. 206–8).
175   File 415 AR 314/81, p. 441.
176   Two recent examples of this phenomenon in the field of Gypsy studies are Baumiller (1992, pp. 103–11) and Krokowski (1992, p. 133); also the study of Seidler and Rett (1988, pp. 234–8) in which they draw the erroneous conclusion that anthropological research determined the racial categorization of Gypsies. A contradictory conclusion can be derived, to cite one source, from the statements made by Brigitte Richter on 28 August 1986, employed by Ritter from October 1939 to July 1943. She declared that *Sippentafeln* were drawn up on a basis of genealogical data, that the names of all persons included were then written on file cards which later formed the basis for racial diagnoses that usually bore a stamp of Ritter's signature. See preliminary investigation file no. 414 AR 540/83, StA Hamburg 2200 Js 2/84, as well as the comments of Adolf Würth during the same case.
177   Here, respectively, the figures cited are the Doctor of Law Avé-Lallemant (1858, Part 1: 25–36, Part 2: 38–40); Liebich, who, in 1863 after 30 years of detective work, looked back at his career and, as he himself said, personally noted down words from the mouths of the members of Gypsy bands, recording what they had to tell about their lives; the examining magistrate Gross, in his popular handbook of 1894, devoted a short chapter to Gypsies (pp. 328–49); the head of the Central Bureau for Gypsies (*Zigeunerzentrale*) in Munich, whose work fell under the Ministry for the Interior, Dillmann, brought the first general search and registration system for Gypsies into the world with his book on Gypsies in 1905; the lawyer Aichele, finally, expatiated in his strongly historically-oriented dissertation (1912) on how the police and governments could best solve the Gypsy problem.
178   See Fricke (1991, pp. 137-42) for the increasingly open judicial discrimination in Württemberg against Gypsies with itinerant vocations. In '*Zigeuner*' (1997), Leo Lucassen defends the hypothesis that the centralization and specialization of the German police at the end of the nineteenth century led to an expansion of the category 'Gypsies' to include all kinds of other people who moved about with their families and who were not previously labelled as such.
179   Dillmann (1905, p. 5). According to Dillmann, authentic native Gypsy dynasties still lived only in Spain, Hungary and other East European countries. Aichele (1912, pp. 22–3) also referred to the intensive mixing of Gypsies with native (wandering)

Germans which, he concluded on the authority of Grellmann and Biester, had already occurred on a large scale in the eighteenth century, and even – based on Sebastian Münster – in the sixteenth century.

180 Dillmann (1905, pp. 6–7).

181 See Cottaar et al. (1992, pp. 51–5) for a concise account of shifting definitions of Gypsies used in policy towards them, from German unification in 1870 up to the social projects undertaken in the 1980s in the framework of the *Wiedergutmachung*.

182 Dillmann (1905, p. 8).

183 It is revealing how frankly these local activities to compile complete regional records in the 1930s of all 'gypsy-like' persons were described at the time in a short article by Bader (1935, pp. 265–8). We can conclude from this piece that people with an itinerant vocation were incapable of doing any good in the eyes of the police. On the one hand their roaming way of life was made impossible; on the other, people did not believe they could become sedentary, driven as they were by a congenital compulsion to move about.

184 Gross (1894, pp. 328, 335), who had far less of an eye for the phenomenon of half-castes, even believed: 'No man of culture, even the most depraved, remains among the Gypsies for long.' Aichele (1912, p. 34) appears, some decades later, to have been much more strongly influenced by ideas about the harmful consequences of mixing.

185 Aichele (1912, p. 35).

186 Ibidem, pp. 7–9.

187 See Proctor (1988, pp. 202–4) about the work methods of the *Kriminalbiologische Sammelstellen*.

188 This therefore provoked strenuous resistance on the part of the national group defending the interests of those with itinerant vocations. In 1924 this group protested immediately when the initial legislative proposal was made public. It did not want its members to be equated with Gypsies and the workshy. Those with an honourable occupation and a fixed abode also, formally, did not fall under the law but, in practice, the police had a difficult time making such subtle distinctions. See Hehemann (1987, pp. 301–4).

189 For a systematic treatment of these laws, see Milton (1992, pp. 1–18), but also Zülch (1982, pp. 27–45).

190 See Döring (1964, pp. 35–8) and Milton (1992, p. 11, note 8).

191 There is a draft by Dr Zindel of the Ministry of the Interior for a *Reichszigeunergesetz* (Law on Gypsies) dated 4 March 1936 in the State Archives in Koblenz (sign. R 018/005644, Rep. 320, no. 644, pp. 1069–75). On the eve of WW II Reiter (1939, p. 357) wrote that on the basis of race biological research conducted among non-sedentary groups in Germany by Ritter's *Rassenhygienische und bevölkerungs-biologische Forschungsstelle* proposals were being drawn up for a Gypsy law.

192 From Gruchmann (1972, pp. 235–79).

193 Hohmann (1991, pp. 84–132) has included these decrees and laws-in-the making in his book, for the most part literally transcribed, comparison reveals, just as he found them in File no. StA Cologne 24 Js 429/61 (*Zentralstelle Ludwigsburg*), but also to some extent paraphrased.

194 This interpretation I have borrowed from Gruchmann (1988, pp. 1115–46).

195 For these actions see especially Gruchmann (1972, pp. 235–79) and Burleigh (1991, pp. 453–73), who presents a summary of the discussion then going on about the growing public unrest in relation to the secret euthanasia programme in Germany of which the Ministry of Justice was for a long time ignorant.

196 Ganssmüller (1987, p. 181).

197 In a letter dated 13 October 1942 Thierack petitioned Martin Bormann, head of the chancellery, for Hitler's permission to transfer to Himmler, the authority to prosecute these four groups, whom he regarded as a threat to the German people.

To keep them in prisons and houses of correction cost the German state money unnecessarily, whereas the SS could settle accounts with them very nicely. In a letter from the Ministry of Public Health dated 5 November 1942 and sent to all *Kriminal-, Sicherheits- und Staatspolizeistellen* they were informed of this Thierack–Himmler agreement. From a letter from Thierack to Himmler dated 16 November 1942 it emerges, however, that district leaders in the Eastern territories protested profusely against the proposal to mete out such treatment to Poles and Russians because of the many family ties there were with the people who were living there. Special treatment of Jews and Gypsies, on the other hand, did not trouble them at all. From Nuremberg-documents No. 2927 and NG 558, PS 1750 and NG 1255.

198 From Milton (1992, p. 5) and File StA Cologne 24 Js 429/61 (*Zentralstelle Ludwigsburg*), in which can be read that Minister Frick of the Interior in his guidelines of 4 April 1938 went more deeply into the matter of exactly whom should be considered asocial. The term 'Gypsies' appeared at the time to pertain to 'wandering people'.

199 See Milton (1992, p. 6).

200 Nevertheless until the end of 1942 the Minister of Labour still decreed that pure Gypsies and half-castes of predominantly Gypsy descent should be put to work to the greatest extent possible because otherwise the production process, given the labour-devouring demand of the army, would stagnate. See the reference to this ordinance dated 13 March 1942 in an article by Küppers (20 May 1942, no. 125). In a communication from the same bureau, no. 128, dated 20 August 1942, the subject was once more finding employment for Gypsies and Gypsy half-castes. The employment bureaus were encouraged to mediate, although Gypsies were not so easily permitted to leave the places they were staying.

201 Thus Milton (1992, pp. 4–5, 13–14, note 22) who cites the transit camps in Cologne, Düsseldorf, Essen, Frankfurt and Hamburg, and refers to different regional studies on these (temporary) Gypsy camps. Milton further comments that only inadequate research has been done so far into the deportation of Gypsies prior to the outbreak of the war.

202 Derived from a communication about the discussion between Heydrich and others in Berlin, on 30 January 1940, concerning the pending evacuation of groups, on Hitler's and Himmler's orders, to the *Generalgouvernement* (NO 5322, State Archives of Nuremberg) and from an overview as of 14 November 1940 of the evacuations actually carried out by the *Chef der Sicherheitspolizei und des SD* (without date), reporting 294,336 Poles, 6,053 Jews and 2,800 Gypsies (NO 5150, State Archives of Nuremberg). According to Döring (1964), until the autumn of 1944 they lived in Poland under circumstances comparable to the ghetto. They were also obliged to wear an armband with a Z.

203 See the official decree of the Ministry of Public Health dated 11 January 1943; integral text in Hohmann (1991, pp. 110–11, 115).

204 Derived from a statement by the public prosecutor in the preliminary investigation (20 April 1963) of all institutions implicated in the persecution of Gypsies. See File StA Cologne 24 Js 429/61 (*Zentralstelle Ludwigsburg*).

205 See, among others, Broad (1966, pp. 3–53, here p. 41). See, too, Zimmermann (1989, pp. 40–2 and 1992, pp. 362–3) where he points out that some municipalities seized the deportation regulations as a chance to rid themselves of their socially integrated Gypsies.

206 Milton (1992, p. 9).

207 References to Gypsies in the reports of *SS-Einsatzkommandos* in the Eastern occupied zones have, to be sure, never been analysed systematically.

208 From different articles in Berenbaum (no year). According to Wiesenthal (1967, pp. 216–19) all the Gypsies in the Ukraine and the Crimea were killed by *SS-*

Einsatzkommandos. See Lucassen (1990, pp. 221–3) for the situation in the Western occupied territories.

209 Already in a letter dated 12 February 1935, Ritter had written to the DFG that his research among the wine growers of Tübingen, who were burdened by alcoholism and in-breeding, had led him to the study of the Gypsy half-caste population and its influence on this population group. See the State Archives in Koblenz, sign. R 73/14005.

210 In a letter to the DFG dated 6 January 1940, the chief of the *Sicherheitspolizei und des SD* wrote that Ritter's research was of exceptional importance to the state and therefore deserved additional subsidy. He continued: 'That is of course principally a racial problem, but in its practical ramifications above all a problem of asociability.' He regarded the registration of Gypsies as indispensable for the solution of problems faced by the police. See the State Archives in Koblenz, sign. R 73/14005.

211 Ritter (1945, p. 49).

212 She received her Ph.D. from the Friedrich-Wilhelm University of Berlin on 5 November 1943; the faculty members who sat on her degree committee were Eugen Fischer, Richard Thurnwald (an anthropologist and one of the earliest racial hygienists) and Robert Ritter. For Justin's Ph.D. dossier, see the archives of what today is Humboldt University in Berlin, Department of Mathematics and Natural Sciences, sign. 192.

213 Ritter (1945, p. 52).

214 See, for example, the memoirs of Von Mahlsdorff (1992, pp. 58–62). This transvestite, born in 1928 as Lothar Berfelde, bludgeoned his father to death and was then sent to Tübingen for observation. Here Ritter took charge of his treatment.

215 He even referred to these '*Asozialen-Reservaten*' in the self-defence he prepared from Mariaberg for presentation to the French occupying authorities on 20 May 1947. See the City Archives in Frankfurt, sign. 2009, p. 39.

216 From Ritter's letter to the DFG on March 6, 1944. See the State Archives in Koblenz, sign. R 73/14005.

217 To resort under *Gruppe V D* of the *Reichssicherheitshauptamt*. See the Berlin Document Centre, File Robert Ritter, for correspondence concerning this appointment between *SS-Obersturmbannführer Oberregierungs- und Kriminalrat* Werner of the RSHA and *SS-Gruppenführer* Hofmann, *Chef des Rasse- und Siedlungshauptamtes-SS* (dated 15/7, 4/8, 8/8/1941).

218 In a letter to the RKPA dated 12 November 1943. See State Archives in Koblenz, sign. R. 165/145, folder with correspondence concerning the Gigl family.

219 From Eva Justin's letter to Manfred Betz in Tübingen dated 12 January 1939. See State Archives in Koblenz, sign. R 165/ 000239, Tübingen division, p. 45.

220 Laqueur (Dutch translation 1980, p. 230). Precisely the fact that Auschwitz was a 'mixed camp' would have confused many people.

221 Thus Laqueur (1980, pp. 196–208) who writes of a suppressed *Endlösung* (Final Solution).

222 Ritter (1945, p. 104).

223 This, at any rate, is what Kogon (no date, pp. 144–5) thinks. He concluded that Nebe was assuredly not the pitiless SS-functionary and conjuncture-profiteer people took him to be shortly after the war. In a certain sense Kogon even found him tragic although he blames him for being too heartless in his double role. Welsh Dulles (1947, pp. 4, 45) reached the same conclusion. There are various passages about Nebe in Bernd Gisevius' personal testimonies (1946).

224 Ritter (1945, p. 110).

225 Ibidem, p. 126.

226 From a letter written on 19 May 1947 by Paul Wiedel, Vice President of the Ministry of Public Health to the state directorate for purging the police in Reutlingen. See

the State Archives in Sigmaringen, sign. Wö 13/10/C/ 3206 no. 1600.

227 Ritter (1945, p. 149).

228 This institute took over co-ordination in this area (including 19,000 dossiers) from the *Zigeunerzentrale* in Munich.

229 See Milton (1992, p. 6).

230 From a letter of Eva Justin's dated 12 January 1939 to her colleague Betz (State Archives in Koblenz, R 165/000239, *Zweigstelle Tübingen*, p. 45).

231 From a letter sent by the *Staatliche Kriminalpolizei* in Darmstadt on 27 May 1940 to the subdivision in Frankfurt am Main concerning the evacuation of Gypsies; the communication reveals that in drawing up the lists of Gypsies for transport the authorities sorely missed the racial biological research data of the Ministry of Public Health. See File 415 AR 314/81, StA Stuttgart 19 Js 928/81 (*Zentralstelle Ludwigsburg*).

232 From File 415 AR 930/ 61, StA Cologne 24 Js 429/61 (*Zentralstelle Ludwigsburg*) concerning the preliminary investigation of Hans Maly; document no. 54 (family members: nrs. 52, 53, 55, 56). See, also, Hohmann (1991, pp. 380–416) who deals with this case at length, albeit from a different angle.

233 In 1958 the canton judge ruled that Maly had acted illegally by treating Liselotte W. as an asocial who fell under the *Schutzhaft*-decree. She lived a socially adapted life, had not entered into marriage with Meissinger, and had voluntarily proposed termination of her pregnancy. The prison doctor, moreover, had declared her, in her pregnant condition, unfit for camp admission. The judge found that one could speak of an excessive, arbitrary action and proposed that Maly be tried before a jury in Cologne. No judgment was ever obtained against him in this case, however, for the accused died in October 1971.

234 Hohmann (1991, p. 385 and other passages).

235 From the Nuremberg-documents, NG 1008 and NG 1619.

236 In a subsidy application to the DFG dated 23 March 1943, Ritter wrote that, as of that moment, they had come up with a racial biological solution for 21,498 Gypsy cases. He added that after the conclusion of his research, 9,000 Gypsy half-castes had been amassed in a special Gypsy camp in Sudetenland. See State Archives in Koblenz R 73/14005, letter 35.

237 Tobler gave her testimony on 23 September 1960. See File 415 AR 314/81, StA Stuttgart 19 Js 928/81 (*Zentralstelle Ludwigsburg*). Her interpretation is confirmed by evidence from Brigitte Richter, miss Thiele, Ruth Greuling and Herta Wolek; the latter pair were witnesses in the case StA Frankenthal 1 U Js 947/79 file no. 110 AR 315/79.

238 See File no. StA Cologne 24 Js 429/61 (*Zentralstelle Ludwigsburg*). See, also, Lifton (1986, pp. 348–73) on Mengele's attitude towards Gypsies, especially the children.

239 In one of Ritter's work reports from 1942, among the topics raised was impending Gypsy legislation. From File StA 4 Js 220/59 Frankfurt/M (*Zentralstelle Ludwigsburg*). For a detailed analysis up to April 1945 of how the *Gemeinschaftsfremdengesetz* came into being, including allusions to Ritter's contributions, see Wagner (1988, pp. 75–100). Among factors that stood in the way of enactment were the problem of definition, which was never adequately settled, and the jurisdictional dispute between the RKPA and the Ministry of Justice's sterilization courts.

240 From a letter dated 20 May 1947 from Ritter in Mariaberg to his wife in Berlin. Copies in my possession.

241 See Humboldt University, Berlin, Law Faculty, sign. 590, pp. 1–26 for correspondence concerning this appointment which was made on 7 March 1940.

242 From a letter dated 18 January 1946 from the Dean of the Law School to the rector of the University in Tübingen. University Archives in Tübingen, sign. 126a/043.

243 Letter from *Landeskommissar* Kirchheimer dated 12 February 1946 to the District commissioner and the rector of the university; further, a letter from the Dean of

the Law Faculty to the Rector dated 4 August 1946 in which, after consultation with Professors Kern and Ernst Kretschmer (psychiatrist), he wrote that there was no longer such an urgent need to fill the proposed chair. University Archives in Tübingen, sign. 126a/ 043. There are also copies of letters from Gaupp dated 24 March 1946, Oehme from Heidelberg dated 28 March 1946 and Paul Wiedel (vice-president of the Ministry of Public Health) dated 26 March 1946, all of which shower praise on Ritter, in the University Archives in Tübingen, sign. 601/65.

244 Protocol no. 1912 of the *Untersuchungsausschuss für den Kreis Reutlingen, zur Säuberung der Verwaltung von nationalsozialistischem Einfluss* dated 22 January 1946 in which it stands that Ritter had not participated in running – administratively or otherwise – the areas Germany had occupied. Excerpt from the State Archives in Sigmaringen file Robert Ritter, where several documents are stored concerning his political purgation. In the context of de-Nazification, the French had set up investigatory committees in the territory that they occupied. These examined whether someone's past under the Nazi regime gave cause to bar him or her from a public function. On 1 November 1946, this resulted in the French zone in 36,216 dismissals. Borrowed from Henke (1991, pp. 21–83, here p. 42).

245 Derived from a communication of 15 pages dated 3 September 1945 which Ritter sent to the *Württembergische Landesdirektion für Justiz* in Stuttgart. University Archives in Tübingen, sign. 601/65.

246 From a letter to Robert Ritter dated 17 February 1949 from the *Stadtgesundheitsamt* of Frankfurt am Main. Copies in my possession.

247 See Ritter's letter to Alderman Menzer dated 17 May 1947 about his applying for the position of youth physician. In the letter he emphasized that if it was true in Frankfurt that as soon as people heard the phrase 'racial hygiene' they thought of Nazi race ideology, then he'd rather forget the job, a reaction that prompts the suspicion that he was asked to solicit for it. See, too, Alderman Prestel's letter to Alderman Menzer, 12 July 1947; a report of a discussion with Ritter about his independent post as youth doctor (no date); the letter from Chief Physician Schmith to Prestel, 13 August 1947 (in which he alludes to an earlier talk with Ritter). All these letters are in the University Archives in Tübingen, sign. 601/65.

248 From Bauer et al. (1992, p. 87).

249 Ibidem, pp. 109–10 and 176, on new appointments to the municipal health services in Frankfurt after the war. In Eva Justin's employee file (City Archives in Frankfurt am Main, sign. 92.546), there is a letter from Ritter dated 4 December 1947, in which he explains why his bureau needs a new addition, someone to fill the position of criminological psychologist, and there is approval of the suggestion by the mayor and city aldermen, dated 15 March 1948. Justin's certificate of de-Nazification dated 30 August 1947, is in there as well. She continued to work for the municipal services until her death on 11 September 1966, albeit in different functions.

250 According to a letter from Wiesbaden dated 13 January 1949 the Minister entrusted with the political purgation of the *Hessische Staatsministerium* began a preliminary investigation of Ritter because it was said to be reported in the *Analysis of Nazi Criminal Organizations* (p. 31) that he had been an SS officer. Inquiry at the Berlin Document Centre revealed this to be inaccurate. Moreover, in a declaration of the chancellery dated 1 March 1949, reference is made to Ritter's certificate of de-Nazification dated 3 March 1948, signed by State Commissioner Künzel who was in charge of political cleansing. These documents are in the University Archives in Tübingen, sign. 601/65.

251 In the *Zentralstelle Ludwigsburg* there is a small file on Robert Ritter (sign. 415 AR 55/82, StA Frankfurt 55/3 Js 5582/48) in which a reference appears to the preliminary investigation of 28 August 1950. On 25 February 1982 the *Zentralstelle* asked the public prosecutor in Frankfurt for the relevant paperwork on this inquiry concerning Ritter, but it all turned out to have been disposed of.

252 See Hohmann (1991, pp. 167–84). On 25 March 1992 I wrote Hohmann asking permission to examine the documents (including letters prepared by Attorney General Kosterlitz), which he alludes to in his text without mentioning where to find them. I had not come across any trace of them during my research. On 5 April 1992 he replied that he couldn't help me.

253 Hohmann (1991, p. 180). On 18 May 1994 I sent a letter to Hohmann with the request that he cite the whereabouts of this document, but he never responded.

254 Thus, in a letter of defence dated 12 October 1949, which he wrote to Alderman Prestel in Frankfurt about the accusations of these Gypsies, Ritter remarked: 'Some Bavarian Gypsy families are always trying to come up with new, fantastic stories.' In the University Archives in Tübingen, sign. 601/65. Hermann Stolting II, Ritter's lawyer, wrote in a condolence note dated 2 April 1951 to Hildegard Ritter that he was pleased to have been able to establish his client's innocence: 'To refute all the arguments that criminal and dishonourable elements had assembled.' I have a copy of this letter in my possession.

255 Statement by the director of the *Landespersonalamt Hessen* on 4 December 1950 to the personnel division of the city of Frankfurt. In the University Archives in Tübingen, sign. 601/65.

256 From Henke and Woller (1991, pp. 38–9).

257 One can trace the history of his illnesses in an employee dossier under his name in the City Archives in Frankfurt, sign. 2009. The most important items on file are the letter of Dr Hübener of the Caritas Sanatorium dated 14 August 1948; the diagnosis of Prof. Hauss, MD, dated February 1951, addressed to the personnel division of the public health services in Frankfurt; an overview of Ritter's absenteeism owing to illness dated 21 February 1951.

258 From a communique dated 26 April 1951 sent by the *Stadtgesundheitsamt* to the personnel division. Ritter's contract was not ended until 30 September that same year.

259 According to Gilsenbach (1988, pp. 101–34, here p. 134, note 65), during the last days of the war *Sicherheitspolizisten* and *SS-Männer* destroyed the documents kept in this *Führerschule*. His comment that the headquarters of Ritter's institute were situated there is, however, inaccurate.

260 Thus Krokowski (1992, p. 61), with reference to a dossier in the State Archives in Koblenz, sign. R 165/45.

261 Specifics about the conflicts between Ritter and the management of this psychiatric nursing institution which fell under the *Landesverband der Inneren Mission*, in particular his clashes with *Schulrat* Wittmann and later with Director Kraft, a newly returned prisoner of war, can be read in a thin dossier containing correspondence which spans the period 17 May 1944 to 5 August 1946 (Mariaberger Heime, Archive, inventory no. 78.3). See also Hohmann (1991, pp. 162–6).

262 Per 9 November 1943, with a basic monthly salary of RM 700. See the letter from the Ministry of the Interior dated 19 November 1943 naming him to the post and the letter confirming the salary of the President of the Ministry of Public Health dated 7 February 1944. The originals of both letters are in my possession.

263 Ritter (1945, p. 134).

264 See the University Archives in Tübingen, sign. 126 a/403, which contains correspondence about this appointment. We can infer that Ritter himself had taken the initiative to give a series of lectures. See, too, Humboldt University Berlin, Law Faculty, sign. 560, pp. 4–5, about the proposal (and also request) to prolong his teaching stint in Tübingen which lay in close proximity to Mariaberg (in Reutlingen).

265 Hepp (1987, p. 212) has pointed out that, for a long time after the war, a discussion was carried on about the question of whether or not Moringen and Uckermark were concentration camps for juveniles. According to him they were exceptional camps which were administered until mid-1943 under the *Inspektion der KZ's*.

What's more, all girls and young women from Uckermark would be transported in January 1945 to the concentration camp at Ravensbrück.

266 See Körber (1988, pp. 165–75) about resistance on the part of the courts to taking the testimony of Gypsies seeking compensation seriously.

267 See Hohmann (1991, pp. 380–416) for an overview of these legal inquiries. According to Henke and Woller (1991, p. 82) between 8 May 1945 and 31 December 1989 a preliminary investigation or criminal case was undertaken against 98,043 persons accused of crimes committed during the Nazi regime. This led to 6,486 convictions. According to Schwarberg (1990, p. 131) most defendants escaped without punishment because the statute of limitations for their crimes had expired or the testimony against them was inconsistent.

268 Borrowed from Zimmermann (1992, p. 366); he relies on Wolfgang Feuerhelm's *Polizei und 'Zigeuner'. Strategien, Handlungsmuster und Alltagstheorien im polizeilichen Umgang mit Sinti und Roma* (1986).

269 Thus Gilsenbach (1988, p. 134, note 65); the public prosecutor in the case against Dr Maly (file 415 AR 930/61, StA Cologne 24 Js 429/61, here p. 15) also discovered during his preliminary investigation that all the RKPA documents had been destroyed. For this trial at the beginning of the 1960s he amassed his own collection of 15,000 Gypsy files, using information acquired from local police stations. From a documentary and scholarly point of view it is highly regrettable that these basic files no longer exist in their original form.

270 In a letter from Ritter to Alderman Menzer of Frankfurt am Main dated 26 June 1947, he wrote that he still needed two to three weeks to collect all his scientific material dispersed in various places and that then he wished to confer about where it could be housed. See the City Archives in Frankfurt, personal file Robert Ritter, sign. 18.576.

271 See the City Archives in Frankfurt, personal file Eva Justin, sign. 92.546.

272 Winter's *Magisterarbeit* (1991) constitutes a valuable start towards the reconstruction of the way in which the empirical material of Ritter and his helpers was handled after the war. Sadly enough, Winter did not get around to a closer analysis of the archival material that Arnold deposited in the State Archives in Koblenz (sign. ZSG 142, especially the second '*gesperrte*' section). The brevity of my visit to Koblenz obliged me to restrict my work to acquainting myself with a portion of the material on hand (after gaining Arnold's written consent to see what was there).

273 According to Winter (1991, pp. 59–60) prior to 1945 Uschold had been employed at the *Reichszentrale zur Bekämpfung des Zigeunerunwesens* and he and Eva Justin knew each other from that period. In that event it would not have been illogical to appeal for help from Ritter's registration system during the building up of a new 'Gypsy Bureau' in Munich because of the material destroyed in 1945. Since at that moment, however, he himself was disabled by illness, Justin would have stood in for him.

274 On 22 December 1953 a Bavarian ordinance was also again enacted for *Landfahrer* (travellers); in 1954 its validity was extended throughout West Germany. The wording used in large part duplicated the 1926 law. Only on 30 July 1970 was this law rescinded under acute pressure from Gypsy Interest-Promoting Groups, for it turned out to conflict with the Constitution. What's more, the European Council recommended its repeal. See Winter (1991, pp. 61–2) and Cottaar et al. (1992, pp. 51–5, 59–61) for a succinct sketch of the post-war situation in Germany and references to relevant literature.

275 Uschold (1951, pp. 60–2, here p. 62). We also encounter Ritter's ideas about scarcely criminal racially pure Gypsies and arch criminal and asocial Gypsies with mixed blood in an article by Uschold from 1957, pp. 38–40.

276 See Geyer (1957, no. I, pp. 6–8) and (1957, no. II, pp. 22–3), where reference is made to Article 1 of the Bavarian *Landfahrerordnung* of 1953.

277 Zimmermann (1992, p. 369) points out that the police criminal statistics in the 1990s, after various attacks on separate ethnic registration, switched over to using the designation HWAO-er, standing for persons with a *'häufig wechselnder Aufenthaltsort* (frequently changing domicile)'.

278 In a letter dated 29 June 1978 to Prof. Gunzert, when Arnold requested permission to see the contents of the personal file of Dr Robert Ritter, he wrote that he had executive authority over Ritter's scientific legacy and wished to protect him from accusations of implication in the mass murder of Gypsies. He added a statement by Ritter's widow in support of his request. See the State Archives in Koblenz, ZSG 142/000022 (part 2).

279 Letter dated 11 January 1965 in the State Archives in Koblenz, Arnold-collection, sign. ZSG 142/000032, fol. 1–3.535. In the years 1965 to 1968 he also corresponded with Antje Gerlach from Berlin who was hard at work studying Gypsies' family trees. This enables us to conclude that, in certain circles, it was known that he had control over Ritter's genealogical materials (sign. ZSG 142/000026, fol. 1–3.12).

280 See Winter (1991, pp. 102–24, 152–64).

281 Arnold's preference for eugenic measures is apparent in a letter he sent, dated 28 March 1964, to a professor in Heidelberg whose name is not given. In the State Archives in Koblenz, sign. ZSG 142/000039, fol. 1–4.42. The letters from Döring date from 17 October 1959 and 4 February 1961 (ZSG 142/000021, fol. 1–1.921).

282 See Winter (1991, pp. 102–24, 152–64).

283 According to Winter (1991, pp. 65–6), who relies here upon a press statement of the *Zentralrat* on 6 April 1984, there was said to be a note dated 23 July 1964 in a dossier of the *Landfahrerzentrale* which explicitly mentioned racial diagnoses among the second shipment of materials to Arnold. In the legal inquiry initiated by the *Zentralrat* against Arnold, the prosecutor concluded that it was impossible to conclude from the notation whether the racial diagnoses had indeed been handed over and, if so, how many there were. Searches of Arnold's house by Hamburg detectives in 1961 and 1963 only turned up a few such diagnoses. File 414 AR – Z 42/83, StA Landau Js 7091/83 (*Zentralstelle Ludwigsburg*).

284 Winter (1991, pp. 89–90).

285 Letter dated 17 November 1959 from Hans W. Jürgens, affiliated with the anthropological institute of Kiel University, to Arnold. This letter can be found in the back of the dossier Franz (genealogical table 'Lalleri'), State Archives in Koblenz, R 165/44.

286 Winter (1991, pp. 73–7) refers in this context to the following studies: Hanneliese Duvernoy *Fingerleistenmuster bei Zigeunern Mitteldeutschlands* (1946) and Annelore Oertle *Über die Hautleisten bei Zigeunern* (1947). Reading taught me that they attempted to confirm anthropometrically–dactyloscopically the extent to which Gypsies had mixed blood as determined through genealogical research by Ritter's institutes.

287 Thus Winter (1991, pp. 78–9). On 6 May 1942 Sophie Ehrhardt joined Ritter's institute and worked for it in Munich under the notorious Nazi anthropologist Hans Günther. See the personal file about her employment there between 1935 and 1942 in the State Archives in Potsdam, sign. 49.01 REM, nrs. 1403 and 1483.

288 Sophie Ehrhardt, born on 31 October 1902 in Kazan (Russia) died in Tübingen on 22 October 1990. See the City Archives in Tübingen, *Einwohnermeldeamt*.

289 Winter (1991, pp. 82–3). See, too, the report dated 21 September 1981 prompted by this affair, prepared by the archivist Dr Schäfer of the Eberhard-Karl-University in Tübingen, and also Ehrhardt's provisional overview of the uninventoried Gypsy material, consisting of a card system, morphological data, plaster casts of Gypsy heads, photographs and slides and genealogical material. In the University Archives in Tübingen, sign. Rep. 283.

290 Winter (1991, p. 83); from the *Tageszeitung* of 21 September 1990.

6

Conclusions

THE GYPSY IDENTITY:
DISCOVERY OR CONSTRUCTION?

In his general overview, *The Gypsies* (1992), Angus Fraser concludes that Grellmann at the end of the eighteenth century restored the ethnic identity of Gypsies by revealing their origins by examining their language.[1] With this study I have tried to convince the reader that it was more a matter of him constructing a Gypsy identity which previously had not existed as such. What took place was not the historical retrieval of knowledge that had been lost, but the synthesis of different approaches and the creation of unity in ways of thinking about diverse population groups. Grellmann's conclusions were generalizations based on a collection of sources about dissimilar groups which, to his mind, had a number of traits in common. They were said to have differed from others in their surroundings by virtue of their itinerant way of life, their being foreigners of oriental descent and their being devoid of religion wherever in the world they resided. In short, he created an image of mutually related, alien heathens who lived parasitic, highly mobile lives. They might be called by different names in different places, but Grellmann gathered them all under the label of 'Gypsies'. In so doing he made them into one people, endowed with a general ethnographic profile.

As we have seen, Grellmann derived his most important information from a series of articles about the lives and works of Gypsies in Hungary and Transylvania written by a Hungarian minister, Samuel Augustini Ab Hortis. We don't know whether Ab Hortis had his own observations to thank for his expertise. In any event his pronouncements were extrapolated by Grellmann to apply to all groups that matched his idea of Gypsy characteristics known to him from the literature. Thus there emerged the portrait of an ethnic group which, by comparing lists of words from a parental language, *Romani*, he subsequently provided with a surprising new land of origin, namely India. He had no idea of the extent to which all the people whom he called Gypsies had a command of *Romani*. He was also in the dark about the reasons why they left their original homeland at the start of the fifteenth century, yet he did not hesitate to point out parallels with the way of life of outcasts in Indian society, making use of travellers' accounts. By proceeding in this way he provided all Gypsy groups with a common descent. He also constructed a national history by compiling every scrap of information about them that he could find in chronicles, cosmographies, theological tracts, legal documents and other such sources. So he believed he had penetrated to the essence of the Gypsy people. Until now he has had the support of most gypsiologists – to use a collective term to cover authors who rely on this ethnographic perspective in carrying out their research on Gypsies.

Critical examination of Grellmann's sources and work methods reveals, however, a deficiency of reliable empirical information, an approach which, in the last analysis, shows little originality, and a set of dubious presuppositions. No consensus existed in the periods preceding Grellmann about the way in which Gypsies were defined. On one occasion they comprised one category in the midst of many kinds of vagrants; on another they were the degraded descendants of fifteenth-century pilgrims or the criminal allies of indigenous villains and impostors who, for opportunistic reasons, called themselves Gypsies. Some chronicles report their exceptional wealth, other tracts emphasize only their behaviour as social deviants. Epithets such as 'alien heathens', 'spies for the Ottoman enemy' or even 'pseudo-Jews' continued to be heard. In authoritative texts of the seventeenth century, in keeping with the perspective of the state, they were portrayed as a mixed population of half-criminals, beggars and other 'lawless wastrels'. This came to an end with the appearance of Grellmann's book, which introduced a categorization of Gypsies as a *distinct people*. This approach caught on with Grellmann's contemporaries and with later writers. A number of factors contributed to its success.

First of all there were current, timely motives for taking a scientific look at the origins of Gypsies; the subject hung, as it were, in the air. From private correspondence we know that the visit of an English professor to Göttingen to collect material about Gypsies prompted Grellmann himself – who was still a history student in those days – to write an essay on the subject, possibly inspired in part by a Swedish Academy essay competition during the seventies. The reason that his paper grew and grew was that two of his teachers, August Schlözer and Christian Büttner, put their historical and linguistic sources at his disposal, which made a more extensive analysis possible. While he was busy, news reached him about the notorious Hungarian accusation in 1782 that Gypsies had practised cannibalism. The media covered the drawn-out yet dramatic trial that ensued in all its gory detail. Grellmann's book thus profited from a public appetite for knowing more about these 'heathen and uncivilized foreigners' who were fomenting the wildest fantasies. We should also not forget that most people at this time already had some notion of Gypsies who had for centuries been a favourite literary theme and part of an iconographic tradition. The literate public knew them as beautiful young women and terrifying witches, as magicians and agents from a magic realm, as highwaymen and exotic misfits. As figures in literature they created a sensation and in the plastic arts they tickled the imagination. Grellmann's book made people aware that these mythical representatives from some in-between world also existed in reality. The scientifically presented group portrait evidently dovetailed well into the prevailing picture. Here fascination and dread for Gypsies vied for supremacy and, to my mind, this same ambivalence of feeling has continued down into the present.

Grellmann's success with his book about these exotic groups of outsiders welded together a number of scientific traditions. Academic debate at that time was dominated by an interest in the mysterious anti-world shadowland of vagabonds, beggars, criminals and other non-conformist denizens, and a disposition to concentrate on the historical roots of one's own state. Enlightened historiographers in Germany combed chronicles and other sources that seemed to enable them to reconstruct their own common past. Moreover, ethnographic interest increased in those peoples about whom contemporary travellers to the far corners of the world published reports. Physical anthropology – the study of skulls and physiognomy – contributed its anatomical findings and Johann Gottfried Herder introduced the concept of a people as the expression of a *Nationalgeist*. This gave impetus to a grail-like search for the elemental foundations of the national past, but the methods of arrangement and classification led inevitably to a hierarchy of peoples, values and ways of living within which the Gypsies were allocated a lowly position. Grellmann's assumption that Gypsy groups, wherever in the world they happened to be, all belonged to one people with an immutable national spirit was wholly consistent with the principles formulated by Herder, including his assertion that language reveals the essence of a people. This helps explain why the link Grellmann makes – following others – between the Gypsy language and Hindustani prompts his conclusion that Gypsies come from India.

One people, one language, a homeland that was left behind long ago. The way in which Grellmann supplied a common ethnic base to Gypsy groups living scattered from each other by characterizing them extensively as a group with a static culture and way of life, is familiar to us from popular west European conceptions about Jews in the diaspora.

Indeed various authors before him had actually worked out the hypothesis that Gypsies were a group that had split off from the Jews. In a certain sense Grellmann joined ranks with this tradition by modelling his ideas about Gypsies on the accepted image of Jews. In the case of both Gypsies and Jews, the idea existed that a separate people was involved, living as a state within the state, with its own morals and customs, a language of its own, an endogamous marriage pattern, and an oriental appearance. Both were said not to be assimilable, for in essence they always remained themselves and only appeared to adapt to their surroundings. A primordial standpoint through and through. This analogy underpinned Grellmann's notions about Gypsies as a distinct people. Only their language pointed the way to a different ethnic origin. None the less the parallels continued to surface in various publications during the two centuries after him and in the Nazi era they were emphasized even more than ever: 'Der Jude und der Zigeuner sind heute weit von uns entfernt, weil ihre Asiatische Vorfahren völlig andersartig als unsere nordische Ahnen waren.' ('The Jew and the Gypsy are very far away from us nowadays, since their Asian forefathers were altogether different (*andersartig*) from our Nordic ancestors.')[2]

One last aspect which deserves mention in connection with the success of the first major work about Gypsies is that it matched the political climate of the time. On a number of occasions Grellmann reported that he had been inspired by the guidelines for civilizing the Gypsies (and other 'deviant groups') that the Habsburg monarchs Maria Theresa and Joseph II had promulgated; accordingly he emerged as a policy researcher *avant la lettre*. He made no evaluation of the directives but acted like a loyal follower intent on providing scientific justification for what he praised as an enlightened government approach. Critics and other contemporaries praised him for his efforts and the university rewarded him with a professor's chair.

In this context there is an ambivalence in Grellmann's thinking, the traces of which remain detectable into the twentieth century. At the core of the Enlightenment is the thought that people can be improved and which condones government policy directed towards this end. In such a perspective, culture is presumed to be more potent than nature. The Herderian idea of a people was incompatible with this; it was a notion founded on the essence of a *Nationalgeist*, thus on a principle of exclusivity. What is essentially innate is by its very nature unchangeable. According to Grellmann, Gypsies, as Orientals, clung very tightly to their own norms and values, which explained why they had been able to preserve their essence as a people for so many centuries. Yet he still thought it necessary that they be ruled with an iron hand so that they would obey the orders of Joseph II. This ideologically tinted belief in change contends for primacy in his book with his rational scepticism concerning the success of the undertaking. This ambiguity is characteristic of general European thinking about Gypsies.

THE EVOLUTION OF THE GYPSY IDENTITY

By consulting written sources exclusively, Grellmann had constructed an ethnic homogeneity and a coherent picture of the history of the Gypsies. Various later writers moved among the Gypsies themselves and reported at length about their personal encounters and experiences. The question is whether George Borrow, and in his wake the English and Austro-Hungarian gypsiologists increased the subtlety of the image of Gypsies through their observations. Did they leave the 'paper Gypsies' behind them and come forward with trustworthy ethnographic articles?

First of all they were responsible for a major shift in the categorizing of Gypsies. The fact is that it was difficult for them to fit the reality that they discovered with the image handed down through the literature. Nevertheless, they did not challenge earlier authoritative texts. They did, however, begin to differentiate among Gypsies. The nineteenth-century Gypsy specialists were soon convinced that the true Gypsies, as they knew them from the ethnographic sketches that had been published since their appearance in Europe, hardly existed any longer. Only occasionally did one meet a solitary example of the ancient race, as Borrow called them, and such individuals were therefore a valuable source of information. These were the informants on whom Gypsy researchers depended, for a price, to initiate them into the secrets of their vanishing people. This method, however, did not altogether correspond with the prevailing image of Gypsies as people who were not willing to reveal anything about their language or customs to non-Gypsies. The complaint about an inclination to secrecy is one that had already been voiced by Grellmann and his predecessors. What was new about Borrow and those who came after him was that they prided themselves on having demolished the wall of suspicion. Thus on paper they created the romantic image of the 'Romany Rye' who was a regular visitor to the tents and was accepted as an intimate: the Gypsies' friend, who, obviously, was privy to the rituals of their lives. The way in which they accounted for this triumph became a (tautological) pat line of reasoning in Gypsy study circles.

The reasoning goes as follows. Someone wins a Gypsy's trust by virtue of his duly valued interest, upon which the Gypsy declares that he is ready to reveal to him the basic principles of his language. Actually money or gifts were usually necessary to induce such willingness, but this for the most part was passed over in silence. Subsequently the person in question, either by chance or in the course of an active search, meets another Gypsy or a whole group, and after speaking a few words the 'Romany Rye' is immediately recognized as one of them. In this way, as time passes, the person's command of the Gypsy language steadily improves. It could also transpire that someone who had picked up a handful of Gypsy words from one of the many vocabulary lists published in the nineteenth century let a few of them drop at an opportune moment. Whoever looks back at the history of these accounts notices that most 'Romany Ryes' managed to locate an out-of-the-ordinary Gypsy to teach them his language. Gypsies were thus indeed prepared to lift the corner of the veil if someone showed curiosity or took the trouble to get to know them, only for this favour something was expected in return. In that connection I have also pointed out a number of other arguments that, since Borrow, belong to the standard reper- toire of writers who feel called upon to justify their interest in Gypsies – as personifications of social outsiders. Popular reasons given for acceptance by the Gypsies are a (partial) Gypsy descent, a love relation with a Gypsy, a meeting of like spirits, and a shared preference for an itinerant way of life. In folklorist circles, in particular, we regularly run into these self-justifications.[3]

The obdurate reality that Gypsy researchers confront in the field brings them time and again to the conclusion that authentic Gypsy culture is on the brink of disappearing. This notion has held them captive for a good century-and-a-half and constitutes an important argument for their own existence, for they feel called upon, rather like archaeologists, to collect the surviving relics of a centuries-old culture, to analyse but, above all, to preserve them. In the course of this they demonstrate a special interest in folklore: Gypsy motifs in art and literature, their songs and verses, magic rituals and religion, kinds of healing, apparel, music and dance. The study of language variants has also enjoyed continuing interest (with a burst of popularity during the 1980s) and articles regularly appear in which the author makes known a previously lost text from the early Middle Ages in which reference is said to be made to the presence of Gypsies in, for example, Persia, Greece or central Europe. By now a small reference library full of books has been written about the origin of Gypsies and their first appearance in Europe. Whether all these inventories of words, musical forms and customs rightly belong in one collection is a question that only a few ask themselves. As a rule Gypsy specialists concentrate on striking likenesses and have far less keen an eye for differences. Stronger yet is their belief that the way of life of those who, to their way of thinking, do not belong to the true 'Gypsy race' sullied the reputation of the whole category of itinerants in the distant past. This development in thinking about Gypsies was initiated by George Borrow.

This fixation on the supposed uniqueness of Gypsies has meant that no comparative studies of people in roughly the same circumstances were forthcoming. When, several years ago, a colleague of mine in the company of a number of British anthropologists, including Judith Okely, visited a caravan camp in Leiden, they saw parallels with British and Irish Gypsy-Travellers.[4] They knew for certain that these were Gypsies. The Dutch women living in the caravans, however, were having none of it and stressed that they were native Dutch. That social surroundings can, as it were, compel people to behave in a certain way is something that Gypsy specialists do not acknowledge sufficiently. The writers of an analysis of the begging of Gypsies in seventeenth-century western Europe omit to mention that at the time the number of beggars was, in any event, large. Elaborate discussions of the deceptions perpetrated by Gypsies throughout the German countryside in the eighteenth century lose much of their ethnic charge if we realize that a legion of drifters struggled to extract themselves from the swamp of poverty through ruses and tricks. That is not to say, however, that all tales about begging and thieving Gypsies were based on false reports. It does go to show, however, what little historical sense it makes to present such conduct as a group-specific characteristic.

In the 1930s German eugenists added a biological component. In my analysis of the work of Robert Ritter I pointed out that he, too, albeit in a much more indirect fashion, maintained the idea of the 'true Gypsy' as the prototypical nomad. In his portrait of this practically mythological figure we recognize the traits that Grellmann had collected, but we can also observe an element stemming from the tradition in which natural peoples are contrasted to cultured ones. He compared them specifically with hunters and gatherers from prehistoric times, who were said to be incapable of keeping pace with the forward march of civilization. The stagnation in their mental growth, as he saw it, explained their restive and parasitical behaviour; he even attributes their itineracy to this prehistoric core. The socially unacceptable conduct of those with 'mixed blood' who came later was alleged to derive from their biological inheritance. Through relations across group lines, a gene for rootlessness made its way into the blood of previously sedentary Germans. The biological legacy of the latter had, in its turn, seen to it that 'halfbloods' were more asocial and criminal than 'true Gypsies' because their potential for deviance was strengthened by their German cleverness and enterprising boldness. Relations between sedentary and non-sedentary peoples were, according to Ritter, invariably disadvantageous for both. His anxiety about contamination with inherited Gypsy characteristics was so strong that he wrote that a single mixed match could stain the blood for many generations. Such notions of purity, and a belief in the determinant force of the genetic, underpinned all his research. From that point of view 'Gypsy halfbreeds' were the root of social and biological evil.

The irony of this is that Ritter, with his genealogical research on people labelled 'Gypsies' by the government, demonstrated that their ethnic identity was non-existent, at least not in the primordial form that Grellmann had constructed. Consequently he felt obliged to break the all-embracing category down into a number of vaguely defined subcategories, dominated in the first instance by that of the mixed population. They constituted, both for Ritter and for the Nazis whose policy he prepared, a threat to the racial purity of the German people – a view that engendered proposals for sterilization and, in a later phase, all but inevitably, deportation to Auschwitz.

THE DICTATES OF AUTHORITATIVE TEXTS

The manner in which Gypsies have been defined at the governmental level down through the centuries – and still are defined – demonstrates, as I have wished to portray in this study, a clear connection with changing notions of the process of categorization in science. The labelling of Gypsies as deviants appears to have been subject to revision, and this also holds true for the accompanying argumentation. The extent to which the scientific construction of the Gypsy identity mirrored the (historical) existence of the different groups discernible behind the name is far from clear. Although, until the middle of the eighteenth century, authoritative texts promulgated the definition used by governments in the implementation of their policies, after Grellmann a shift came about in that process with the publication of his historical survey, the ethnic element of the Gypsy people moved squarely into the foreground. Subsequent portraits of Gypsies have largely been inventories of their ethnic characteristics. Judicial authorities, in particular, subsequently adopted Grellmann's view of things and used it to legitimize their stigmatizing policy. There can be no mistaking this development when one traces the criminological tradition within Gypsy studies, culminating in its criminological biological variant during the Nazi era. In the practice of law enforcement, however, it did often prove difficult to base the combating of vagrancy, or the limitation of possibilities for earning a living by means of an itinerant vocation, on an ethnic categorization. The complicated relationship between labelling and policy in Germany is something, however, that I have not worked out in any detail.[5]

Thus, since Grellmann, academics and amateur scientists have been at the vanguard of the process of defining Gypsies. He has seen to it that the notion of a Gypsy people has become dominant and other group categories such as pilgrims, spies, criminal vagabonds, heathens and the mixed category of social outsiders have faded into the background. The concept of the Gypsies as a people appears to have meshed together so well with the founding myths of nineteenth-century nationalism that it remained in use even after evidence of integration (sedentarism, intermarriage, social mobility) kept gradually accumulating. This was true both for governments and for the experts on Gypsies whose work has been central to this study, and this leads us to the question of why scholarship has changed so little in its vision of Gypsies' history and way of life with the passage of time.

The most important explanation for such steadfastness is the tradition of imagery, the dictates of authoritative texts or the family tree of ideas, as Edward Said illustrates in his inspiring study *Orientalism* from 1978. Said shows how, in the European process of exercising hegemony and domination, one's own culture is constantly defined in terms of its opposite. Thus the identity of Europe is, for example, presented as the mirror image of the Orient, a designation for the other half of the world. Similar analyses are perpetrated in Western literature concerning America, Indians and black populations in Africa.[6] Each image of another, so it appears, is always a reflection of a facet of the image of self. Said, to be sure, is not so much interested in imagery for its own sake as in the power relations of which imagery is an expression. He points out that writers on the Middle East, whom he groups together under the institutionalized collective term of orientalists, have, through their texts, wielded definitional power over the people whom they describe. As a consequence a static cultural picture has come into existence of the Orient which, to a large extent, obfuscates the historical identities of the inhabitants of Eastern countries. Ideas that have been formulated about Orientals, Said contends, correspond with reality only in a small way, for many administrative civil servants, adventurers, philologists and writers who spent some time in an Eastern country and then took up a pen closed ranks, as a rule, behind a tradition of authoritative texts within which a Western image of the Orient held sway. We encounter a similar chain of events, I feel, where Gypsy studies are concerned.

An historical canon of publications on Gypsies already existed prior to Grellmann. Authors had primarily followed in each other's footsteps. This tradition of the ongoing reproduction of the same sources and sentences did not undergo demonstrable disruption with the appearance of Grellmann's study. In the final analysis his book is first and foremost a compilation of existing texts, a summary of the current state of knowledge on the subject. By combining a number of scientific traditions he introduced a fundamental change in how Gypsies were defined but without disclosing any new sources about them. He derived his interpretation of their history from authoritative writers who, in their brief passages on the subject, had often based their ideas on the chronicles of a century or longer before. His ethnographic portrait of the essence or the character of Gypsies was likewise culled from the text of others and not from his own observations. He continued the pattern of his predecessors and little changed after him, for Borrow and countless other authors also depended upon earlier texts on the subject and weighed their own experiences against what had been written. In this way it was practically inevitable for them to reach the conclusion that 'true Gypsies' hardly survived any longer, except for – and in this sense they constrained reality to suit their purposes – those whom they knew best, because of all Gypsies these in their eyes were (morally) the most pure. The process of identifying exceptions was adopted by Pushkin, Borrow, Leland and Von Wlislocki, but also by Himmler and Ritter with their 'racially pure' Gypsy families. The idea of 'the Gypsy' was thus preserved, while the actual Gypsies whom they came across continued to constitute a problem.

Through comparison with Said's analysis of Orientalism it also becomes possible to understand why writings about Gypsies were so readily accepted as the truth in educated circles. The extant, negative imagery led a life of its own since the social distance separating these authors from the people whom they wrote about was so considerable that correction of the picture through first-hand contact seldom occurred. Another important reason for the continuity of thinking about Gypsies is the particularizing of this group (or these groups). As a result of their fixation with the 'different' nature of Gypsies, experts in Gypsy studies appear unable to perceive that they are dealing with people who are attempting to survive economically and therefore in many respects are comparable to other groups in the same jeopardy. For these reasons countless obvious questions are seldom asked, such as: how did other economically weaker categories of people manage to live? What economic functions did groups of Gypsies fulfil with their specific occupations? Were these occupations indeed so specific? And how general were the phenomena of begging and itinerancy in the periods studied in diverse countries? Practically no one makes an effort to discuss the existing image of Gypsies or to test the tenability of generalizations about their history and expressions of their culture. Even when authors discover positive or functional aspects of the Gypsy way of life, this seldom leads to a more subtle appraisal of their social existence. What we observe happening is that an exceptional category of 'true Gypsies' is created by means of which the image of the entire group as parasites, primitives, criminals, thieves or persecuted victims can be maintained. The overarching denominator – already a stigma *par excellence* early in history – affects every observation. People's (comparative) ignorance of Gypsies encourages reduction and generalizations. There is stagnation of the kind of individual interpretation necessary to break away from the prevalent stigmatizing perspective.

In addition there appears to be a dichotomy in thinking about Gypsies. At least it is certainly not true that there was a total lack of nuance or refreshing opinions about Gypsies in all the studies which I consulted. Some of Grellmann's critics, but Borrow, too, and the evangelically inspired authors on whom he relied, proved now and then to be accurate portraitists of the daily lives of Gypsies. With feeling for detail, they knew how to bring individuals alive on paper or they offered a glimpse of their economic circumstances from which it is possible to conclude that they actually did look around them and did not always let themselves be blinded by their prejudices. Yet for most authors any such subtle touches ultimately turn out to be trivial compared to their exceptionally negative sweeping statements about 'the Gypsy people' in which, above all, we can recognize inherited thinking. Stigma apparently offers but scant room for alternative opinions, for even when a writer's empirical findings contradicted traditional representations it was not permitted to alter the general picture. Because of the limited perspective of most scholarly historical studies hardly any accumulation of historical information occurred, and the absence of sound social-scientific research caused the one-sided image of the Gypsy to persist. As a result we still know little about the socio-economic and cultural history of diverse Gypsy groups in Europe during the timespan stretching from the beginning of the fifteenth century to the end of the Second World War.

THE FAMILY TREE OF EUROPEAN THINKING ABOUT GYPSIES

In the diagram that follows the authoritative texts that I have dealt with in this study have been arranged into a kind of family tree in order to portray 'family relations'. It enables us to trace the influence that authors have exercised through time on diverse social responses towards

FIGURE I
FAMILY TREE OF EUROPEAN THINKING ABOUT GYPSIES

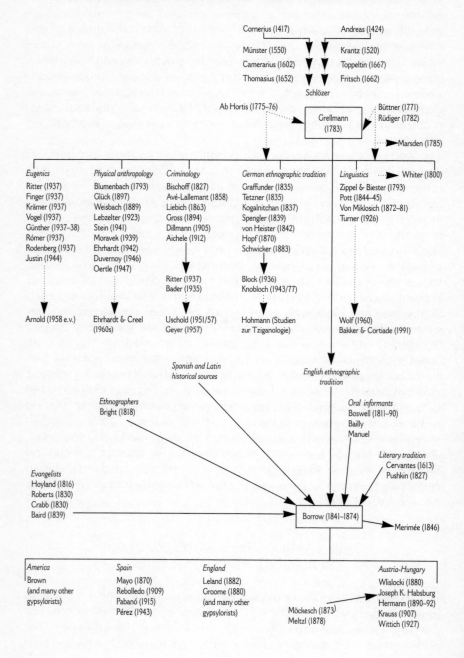

Gypsies and on various lines of research. It also illustrates which writers generated which branches. The diagram does not in the least pretend to be exhaustive but the reader will recognize a great number of names of well-known Gypsy experts.

A selection of ur-texts from the early history of Gypsies has been made; after Grellmann, however, all authors who put in an appearance in the preceding chapters have been included, so we see not only which traditions Grellmann bundled but above all which branches sprouted after him. The criminology offshoot can be followed as far as Ritter and his post-war heirs. Linguistics is probably the most consistent line. By way of Borrow it reached even the folklorists in England and by way of continental texts the folklorists in central Europe. Most traditions have had adherents down to the post-Second World War period.

THE SPLENDID ISOLATION OF GYPSY STUDIES

For anyone surveying the history of Gypsy studies, it is striking that practically all perspectives that have been developed still persist. Every way of thinking has its own history and a strong claim to a right to exist. In the tradition of the Romantics, who have always emphasized that Gypsies are the most free of primitive peoples, the accepted line at present is that they live in resistance to the conformist world. Evangelically inspired or other civilizing movements stress, even today, that Gypsies, as deprived outsiders living in pathetic conditions, require special attention. Folklorists carry on with their search for authentic traces of Gypsy culture with undiminished zeal, including linguists who have elevated Romani-philology to a special status. In judicial circles, in the course of the twentieth century, the criminological tradition in Gypsy studies has even expanded and become more intricately entwined than ever with government policy in a general sense, policy which even after the Second World War has remained strongly oriented to the promotion of assimilation within existing social structures. If in the past it was felt that Gypsies needed to be tamed, nowadays governments are intent on integrating them while assuring the preservation of their own (ethnic) identity as – at any rate in the West – policy jargon would put it. Although all these approaches may have their own motives for engagement with Gypsies, the image of the Gypsy has not lost any of its uniformity. Fascination with the Gypsies' life has endured, together with disapproval. In a certain sense they are romantic outcasts without equal.

The social isolation of Gypsies, together with the failure, until the 1970s, of special interest groups to tackle existing prejudices against

Gypsies in an organized way or to occupy themselves with helping Gypsies to catch up, probably explain why historians never demon- strated much interest in their past. To the extent that there was interest it usually was complementary to the perspective of the governments then in power.[7] Yet even historians who regarded their invariably biased sources critically do not, for the most part, appear to have been capable of adding subtler shades of meaning to the one-sided picture presented there,[8] with the exception of a number of recent studies.[9] Scrutiny of Gypsy persecution under the Nazi regime has, to be sure, increased sharply, especially in Germany since the beginning of the 1980s. Virtually all the writers involved, however (a not inconsiderable proportion of whom had been commissioned by organizations which promote Gypsies' interests), similarly accept as their point of departure the notion that Gypsies comprise one people, a folk which since its assumed departure from its homeland in India in the early Middle Ages has barely mingled with others and therefore has been able to maintain a character of its own. This is despite the fact that there are countless indications and pieces of evidence establishing that the term 'Gypsy' was applied in a number of instances rather generally by sitting governments, and certainly not simply to denote the ancestors of today's *Sinti* and *Roma*. The entanglement of science and politics on this (post-war) terrain has thus generated a number of analyses that are critical of government policy but at the same time it has confirmed some stereotypical ideas about the folk character of *the* Gypsies.

Another academic discipline whose absence from Gypsy studies has sorely been missed is anthropology, a field that has become insti- tutionalized within universities since the final quarter of the nineteenth century. Until long after the Second World War, no original anthro- pological fieldwork was undertaken among Gypsies. Only guesswork is possible about the reasons for this omission. Was it that, at the uni- versity level, people simply didn't consider the morals and customs, cultural manifestations and way of life of Gypsy groups, recognized as marginal, worth serious study? Or is access to Gypsy groups for scientific research more difficult than access to other ethnic (minority) groups? Only folklorists have seemed to attach any value to what the members of a – for them – disappearing primitive people have left behind. The conclusion is even justified that Gypsy studies is actually only intensively pursued in these circles. That is likely to be one of the reasons why the field idles in such splendid isolation. Gypsy folklore, with its upgraded amateurism and, since 1888, its own journal, has always dominated the field. As we saw, it was an enclave of enthusiastic 'Romany Ryes' and 'Romany Rawnies' who, in their longing for specialization, stuck to their own, delimited work terrain. They moved among like-minded spirits who shared practically identical ideas about how to approach their subject. As a result, connections with historical and social sciences were only established after the Second World War and, even then, only on a modest scale. What hindered progress was a lack of reflection concerning historical sources. From whom, for example, must anthropology derive material for comparisons? There are hardly any reliable empirical studies available from either the eighteenth or nineteenth century and, moreover, most studies confined themselves to narrowly delineated groups in diverse countries, the extent of whose mutual ethno-historical ties is unknown. The danger of unjustified generalizations still looms large as life.

According to Edward Said, Orientalism was only attacked and (in part) exposed for what it is once the decolonization of formerly oppressed peoples or nations had been achieved. Since, for some Gypsy groups in Western European countries, the process of emancipation has only commenced recently, hardly any revaluation of extant historical knowledge has yet taken place. It remains questionable, moreover, whether corrections are to be anticipated from this corner since the intelligentsia in Gypsy circles are not likely to profit very much by challenging the core concepts of Gypsy studies. For political and pragmatic reasons they will sooner close ranks in support of the idea of a *collective* Gypsy identity, including a language that belongs to them, as we observed when discussing the so-called Yugo-Egyptians. Recognition as an ethnic minority certainly culminates in more agreements pertaining to specific rights. It will, in part, depend upon the choices made by Gypsy leaders and representatives to what extent and in what way the definition of Gypsies from above and the stigma it entails will be set right with all the social and political ramifications of such correction. However this tentatively launched process may develop further; until now practitioners of Gypsy studies have appeared to be preaching simply to their own parishioners. The study of the history of workers' groups and of women may, by now, constitute recognized academic specialities and social scientific studies of (ethnic) minorities may already have been burgeoning for years, but the number of Gypsy studies incorporated within standard curricula has so far remained small. In that connection those engaged in Gypsy studies face the threat of being marginalized themselves, as academic outsiders. Only if that isolation is shattered and a fundamental debate about the premises of Gypsy studies takes place in prestigious periodicals and addressed to a broad academic public can we expect, perhaps, to arrive at a deeper understanding of the history of Gypsies in the future.

PLEA FOR A DIFFERENT APPROACH

The process of the social construction of Gypsies as a *people apart*, to my mind, has been similar to that which accompanies the emergence of many nation states, as analysed with such brilliance by Benedict Anderson in *Imagined Communities*.[10] There is a difference, however: as a rule those designing the nation states of the nineteenth and twentieth centuries were members of the communities concerned whereas, for centuries, Gypsies themselves have scarcely been able to exercise any influence on the way in which their identities have been constructed. The study of language as an indicator of the origins of a people has led to many speculations, not at least in the field of Gypsy studies. Because of their strong determination to designate a country of origin, scholars have not paused to reflect sufficiently on a number of questions that, from a historical point of view, are at least equally interesting such as the reasons for the departure of Gypsy groups from central and north-west India, or their social-economic position and cultural background in that putative homeland. We do not even know what kinds of relations these Gypsy groups, who lived everywhere in disparate circumstances, maintained with each other over time. Linguistics will never be able to give conclusive answers to all such questions concerning the reconstruction of the Gypsies' history. Moreover, the criterion of language is utterly inadequate for explaining why people were (or still are) defined as Gypsies. Where governments were busy stigmatizing Gypsies, language appears never to have been ultimately of decisive importance.

If we wish to be in a position to shed new light on the history of Gypsy groups in Europe since the Middle Ages then, to my mind, we should consider them in the first place as migrants, like other groups of newcomers: migrants with widely different backgrounds who have settled at different times in diverse European countries where they either managed to integrate successfully or did not. In those instances where they turned into a minority, the negative image of them that took shape will have possibly corresponded in part with the social reality of the situation in which the groups concerned found themselves. The settlement process will not have been identical everywhere and the factors that influenced it surely deserve closer investigation. Experts in Gypsy studies – and in this respect they resemble generations of historians – have never postulated that migration constitutes a structural element of human societies. They have primarily had eyes for the spectacular, abrupt and unique exodus of certain Gypsy castes from India, presumably propelled by the threat of war. That picture of people who, in a state of panic, resolve to try their luck elsewhere, burning their ships behind them so that, rootless and disoriented, they arrive on foreign soil has, as a general profile of migrants, also had its day.[11] If we consider Gypsies as clans of artisans who, through the centuries, have acquired a certain identity under the influence of circumstances that remain to be studied more closely, it becomes possible to analyse their socio-economic mobility and their emergence as minorities in various countries with a much greater degree of differentiation. The identity that these groups of migrants developed must in any event have been comparatively open, for there are many indications that they soon began to mix with indigenous peoples. We know, moreover, that certain indigenous groups became Gypsies, some voluntarily, some not, so that a guildlike segmentation of vocations could have existed that offered outsiders the possibility of entry.

Such an approach, to my mind, provides more points of contact than the ethnographic perspective for making sense of the historical differences that have been established among groups of Gypsies. By making creative use of historical sources that have remained unexplored until now,[12] and by choosing a socio-economic perspective to analyse the history of these groups, perhaps we will succeed in discovering creatures of flesh and blood behind the social construction of a separate Gypsy people. For we should not content ourselves simply with an attempt to tear off the mask of identity that has been imposed on Gypsies. We should also set ourselves the task of according the Gypsy, idealized by some but despised by most, his proper place on the stage of European history. To put it in the words of Robert Hughes:

> You cannot remake the past in the name of affirmative action. But you can find narratives that haven't been written, histories of people and groups that have been distorted or ignored, and refresh history by bringing them in.[13]

NOTES

1 Fraser (1992, p. 196): 'However imperfect the details, Grellmann's indubitable achievement was that, by deploying linguistic evidence as it was then understood, he ensured that the general proposition of the Indian origin of the Gypsies' language became widely accepted and that their ethnic identity was restored in the eyes of many. For him, latter-day Gypsies were clearly lineal descendants of the early arrivals.'

2 See R. Körber *Volk und Staat* (1936), cited in Zülch (1982, p. 31).

3 One illustrative example is the American folklorist, deeply influenced by Borrow's work, Irving Brown (1888–1940). For a biographical portrait of his somewhat tragi-comic attempts to become a real 'Romany Rye', see Nemeth (1994, pp. 7–31).

4 This visit was described to me personally by the Leiden University historian

Annemarie Cottaar whose doctoral dissertation on the history of caravan dwellers in the Netherlands (1870–1945) was recently published.

5   For this subject, I refer the reader to historian Leo Lucassen's study *Zigeuner* (1997).

6   See Mason (1990), T. Lemaire *De Indiaan in ons bewustzijn. De ontmoeting van de Oude met de Nieuwe wereld* (1986), and Corbey (1989). Their approach which is strongly cultural philosophic has little affinity, however, with mine.

7   What the English historian Tawney once remarked about the vagabond applies just as aptly to the Gypsy: 'His history is inevitably written by his enemies.' Cited by Lucassen and Willems (1993, pp. 295–9).

8   See Lucassen (1993, pp. 209–35) for a critical review of these studies.

9   See, among others, Mayall (1988), Lucassen (1990), Fricke (1991) and Cottaar (1996).

10 Anderson (1991). See especially the chapters, 'The Origins of National Consciousness' and 'Old Languages, New Models'.

11 See, for example, the introduction by Jan and Leo Lucassen to the volume *Migration, Migration-History, History: old Paradigms and New Perspectives* (1997), which they also edited.

12 See Lucassen (1993, pp. 209–35) for a plea in this direction.

13 From Hughes (1993, p. 104).

Annex 1: the publications of H.M.G. Grellmann[1]

De prudentia, qua negotium Augustanae confessionis peregerunt confessores. Oratio solemnis in aede acad. habita (Jena, 1780).

'Ursprung der Zigeuner', *Staatsanzeigen* (Göttingen, 1783) pp. 444–50.

Die Zigeuner. Ein historischer Versuch über die Lebensart und Verfassung, Sitten und Schicksale dieses Volks in Europa, nebst ihrem Ursprunge (Dessau/Leipzig, 1783). Second, expanded edition (Göttingen: Johann Christian Dieterich, 1787).

'Ilmenauer Bergbau; ein Auszug aus den Nachrichten von dem ehemaligen Bergbau der Ilmenau', *Schlözers Staatsanzeigen*, 16 (Göttingen, 1784) pp. 425–34.

Kurze Geschichte der Stohlgebühren oder geistlichen Accidenzien, nebst andern Hebungen, nach ihrer ersten Entstehung und allmähligen Entwicklung abgehandelt (Göttingen: Dieterich, 1785).

Italiänische Staatsanzeigen Part I. St. 1 und 2 (Göttingen, 1785. St. 3, Göttingen, 1786).

'Geschichte der Pfarrgebühren', *Staatsanzeigen* (Göttingen, 1785) pp. 227–59.

De pontificibus Romanis Christianae religionis in Germania auctoribus. Prolusio (Göttingen, 1787).

'Geschichte der Hochzeitkränze und Brautringe', *Göttingischen Taschencalender* (Göttingen, 1787) pp. 153–63.

'Vom Recht der Hagestolze bey Deutschen, Römern und Griechen', *Göttingischen Taschencalender* (Göttingen, 1787) pp. 178–92.

Dissertation on the Gipsies, being an historical enquiry, concerning the manner of life, economy, customs, and conditions of these people in Europe, and their origin. Translated into English, by Matthew Raper (Londen: Elmsley, 1787).

'Geschichte der Handwerker und Zünfte in Teutschland, und ihres blauen Montags', *Göttingischen Taschencalender* (Göttingen, 1788) pp. 81–104.

Mémoire historique sur le peuple nomade, appelé en France Bohémien, et en Allemagne Zigeuner; avec un vocabulaire comparatif des langues indienne et bohémienne. Translated from German by M. de B. de Bock (Metz: Lamort, 1788).

'Pluderhosen und Teufeleyen, ein Paar Modesachen des sechszehnten Jahrhunderts', *Göttingischen Taschencalender* (Göttingen, 1789) pp. 148–58.

'Wie Gottesäcker auf Kirchhöfen und Begräbnisse in den Kirchen entstanden sind', *Göttingischen Taschencalender* (Göttingen, 1790), pp. 81–91.

'Was es eigentlich mit dem Geschenke der Bräutigamshemden und des Schlafrocks bey Hochzeiten für eine Bewandniss habe', *Göttingischen Taschencalender* (Göttingen, 1790) pp. 92–100.

Staatskunde der vornehmsten welt- und geistlichen Staten von Deutschland. Ein Grundriss zum Gebrauch seiner Vorlesungen, 1: A general description of the German state (Göttingen, 1790).

Geschiedkundige verhandeling over de Heidens, betreffende hunne herkomst, leevenswijze gesteldheid, zeden en lotgevallen, sedert hunne verschijning in Europa. Dutch translation based on the expanded second edition (Dordrecht: Blussé & Zn., 1791).

Gegenwärtiger Zustand des päbstlichen Staats vornehmlich in Hinsicht seiner Justizpflege und politischen Oekonomie (Helmstadt, 1792).

Historische Kleinigkeiten, zum Vergnügen und Unterricht aus der Zerstreuung gesammelt (Göttingen, 1794).

Statistische Aufklärungen über wichtige Theile und Gegenstände der österreichischen Monarchie, 1 and 3 (Göttingen, 1795, 1797 and 1802).

Historisch Statistisches Handbuch von Teutschland und den vorzüglichsten seiner besondern Staaten, 1: A general survey of the German state (Göttingen, 1801) and 2: The Austrian monarchy, part 1, History of the State (Göttingen, 1804).

De natura et fructu Statisticae. Oratio aditialis (University of Moscow, 31 August 1804).

Dissertation on the Gipseys: representing their manner of life, family economy, occupations and trades, marriages and education, sickness, death and burial, religion, language, sciences and arts, etc. etc. etc.. With an historical enquiry concerning their origin and first appearance in Europe (London: Effingham Wilson, 1807).

Histoire des Bohémiens, ou Tableau des moeurs, usages et coutumes de ce peuple nomade; suivie de recherches historiques sur leur origine, leur langage et leur première apparition en Europe. Translation from German based on the second edition, by M.J. (Paris: Chaumerot, 1810).

In addition Grellmann wrote some 85 reviews in the *Göttingische Gelehrte Anzeigen*, over a period of 16 years.[2] A summary of these pieces follows below, arranged by year with the numbers of the pages on which the reviews begin. Political science: *1785:* 1884, *1786:* 1211, 1413, 1661,

1710, 1840, 2038, 2108, *1787*: 221, 233, 333, 421, 425, 457, 485, 489, 551, 567, 665, 705, 853, 854, 1023, 1302, 1454, 1629, 1630, 1631, 1701, 1885, 1892, *1788:* 646, 778, 924, 1216, 1239, 1317, 1319, 1751, 1760, 1781, 1801, *1789*: 53, 161, 193, 1669, *1790*: 481, 912, 1081, 1101, 1657, 1666, *1791*: 43, 513, 751, 1497, *1792*: 940, 1359, 1365, 1410, 1420, 1422, 1897, *1793*: 156, 169, 701, 742, *1795*: 1363, *1796*: 2034, 2073, *1797*: 654, 999, 1036, 1152, 1169, 1425, 1428, 1505, 1692, 1703, 1810, *1798*: 127, 1521, *1799*: 628, *1801*: 1297. For the purposes of orientation, I examined the first 17 reviews. Besides statistical works he reviewed a strikingly large number of books about India. These roused considerable enthusiasm in Grellmann.

NOTES

1 Derived from the *Index deutschsprachiger Zeitschriften 1750–1815*, compiled by Klaus Schmidt (Göttingen, 1990), under 'Grellmann'. This is not an exhaustive list, for Grellmann also made various anonymous contributions to the *Teutschen Merkur* and the *Göttingischen Taschencalender*. Schmidt collected the latter but not the former. Reviews of Grellmann's writings and other comments on his work in the *Göttingische Gelehrte Anzeigen* (GGA) were consulted through Hartmann (1829, pp. 239–40).

2 From the survey by Fambach (1976, p. 445), according to the copy with written comments by Jeremias David Reuss in the library of the University of Tübingen.

Annex 2: reviews of H.M.G. Grellmann's book on the Gypsies[1]

Anzeiger des Deutschen Merkur (December 1783) p. 181 (by C.M. Wieland).

Historische Litteratur für das Jahr 1784, 4, 1 (Erlangen, 1784) pp. 123–8 (published by Johann Georg Meusel).

Gothaische gelehrte Zeitungen (Gotha, May 1 1784) pp. 293–4.

Göttingische Anzeigen von gelehrten Sachen, 1 (Göttingen, 1784) pp. 83–7 (by C.G. Heyne; under the auspices of the 'Königl. Gesellschaft der Wissenschaften').

Wöchentliche Nachrichten von neuen Landcharten, geographischen, statistischen und historischen Büchern und Schriften, 12, 1784 (Berlin, 1785) pp. 298–9 (by D. Anton Friderich Büsching).

Allgemeine Literatur-Zeitung vom Jahre 1787, 3 (Jena/Vienna, 1787) pp. 293–5.

Göttingische Anzeigen von gelehrten Sachen (Göttingen, 1787) pp. 1885–6 (under the auspices of the 'Königl. Gesellschaft der Wissenschaften'; on the French version).

Göttingische Anzeigen von gelehrten Sachen, 1 (Göttingen, 1787) pp. 489–90 (by Grellmann himself).

Critical Review (1788 VII) pp. 56–60 (on the English version).

Monthly Review (1788 VI) pp. 464–8 (on the English version).

Journal Encyclopédique ou Universel Dédié, 1 (Bouillon, 1788) pp. 419–33 (on the French version).

Nieuwe Algemeene Vaderlandsche Letter-Oefeningen, 3 (Amsterdam, 1788) pp. 357–63, 406–13, 456–60 (second article, by A. van der Kroe and J. Yntema).

Allgemeine Literatur-Zeitung, vom Jahre 1789, 3 (Jena/Leipzig/Vienna, 1789) pp. 725–6 (on the French version).

Efemeridi Letterarie di Roma (Rome, 1789) p. 16 (on the French version).

Allgemeinen Deutschen Bibliothek, (annex to) 53–86 (Berlin/Stettin, 1791) pp. 2253–6.

NOTES

1 To retrieve these reviews first of all I consulted the microfiches of the *Index deutschsprachiger Zeitschriften 1750–1815*. I located complementary material about

reactions to Grellmann in Lawätz, Vol. 1 (1788, pp. 687–8: no. 4083, 4084, 4085); Lawätz (1791, p. 490: no. 4018); Lawätz (1794, p. 352: no. 2780, 2781, 2782); *Allgemeines Repertorium der Literatur für die Jahre 1785 bis 1790*. Vol. 3 (1794, p. 147); *Allgemeines Repertorium der Literatur für die Jahre 1785 bis 1790*. Vol. 2 (1793, no. 2585c, 2905a, 2905b, 2905c); Ersch (1790–92) Vol. 1, pp. 95–6; Vol. 3, p. 271; Ersch and Gruder, Vol. 90 (1871, p. 136–7). I also looked at the issues that appeared in certain years (1783/84, 87/88) in a whole series of other leading German periodicals, not all of which will be cited here. To the extent that I came across reviews in them, the reader will find them listed.

Annex 3: sources for *The Zincali*

Adelung, Johann Christoph, *Mithridates; oder allgemeine Sprachenkunde*, 1 (Berlin, 1806).

Alcalá Yañez y Rivera, Geronimo (1563–1632), *Alonso, mozo de muchos amos (o eldonado hablador)* (Madrid: Guzman, 1624).

Arabschah, *Life of Timour* (further data missing).

Aventinus, *Annales Boiorum* (Ingolstad, 1554) (chronicle for the year 1439).

Barbosa, Agostinho, *Collectanea doctorum*. 5 Vols (1697).

Biesius, Nicolaus, *De Republica* (Antwerp, 1556).

Boissard, Jean Jacques, *Tractatus postumus. De Divinatione et magius practigiis, cum effigiebusaere incusis per Jo. Theod. Debry* (Hopemheinisi: Gallet, no year).

Bonifacio, Juan, *Christiani Puen Institutir adolescentiae* (Bergis, 1586).

Caballus, Petrus, *Resolutiones Criminales* (Venice, 1672).

Castillo de Bobadilla, Jerónimo (b. 1547), *Politica para corregidores y señores de vassallos en tiempo de paz y guerra* (Madrid, MDXCVII).

Cervantes Saavedra, Miguel de (1547–1616), *Novelas exemplares* (Brussel: Velpio & Antonio, 1614).

Córdoba, Francisco Fernández de, *Didascalía multiplex* (Leiden: Cardon, 1615).

Felisius, Matthias, *Institutionis christianae catholica et erudita elucidatio, secundum methodum, à magistro in secundum sententiarum observatam: autore Reverendu P. Matthia Felisio* (Antwerp: Plantijn, 1575).

Genebrard, Gilbert (Archbishop of Aix), *Chronographia. Libri quator*. 3 Vols (Paris, 1580).

Geronimo of Alcalá, Historia de Alonso, mozo de muchos amos (seventeenth-century tale, no further data).

Gregoire, Pierre, *Syntagma Iuris Universi atque legum pene omniuni Gentunu* (Leiden, 1582).

Hervás y Panduro, Lorenzo (S.I), *Catálogo de las lenguas de las naciones conocidas*. Por el abate don L. Hervás; noticia introductoria por Augustín Hevia Ballina, Madrid 1800–05 (Madrid, 1979).

Hidalgo, Juan, *Romances de Germanía, de varios autores, con el vocabulario* (Barcelona: De Cormellas, 1609).

J.M., *Historia de los Gitanos* (Madrid, 1802).

Krantzius, Albert (d. 1517), *Saxonia Alberti Krantz* (Cologne, 1520).

Leon, François (Carmelite), *Studium sapientae universalis* (Paris, 1657).

Magero, Martin (fl. 1583–1625), *Gratulatio cum virtutum et literarum ornamenti*. No. 8 of a collection of poetic variations (1583).

Mendoza, Pedro Salazar de (d. 1629), *Origen de las dignidades seglares de Castilla y Leon*. Para el principe de Espana Don Felipe nuestro senor. Por el doctor Salazar de Mendoca (Toledo, 1618–19).

Moncada, Sancho de, 'Expulsión de los Gitanos, discurso ...', In: Hidalgo, Juan (Ed.), *Romances de Germanía* (Madrid: De Sancha, 1779).

Muratori, Ludwig Anton, 'Cinganorum adventus in Italiam, 1422'. In: *Rerum Italicarum Scriptores*. Vol. 18 of the supplement to this work, by Forli (Milan, 1731).

Navarro, Martin de Azpilcueta (1492[?]–1586), *Manual de confessores y penitentes* (Medina del Campo, 1554).

Ortelius, Abraham (1527–98), *Thesaurus geographicus* (Antwerp, 1587).

Palmireno, Lorenzo, *El estudioso Cortesano* (Alcalá de Henares, 1587).

Philips II (Felipe II), *Nueva Recopilación de las leyes de España; Recopilación de las leyes de stos Reynos hecha por mandado del Rey don Felipe Segundo* (Alcalá de Henares, 1592).

Philips III (Felipe III), *Las Cortes de Madrid*. Cuaderno de las leyes y prematicas reales (Toledo, 1528; Alcalá, 1546; Madrid, 1588).

Quiñones de Benavente, Juan de (1600–50), Al Rey nvestra Señor el doctor Ivan de Quiñones, alcalde de su Casa y Corte, *Discurso contra los Gitanos* (Madrid, 1631).

Reinking, Dietrich (also Theodor) (1590–1664), *Tractatus de regimine seculari et ecclesiastico; cum indicibus, capitum et rerum* (Frankfurt am Main, 1653).

Río, Martin Antoine del (1551–1608), *Disqvisitonvm magicarum*. Libri sex, in tres tomos partiti (Leuven, 1599–1600).

Rovito, Scipione (1556–1636), *In singuluas Regni Neapolitani pragmaticas sanctiones luculentacomentaria, cum declaratione juris communis per eas confirmati* (Venice, 1600).

Schönborner, Georg (1597–1637) see Wendelin, Marcus Friedrich.

Torreblanca Villalpando, Francisco (1615), *Epitome delictorum, sive, De Magia*. In qua aperta vel occulta invocatio daemonis intervenit. New edition (Leiden, 1678).

Vigne, *Cashmire and Panjab* (no further data).

Wendelin, Marcus Friedrich (1584–1652), *Institutionum politicarum. Libri III e septem Georgii Schonborneri* (Frankfurt, 1638).

Vocabulario de Germanía, see: *Orígenes de la lengua española*, Ed. D. Gregorio Mayans y Siscar (Madrid, 1737).

Index 4: reviews of the works of George Borrow[1]

THE ZINCALI (LONDON, 1841)

Allgemeine Literatur-Zeitung, Ergänzungsblättern, 68–70 (Halle/Leipzig, August 1942) pp. 537–41, 556–60 (by L. Diefenbach).

Athenaeum (The) (London, 1841), April 24, pp. 318–29; 1 May, pp. 334–6; May 8, pp. 362–4.

Blackwood's Edinburgh Magazine, 50 (Edinburgh/London, 1841) pp. 352–62.

Blätter für literarische Unterhaltung, 2 (Leipzig, 1841) p. 1164.

British and Foreign Review, 27 (London, 1841) p. 468; 13 (London, 1842) pp. 367–415 (by R. Ford).

Dublin University Magazine (The), 21 (Dublin, 1843), pp. 248–68 (also a review of '*The Bible in Spain*').

Edinburgh Review (The), 74 (Edinburgh, 1842) pp. 45–67 (reprinted in *The American Eclectic*, 3 (New York, 1842) pp. 102–22).

Göttingische gelehrte Anzeigen, 2 (Göttingen, 1844) pp. 996–9.

Jahrbücher für wissenschaftliche Kritik, 1 (Berlin, 1842) pp. 367–96 (by L. Diefenbach).

Lesefrüchte von Felde der neuesten Litteratur (1841) (not located).

Literary Gazette (The) (London, 1841) pp. 243–7, 277–9.

Magazin für die Literatur des Auslandes, 67 (Berlin, 1841) pp. 265–6.

Miscellen aus der neuesten ausländischen Literatur (Jena/Hamburg, 1842) pp. 66–77, 361–97 (ed. F.A. Brans).

Monthly Review (The), 2 (1841) pp. 107–22.

Museum of Foreign Literature, Science, and Art (The), 43 (Philadelphia, 1841) pp. 321–7 (reprinted from *Blackwood's Magazine*).

Museum of Foreign Literature, Science, and Art (The), 44 (Philadelphia, 1842) pp. 476–85 (reprinted from *The Edinburgh Review*).

New Monthly Magazine and Humorist, 2 (London, 1841) pp. 280–2.

North American Review (The), 55 (Boston, 1842) pp. 72–96.

Nyaste dagligt Allehanda, 42–3 (Stockholm, 1842) (3 unnumbered pages).

Revue Britannique ou Choix d'Articles traduits des meilleurs écrits périodiques de la Grande-Bretagne, 1 (Brussels, 1841) pp. 549–59; 2, pp. 59–75, 247–59.

Revue des Deux Mondes, fourth series, 27 (Paris, 1841) pp. 462–79 (reprinted in *Revue des Deux Mondes*, 30 (Brussels, 1841) pp. 203–15).

United States Catholic Magazine (The), 2 (Baltimore, May 1843) pp. 257–69.

United States Magazine and Democratic Review, 11 (New York, 1842) pp. 58–68.

Westminster Review (The) (London, 1841) pp. 268–70.

THE BIBLE IN SPAIN (LONDON, 1842–43)

Athenaeum (The) (London, 17 December 1842) pp. 1080–2; 24 December, pp. 1105–7; 31 December, pp. 1128–31.

Bookman, 17 (London, 1900) p. 145 (by F.H. Groome).

Catholic Magazine, II (1843) p. 321 ff. (not located).

Christian Examiner, 34 (Boston, 1842) pp. 170–86.

Christian Review, 11 (1842) pp. 516–33.

Dial, 20 (New York, 1896) p. 341.

Dublin Review, 14 (May 1843) pp. 443–80.

Dublin University Magazine (The), 21 (1843) pp. 248–68 (also a review of *The Zincali*).

Eclectic Review, 13 (1843) pp. 170–88.

Edinburgh Review (The), 77 (Feb. 1843) pp. 105–38.

Evangelical Magazine (April 1844) p. 190.

Examiner (The) (17 December 1842) pp. 804–5.

Harper's Monthly Magazine, 128 (New York, May 1914) pp. 958–61.

Literary Gazette (The) (London, 17 December 1842) pp. 857–9.

Monthly Review or Literary Journal enlarged (The) (London, 1842–3) pp. 104–15.

Museum, 44 (1843), p. 476 ff. (not located).

New Englander, 1 (New Haven, 1843–56) pp. 278–85.

New Monthly Magazine and Humorist (The) (London, 1843) pp. 140–2.

Quarterly Review (The), 71 (London, 1843) pp. 169–97 (reprinted in *The Eclectic Magazine of Foreign Literature etc.*, 1, pp. 252–67).

Revue Britannique, 1 (Brussels, 1844) pp. 552–67; 2, pp. 290–319.

Revue des Deux Mondes (1 May 1843) pp. 145–67 (by P. Chasles).

Southern Literary Messenger, 9 (Richmond Virginia, August 1843) pp. 465–89.

Spectator (London, December 1842) pp. 1214–5; 203 (London, 1959) p. 561 (by R. Bryden).

Tait's Edinburgh Magazine, 10 (1843) pp. 75–84, 161–74.

LAVENGRO (LONDON, 1851)

American Whig Review, 13 (April, 1851) p. 382.
Athenaeum (*The*) (London, 8 and 15 February 1851) pp. 159–60, 188–90.
Blackwood's Edinburgh Magazine, 69 (1851) pp. 322–37.
Bookman, 49, supplement (London, 1915) p. 48.
Bow's Review of the Southern and the Western States (*The*), 10 (1851) p. 599.
Britannia (*The*) (26 April 1851) pp. 267–8.
Christian Examiner, 50 (Boston, 1851) pp. 504–5.
Dial, 14 (New York, 1893) p. 343.
Dublin University Magazine, 37 (June 1851) pp. 711–20.
Eclectic Review, 1 (April 1851) pp. 438–48.
English Review or quarterly Journal of ecclesiastical and general Literature
    (*The*), 15 (June 1851) pp. 362–77.
Fraser's Magazine, 43 (March 1851) pp. 272–83.
Gentleman's Magazine (March 1851) pp. 292–3.
Harper's New Monthly Magazine, 2 (New York, 1851) pp. 565–6.
International Monthly Magazine (*The*), 3 (New York, 1851) pp. 36, 183–4.
Knickerbocker (*The*), 37 (New York, 1851) p. 268.
Literary Gazette (*The*) (London, 1851) pp. 107–9, 126–7.
Literary World (*The*), 8 (New York, 1851) pp. 148–50, 168–70.
New Monthly Magazine, 91 (March 1851), pp. 290–8; (April 1851)
    pp. 455–61.
People's and Howitt's Journal, 4 (1851) pp. 144–5 (not located).
Quarterly Review (*The*), 101 (London, 1857) pp. 468–501 (also a review
    of *The Romany Rye*).
Revue des Deux Mondes, 21 (January–March 1851) pp. 1106–28 (by E.D.
    Forgues).
Sharpe's London Magazine, 13 (April 1851) pp. 184–8, 229–33.
Sketch (*The*), 'The Book and its Story' (26 April 1893) p. 762.
Spectator, 24 (London, 1851) pp. 206–7.
Tait's Edinburgh Magazine, second series, 18 (May 1851) pp. 270–6.
United States Magazine and Democratic Review, 28 (March 1851) p. 288.

THE ROMANY RYE (LONDON, 1857)

Athenaeum (*The*) (London, 23 May 1857) pp. 653–5.
Harper's New Monthly Magazine, 15 (New York, 1857) p. 405.
Quarterly Review, 101 (London, 1857) pp. 468–501 (also a review of
    Lavengro).
Revue des Deux Mondes, 27 (September 1857) pp. 109–43 (by E.
    Montégut).

Saturday Review (*The*) (23 May 1857) pp. 480–2.
Southern Literary Messenger, 25 (Richmond Virginia, 1857) p. 157.

ROMANO LAVO-LIL (LONDON, 1874)

Academy (*The*), 5 (London, 13 June 1874) pp. 665–7 (by F. Hindes
 Groome).
Academy (*The*) (London, 22 July 1905) pp. 751–2.
Athenaeum (*The*) (London, 25 April 1874) pp. 556–7.
Dial, 40 (New York, 1906) p. 23.
Edinburgh Review, 303 (1878) pp. 117–46.

NOTES

1 References to these reviews are from Black (1914, pp. 21–5); Knapp (1899, Vol. I,
   pp. 355, 376; Vol II, pp. 24, 167–76, 227–32); *The Hispanic Society of America*,
   Borrow-archive, folder Knapp 1842; Stephen (1927, pp. 31–3); Fréchet (1956,
   pp. 358–9); Tilford jr. (1944, pp. 442–56) and 'Combined Retrospective Index to
   Book Reviews', *Humanities Journals*, 1802–1974, Vol. II (1982) p. 32.

Annex 5: summary of Robert Ritter's publications and lectures

(1928) *Das geschlechtliche Problem in der Erziehung. Versuch einer Sexualpädagogik auf psychologischen Grundlage*. Inaugural-Dissertation (Munich: Ernst Reinhardt).

(1929) 'Der neue politische Mensch', *Kölnische Zeitung* (12 September 1930).

(1929a) 'Europäische Jugend. Die politische Jugendbewegung in Deutschland', *Neue Züricher Zeitung* (22 December 1929).

(1931) 'Nationalsozialismus und Jugend', *Kölnische Zeitung* (8 January 1931).

(1931a) 'Mehr gegenseitige Achtung', *Kölnische Zeitung* (22 January 1931).

(1934) *Über Gaunernachkommen*. Unpublished lecture at the University of Tübingen (reference found in the City Archives, Frankfurt, Ritter's dossier, sign. 18.576, p. 13).

(1934a) *Untitled*. Unpublished lecture on vagrants and Gypsies. Congress of Psychiatrists in Giessen (copies are in the State Archives, Koblenz, R 073/014005; 37 pages).

(1934b) *Die Coedukationsfrage*. Unpublished lecture at an international congress on moral upbringing in Kraków (mentioned in Ritter (1945, p. 5)).

(1934c) *Einführung in der Heilpädagogik und Jugendpsychologie*. Course for the psychiatric clinic in Tübingen (mentioned in Ritter's dossier, Frankfurt).

(1935) 'Rothaarigkeit als rassenhygienisches Problem', *Volk und Rasse*, 1 (Munich, January) pp. 385–90.

(1935a) *Über Pubertätskrisen*. Unpublished lecture, University of Tübingen (mentioned in Ritter's dossier, Frankfurt).

(1935b) *Sippenkundliche Untersuchungen über Gaunergeschlechter in Schwaben*. Unpublished lecture to the Society for Genealogical Research in Stuttgart (mentioned in Ritter's dossier, Frankfurt).

(1935c) *Erbgeschichte eines Zigeunerstammes*. Unpublished lecture to the Society for Genealogical Research in Bremen (mentioned in Ritter's dossier, Frankfurt).

(1935d) *Über Erbpflege und Erbgesundheitserziehung*. Course given at the Social Academy for Women in Stuttgart (mentioned in Ritter's dossier, Frankfurt).

(1936) 'Erbbiologische Untersuchungen innerhalb eines Züchtungs-kreises von Zigeunermischlingen und "asozialen Psychopaten"'. In: Harmsen, H. and F. Lohse (eds), *Bevölkerungsfragen, Berichte des Internationalen Kongresses für Bevölkerungswissenschaft 1935 in Berlin*, 7, pp. 713–18.

(1936a) 'Zur Frage der Vererbung der allergischen Diathese. (Mit zwei Erbtafeln)', *Archiv für Rassen- und Gesellschaftsbiologie. Einschliess-lich Rassen- und Gesellschafts-Hygiene*, 30, 4, 15. XI. (Munich, 1936) pp. 289–303 (expanded rewrite of an unpublished Masters thesis, Faculty of Medicine, Heidelberg 1930).

(1936b) *Erbgeschichte einer asozialen und kriminellen Sippschaft*. Unpublished lecture, University of Tübingen (mentioned in Ritter's dossier, Frankfurt).

(1937) *Ein Menschenschlag. Erbärztliche und erbgeschichtliche Untersuchungen über die – durch 10 Geschlechterfolgen erforschten – Nachkommen von 'Vagabunden, Jaunern und Räubern'. [Mit 3, teilweise farbigen Erbtafeln]*. Med. Habilitationsschrift (Leipzig: Georg Thieme).

(1937a) 'Mitteleuropäische Zigeuner: ein Volkstamm oder eine Mischlingspopulation?', *Congrès de la Population*, 8 (Problèmes qualitatifs de la population) (Paris), pp. 51–60.

(1937b) *Über die jenische Bevölkerungsgruppe*. Unpublished lecture to the Society for Anthropologists in Berlin (mentioned in Ritter's dossier, Frankfurt).

(1938) 'Zur Frage der Rassenbiologie und Rassenpsychologie der Zigeuner in Deutschland', *Reichs-Gesundheitsblatt*, 22 (Berlin) pp. 425–6.

(1938a) 'Zigeuner und Landfahrer', *Der nichtsesshafte Mensch. Ein Beitrag zur Neugestaltung der Raum- und Menschenordnung im Grossdeutschen Reich* (Munich) pp. 71–88.

(1939) 'Die Zigeunerfrage und das Zigeunerbastardproblem', *Fortschritte der Erbpathologie, Rassenhygiene und ihrer Grenzgebiete*, III (Leipzig) pp. 2–20.

(1940) 'Les vagabonds asociaux en Allemagne', *Bulletin mensuel de l'Office International d'Hygiène publique*, part XXXII (Paris) pp. 446–8 (there are three identical versions of this article attributed to three different names: R. Ritter, K. Ritter en K. Reiter).

(1940a) 'Primitivität und Kriminalität', *Monatsschrift für Kriminalbiologie und Strafrechtsreform. Organ der Kriminalbiologischen Gesellschaft*, 31, 9 (Munich und Berlin) pp. 197–210.

(1940b) *Das Asozialenproblem und die Möglichkeiten seiner Lösung*. Unpublished lecture to the *Wissenschaftliche Gesellschaft* in Bremen (copies of the original in the State Archives in Koblenz ZSG 142/22, Arnold Collection, 36 pages).

(1940c) *Zigeunerwesen und Kriminalpolizei*. Unpublished lecture (mentioned, but no text, in the State Archives in Koblenz ZSG 142/22, Arnold Collection).

(1940d) *Das deutsche Zigeunerproblem der Gegenwart*. Unpublished lecture (mentioned, but no text, in the State Archives in Koblenz ZSG 142/22, Arnold Collection).

(1940e) *Brief an die Pfarrämter*. Unpublished lecture (mentioned, but no text, in the State Archives in Koblenz ZSG 142/22, Arnold Collection).

(1941) 'Die Bestandsaufnahme der Zigeuner und Zigeunermischlinge in Deutschland', *Der Öffentliche Gesundheitsdienst*, 6, 21 (Leipzig, 5 February) pp. 477–89 (also in: *Zeitschrift für Standesamtswesen, Personenstandsrecht, Eherecht und Sippenforschung*, 22, 11 (Berlin, 10 June 1942) pp. 87–90, 99–102).

(1941a) 'Die Aufgaben der Kriminalbiologie und der kriminalbiologischen Bevölkerungsforschung', *Kriminalistik. Monatschrift für die gesamte kriminalistische Wissenschaft und Praxis*, 15 (Berlin) pp. 38–41.

(1941b) 'Die Asozialen, ihre Vorfahren und ihre Nachkommen', *Fortschritte der Erbpathologie, Rassenhygiene und ihrer Grenzgebiete*, V, 4 (Leipzig) pp. 137–55.

(1941c) *Jugendpsychiatrische Erfahrungen im Jugendschutzlager*. Lecture to the *Deutsche Vereinigung für Jugendgerichtshilfer* in Berlin (mentioned in Ritter (1945, p. 5)).

(1941d) *Über Jugendbewahrung*. Unpublished lecture to the *Gesellschaft für Jugendgerichtshilfe* in Berlin (mentioned in Ritter's dossier, Frankfurt).

(1942) 'Erbärztliche Verbrechensverhütung', *Deutsche Medizinische Wochenschrift*, 68, 21 (Leipzig, 22 May) pp. 535–9 (off-print copy in: *Veröffentlichungen der Berliner medizinischen Gesellschaft*, 21 (Leipzig) p. 535 ff.).

(1942a) 'Das Kriminalbiologische Institut der Sicherheitspolizei', *Kriminalistik. Monatshefte für die gesamte kriminalistische Wissenschaft und Praxis*, 16, 11 (Berlin, November) pp. 117–19.

(1943) *Fragen der Bewahrung und Kriminalpädagogik*. Lecture at a Congress of Youth Judges in Thorn (mentioned in Ritter (1945, p. 5)).

(1944) 'Die Artung jugendlicher Rechtsbrecher', *Deutsches Jugendrecht. Beiträge für die Praxis und Neugestaltung des Jugendrechts*, 4 ('Zum neuen Jugendstrafrecht') (Berlin) pp. 33–60.

(1944a) *Kriminalbiologische Grundlagen und Praxis der Jugendbewahrung*. Lecture at a Congress of Youth Custodial Judges in Burg Cochem (mentioned in Ritter (1945, pp. 5, 151); with the annotation that it would later appear in print).

(1944b) *Die Beziehungen zwischen Geisteskrankheit und Jugendkriminalität*. Lecture to the directors of prisons for youthful offenders in Cochem (mentioned in Ritter (1945, pp. 5, 151); with the annotation that it would later appear in print).

(1945) *Autobiography* (Mariaberg) (copies in my possession, 158 pages).

Annex 6: reviews of Robert Ritter's *Ein Menschenschlag*[1]

Anzeiger, Anthropologische, 14 (Stuttgart, 1937) p. 133 (by A. Harrasser).

Anzeiger, ethnologischer. Bibliographie und Bericht über die völker-kundliche Literatur, 4 (Stuttgart, 1942) pp. 358–9 (by R. Grau).

Archiv für Bevölkerungswissenschaft und Bevölkerungspolitik, 5 and 6 (Leipzig, 1937) pp. 429–30 (by H.W. Kranz).

Archiv für Kriminologie, 100 (1937) p. 293.

Archiv für Rassen- und Gesellschaftsbiologie, 31 (Munich, 1937) p. 270 (by F. Stumpfl) and pp. 459–60 (by F. Reinöhl).

Archiv für Rechts- und Sozialphilosophie, 31 (1937/38) pp. 530–2 (by A. Vierkandt).

Archivio di antropologia criminale, 58 (Turin, 1937/38) pp. 956–7.

Berichte über die wissenschaftliche Biologie, 43, 7/8 (Berlin, 8 September 1937) p. 399 (by Agnes Bluhm).

Blätter, Hessische, für Volkskunde, 35 (Giessen, 1937) pp. 148–50 (by Gerhard Pfahler).

Blätter für Württembergische Familienkunde, 73–6 (Stuttgart, 1937) p. 77 (by R. Sch.).

Bulletin de la société clinique de France, 34 (Paris, 1936/37[?]) p. 254 (by Hohlfeld).*

Erbarzt, der. Beilage zum 'Deutschen Ärzteblatt', 4, 9 (Berlin, 18 September 1937) p. 127 (by F. Steiner).

Fortschritte der Therapie, 13, 10 (Leipzig, 1937) p. 592 (by Prof. J.H. Schultz).

Gesundheitsdienst der öffentliche Volksgesundheitspflege, 3 (1937) p. 374 (by Friese).

Geisteskrankenpflege (before *Die Irrenpflege*), 41 (Halle/Stuttgart, 1937) p. 143.

Jahrbuch für Gesetzgebung, Verwaltung und Volkswirtschaft im Deutschen Reiche, 62 (1937/38[?]) pp. 122–3 (by H. Gottschalk).*

Journal of nervous and mental disease, 90 (Richmond, 1938) p. 545.

Landartzt, der. Wochenschrift für arztlichen Meinungsaustausch, 18, 46 (Stuttgart, 17 November 1937) pp. 625–6 (by Dr Fenner).

Monatsblätter für Straffälligenbetreuung und Ermittlungshilfe, 13 (Berlin, 1941[?]) p. 62 ff. (by E. Raesner).*

Monatschrift für Kriminalbiologie und Strafrechtsreform, 29, 1 (Munich, 1938) pp. 54–5 (by F. Stumpfl).

Nederlandsch Tijdschrift voor Geneeskunde, 81, 3 (Amsterdam, 17 July 1937) p. 3460 (by J. Sanders).

Nervenarzt, der, XI (Berlin, 1938) pp. 222–3 (by Brugger).

Rheinische Sippen, I (Frankfurt am Main, 1940) p. 83.

Sachverständigen Zeitung, 43 (Berlin, 1937) p. 284 (by H. Voss).

Schwäbische Merkur, Beilage zum (Stuttgart, 27 June 1937) p. 11 (by H.D. Roecker).

Schwester, deutsche, VI (Osterwieck, 1941[?]) p. 27 (by H. Weiss).*

Volk und Rasse. Illustrierte Monatsschrift für Deutsche Volkstum, Rassenkunde, Rassenpflege, XII (Munich/Berlin, 1937) pp. 333–4 (by B.K. Schultz).

Welt, die medizinische: ärztliche Wochenschrift, II, 44 (Stuttgart, 1937) p. 1542 (by F. Curtius).

Wochenschrift, Deutsche Medizinische, 64 (Leipzig, 1938) pp. 1745–6 (by Prof. Rodenwaldt).

Wochenschrift, klinische. Organ der Gesellschaft Deutscher Naturforscher und Ärzte, 17, 4 (22 January 1938) p. 137 (by Johannes Lange).

Wochenschrift, Wiener klinische, 50, 38 (1937) p. 1340 (by J. Wagner-Jauregg].

Wochenschrift, Münchener medizinische, 84 (29 October 1937) p. 1749 (by H. Luxenburger).

Wochenschrift, Psychiatrisch-Neurologische, 39, 43 (23 October 1937) p. 492 (by Prof. Bürger-Prinz).

Zeitschrift, deutsche für die gesamte gerichtliche Medizin, 29 (1937) p. 124 (by Von Neureiter).

Zeitschrift für Menschenkunde und Zentralblatt für Graphologie, XIII (Kampen, 1937) pp. 208–9 (by Conrad).

Zeitschrift für Morphologie und Anthropologie, 38 (1940) p. 174 (by Eugen Fischer).

Zeitschrift, Prager Juristische, XVIII, 8 (Reichenberg, 1938) p. 256 (by Erich Schmied).

Zeitschrift für angewandte Psychologie und Charakterkunde, 56, 5 and 6 (Leipzig, 1939) pp. 389–90 (by R. Scholl).

Zeitschrift für Psychologie, 141, 3–6 (1937) pp. 367–8 (by F. Köhrle).

Zeitschrift für menschliche Vererbungs- und Konstitutionslehre, 25 (Berlin, 1942) pp. 626–7 (by W. Villinger).

Zeitschrift für Rassenkunde und die gesamte Forschung am Menschen, 6 (Stuttgart, 1937) p. 348 (by M. Werner).

Zeitung, illustrierte, 100 (Leipzig, 1943) p. 34 (by H. Hartmann).

Zentralblatt für die gesamte Hygiene, 39 (Berlin, 1938) p. 625 (by Dornedden).

Ziel und Weg, Zeitschrift des Nationalsozialistischen Deutschen Ärzte-bundes, 8 (1938) pp. 100–1.

NOTES

1   Derived from *Bibliographie der deutschen Zeitschriftenliteratur mit Einschluss von Sammelwerken. Bd. 1 (1896) – 128 (1964)* (Leipzig: Dietrich, 1896–1964). Fused with *Bibliographie der fremdsprachigen Zeitschriftenliteratur* and continued as *Internationale Bibliographie der Zeitschriftenliteratur aus allen Gebieten des Wissenschafts* (with a joint index). For *Ein Menschenschlag* I consulted the Volumes 64, 65, 66, 67, 68, 69, 70, 72, 74, 76 (1937 through 1943). I traced additional reviews by examining whatever issues I came across of magazines from the Nazi era published in 1937 or 1938. To four titles an asterisk [*] has been affixed to indicate that I could not obtain the review in question by means of an inter-library loan. The indicated titles are presumably inaccurate.

Archives

GERMANY/AUSTRIA

Berlin, Berlin Document Centre
Dossier Manfred Betz
Dossier Sophie Ehrhardt
Dossier Robert Ritter
Dossier Ernst Rüdin

Berlin, University Archives, Humboldt University
Faculty of Mathematics and Natural Sciences
Sign. 192: Ph.D. Dossier Eva Justin
Law Faculty
Sign. 590, Bl. 1-26: Dossier Robert Ritter (1940–44)

Frankfurt am Main, Municipal Archives
Sign. 92.546

Frankfurt am Main, City Archives
Sign. 2009: Dossier Robert Ritter (1947–51)
Sign. 18.576: Dossier Robert Ritter
Sign. 89.849: Dossier Eva Justin
Sign. 92.546: Dossier Eva Justin

Germanisches National Museum
Autographs H.M.G. Grellmann, no numbering: one letter dated 2 May
   1787

Göttingen, State Library
Manuscript catalogue, Autographs (Grb–Han)
Ms. Philos., 182
Stammbuch Eintr. Göttingen 19-9-1786, no. 80 H lit. 48 ha, 205
Register of the Göttingen Manuscripts Overview, Philos. 133 iv 269,
   p. 74

Göttingen, University Archives
Dossier KA 4) Vb 55, (12-8-1793): on H.M.G. Grellmann

Greifswald, National Archives
Pers. akt. 15721/242

Hannover, City Archives
Sign. no. 168-2173: letter from H.M.G. Grellmann, 18 October 1794

Heidelberg, University Archives
Sign. H-III-862/56: dossier on the student Robert Ritter (1926–30)

Jena, Evangelisch-Lutherische Kirchgemeinde
Baptismal register, Vol 6, p. 481: baptismal certificate H.M.G. Grellmann

Jena, University Archives
Section M, no. 180, Philosophy Faculty 1783–84: on H.M.G. Grellmann

Koblenz, State Archives
Sign. 018/005644, Rep 320, no. 644: Gypsy documents from the Ministry of the Interior
Sign. R 73/14005: work reports by Robert Ritter for the *Deutsche Forschungs Gemeinschaft*
Sign. R 165: inventory *Rassenhygienische und Bevölkerungsbiologische Forschungsstelle Reichsgesundheitsamtes*
Sign. R 165/137, 139, 141, 144, 145, 147, 164, 165, 166: genealogical dossiers of Gypsies
Sign. R 165/233, 237, 238, 239, 241, 242, 243: Tübingen branch (correspondence with Manfred Betz)
Sign. ZSG 142, no. 1.9222 and 1.924: Hermann Arnold Archive, documents related to Gypsy policy during the Nazi regime
Sign. ZSG 142/000022 (Vol. 2): Hermann Arnold Archive (restricted access): diverse documents
Sign. UAT 164: inventory of documents from the branch in Tübingen

Ludwigsburg, Zentrale Stelle der Landesjustizverwaltung
Dossier 110 AR 315/79, StA Frankenthal 1 U Js 947/79: Ritter's institutes
Dossier 402 AR 12.519/88, ZSt Cologne-130 Js 7/88: Anton Böhmer
Dossier 414 AR-Z 42/83, StA Landau Js 7091/83: Hermann Arnold
Dossier 414 AR 540/83, StA Hamburg 2200 Js 2/84: Ruth Kellermann
Dossier 415 AR 55/82, StA Frankfurt 55/3 Js 5582/48: Robert Ritter

Dossier 415 AR 314/81, StA Stuttgart 19 Js 928/81: Sophie Ehrhardt/
  Adolf Würth
Dossier 415 AR 930/61, StA Cologne 24 Js 429/61: Hans Maly
Dossier 415 AR 531/92, StA Frankfurt 4 Js 220/59: Eva Justin

Magdenburg, Landeshauptarchiv Sachsen-Anhalt
C 29 Anhang II no. 84/1, 54 R: police dossiers on individual Gypsies

Magdenburg, State Archives
Sign. nr. Rep. C 29: police dossiers on individual Gypsies

Munich, Institute of Contemporary History
Sign. MA 423: ministerial documents relating to the treatment of
  Gypsies during wartime
Sign. MA 1159: publications about Gypsies in *Informationsblatt Rassen-
  politisches Amt der NSDAP* (1940–42)
Eichmann Trial, documents submitted in evidence no. 1505: concerning
  the 'Gypsy question' in Bialystok

Munich, University Archives
Sign. O–N prom. SS 1927: dossier student Robert Ritter (1926)

Nuremberg, State Archives
NG 1008: testimony on camp observations by R. Hecker, 17 March 1947
NG 1619: testimony by H. Mayr, 28 April 1947
Nr. 2927: Min. of Justice Thierack to Bormann, 16 November 1942;
  about the transfer of the prosecution of Poles, Soviet Russians, Jews
  and Gypsies to Himmler's SS (for this Thierack–Himmler accord, see
  also the following documents: NO 2926, 25 November 1942, NO
  1784, 9 October 1942, NG 558, 13 October 1942, NG 1255, 16
  November 1942 and PS 1750, 5 November 1942)
NO 1499: message from *Rassenamt* 28 September 1942 about the
  evacuation and deportation of undesirable groups from the occupied
  Elzas region
NO 1725: communication from *Amt Ahnenerbe* 14 January 1943
  concerning proposed Gypsy research in Camp Lackenbach by
  Knobloch from Vienna
NO 5150: summary 15 November 1940 of evacuations sent to the
  Generalgouvernement
NO 5322: meeting between Heydrich et al. 30 January 1940
  concerning the deportation of Jews, Poles and Gypsies

Potsdam, Government Archives
Sign. 49.01 REM, no. 1403 en 1483: dossier Sophie Ehrhardt

Potsdam, Brandenburgisches Landeshauptarchiv
Rep. 30 Berlin G Polizeipräsidium tit. 198 A 3: police dossiers on individual Gypsies

Reutlingen, Mariaberger Heime Archive
Inventory no. 78.3: dossier on the stay of Robert Ritter and colleague (1944–47)

Sigmaringen, State Archives
Sign. WÜ 13/10/C/3206 no. 1600: dossier Robert Ritter

Tübingen, City Archives
Sign. A 150/4857: announcement of a lecture by Robert Ritter on 'Gypsy mixed-bloods' 28 January 1935
Sign. A 150/4859: dossier on the *Eheberatungsstelle* in Tübingen
Einwohnermeldeamt, Hauptregister 1920–75: personal data Sophie Ehrhardt

Tübingen, University Archives
Sign. 117/565: dossier Robert Ritter (1935)
Sign. 125/95: faculty register (1935–36)
Sign. 125/159: Hoffmann's evaluation of Ritter's dissertation, 8 June 1936
Sign. 126 a/403: dossier Robert Ritter (1945–46)
Sign. 308/1804: dossier Eva Justin
Sign. 308/3201: dossier Robert Ritter (1931–36, 1951–52)
Sign. 601/65: dossier Robert Ritter (1944–46)
Sign. Rep. 283: report by archivist Schäffer about the Gypsy occupation

Weimar, Evangelisch-Lutherische Kirchgemeinde
Marriage register of the court church, 1762–1800, Vol. 1791, p. 422: H.M.G. Grellmann

Weimar, Goethe und Schiller Archive
70 letters from H.M.G. Grellmann to F.J. Bertuch; 1780 to 1800

Vienna, Austrian National Library
Autograph 134/110 (1–20): letters from F.H. Groome to F. von Miklosich

ENGLAND

Leeds, Brotherton Collection
Romany collection

Norwich, Norfolk Record Office

Ms 508 T 137 D: manuscript of Dean Beeching's *Life of Borrow* (no year)

Ms 4664, T 138 E: first printer's proofs with changes in the manuscript of *Romano-Lil*

Ms 4665, P 140 A: printer's proofs of *Life of GB* by W.I. Knapp

Ms 11312, P 138 C: Borrow's notes on Gypsies

Ms 11318, P 138 C: advertisement for *Romany Rye*, 1857

Ms 11319, P 138 C: letters to Borrow, 1826–62

Ms 11321 A, P 138 C: folder with newspaper reviews about W.I. Knapp

Ms 11322, P 138 C: letters from J.T. Hasfeldt to Borrow (1844, 1853, 1875)

Ms 11337, P 138 C: 'How Lavengro learned Languages'

Ms 11338, T 134 D: manuscript journal 1823 of Mary Clarke

Ms 11342, T 138 D: 4 folders with newspaper clippings from 1910 to 1920

HUNGARY

Budapest, Hungarian Academy of Sciences, manuscript collection
Section 'Ungarische Literaturkorrespondenz' (Magyar irodalmi levelezés), 4 r. 60. no. 81

Budapest, Hungarian National Archives
Archiv des ungarischen Statthaltereirates (OL – C 43), Acta secundum referentes (Emericus Csáky – 1783 – F. 15, Pos. 7, 8, 11; Fabiankovics – 1783 – F. 4, Pos. 172; Fabiankovics – 1783 – F. 19, Pos. 39): the case of cannibalism 1782
Archiv der ungarischen Hofkanzlei (OL – A 39), Acta generalia – 1782, no. 6045, 6046, 6063, 6693, 6999, 7081: the case of cannibalism 1782

THE NETHERLANDS

Amsterdam, University Library, Manuscript Dept.
Sign. 70 Bt. 1 + 2: 2 letters from H.M.G. Grellmann to G. Hufeland in Jena, 26 December 1787 and 1 January 1788

The Hague, personal archives of Wim Willems
Autobiographical manuscript Robert Ritter (Summer 1945)
Personal letters (32) written by Robert Ritter from the years 1908 to 1925, 1932 and 1945 to 1947

UNITED STATES

New Brunswick, New Jersey, Rutgers University Library, Symington Collection
Sign. Borrow, George:
- eight handwritten letters from George Borrow to Henrietta, from 1873 on
- rough draft of a letter from George Borrow to the Rev. Francis Cunningham, 18 October 1833, St Petersburg
- fragment of a manuscript entitled 'Alonso, Servant of Many Masters'

New York, Fales Library, New York University
Sign. George Borrow file
No. 20.2: Four letters from George Borrow:
- to Captain Narburton, Oulton, 11 December 1851
- to Mrs. Ropes, St Petersburg, 10 May 1835
- to Mr. Wiseman, Oulton (no year)
- to John Murray (no address, no year)
No. 20.4: *The Gospel of St. Luke*. Translated into the dialect of the 'Gitanos of Spain'. Original manuscript. c.1835–36.

New York, Hispanic Society
Sign. George Borrow Collection. With folders arranged by year. Of importance for this study:
Knapp 1824 a; Knapp 1836 a; Knapp 1837 b; Knapp 1838 a; Knapp 1841 a; Knapp 1842; Knapp 1844 a; Knapp 1846 a; Knapp 1848; Knapp 1851 a–g; Knapp 1861–62; Knapp 1863–66; Knapp 1887 a; Knapp 1888 a–e; Knapp 1889
Sign. Charles Godfrey Leland (1824–1903)
Sign. Frances Hindes Groome (1851–1902)
Sign. John Borrow
Sign. Knapp – letters to Huntington
Sign. letters from Richard Ford (1796–1858) to George Borrow

New York, Public Library, Berg Collection
Sign. 103508 B: Handwritten letter from George Borrow to his mother, signed 27 July 1838
Sign. 106185 B: Original manuscript for part of *The Romany Rye*
Sign. 209734 B: Handwritten letter from George Borrow to Mrs. Clarke, Toledo Spain, 5 December 1837
Sign. 310947 B: Handwritten, signed letter from George Borrow to Mrs. Clarke, Seville, 10 January 1839 (with typed commentary by an unknown person)

Sign. 64 B 4845: Biographical sketch of George Borrow, handwritten (unsigned and undated)

Sign. 64 B 4846: Mac Oubrey, Henrietta Mary, *Borrow's works*. Handwritten list of works with a biographical sketch of George Borrow (unsigned, undated)

Sign. 64 B 4848: Whitwell Elwin, *3 Autograph Letters Signed to George Borrow from Norwich*. 21 and 26 October 1853, 5 November 1853

Sign. 64 B 4849: Whitwell Elwin, *4 Autograph Letters Signed to James Hooper*. Booton Rectory, Norwich. October and December 1893, June 1894

Sign. 64 B 4851: H.M. Mac Oubrey, *5 Autograph Letters Signed to George Borrow*. London (no year)

Sign. 64 B 4852: H.M. Mac Oubrey, *2 Autograph Letters Signed to Mr. Cooke* (no year)

Sign. 64 B 4853: H.M. Mac Oubrey, *Autograph Letter Signed to James Hooper*: 10 October 1894

Sign. 64 B 7197: Francis Hindes Groome, *9 Autograph Letters Signed to Theodore Watts-Dunton*: 31 December 1885 – 2 August 1898

Letters to his mother Ann Borrow and Other Correspondents. By George Borrow. London: privately printed edition, 1913

Bibliography

Acton, Thomas, *Gypsy Politics and Social Change. The development of ethnic ideology and pressure politics among British Gypsies from Victorian reformism to Romany nationalism* (London/Boston: Routledge & Paul, 1974).

Aichele, Hermann, *Die Zigeunerfrage mit besonderer Berücksichtigung Württembergs* (Stuttgart: Vereinsdruckerei, 1912).

Album Studiosorum, Academiae Rheno-Traiectinae (1636–1886), Accedunt Nomina Curatorum Professoru. Per Eadem Secula (Utrecht: Beijers & Van Broekhove, 1886).

Allderidge, Patricia H., 'The Horrors: A Preliminary Report'. In: Gillian Fenwick (ed.), *Proceedings of the 1989 George Borrow Conference* (Toronto: Published for The George Borrow Society, 1990) pp. 44–53.

Allgemeine Deutsche Biographie, 1 (Leipzig: Duncker & Humblot, 1879) pp. 636–7.

Anderson, Benedict, *Imagined Communities. Reflections on the Origin and Spread of Nationalism*. Revised edition (London/New York: Verso, 1991).

'An old Romany', *Eastern Daily Press* (19 August 1896).

Arkel, Dik van, 'De groei van het anti-Joodse stereotype. Een poging tot een hypothetisch-deductieve werkwijze in historisch onderzoek', *Tijdschrift voor Sociale Geschiedenis*, 10, 33 (1984) pp. 34–70.

(A) Summary Account of the Proceedings of a Provisional Committee Associated at Southampton, with a View to the Consideration and Improvement of the Condition of the Gipseys (no further details).

Autobiography and select remains of the late Samuel Roberts (London, 1849).

Avé-Lallemant, Friedrich Christian Benedict, *Das Deutsche Gaunerthum in seiner social-politischen, literarischen und linguistischen Ausbildung zu seinem heutigen Bestande*. Two Volumes (Leipzig, 1858).

Bader, Dr., 'Bekämpfung des Zigeunerunwesens', *Kriminalistische Monatshefte. Zeitschrift für die gesamte kriminalistische Wissenschaft und Praxis*, 9, 12 (1935) pp. 265–8.

Baird, John, *The Scottish Gipsy's Advocate: Being a short Account of the Gipsies of Kirk-Yetholm, in connection with a plan proposed to be adopted for the improvement of the Gipsy Population of Scotland* (Edinburgh: Lindsay & Co., 1839).

Bakker, Peter and Marcel Cortiade (eds), *In the Margin of Romani. Gypsy Languages in Contact*. Studies in Language Contact I. Publication no. 58, Instituut voor Algemene Taalwetenschap (Amsterdam, 1991).

Barth, Frederik (ed.), *Ethnic Groups and Boundaries* (Boston: Allen & Unwin, 1969).

Bataillard, Paul, *Les derniers travaux relatifs aux Bohémiens dans l'Europe orientale*. Excerpts from the 'Revue Critique', 171 and 181, pp. 191–218 and 277–323 (Paris, 1872).

Bauer, Thomas, Heike Drummer and Leoni Krämer, *Vom 'stede arzt' zum Stadtgesundheitsamt. Die Geschichte des öffentlichen Gesundheitswesens in Frankfurt am Main* (Frankfurt am Main, 1992).

Bäumer, Anna, *NS-Biologie* (Stuttgart: Hirzel, 1990).

Baumiller, Irmgard, '"Getarnter Schwachsinn". Der Tübinger Beitrag zur nationalsozialistischen "Zigeuner" Verfolgung'. In: *Nationalsozialismus in Tübingen – vorbei und vergessen*. Exhibition Catalogue (Tübingen: Kulturamt, 1992).

Becker, Peter Emil, 'Die Protagonisten und ihre Wege ins Dritte Reich'. In: *Sozialdarwinismus, Rassismus, Antisemitismus und Völkerische Gedanke. Wege ins Dritte Reich*, II (Stuttgart/New York: Thieme, 1990) pp. 500–620.

Beekes, R.S.P., *Vergelijkende taalwetenschap: een inleiding in de vergelijkende Indo-Europese taalwetenschap* (Utrecht: Het Spectrum, 1990).

Berbüsse, Volker, 'Das Bild der *Zigeuner* in deutschsprachigen kriminologischen Lehrbüchern seit 1949. Eine Bestandsaufnahme'. In: *Jahrbuch für Antisemitismusforschung*, I (Frankfurt: Campus Verlag, 1992) pp. 151–71.

Berenbaum, Michael, *A mosaic of victims. Non-Jews persecuted and murdered by the Nazis* (London/New York: Tauris, no year).

Berger, H., *Das Zigeunerbild in der Deutschen Literatur des 19. Jahrhunderts* (Waterloo, 1972) (unpublished doctoral dissertation).

Bernard, Paul B., *The limits of enlightenment; Joseph II and the law* (Urbana: University of Illinois Press, 1979).

Bernd Gisevius, H., *Bis zum Bittern Ende*, 1 and 2 (Zürich: Fretz & Wasmuth, 1946).

Beschreibung der jenigen Jauner, Zigeuner, Mörder, Strassenräuber, Kirchen-, Markt-, Tag-, und Nacht-Diebe und andern herumvagierenden liederlichen Gesindels, welche teils in Schwaben, meistenteils aber in der Schweiz würklich noch herumschwärmen, und von denen dahier ... in Verhaft ... gestandenen ... sieben Erzjaunern und Jaunerinnen ...

entdeckt worden sind ... aus denen ... Untersuchungs-Acten herausgezogen (Stuttgart, 1784).

Bibliographie der deutschen Zeitschriftenliteratur mit Einschluss von Sammelwerken, 1–128 (Leipzig: Dietrich, 1896–1964).

Bischoff, Ferdinand, *Deutsches-Zigeunerisches Wörterbuch* (Ilmenau: Voigt, 1827).

Black, George F., *A Gypsy Bibliography* (London: Constable, 1914).

Block, Martin, *Zigeuner. Ihr Leben und ihre Seele, dargestellt auf Grund eigener Reisen und Forschungen* (Leipzig: Bibliographisches Institut, 1936).

Blok, Anton, 'Infame beroepen', *Symposion*, III, 1/2 (1981) pp. 104–28.

Bloshteyn, Maria, 'The Russian Gypsy Borrow'. In: *The Second Research Colloquium on the Works of George Borrow* (Toronto: York University, 1992) pp. 24–9.

Bloshteyn, Maria, 'Borrow in St Petersburg: Some 19th Century Russian Reactions to his Work'. In: *The Third Research Colloquium on the Works of George Borrow* (Toronto: York University, 1993) pp. 10–17.

Blumenbach, Johann Friedrich, *Decas altera Collectionis suae Craniorum diversarum gentium illustrata* (Göttingen, 1793).

Boas, Wilhelm, *Die Zigeunerromantik im englischen Roman* (Erlangen, 1929) (unpublished doctoral dissertation).

Bock, Gisela, *Zwangssterilisation im Nationalsozialismus* (Opladen: Westdeutscher Verlag, 1986).

Bödeker, Hans Erich, 'Das staatswissenschaftliche Fächersystem im 18. Jahrhundert'. In: R. Vierhaus (ed.), *Wissenschaften im Zeitalter der Aufklärung* (Göttingen: Vandenhoeck & Ruprecht, 1985) pp. 143–62.

Bogeng, G.A.E., *Die grossen Bibliophilen: Geschichte der Büchersammler und ihrer Sammlungen*, 1 (Leipzig: Seemann, 1922).

Borenius, Tancred, 'Arthur Thesleff: A Friend's Memoir', *JGLS*, 22 (1943) pp. 1–9.

Borrow, George, *The Zincali; or, An Account of the Gypsies of Spain. With an Original Collection of their Songs and Poetry, and a Copious Dictionary of their Language*. Two Parts (London: Murray, 1841).

Borrow, George, *Wild Wales: Its People, Language and Scenery* (London: Murray, 1862).

Borrow, George, *The Zincali. An Account of the Gypsies of Spain*. New edition (London: Murray, 1901).

Borrow, George, *The Romany Rye; A Sequel to 'Lavengro'* (London: Murray, 1903) (original edition 1857).

Borrow, George, *The Bible in Spain; or, The Journeys, Adventures, and Imprisonments of an Englishman in an Attempt to Circulate the Scriptures in the Peninsula* (London: Murray, 1904) (original edition 1842).

Borrow, George, *Lavengro; The Scholar – The Gypsy – The Priest*. New edition (London: Murray, 1904) (original edition 1851).

Borrow, George, 'A Visit to Moscow in 1835. From an Unpublished Report'. In: *The Bible in the World* (March 1905) pp. 71–5.

Borrow, George, *Romano Lavo-Lil Word-Book of the Romany or, English Gypsy Language with Specimens of Gypsy Poetry, and an Account of certain Gypsyries or Places inhabited by them, and of various Things relating to Gypsy Life in England* (London: Murray, 1905) (original edition 1873).

Borrow, George, *Letters to John Hasfeld 1835–1839* (Edinburgh: Tragara, 1982) (Ed. by Angus M. Fraser).

Borrow, George, *Letters to John Hasfeld 1841–1846* (Edinburgh: Tragara, 1984) (Ed. by Angus M. Fraser).

Boswell, Gordon Sylvester, 'Wester Boswell's Medal', *JGLS* 34 (1955), pp. 129–33.

Boswell, Gordon Sylvester, *The Book of Boswell. Autobiography of a Gypsy* (London, 1970) (Ed. by John Seymour).

Boterman, Frits, *Oswald Spengler en Der Untergang des Abendlandes. Cultuurpessimist en politiek activist* (Assen/Maastricht: Van Gorcum, 1992) (doctoral dissertation).

Breuner, Peter J. (ed.), *Der Reisebericht. Die Entwicklung einer Gattung in der deutschen Literatur* (Frankfurt am Main: Suhrkamp, 1989).

Bright, Richard, *Travels from Vienna through Lower Hungary; with some remarks on the state of Vienna during the Congress, in the Year 1814* (Edinburgh: Constable, 1818).

Broad, Pery, *KZ-Auschwitz. Erinnerungen eines SS-Mannes der Politischen Abteilung in dem Konzentrationslager Auschwitz*. Auschwitz no. 9 (Kraków, 1966) pp. 3–53.

Brockie, William, *The Gypsies of Yetholm: Historical, Traditional, Philological, and Humorous* (Kelso: Rutherfurd, 1884).

Buchheim, Hans, 'Die Zigeunerdeportation vom Mai 1940'. In: *Gutachten des Instituts für Zeitgeschichte*, 1 (Munich, 1956) pp. 51–60.

Bühle, J.T., *Elogium Virti quondam illustris Henrici Mauritii Theophili Grellmann*. Recitatum in Conferssu Academico Mosquensi (January 1805).

Burleigh, Michael, 'Racism as social policy: the Nazi "euthanasie" programme, 1939–1945', *Ethnic and Racial Studies*, 14, 4 (1991) pp. 453–73.

Büttner, Christian Wilhelm, *Vergleichungstafeln der Schriftarten verschiedener Völker in den vergangenen und gegenwärtigen Zeiten* (Göttingen, 1771).

Calvelli-Adorno, 'Die rassische Verfolgung der Zigeuner vor dem 1. März 1943', *Rechtsprechung zum Wiedergutmachungsrecht*, 12 (1961) pp. 529–37.

Cann, Kathleen, 'George Borrow and Religion'. In: Gillian Fenwick (ed.), *Proceedings of the 1989 George Borrow Conference* (Toronto: Published for The George Borrow Society, 1990) pp. 55–63.

Collie, Michael, *George Borrow. Eccentric* (Cambridge: Cambridge University Press, 1982).

Collie, Michael and Angus Fraser, *George Borrow. A Bibliographical Study* (Winchester: St Paul's Bibliographies, 1984).

'Combined Retrospective Index to Book Reviews', *Humanities Journals*, 2 (1802–1974) (Woolbridge, 1982).

Corbey, R., *Wildheid en beschaving* (Baarn: Ambo, 1989).

Cottaar, Annemarie, *Kooplui, kermisklanten en andere woonwagen-bewoners. Groepsvorming en beleid 1870–1945* (Amsterdam: Het Spinhuis, 1996) (doctoral dissertation).

Cottaar, Annemarie, Leo Lucassen and Wim Willems, 'Justice or Injustice? A Survey of Government Policy Towards Gypsies and Caravan Dwellers in Western Europe in the Nineteenth and Twentieth Century', *Immigrants and Minorities*, 11, 1 (London: Cass, March 1992) pp. 42–66.

Crabb, James, *The Gipsies' Advocate; or Observations on the Origin, Character, Manners and Habits, of the English Gipsies: to which are added Many Interesting Anecdotes on the Success that has attended the Plans of Several Benevolent Individuals who anxiously desire their conversion to God*. Third printing, with additions (London: Nisbet, 1832).

Cunningham, W., *Alien Immigrants to England* (London: Social England Series, 1897).

Darlow, T.H., *Letters of George Borrow to the British and Foreign Bible Society*. (London, 1911).

Das Reichsgesundheidsamt 1933–1945 – eine Ausstellung, 32 (March 1989).

Dillmann, Alfred, *Zigeuner-Buch* (Munich, 1905).

Döring, Hans-Joachim, *Die Zigeuner im nationalsozialistischen Staat* (Hamburg: Kriminalistik Verlag, 1964).

Dorson, Richard M., *The British Folklorists. A History* (London: Routledge & Kegan, 1968).

Dougherty, Frank W.P., 'Christoph Meiners und Johann Friedrich Blumenbach im Streit um den Begriff der Menschenrasse'. In: Gunter Mann & Franz Dumont (eds), *Die Natur des Menschen. Probleme der physischen Anthropologie und Rassenkunde (1750–1850)* (Stuttgart/ New York: Fischer, 1990) pp. 89–111.

Duijzings, Ger, 'De Egyptenaren in Kosovo en Macedonië', *Amsterdams Sociologisch Tijdschrift*, 18, 4 (1992) pp. 24–38 (Also as 'The Making of Egyptians in Kosovo and Macedonia'. In: Cora Govers and Hans Vermeulen (eds), *The Politics of Ethnic Consciousness* (Hampshire: Macmillan, 1997)).

Ebel, W., *Catalogus Professorium Gottingensium 1734–1962* (Göttingen, 1962).

Eekhof, A., 'Hongarije', In: *Gedenkboek van het algemeen Nederlandsch verbond bij gelegenheid van zijn 25-jarig bestaan (1898–mei–1923). Geschiedenis en invloed van den Nederlandschen stam* (Amsterdam: Wereldbibliotheek, 1923) pp. 151–71.

Egmont Hake, A., 'Recollections of George Borrow', *The Athenaeum*, 2807 (13 August 1881) pp. 209–10.

Ehrhardt, Sophie, 'Zigeuner und Zigeunermischlinge in Ostpreussen'. In: *Volk und Rasse* (Munich, 1942) pp. 52–7.

Ergebnisse der in Ungarn am 31. Jänner 1893 durchgeführten Zigeuner-Conscription (Budapest: Buchdruckerei der Actiengesellschaft, 1895).

Ersch, M. Johann Samuel and J.G. Gruder, *Allgemeine Encyklopädie der Wissenschaften und Künste in alphabetischer Folge von genannten Schriftstellern bearbeitet*, 1, A-G (Leipzig, 1871).

Ersch, M. Johann Samuel, *Repertorium über die allgemeinern deutschen Journale und andere periodische Sammlungen für Erdbeschreibung, Geschichte und die damit verwandten Wissenschaften* (Lemgo, 1790–1792).

Etzler, Allan, *Zigenarna och deras avkomlingar i sverige, historia och sprak* (Uppsala: Almqvist & Wiksell, 1944).

Fabian, Bernhard, 'Göttingen als Forschungsbibliothek im 18. Jahrhundert. Plädoyer für eine neue Bibliotheksgeschichte'. In: Paul Raabe (ed.), *Offentliche und Private Bibliotheken im 17. und 18. Jahrhundert. Raritätenkammers, Forschungsinstrumente oder Bildungsstätten?* Wolfenbüttel Forschungen, 2 (Bremen/Wolfenbüttel: Jacobi, 1977) pp. 209–39.

Fairley, John A., *Bailie Smith of Kelso's Account of the Gypsies of Kirk Yetholm in 1815* (Hawick, 1907).

Fambach, Oscar, *Die Mitarbeiter der Göttingischen gelehrten Anzeigen 1769–1836* (Tübingen: Universitätsbibliothek, 1976).

Feest, E., *Geschichte des Wiener Zeitschriftenwesens von 1727 bis 1780* (Vienna, 1945).

Fertig, Georg, 'Eighteenth century transatlantic migration and early German anti-migration ideology'. In: Jan Lucassen and Leo Lucassen (eds), *Migration, Migration-History, History: Old Paradigms and New Perspectives* (Frankfurt am Main: Lang, 1997) pp. 271–90.

Finger, Otto, *Studien an zwei asozialen Zigeunermischlings-Sippen. Ein Beitrag zur Asozialen- und Zigeunerfrage* (Giessen, 1937).

Fings, Karola and Frank Sparing, *Z.Zt. Zigeunerlager. Die Verfolgung der Düsseldorfer Sinti und Roma im Nationalsozialismus* (Cologna, 1992).

First Report of the Committee for the Reformation of the Gipsies in Scotland (Edinburgh: Constable, 1840).

Fraser, A., 'Commentary: Brawo Sinto!' *Newsletter of the Gypsy Lore Society*, 12, 1 (1989) pp. 3, 8.

Fraser, A.M. (ed.), *A Journey to Eastern Europe in 1844. Thirteen Letters by George Borrow* (Edinburgh: Tragara, 1981).

Fraser, Angus, 'A Rum Lot'. In: Matt T. Salo (ed.), *100 Years of Gypsy-Studies*, 5. Gypsy Lore Society, Cheverly (Maryland, 1990) pp. 1–14.

Fraser, Angus, 'Borrow's Unsung Collaborators in Spain'. In: Gillian Fraser (ed.), *Proceedings of the 1993 George Borrow Conference* (Toronto: Published for the George Borrow Society, 1994) pp. 29–44.

Fraser, Angus M., 'Borrow's Captain Bosvile', *JGLS*, 47 (1968) pp. 38–47.

Fraser, Angus M., 'George Borrow's Birthplace and Gypsy Ancestry', *JGLS*, 51 (1972) pp. 60–81.

Fraser, Angus M., 'George Borrow's Wild Wales: Fact and Fabrication'. In: *Transactions of the Honourable Society of Cymmrodorion 1980*, pp. 163–73.

Fraser, Angus M., 'Mérimée and the Gypsies', *JGLS*, 30 (1951) pp. 2–16.

Fraser, Angus, 'Sleeping under the Angel's Wing: George Borrow's Imprisonment in Madrid'. In: Gillian Fraser (ed.), *Proceedings of the 1991 George Borrow Conference* (Toronto: Published for the George Borrow Society, 1992) pp. 25–47.

Fraser, Angus, 'The Dismemberment of George Borrow's Remains', *Antiquarian Book, Monthly Review* (May 1990) pp. 182–9.

Fraser, Angus, *The Gypsies* (Oxford (GB)/Cambridge (USA): Blackwell, 1992).

Fraser, Angus, 'The Unveiling of the Veiled Period'. In: Gillian Fenwick (ed.), *Proceedings of the 1987 George Borrow Conference* (Toronto: Published for The George Borrow Society, 1988) pp. 2–13.

Fréchet, René, *George Borrow (1803–81), Sa Vie – Son Oeuvre* (Paris: Didier, 1956).

Frensdorff, F., *Von und über Schlözer*. Königlichen Gesellschaft der Wissenschaften, Göttingen. Philologisch-Historische Klasse. xi, 4 (Berlin: Weidmann, 1909).

Fricke, Thomas, *Zwischen Erziehung und Ausgrenzung. Zur württembergischen Geschichte der Sinti und Roma im 19. Jahrhundert* (Frankfurt am Main: Lang, 1991).

Frijhoff, W.Th.M., *La Société Néerlandaise et ses Gradues, 1575–1814* (Amsterdam: Holland University Press, 1981) (doctoral dissertation).

Führer, Christian, *Die Roma im Westungarisch-Burgenländischen Raum zwischen 1850 und 1938* (Vienna, 1988) (unpublished masters thesis).

Ganssmüller, Christian, *Die Erbgesundheitspolitik des Dritten Reichs. Planung, Durchführung und Durchsetzung* (Cologna/Vienna: Böhlau, 1987).

Geremek, Bronislaw, *Het Kaïnsteken. Het beeld van armen en vage-bonden in de Europese literatuur van de 15e tot de 17e eeuw* (Baarn: Anthos, 1992) (original Polish edition 1980).

Geyer, Georg, 'Das Landfahrerwesen, polizeilich gesehen', *Die Neue Polizei*, 1 and 2 (1957) pp. 6–8 and pp. 22–3.

Gilsenbach, Reimar, 'Wie Lolitschai zur Doktorwürde kam'. In: *Feinderklärung und Prävention. Kriminalbiologie, Zigeunerforschung und Asozialenpolitik* (Berlin: Rotbuch, 1988) pp. 101–34.

Gilsenbach, Reimar, *Weltchronik der Zigeuner. 2500 Ereignisse aus der Geschichte der Roma und Sinti, der Luri, Zott und Boza, der Athinganer, Tattern, Heiden und Sarazenen, der Bohémiens, Gypsies und Gitanos und aller anderen Minderheiten, die 'Zigeuner' genannt werden. Teil 1: Von den Anfängen bis 1599* (Frankfurt am Main: Lang, 1994).

Giménez, Antonio, 'George Borrow and the Spanish Press'. In: Gillian Fenwick (ed.), *Proceedings of the 1989 George Borrow Conference* (Toronto: Published for the George Borrow Society, 1990) pp. 19–31.

Glazer, N. and D.P. Moynihan (eds), *Ethnicity, Theory and Experience* (Cambridge/Massachusets: Harvard University Press, 1975).

Goethe, J., *Sämtliche Werke*, 25, 30, 38, 39, 40 (Stuttgart/Berlin: Cotta, 1902–7).

Goor, J. van, *Jan Kompenie as Schoolmaster. Dutch Education in Ceylon 1690–1795* (Groningen: Wolters-Noordhoff, 1978) (doctoral dissertation).

Goss, John, *The Mapmaker's Art* (London: Studio Editions, 1993).

Gräffer, F., *Österreichische Nationalencyklopädie* (Vienna, 1833).

Graffunder, *Ueber die Sprache der Zigeuner. Eine grammatische Skizze* (Erfurt:Otto, 1835).

Griselini, Francesco, 'Etwas von den Zigeunern überhaupt und insbesondere von den Zigeunern im Temeswarer Banat', *Neueste Mannigfaltigkeiten*, Week 157, pp. 3–13; Week 158, pp. 17–25.

Gronemeyer, Reimer, *Zigeuner im Spiegel früher Chroniken und Abhandlungen. Quellen vom 15. bis zum 18. Jahrhundert* (Giessen: Focus, 1987).

Groome, F.H., *In Gipsy Tents* (Yorkshire: Nimmo & Co., 1973) (reprint of the original edition of 1880).

Gross, Hans, *Handbuch für Untersuchungsrichter, Polizeibeamte, Gendarmen u.s.w.* 2nd printing (Graz: Leuschner & Lubensky, 1894).

Grosvenor, Lady Arthur, 'Whiter's Lingua Cingariana', *JGLS*, 2 (1909) pp. 161–79.

Gruchmann, Lothar, 'Euthanasie und Justiz im Dritten Reich'. *Vierteljahrshefte für Zeitgeschichte*, 20 (1972) pp. 235–79.

Gruchmann, Lothar, *Justiz im Dritten Reich, 1933–1940. Anpassung und Unterwerfung in der Ära Gürtner* (Munich: Oldenbourg, 1988).

Günther, 'Die Zigeunerverhältnisse in Berleburg', *Ziel und Weg*, 7 (1937) pp. 262–8.

Gutkas, Karl, 'Kampf gegen die Armut'. In: *Was blieb von Joseph II?* Documentation from an international Symposium in Melk (Vienna: Niederösterreichisches Pressehaus, 1980) pp. 77–85.

Gutkas, Karl, 'Die Josephinischen Reformen'. In: *Sonderausstellung* (Vienna, 1989) pp. 84–7.

Gutkas, Karl, *Joseph II* (Vienna, 1989).

Harmsen, H. and F. Lohse (eds), *Bevölkerungsfragen, Berichte des Internationalen Kongresses für Bevölkerungswissenschaft 1935 in Berlin*, 7.

Harriot, John Staples, (Bengal Infantry) 'Observations on the Oriental Origin of the Romnichal, or Tribe miscalled Gypsey and Bohemian', in: *Transactions of the Royal Asiatic Society of Great Britain and Ireland*, 2 (London, 1830) pp. 518–58.

Hartmann, Johann Melchior, *Allgemeines Register über die Göttingischen gelehrten Anzeigen von 1783 bis 1822*. Part three (Göttingen: Universitätsbibliothek, 1829).

Hasenberger, Michael, *Die Zigeuner in Europa mit besonderer Berücksichtigung des Mittel- und Südosteuropaïschen Raumes* (Vienna, 1982–83) (unpublished masters thesis).

Haslinger, Michaela, *Rom heisst Mensch. Zur Geschichte des 'geschichtslosen' Zigeunervolkes in der Steiermark (1850–1938)* (Lieboch, 1985) (unpublished doctoral dissertation).

Hehemann, R., *Die 'Bekämpfung des Zigeunerunwesens' im Wilhelminischen Deutschland und in der Weimarer Republik, 1871–1933* (Frankfurt am Main: Haag & Herchen, 1987).

Heinschink, Mozes F., 'E Romani Chib – Die Sprache der Roma'. In: Mozes F. Heinschink and Ursula Hemetek (eds), *Roma, das unbekannte Volk. Schicksal und Kultur* (Vienna: Böhlau, 1994) pp. 110–28.

Heister, Carl von, *Ethnographische und geschichtliche Notizen über die Zigeuner* (Königsberg: Gräfe & Unzer, 1842).

Henke, Klaus-Dietmar, 'Die Trennung vom Nationalsozialismus. Selbstzerstörung, politische Säuberung, "Entnazifizierung", Strafverfolgung'. In: Klaus-Dietmar Henke and Hans Woller (eds), *Politische Säuberung in Europa. Die Abrechnung mit Faschismus und Kollaboration nach dem Zweiten Weltkrieg* (Munich: Deutscher Taschenbuch Verlag, 1991) pp. 21–83.

Hepp, Michael, 'Vorhof zur Hölle. Mädchen im 'Jugendschutzlager' Uckermark'. In: A. Ebbinghaus (ed.), *Opfer und Täterinnen. Frauenbiographien des Nationalsozialismus*, 2 (Nördlingen: Greno, 1987).

Hermann, Anton, *Ethnologische Mitteilungen aus Ungarn* (Budapest, 1890–92).

Herrlitz, Hans-Georg and Horst Kern (eds), *Anfänge Göttinger Sozialwissenschaft. Methoden, Inhalte und soziale Prozesse im 18. und 19. Jahrhundert* (Göttingen: Vandenhoeck & Ruprecht, 1987).

Heymowski, Adam, *Swedish 'Travellers' and their Ancestry. A Social Isolate or an Ethnic Minority?* (Uppsala: Almqvist & Wiksell, 1969).

Hitchcock, Richard, 'The Bookseller of Logroño'. In: Gillian Fraser (ed.), *Proceedings of the 1993 George Borrow Conference* (Toronto: Published for the George Borrow Society, 1994) pp. 45–52.

Hohmann, Joachim S., *Zigeuner und Zigeunerwissenschaft* (Marburg: Guttandin & Hoppe, 1980).

Hohmann, Joachim S. (pub.), *Brawo Sinto! Lebensspuren deutscher Zigeuner* (Frankfurt am Main: Lang, 1984).

Hohmann, Joachim S., *Brawo Sinto! Auf den Spuren eines geächteten Buches* (Fernwald, 1986).

Hohmann, Joachim S., *Robert Ritter und die Erben der Kriminalbiologie. 'Zigeunerforschung' im Nationalsozialismus und in Westdeutschland im Zeichen des Rassismus* (Frankfurt am Main: Lang, 1991).

Hohmann, Joachim S., *Neue deutsche Zigeunerbibliographie. Unter Berücksichtigung aller Jahrgänge des 'Journals of the Gypsy Lore Society'* (Frankfurt am Main: Lang, 1992).

Holmes, Colin, 'Samuel Roberts and the Gypsies'. In: S. Pollard and C. Holmes (eds), *Essays in the Economic and Social History of South Yorkshire* (Barnsley: South Yorkshire County Council, 1976) pp. 233–46.

Holzinger, Daniel, *Das Rómanes. Grammatik und Diskursanalyse der Sprache der Sinte* (Innsbruck: Verlag des Instituts für Sprachwissenschaft der Universität Innsbruck, 1993).

Hopf, Carl, *Die Einwanderung der Zigeuner in Europa. Ein Vortrag* (Gotha: Friedrich Andreas Perthes, 1870).

Howitt, William, *The Rural Life of England*. Two parts, Part I (London: Longman, 1838) pp. 219–50.

Howsam, Leslie, 'The Readers in Borrow's Text'. In: Gillian Fenwick (ed.), *Proceedings of the 1987 George Borrow Conference* (Toronto: Published for the George Borrow Society, 1988) pp. 43–55.

Howsam, Leslie, *Cheap Bibles. Nineteenth-Century Publishing and the British and Foreign Bible Society* (Cambridge: Cambridge University Press, 1991).

Howsam, Leslie, 'Under the Rose: George Borrow's Literary Apprenticeship with Sir Richard Phillips'. In: *The Third Research Colloquium on the Works of George Borrow* (Toronto: York University, 1993) pp. 1–9.

Hoyland, John, *A Historical Survey of the Customs, Habits & Present State of The Gypsies; designed to develope The Origin of this Singular People, and to promote The Amelioration of their Condition* (York: Alexander, 1816).

Hughes, Everett C., 'Dilemmas and contradictions of status', *American Journal of Sociology* (March 1945) pp. 353–9.

Hughes, Robert, *Culture of Complaint. The Fraying of America* (Oxford: Oxford University Press, 1993).

Index deutschsprachiger Zeitschriften 1750–1815. A set of micro-fiches, compiled by a workgroup under Klaus Schmidt (Göttingen, 1990).

Ives, Herbert, 'George Borrow in Russia', *National Review*, 54 (1910) pp. 71–84.

Jäger, Hans-Wolf, 'Reisefacetten der Aufklärungszeit'. In: Peter J. Breuner (ed.), *Der Reisebericht. Die Entwicklung einer Gattung in der deutschen Literatur* (Frankfurt am Main: Suhrkamp, 1989) pp. 261–83.

Jenkins, Herbert, *The Life of George Borrow* (London: Murray, 1912).

Jessopp, Augustus, 'Lavengro', *The Athenaeum*, 3428 (8 July 1893) pp. 65–6.

Jessopp, Augustus, 'Dr. Jessopp's Reminiscenses of George Borrow', *The Norwich Mercury* (19 July 1893).

Jessopp, A., 'Lights on Borrow', *The Daily Chronicle* (30 April 1900) p. 8.

Justin, Eva, *Lebensschicksale artfremd erzogener Zigeunerkinder und ihrer Nachkommen* (Berlin, 1944) (doctoral dissertation).

(Kaiserlich-Königlich allergnädigst privilegierte) Anzeigen aus sämmtlich-kaiserlich-königlichen Erbländern. By Samuel Augustini Ab Hortis (Vienna, 1775–76).

Kaprow, Miriam Lee, 'Celebrating Impermanence: Gypsies in a Spanish City'. In: Philip R. De Vita (ed.), *The Naked Anthropologist: Tales from Around the World* (Belmont: Wadsworth, 1991) pp. 218–31.

Karoly, Vajna, *Hazai Régi Büntetések* (Budapest, 1907) pp. 251–95, 479–97.

Keller, Mechtild, *Russen und Russland aus deutscher Sicht, 18. Jahrhundert: Aufklärung* (Munich: Fink, 1987) pp. 184–260.

Kern, Horst, 'Schlözers Bedeutung für die Methodologie der empirischen Sozialforschung'. In: Hans-Georg Herrlitz and Horst Kern (eds), *Anfänge Göttinger Sozialwissenschaft. Methoden, Inhalte und soziale Prozesse im 18. und 19. Jahrhundert* (Göttingen: Vandenhoeck & Ruprecht, 1987) pp. 55–71.

Király, Béla K., *Hungary in the late eighteenth century; The Decline of Enlightened Despotism* (New York/London: Columbia University Press, 1969).

Kirchner, J., *Bibliographie der Zeitschriften des deutschen Sprachgebietes bis 1900* (Stuttgart: Hiersemann, 1966).

Knapp, W.I., 'George Borrow in Spain', *The Nation* (11 February 1886) pp. 121–3.

Knapp, William I., *Life, Writings and Correspondence of George Borrow (1803–81)*. Two parts (New York/London: Murray, 1899).

Knobloch, Johann and Inge Sudbrack (eds), *Zigeunerkundliche Forschungen I* (Innsbruck: Amoe, 1977).

Köbben, A.J.F., *Van primitieven tot medeburgers*. (Assen: Van Gorcum, 1971).

Koeman, Jakob, *Die Grimmelshausen-Rezeption in der fiktionalen Literatur der Deutschen Romantik* (Amsterdam: Rodopi, 1993) (doctoral dissertation).

Kogalnitchan, Michel de, *Esquisse sur l'histoire, les moeurs et la langue des cigans* (Berlin: Behr, 1837).

Kogon, Eugen, *The Theory and Practice of Hell. The German Concentration Camps and the System Behind Them* (New York: Farrar, no year) (originally published in German, 1946).

Königlichen Commissarien (Die), Prorectoren und Rektoren der Georg-August-Universität zu Göttingen 1734 bis 1957. With commentary by Ernst Gundelach (Göttingen, no year).

Körber, Ursula, 'Die Wiedergutmachung und die "Zigeuner"'. In: *Feinderklärung und Prävention* (Berlin: Rotbuch, 1988) pp. 165–75.

Krämer, Robert, 'Rassische Untersuchungen an den "Zigeuner"-Kolonien Lause und Altengraben bei Berleburg (Westf.)', *Archiv für Rassen- und Gesellschaftsbiologie, einschliesslich Rasse- und Gesellschaftshygiene*, 31 (Munich, 1937) pp. 33–55.

Kranz, H.W., 'Zigeuner, wie Sie wirklich sind', *Neues Volk*, 9 (1937) pp. 21–7.

Krauss, Friedrich Salomo, *Zigeunerhumor. 250 Schnurren, Schwänke und Märchen* (Leipzig: Deutsche Verlagsactiengesellschaft, 1907).

Krokowski, Heike, *Die Rassenhygienische und Bevölkerungsbiologische Forschungsstelle am Reichsgesundheitsamt (1936–1945) unter besonderer Berücksichtigung von Sinti und Roma* (Hannover, 1992) (unpublished masters thesis).

Küppers, G.A., 'Begegnung mit Balkanzigeunern', *Volk und Rasse*, 6 (1938) pp. 183–93.

Küppers, H., 'Die Beschäftigung von Zigeunern'. In: *Informationsdienst, Rassenpolitisches Amt der NSDAP*, 25 (20 May 1942).

Küther, Carsten, *Räuber und Gauner in Deutschland* (Göttingen: Vandenhoeck & Ruprecht, 1976).

Laqueur, Walter, *The Terrible Secret. An Investigation into the Suppression of Information about Hitler's 'Final Solution'* (London: Weidenfeld & Nicolson, 1980).

Lawätz, Heinrich Wilhelm, *Handbuch für Bücherfreunde und Bibliothekare*. Part I, 1 (Halle, 1788).

Lawätz, Heinrich Wilhelm, *Erster Nachtrag zu den drey ersten Bänden des ersten Theiles des Handbuches für Bücherfreunde und Bibliothekare* (Halle, 1791).

Lawätz, Heinrich Wilhelm, *Allgemeines Repertorium der Literatur für die Jahre 1785 bis 1790*, 2 (Jena, 1793).

Lawätz, Heinrich Wilhelm, *Allgemeines Repertorium der Literatur für die Jahre 1785 bis 1790*, 3 (Jena, 1794).

Lawätz, Heinrich Wilhelm, *Zweyter Nachtrag zu den drey ersten Bänden des ersten Theiles des Handbuches für Bücherfreunde und Bibliothekare* (Halle, 1794).

Lee, Sidney and Leslie Stephen (eds), *Dictionary of National Biography* (London: Smith & Elder, 1887–91).

Leland, Charles, *The Gypsies* (Boston/New York: Houghton, Mifflin & Co., 1924) (reprint of the original 1882 edition).

Lerche, O., *Goethe und die Weimarer Bibliothek* (Leipzig: Harrassowitz, 1929).

Lewin, Karl, *Die Entwicklung der sozialwissenschaften in Göttingen im Zeitalter der Aufklärung 1734 bis 1812* (Göttingen, 1971) (unpublished doctoral dissertation).

Lichtenbergs Briefe, 1, 1766–81 (Leipzig: Leitzmann & Schüddekopf, 1901).

Liebich, Richard, *Die Zigeuner in ihrem Wesen und in ihrer Sprache. Nach eigenen Beobachtungen dargestellt* (Leipzig: Brockhaus, 1863).

Lifton, Robert Jay, *The Nazi Doctors. Medical Killing and the Psychology of Genocide* (New York: Basic Books, 1986).

Lis, Catharina, Hugo Soly and Dirk van Damme, *Op vrije voeten? Sociale politiek in West-Europa (1450–1914)* (Leuven: Kritak, 1985).

Luca, I. de, *Das gelehrte Österreich* (Vienna, 1776–78).

Lucas, Joseph, *The Yetholm History of the Gypsies* (Kelso: Rutherfurd, 1882).

Lucassen, Jan & Leo Lucassen (eds), *Migration, Migration-History, History: Old Paradigms and New Perspectives* (Frankfurt am Main: Lang, 1997).

Lucassen, Leo, *'En men noemde hen zigeuners'. De geschiedenis van Kaldarasch, Ursari, Lowara en Sinti in Nederland: 1750–1944* (Amsterdam/'s-Gravenhage: IISG/SDU, 1990) (doctoral dissertation).

Lucassen, Leo, 'A Blind Spot: Migratory and Travelling Groups in Western European Historiography', *International Review of Social History*, 38 (1993) pp. 209–35.

Lucassen, Leo, 'Eternal vagrants? State formation, migration and travelling groups in Western-Europe, 1350–1914'. In: Jan & Leo Lucassen (eds) *Migration etc.* (Frankfurt am Main: Lang, 1997) pp. 225–51.

Lucassen, Leo, 'Zigeuner in Deutschland 1870–1945: ein kritischer historiographischen Ansatz', *1999. Zeitschrift für Sozialgeschichte des 20. und 21 Jahrhunderts*, 1 (Hamburg, 1995) pp. 82–100.

Lucassen, Leo, *'Zigeuner'. Die Geschichte eines polizeilichen Ordnungs-begriffs in Deutschland (1700–1945)* (Cologne/Vienna: Böhlau, 1996).

Lucassen, Leo & Wim Willems, 'Zijn er nog wel buitenstaanders? De geschiedenis van sociale groepen', *Skript. Historisch tijdschrift*, 15, 4 (Amsterdam, 1993) pp. 295–9.

Lucassen, Leo & Wim Willems, 'Wanderers or Migrants? Gypsies from Eastern to Western Europe, 1860–1940'. In: Robin Cohen (ed.), *The Cambridge Survey of World Migration* (Cambridge: Cambridge University Press, 1995) pp. 136–41.

MacRitchie, David, 'Heinrich von Wlislocki', *Gypsy and Folk-lore Gazette*, II, 2 (1913) pp. 46–55.

Magyar életovjti Lexikon, I (Budapest, 1881).

Mahlsdorf, Charlotte von, *Ich bin meine eigene Frau. Ein Leben* (St. Gallen/Berlin: Edition dia, 1992).

Mallory, J.P., *In Search of the Indo-Europeans. Language, Archaeology and Myth* (London: Thames & Hudson, 1989).

Marsden, William, 'Observations on the Language of the People Commonly Called Gypsies. In a Letter to Sir Joseph Banks', *Archaeologia*, 7 (London, 1785) pp. 382–6.

Martins-Heuss, K., *Zur mythischen Figur des Zigeuners in der deutschen Zigeunerforschung. Mit einem Vorwort von Romani Rose*. Forum für Sinti und Roma, 1 (Frankfurt am Main: Haag & Herchen, 1983).

Mason, Peter, *The Deconstruction of America* (Utrecht, 1990) (unpublished doctoral dissertation).

Mayall, David, *Gypsy-travellers in nineteenth-century society* (Cambridge: Cambridge University Press, 1988) (doctoral dissertation).

Mazzolini, Renato G., 'Anatomische Untersuchungen über die Haut der Schwarzen (1700–1800)'. In: Gunter Mann & Franz Dumont, *Die Natur des Menschen. Probleme der physischen Anthropologie und Rassenkunde (1750–1850)* (Stuttgart/New York: Fischer, 1990) pp. 169–87.

McClellan III, James, *Science Reorganized. Scientific Societies in the Eighteenth Century* (New York: Columbia University Press, 1985).

McGrigor Phillips, D.U., *Catalogue of The Romany Collection* (University of Leeds: Brotherton Collection, 1962).

Meester, Mariët, *De Stilte voor het Vuur* (Amsterdam: Meulenhoff, 1992).

Meyer, Gustav, 'Zigeuner-Philologie', *Essays und Studien zur Sprachgeschichte und Volkskunde*, 2 (Straatsburg, 1893) pp. 107–17.

Miklosich, Franz Ritter von, *Über die Mundarten und die Wanderungen der Zigeuner Europa's*, 21, 22, 23, 25, 26, 27, 30, 31 (Vienna: Kaiserliche Akademie der Wissenschaften, 1872–81).

Milkau, F., *Handbuch der Bibliothekswissenschaft*. Second expanded edition (Wiesbaden: Harrassowitz, 1957).

Milton, Sybil, 'Nazi Policies Toward Roma and Sinti, 1933–1945', *JGLS*, 5-2, 1, (1992) pp. 1–18.

Moch, Leslie Page, *Moving Europeans. Migration in Western Europe since 1650* (Bloomington: Indiana University Press, 1992).

Möckesch, Martin Samuel, *Haideblümchen. Zigeunerische Dichtungen und Sprichwörter* (Bucharest, 1873) (translated into German).

Moore, R.I., *The formation of a persecuting society* (Oxford: Blackwell, 1987).

Moravek, Karl, *Ein Betrag zur Rassenkunde der Burgenländischen Zigeuner* (Vienna, 1939) (unpublished masters thesis).

Mosse, George L., *Toward the Final Solution. A History of European Racism* (New York: Fertig, 1978).

Müller-Hill, Benno, *Murderous Science. Elimination by scientific selection of Jews, Gypsies, and others, Germany 1933–1945* (Oxford: Oxford University Press, 1988) (translation of *Tödliche Wissenschaft*, 1984).

Napier, *Excursions along the Shores of the Mediterranean*, II (London, 1842).

Nemeth, David J., 'Irving Brown. The American Borrow?', *JGLS*, 4, 1 (February 1994) pp. 7–31.

Neue Deutsche Biographie, 3 (Berlin: Duncker & Humblot, 1957).

Nevri Nagy Lexikon, 2 (Budapest, 1811).

Niemandt, Hans-Dieter, *Die Zigeunerin in den romanischen Literaturen* (Frankfurt am Main: Lang, 1992) (reprint of the original 1954 edition).

Noakes, Jeremy, 'Nazism and Eugenics: the Background to the Nazi Sterilisation Law of 14 July 1933'. In: B.J. Bullen et al. (eds), *Ideas into Politics* (London: Barnes & Noble, 1984) pp. 75–94.

Northup, George T., 'The Influence of George Borrow upon Prosper Mérimée', *Modern Philology*, 13 (July 1915) pp. 143–56.

Odom, W., *Hallamshire Worthies. Characteristics and Works of Notable Sheffield Men and Women* (Sheffield, 1926) pp. 99–101.

Okely, Judith, *The Traveller-Gypsies* (Cambridge: Cambridge University Press, 1983) (doctoral dissertation).

Pallas, Peter Simon, *Neye nordische Beyträge zur phisikalischen und geographischen Erd- und Völkerbeschreibung*, 3 (Saint Petersburg, 1781–96).

Paunel, Eugen, 'Goethe als Bibliothekar', *Zentralblatt für Bibliothekswesen*, 63, 7/8 (July/August 1949) pp. 235–69.

Pennell, Elizabeth Robins, *Charles Godfrey Leland. A Biography*. Two Parts (Boston/New York: Houghton, Mifflin & Co., 1906).

Pettrits, Maria, *Das Göttingen des 18. Jahrhunderts im Spiegel der Briefe und Erinnerungen Ungarischer Studenten und Gelehrter* (Göttingen, 1984) (unpublished masters thesis).

Pischel, Richard, *Beiträge zur Kenntnis der deutschen Zigeuner* (Halle: Niemeyer, 1894).

Poliakov, Léon, *The Aryen Myth. A History of Racist and Nationalist Ideas in Europe* (London: Chatto & Heinemann for Sussex University Press, 1974) (originally *Le mythe aryen*, 1971).

Pott, A.F., *Die Zigeuner in Europa und Asien. Ethnographisch-linguistische Untersuchung, vornehmlich ihrer Herkunft und Sprache, nach gedruckten und ungedruckten Quellen*, 1 (Halle: Heynemann, 1844); 2 (Halle: Heynemann, 1845).

Proctor, Robert, *Racial Hygiene, Medicine under the Nazis* (Cambridge/London: Harvard University Press, 1988).

Pross, Christian and Götz Aly (eds), *Der Wert des Menschen. Medizin in Deutschland 1918–1945* (Berlin: Hentrich, 1989).

Pushkin, A.S., *The Gipsies*. With an introduction by P. Henry (Liverpool, 1962).

Raabe, P. (ed.), *Offentlichte und Private Bibliotheken im 17. und 18. Jahrhundert. Raritätenkammer, Forschungsinstrumente oder Bildungsstätten?* Wolfenbüttel Forschungen, 2 (Bremen/Wolfenbüttel: Jacobi, 1977).

Rao, Aparna and Michael J. Casimir, 'A Stereotyped Minority. "Zigeuner" in Two Centuries of German Reference Literature', *Ethnologia Europaea*, 23 (1993) pp. 111–24.

Rechtsprechung zum Wiedergutmachungsrecht. Volumes: 1953, 1955, 1956, 1957, 1958, 1959, 1960, 1961, 1962, 1963, 1964, 1965, 1966, 1967, 1968, 1972, 1974.

Reill, Peter Hanns, 'Die Geschichtswissenschaft um die Mitte des 18. Jahrhunderts'. In: R. Vierhaus (ed.), *Wissenschaften im Zeitalter der Aufklärung* (Göttingen: Vandenhoeck & Ruprecht, 1985) pp. 163–93.

Reiter, Hans, *Das Reichsgesundheitsamt 1933–1939. Sechs Jahre nationalsozialistische Führung* (Berlin: Springer, 1939).

Renfrew, Colin, *Archaeology and Language. The Puzzle of Indo-European Origins* (London: Cape, 1987).

Report of the Southampton Committee, for the Amelioration of the State of the Gipsies; and for their religious Instruction, and Conversion. From August, 1827; to May, 1832 (Southampton, 1832).

Richter, H.M., *Geistesströmungen: Die Wiener literarischen Zeitschriften* (Berlin, 1875).

Ridler, Ann M., 'Sidelights on George Borrow's Gypsy Luke', *The Bible Translator*, 32 (3 July 1981) pp. 329–37.

Ridler, Ann Margaret, *George Borrow as a Linguist: Images and Contexts* (Oxford, 1983) (unpublished doctoral dissertation).

Ridler, Ann, 'The Relationship between "The Bible in Spain" and "Lavengro/The Romany Rye"'. In: Gillian Fenwick (ed.), *Proceedings of the 1987 George Borrow Conference* (Toronto: Published for The George Borrow Society, 1988) pp. 27–33.

Roberts, Samuel, *The Blind Man and his Son. A Tale for young People. The four Friends: A Fable. And a Word for the Gypsies* (London: Taylor & Hessey, 1816).

Roberts, Samuel, *Parallel Miracles; or, the Jews and the Gypsies* (London: Nisbet, 1830).

Roberts, Samuel, *The Gypsies: their Origin, Continuance, and Destination; or, the sealed Book opened*. Fifth edition (London: Longmans, 1842).

Roberts, Samuel, *The Jews, the English Poor, and the Gypsies; with a proposal for an important improvement in the British Constitution* (London, 1848).

Roberts, Samuel, 'Samuel Roberts of Park Grange, Sheffield A.D. 1763–1848', *JGLS*, 5 (1911–12) pp. 161–6.

Roberts, Samuel, *Some Memorials of the Family of Roberts, of Queen's Tower, Sheffield, as exemplified by kindred, affinity, and marriage*. Third edition (Sheffield, 1924).

Robertson, Ian, 'George Borrow in Portugal'. In: Gillian Fraser (ed.), *Proceedings of the 1991 George Borrow Conference* (Toronto: Published for The George Borrow Society, 1992) pp. 9–23.

Rodenberg, Carl-Heinz, 'Die Zigeunerfrage', *Der Öffentliche Gesundheitsdienst*, 3, 12 (Berlin, 1937) pp. 437–46.

Rollman, Margrit, *Der Gelehrte als Schriftsteller. Die Publikationen der Göttinger Professoren im 18. Jahrhundert* (Göttingen, 1988) (unpublished doctoral dissertation).

Rómer, Joachim, 'Zigeuner in Deutschland', *Volk und Rasse* (1934) pp. 112–13.

Rómer, Joachim, 'Fremdrassen in Sachsen', *Volk und Rasse* (1937) pp. 281–8, 321–8.

Roth, Karl Heinz (ed.), *Erfassung zur Vernichtung. Von der Sozialhygiene zum 'Gesetz über Sterbehilfe'* (Berlin: Verlagsgesellschaft Gesundheit, 1984).

Ruch, Martin, *Zur Wissenschaftsgeschichte der deutschsprachigen 'Zigeunerforschung' von den Anfängen bis 1900* (Freiburg, 1986) (unpublished doctoral dissertation).

Rudall, John, *A Memoir of the Rev. James Crabb, Late of Southampton* (London: Walton & Maberly, 1864).

Rüdiger, Johann Christian Christoph, *Grundriss einer Geschichte der menschlichen Sprache, nach allen bisher bekannten Mund- und Schriftarten*, 1 (Leipzig, 1782).

Rüdiger, Johann Christian Christoph, *Neuester Zuwachs der teutschen, fremden und allgemeinen Sprachkunde in einigen Aufsätzen, Bücheranzeigen und Nachrichten*, 1 (Leipzig, 1782).

Rüdiger, Johann Christian Christoph, *Neuester Zuwachs*, 2 (Leipzig, 1783).

Rüdiger, Johann Christian Christoph, *Neuester Zuwachs*, 3 (Leipzig, 1784).

Rüdiger, Johann Christian Christoph, *Neuester Zuwachs*, 4 (Leipzig, 1785).

Rüdiger, Johann Christian Christoph, *Neuester Zuwachs der teutschen, fremden und allgemeinen Sprachkunde*, 1. New edition (Halle, 1796).

Rüdiger, Johann Christian Christoph, *Von der Sprache und Herkunft der Zigeuner aus Indien* (Leipzig, 1782) (reprinted as Volume 6 in the series *Linguarum Minorum Documenta Historiographica*; with an introduction by Harald Haarmann (Hamburg, 1990)).

Saage, Richard, 'August Ludwig Schlözer als politischer Theoretiker'. In: Hans-Georg Herrlitz and Horst Kern (eds), *Anfänge Göttinger Sozialwissenschaft. Methoden, Inhalte und soziale Prozesse im 18. und 19. Jahrhundert* (Göttingen: Vandenhoeck & Ruprecht, 1987) pp. 12–54.

Said, Edward, *Orientalism* (New York: Pantheon Books, 1978).

Schäffer, Georg Jacob, *Beschreibung der jenigen Jauner, Zigeuner, Mörder, Strassenräuber, Kirchen-, Markt-, Tag-, und Nacht-Diebe und andern herumvagierenden liederlichen Gesindels, welche teils in Schwaben, meistenteils aber in der Schweiz würklich noch herumschwärmen, und von denen dahier ... in Verhaft ... gestandenen ... sieben Erzjaunern und Jaunerinnen ... entdeckt worden sind ... aus denen ... Untersuchungs-Acten herausgezogen* (Stuttgart: Cotta, 1784).

Schäffer, Georg Jacob, *Sulz. Zigeuner-Liste und genaue Beschreibung des zum Schaden und Gefahr des Gemeinen Wesens meistens in Schwaben, auch in Böhmen, Ungarn, so dann in denen Hessen Hanau-Lichtenbergischen Landen, und besonders bey Pirmasens herum sich aufhaltenden- und herum vagirenden Räuber- und Zigeuner-Gesindels, wie solche von der dahier in Verhafft gelegenen- von denen diesseitigen Oberämter Nagold, Königsbronn und Altenstaig, auch andern Orten anhero eingelieferten-auch zum Theil mit grossen Kosten zu Chur in Graubündten abgeholten Zigeuner- und Mörder-Bande während dem Inquisitions-Process mit äusserst vieler Mühe entdeckt, und beschrieben, auch vor ihrer Hinrichtung, und Abführung auf die Vestung Hohentwiel und in das Zucht- und Arbeitshaus zu Ludwigsburg widerholter bestätiget worden ist. Nebst einem Anhang der aus diesem Mörder- und Räuberhaussen, hie und da justificirten oder sonst entweder natürlichen- oder gewaltsamen Tödes verstorbenen Personen, aus denen in Vierzig starken Tomis bestehenden Untersuchungs-Acten, auf höchst gnädigsten Befehl getreulich herausgezogen und zum Druck befördert* (Stuttgart: Cotta, 1787).

Schenda, Rudolf, 'Mären von deutschen Sagen. Bemerkungen zur Produktion von "Volkserzählungen" zwischen 1850 und 1870', *Geschichte und Gesellschaft*, 9 (1983) pp. 24–48.

Schlichtegroll, F., *Nekrolog der Teutschen für das neunzehnte Jahrhundert*, 1 (Gotha: Perthes, 1802).

Schwarberg, Günther, *Die Mörderwaschmaschine* (Göttingen: Steidl, 1990).

Schwicker, J.H., *Die Zigeuner in Ungarn und Siebenbürgen*, 12 'Die Völker Oesterreich-Ungarns. Ethnographische und culturhistorische Schilderungen (Vienna: Prochaska, 1883).

Seidler, Horst and Andreas Rett, *Rassenhygiene. Ein Weg in den Nationalsozialismus* (Vienna/Munich, 1988).

Seidler, Andrea and Wolfram, *Das Zeitschriftenwesen im Donauraum zwischen 1740 und 1809* (Vienna, 1988).

Shorter, Clement King, *George Borrow and his Circle* (London: Hodder & Stoughton, 1913).

Shorthouse, J.H., 'The Successor of Monsieur Le Sage'. In: *Literary Remains of J.H. Shorthouse* (London: Macmillan, 1905) pp. 61–86.

Smart, Bath C. and H.T. Crofton, *The Dialect of the English Gypsies* (London: Asher & Co., 1875).

Spengler, F.R., *Dissertatio Historico-Juridica de Cinganis sive Zigeunis* (Leiden: Hazenberg & Co., 1839).

Stangl, Reinhard, *Die Verfolgung der Zigeuner im Deutschsprachigen Raum Mitteleuropas von ihren Anfängen bis heute* (Vienna, 1986) (unpublished masters thesis).

Stanicki, Henning, 'Zur Problematik der Ansprüche von Zigeunern nach dem BEG-Schlussgesetz', *Rechtsprechung zum Wiedergutmachungsrecht*, 18, 12 (1968) pp. 529–35.

Starkie, Walter, 'Cervantes and the Gypsies', *JGLS*, 39 (1960) pp. 131–51.

Stein, George J., 'The biological bases of ethnocentrism, racism and nationalism in national socialism'. In: V. Reynold et al. (eds), *The sociobiology of ethnocentrism. Evolutionary dimensions of xenophobia, discrimination, racism and nationalism* (London/Sydney: Croom Helm, 1987) pp. 251–73.

Stein, Gerhard, 'Zur Physiologie und Anthropologie der Zigeuner in Deutschland', *Zeitschrift für Ethnologie, Organ der Berliner Gesellschaft für Anthropologie, Ethnologie und Urgeschichte*, 22 (Berlin, 1941) pp. 74–114.

Stephen, G.A., *Borrow House Museum* (Norwich, 1927).

Streich, Gerhard, 'Die Büchersammlungen Göttinger Professoren im 18. Jahrhundert'. In: Paul Raabe (ed.), *Öffentliche und Private Bibliotheken im 17. und 18. Jahrhundert. Raritätenkammern, Forschungsinstrumente oder Bildungsstätten?* (Bremen and Wolfenbüttel: Jacobi, 1977).

Stuart, Charles, *David Blythe, The Gipsy King: A Character Sketch* (Kelso: Rutherfurd, 1883).

Sutherland, Anne, *Gypsies. The hidden Americans* (Illinois: Free Press, 1975).

Szabó, György, *Die Roma in Ungarn. Ein Beitrag zur Sozialgeschichte einer Minderheit in Ost- und Mitteleuropa*. Studien zur Tsiganologie und Folkloristik, vol. 5 (Frankfurt am Main: Lang, 1991).

Tantö, J., 'Hongaarsche studenten in Nederland', *Stemmen voor Waarheid en Vrede*, 57 (Utrecht, 1920) pp. 120–9, 161–81, 376–89, 441–50.

Tetzner, Theodor, *Geschichte der Zigeuner; ihre Herkunft, Natur und Art* (Weimar/Ilmenau: Voigt, 1835).

'The Scholar Gypsy', *The Nation* (12 July 1913) pp. 560–1.

Thomasius, Jacobus, *Dissertatio philosofica de Cingaris* (Leipzig: Hahn, 1671).

Thompson, Thomas William, 'Borrow's Gypsies: The Relations of Jasper Petulengro', *JGLS*, 3 (July 1909–April 1910) pp. 162–74.

Tilford Jr., John E., 'Contemporary Criticism of *Lavengro*: A Re-Examination', *Studies in Philology*, XLI, 3 (July 1944) pp. 442–56.

Tilford Jr., John E., 'The Critical Approach to *Lavengro–Romany Rye*', *Studies in Philology*, XLVI, 1 (January 1949) pp. 79–96.

Turner, Ralph Liley, 'The Position of Romani in Indo-Aryan'. In: R.L. Turner, *Collected Papers* (London: Oxford University Press, 1975) pp. 251–90.

Uschold, Rudolf, 'Das Zigeunerproblem', *Die Neue Polizei, Fachzeitschrift für die gesamte Polizei*, 4 (1951) pp. 60–2; 3 (1957) pp. 38–40.

Vandenbroeck, Paul, *Beeld van de andere, vertoog over het zelf. Over wilden en narren, boeren en bedelaars* (Antwerp: Tentoonstellings-catalogus Koninklijk Museum voor Schone Kunsten, 1987).

Varesano, Angela-Marie, *Charles Godfrey Leland: The Eclectic Folklorist* (Pennsylvania, 1979) (unpublished doctoral dissertation).

Versuch einer academischen Gelehrten-Geschichte von der Georg-Augustus-Universität zu Göttingen vom geheimen Justizrath Pütter, 2, 1765–88 (Göttingen, 1788); 3, 1788–1820 (Hannover, 1820).

Vesey-FitzGerald, Brian, *Gypsy Borrow* (London, 1953).

Voerst van Lynden, E.M.A. van, *'Gentlemen of the Roads'. Een onderzoek naar het Journal of the Gypsy Lore Society (1888–1892) en zijn protagonisten* (State University Leiden, section Social History, 1993) (unpublished masters thesis).

Vogel, Norbert. 'Die Sippe Delta. Eine Studie über erbliche Minderwertigkeit und asoziales Verhalten', *Ziel und Weg*, 7 (1937) pp. 85–91, 110–21, 147–56.

Wagner, Patrick. 'Das Gesetz über die Behandlung Gemein-schaftsfremder. Die Kriminalpolizei und die "Vernichtung des Verbrechertums"'. In: *Feinderklärung und Prävention* (Berlin: Rotbuch, 1988) pp. 75–100.

Walter, Karl, 'Herder und Heinze. Aus der Geschichte des wei-marischen Gymnasiums'. In: J. Ilberg and B. Gerth (eds), *Neue Jahrbücher für das klassische Altertum, Geschichte und Deutsche Literatur und für Pädagogik*.Part 22, 11 (Teubner, 1908) pp. 36–59.

Watts, Theodore, 'Notes upon George Borrow', Introduction to *Lavengro-edition* (London: Murray, 1893) pp. vii–xxiv.

Webster, Wentworth, 'Stray Notes on George Borrow's Life in Spain', *JGLS*, 1 (July 1888–October 1889) pp. 150–3.

Weindling, Paul, *Health, race and German politics between national unification and Nazism, 1870–1945* (Cambridge: Cambridge University Press, 1989).

Weingart, Peter, Jürgen Kroll and Kurt Bayertz, *Rasse, Blut und Gene. Geschichte der Eugenik und Rassenhygiene in Deutschland* (Frankfurt am Main: Suhrkamp, 1988).

Wellenreuther, Hermann, 'Göttingen und England im 18. Jahrhundert'. In: *250 Jahre Vorlesungen* (Göttingen: Vandenhoeck & Ruprecht, 1985) pp. 30–63.

Welsh Dulles, A., *Germany's Underground* (New York: Macmillan, 1947).

Wiesenthal, Simon, *The Murderers among us* (London: Heinemann, 1967).

Willems, Wim and Leo Lucassen, 'The church of knowledge. The Gypsy in Dutch encyclopedias and their sources'. In: M.T. Salo (ed.), *Hundred years of Gypsy studies*. Publication no. 5 of the Gypsy Lore Society (Cheverley, 1990) pp. 31–50.

Willems, Wim and Leo Lucassen, *Ongewenste vreemdelingen. Buiten-landse zigeuners en de Nederlandse overheid: 1969–1989* (The Hague: SDU, 1990).

Willems, Wim and Leo Lucassen, 'A Silent War: Foreign Gypsies and Dutch Government Policy, 1969–89', *Immigrants and Minorities*, 11, 1 (London: Cass, March 1992) pp. 81–101.

Willems, Wim and Leo Lucassen, 'The return of the Egyptian. The stigmatization of "Gypsies" in Western Europe, 1783–1945'. *Working paper for the New School of Social Research*. Centre for the Studies of Social Change (New York, 1993).

Willems, Wim, 'Victim or Relic? The Ambiguous Gypsy Image of George Borrow'. In: Gillian Fenwick (ed.), *Proceedings of the 1993 George Borrow Conference* (Toronto: Published for The George Borrow Society, 1994) pp. 53–62.

Willems, Wim, *Op zoek naar de ware zigeuner. Zigeuners als studieobject tijdens de Verlichting, de Romantiek en het Nazisme* (Utrecht: Van Arkel, 1995) (doctoral dissertation).

Willems, Wim, 'Aussenbilder von Sinti und Roma in der frühen Zigeunerforschung'. In: Jacqueline Giere (ed.) *Die gesellschaftliche Konstruktion des Zigeuners. Zur Genese eines Vorurteils* (Frankfurt/New York: Campus Verlag, 1996) pp. 87–108.

Winckler, J., *Die Periodische Presse Österreichs* (Vienna, 1875).

Winstedt, E.O., 'Borrow's Hungarian-Romani Vocabulary', *JGLS*, 29 (1950) pp. 46–54, 104–15; 30 (1951) pp. 50–61.

Winter, Mathias, *Von Robert Ritter zu Hermann Arnold – Zur Kontinuität rassistischer Ideologie in der deutschen 'Zigeunerforschung' und 'Zigeunerpolitik'* (Tübingen, 1991) (unpublished masters thesis).

Wischnitzer, Markus, *Die Universität Göttingen und die Entwicklung der liberalen Ideen in Russland im ersten Viertel des 19. Jahrhunderts* (Berlin, 1907).

Wittich, Engelbert, *Blicke in das Leben der Zigeuner* (Hamburg: Advent Verlag, 1927).

Wittich, Engelbert, *Beiträge zur Zigeunerkunde*. Introduced and published by Joachim S. Hohmann. Studien zur Tsiganologie und Folkloristik, 2 (Frankfurt am Main: Lang, 1990).

Wlislocki, H. von, *Eine Hildebrands-Ballade der transsilvanischen Zigeuner* (Leipzig: Friedrich, 1880).

Wlislocki, H. von, *Haideblüten. Volkslieder der transsilvanischen Zigeuner* (Leipzig: Friedrich, 1880).

Wlislocki, H. von, *Die Sprache der transsilvanischen Zigeuner* (Leipzig: Friedrich, 1884).

Wlislocki, H. von, *Vom wandernden Zigeunervolk* (Hamburg, 1890).

Wlislocki, H. von, *Volksglaube und religiöser Brauch der Zigeuner* (Munich: Aschendorff, 1891).

Wolf, Siegmund A., *Grosses Wörterbuch der Zigeunersprache (romani tsiw). Wortschatz deutscher und anderer europäischer Zigeunerdialekte*. Second, revised edition (Hamburg: Buske, 1987).

Woodcock, Henry, *The Gipsies; being a brief account of their History, Origin, Capabilities, Manners and Customs*. With suggestions for the reform and conversion of English Gypsies (London: Lister, 1865).

Wurzbach, C. von, *Biographisches Lexikon des Kaiserthums Österreich*. 58 volumes (Vienna: Zamarski, 1856–1923).

Wurzbach, Wolfgang von, 'Die Preziosa des Cervantes', *Studien zur vergleichenden Literaturgeschichte*, 1 (Berlin: Duncker, 1901) pp. 391–419.

Yates, Dora, *My Gypsy Days. Recollections of a Romani Rawnie* (London, 1953).

Zenker, E.V., *Geschichte der Wiener Journalistik von den Anfängen bis zum Jahre 1848* (Vienna/Leipzig: Braumüller, 1892).

Zimmermann, Michael, *Verfolgt, vertrieben, vernichtet. Die national-sozialistische Vernichtungspolitik gegen Sinti und Roma* (Essen: Klartext, 1989).

Zimmermann, Michael, 'Ausgrenzung, Ermordung, Ausgrenzung. Normalität und Exzess in der polizeilichen Zigeunerverfolgung in Deutschland (1870–1980)'. In: Alf Lüdtke (ed.), *'Sicherheit' und 'Wohlfahrt'. Polizei, Gesellschaft und Herrschaft im 19. und 20. Jahrhundert* (Frankfurt am Main: Suhrkamp, 1992) pp. 344–70.

Zippel and J.E. Biester, 'Über die Zigeuner; besonders im Königreich Preussen', *Berlinische Monatschrift*, 21 (1793) pp. 108–65, 360–93.

Zülch, Tilman, 'Sinti und Roma in Deutschland. Geschichte einer verfolgten Minderheit', *Aus Politik und Zeitgeschichte. Beilage zur Wochenzeitung des Parlament*, 43, 82 (1982) pp. 27–45.

250 Jahre Vorlesungen an der Georgia Augusta 1734–1984. With lectures by Norbert Kamp, Hermann Wellenreuther and Friedrich Hund (Göttingen: Vandenhoeck & Ruprecht, 1985).

Index

Titles of Related Interest

The Politics of Immigration in Western Europe

Martin Baldwin-Edwards, *Queens University, Belfast* and
Martin A. Schain, *Center for European Studies at New York University* (Eds)

This book is devoted to an analysis of how immigration has emerged as a political issue, how the politics of immigration have been constructed, and what have been the consequences in Western Europe. Specific coverage is given to France, the UK, Italy, Austria and Germany, along with the emerging EU policy process and some cross-national comparisons.

200 pages 14 tables, 2 figs 1994 0 7146 4593 1 cloth 0 7146 4137 5 paper

The Territorial Management of Ethnic Conflict

John Coakley (Ed)

'Whatever the difficulties of the subject matter ... this collection of essays reaches a uniformly high standard'.
Edward Moxon-Browne, International Affairs

This volume looks at case studies that illustrate the whole range of ethnic conflict: Kenya and Tanzania, where ethnic groups are territorially mixed; the former USSR and Czechoslovakia, where territorial differentiation has permitted different groups to go their own way; Pakistan and Sri Lanka, where peripheral ethnic groups continue to mount a challenge to the central state; Canada and Belgium, where the central state has responded by conceding considerable regional autonomy; and the special case of Israel, where two groups lay exclusive claims to the same territory.

230 pages 1993 0 7146 3465 4 cloth

The Self-Determination of Minorities in International Politics

Alexis Heraclides

Contributes to the further understanding of the multi-faceted problem of minorities in international politics. Heraclides first examines reasons for violent separatism and then assesses the existing international normative regime against separatism and secession. The main focus is on the international politics of armed separatism and on world reaction and involvement by external parties. Seven secessionist movements are examined – Katanga, Biafra, the Southern Sudan, Iraqi Kurdistan, Bangladesh, Eritrea and the Moros of the Philippines.

291 pages 1991 0 7146 3384 4 cloth 0 7146 4082 4 paper

The Politics of Marginality

Race, the Radical Right and Minorities in Twentieth Century Britain

Tony Kushner and Kenneth Lunn (Eds)

Questions of race, ethnicity and immigration play an increasingly important role in the modern world. The twelve essays in this collection identify some of the significant aspects of this history: studies of groups such as the Jews, Afro-Caribbeans and Germans, the changes and continuities in racism, Fascism, anti-Semitism and more general xenophobia.

195 pages   1991   0 7146 3391 7 cloth